Precolonial Legacies in Postcolonial Politics

Why are some communities able to come together to improve their collective lot while others are not? Looking at variation in local government performance in decentralized West Africa, this book advances a novel answer to this question: Communities are better able to coordinate around basic service delivery when their formal jurisdictional boundaries overlap with informal social institutions, or norms. This book identifies the precolonial past as the driver of striking subnational variation in the present because these social institutions only encompass the many villages of the local state in areas that were once home to precolonial polities. Drawing on a multi-method research design, the book develops and tests a theory of institutional congruence to document how the past shapes contemporary elite approaches to redistribution within the local state. Where precolonial kingdoms left behind collective identities and dense social networks, local elites find it easier to cooperate following decentralization. This title is also available as Open Access on Cambridge Core.

MARTHA WILFAHRT is an assistant professor in the Travers Department of Political Science, University of California, Berkeley.

Cambridge Studies in Comparative Politics

General Editor
Kathleen Thelen *Massachusetts Institute of Technology*

Associate Editors
Catherine Boone *London School of Economics*
Thad Dunning *University of California, Berkeley*
Anna Grzymala-Busse *Stanford University*
Torben Iversen *Harvard University*
Stathis Kalyvas *University of Oxford*
Margaret Levi *Stanford University*
Melanie Manion *Duke University*
Helen Milner *Princeton University*
Frances Rosenbluth *Yale University*
Susan Stokes *Yale University*
Tariq Thachil *University of Pennsylvania*
Erik Wibbels *Duke University*

Series Founder
Peter Lange *Duke University*

Other Books in the Series

Christopher Adolph, *Bankers, Bureaucrats, and Central Bank Politics: The Myth of Neutrality*
Michael Albertus, *Autocracy and Redistribution: The Politics of Land Reform*
Michael Albertus, *Property Without Rights: Origins and Consequences of the Property Rights Gap*
Santiago Anria, *When Movements Become Parties: The Bolivian MAS in Comparative Perspective*
Ben W. Ansell, *From the Ballot to the Blackboard: The Redistributive Political Economy of Education*
Ben W. Ansell and Johannes Lindvall, *Inward Conquest: The Political Origins of Modern Public Services*
Ben W. Ansell and David J. Samuels, *Inequality and Democratization: An Elite-Competition Approach*
Adam Michael Auerbach, *Demanding Development: The Politics of Public Goods Provision in India's Urban Slums*
Ana Arjona, *Rebelocracy: Social Order in the Colombian Civil War*
Leonardo R. Arriola, *Multi-Ethnic Coalitions in Africa: Business Financing of Opposition Election Campaigns*
David Austen-Smith, Jeffry A. Frieden, Miriam A. Golden, Karl Ove Moene, and Adam Przeworski, eds., *Selected Works of Michael Wallerstein: The Political Economy of Inequality, Unions, and Social Democracy*
S. Erdem Aytaç and Susan C. Stokes, *Why Bother? Rethinking Participation in Elections and Protests*
Andy Baker, *The Market and the Masses in Latin America: Policy Reform and Consumption in Liberalizing Economies*

(continued after the Index)

Precolonial Legacies in Postcolonial Politics

Representation and Redistribution in Decentralized West Africa

MARTHA WILFAHRT
University of California, Berkeley

CAMBRIDGE
UNIVERSITY PRESS

University Printing House, Cambridge CB2 8BS, United Kingdom

One Liberty Plaza, 20th Floor, New York, NY 10006, USA

477 Williamstown Road, Port Melbourne, VIC 3207, Australia

314–321, 3rd Floor, Plot 3, Splendor Forum, Jasola District Centre, New Delhi – 110025, India

103 Penang Road, #05–06/07, Visioncrest Commercial, Singapore 238467

Cambridge University Press & Assessment is part of the University of Cambridge.

It furthers the University's mission by disseminating knowledge in the pursuit of education, learning, and research at the highest international levels of excellence.

www.cambridge.org
Information on this title: www.cambridge.org/9781009286183
DOI: 10.1017/9781009286176

© Martha Wilfahrt 2022
Reissued as Open Access, 2022

This work is in copyright. It is subject to statutory exceptions and to the provisions of relevant licensing agreements; with the exception of the Creative Commons version the link for which is provided below, no reproduction of any part of this work may take place without the written permission of Cambridge University Press.

An online version of this work is published at doi.org/10.1017/9781009286176 under a Creative Commons Open Access license CC-BY-NC-ND 4.0 which permits re-use, distribution and reproduction in any medium for non-commercial purposes providing appropriate credit to the original work is given. You may not distribute derivative works without permission. To view a copy of this license, visit https://creativecommons.org/licenses/by-nc-nd/4.0

All versions of this work may contain content reproduced under license from third parties. Permission to reproduce this third-party content must be obtained from these third-parties directly.

When citing this work, please include a reference to the DOI 10.1017/9781009286176

First published 2022

A catalogue record for this publication is available from the British Library.

ISBN 978-1-009-28618-3 Paperback

Cambridge University Press has no responsibility for the persistence or accuracy of URLs for external or third-party internet websites referred to in this publication and does not guarantee that any content on such websites is, or will remain, accurate or appropriate.

Contents

List of Figures		*page* vii
List of Tables		ix
Acknowledgments		xi
	Introduction	1
1	A Theory of Institutional Congruence	22
2	Bringing Old States Back In: Senegal's Precolonial Polities	47
3	The Politics of Decentralization in Senegal	74
4	Political Narratives across Rural Senegal	95
5	Delivering Schools and Clinics in Rural Senegal	128
6	Congruence and Incongruence in Action	155
7	Decompressing Legacies of Public Goods Delivery, 1880–2012	192
8	Institutional Congruence beyond Senegal	218
	Conclusion	244
Appendix		253
Bibliography		269
Index		291

Figures

1.1	Redistribution across political geographies – high congruence and low congruence	*page* 41
2.1	Precolonial polities and historically acephalous regions	54
2.2	Colonial-era dynamics predicting erasure of precolonial legacies	63
3.1	Colonial changes to cantons by cercle and region, 1895–1960	88
4.1	Map of surveyed departments	98
4.2	Difference in means in elite social ties	110
4.3	Evaluations of local government performance	120
4.4	Evaluations of local government performance by family relation	121
4.5	Local government responsibilities (% responses)	122
5.1	Precolonial capitals and discount rate illustration	140
5.2	Effect of institutional congruence on village access to new social services	145
5.3	Effect of alternative explanations on village access to new social services	147
5.4	Trust estimates	149
5.5	Illustration of location-allocation models	152
5.6	Effect of institutional congruence on location-allocation choices	153
5.7	Placebo models – effect of institutional congruence on central-state-allocated goods	153
6.1	Family network relations between village chiefs	166
6.2	Friendship network relations between village chiefs	167
6.3	Network relations between village chiefs and local elected officials	168
6.4	Kebemer public goods delivery	179
6.5	Koungheul public goods delivery	180
6.6	Elite networks in Koumpentoum	185
6.7	Koumpentoum public goods delivery	187

7.1 Effect of institutional congruence on new social service access over time	195
7.2 Basic services over time	197
7.3 Marginal effect of centralization on education and health attainment	198
7.4 Effect of colonial exposure on service access over time	206
7.5 Linear fit between early colonial and subsequent service access	207
7.6 Effect of early investments on later investments	209
7.7 Colonial favoritism on service access over time	212
8.1 Difference of means – DHS data	224
8.2 Difference of means – DHS data, accounting for variation in level of decentralization	228
8.3 Difference in means – Afrobarometer data	230

Tables

2.1	Descriptive data on persistence of village social hierarchies	*page* 65
3.1	Administrative hierarchies over time	81
4.1	Descriptive statistics for local elite survey respondents, by department	100
4.2	Odds ratios of perceived inequality in the local council	124
5.1	Descriptive statistics of large-N dataset	136
6.1	Description of case selection	158
6.2	Descriptive statistics for case study interviewees	159
8.1	Decentralization in West African countries surveyed in Afrobarometer Round 6	221
8.2	West Africa's precolonial states in the nineteenth century	226
A.1	Additional descriptive statistics	254
A.2	Effect of institutional congruence on village access to new social services (Figure 5.2)	256
A.3	Effect of institutional congruence on village access to new social services, increased buffer size	258
A.4	Effect of institutional congruence on village access to new social services, reduced measure of access	260
A.5a	Effect of alternative explanations on village access to new primary schools, odds ratios (Figure 5.3a and b)	262
A.5b	Effect of alternative explanations on village access to new clinics, odds ratios (Figure 5.3c)	264
A.6	Trust estimates (Figure 5.4)	265
A.7	Effect of institutional congruence on location-allocation choices (Figure 5.6)	267
A.8	Placebo models – effect of institutional congruence on central state allocated goods, odds ratios (Figure 5.7)	268

Acknowledgments

This book began as a dissertation at Cornell University, where I was supervised by Nicolas van de Walle. Nic deserves the first and deepest acknowledgment for his guidance during the project's development as well as the generous support he continues to offer long after my departure from Ithaca. I benefited enormously from the other members of my dissertation committee, Kenneth Roberts and Christopher Way, both of whom encouraged me to think beyond Senegal to the broader implications of my ideas. I also thank Richard Bensel and Tom Pepinsky for providing particularly detailed commentary at various points in this project's development. Kevin Morrison also provided valuable feedback at early stages. Like many, my peers were as influential as my professors and my graduate education was greatly enriched by my fellow graduate students. I thank, in particular, Jaimie Bleck, Erin Hern, Lauren Honig, and Danielle Thomsen.

During my repeated visits to Senegal, I received generous help from the staff at the West African Research Center and the Senegalese National Archives. Excellent research assistance was provided by Amina Ba, Mohammed Camara, Balla Diatta, Koly Fall, Moussa Fall, Mairame Ly, and Idrissa Ndiade. El Hadji Almareme Faye deserves special recognition for repeatedly decamping from Dakar with me to the countryside. Hundreds of local elected officials, village chiefs, rural development agents, and government officials graciously took the time to talk with me about local politics. I will never be able to express my gratitude to them for partaking in the Senegalese specialties of political debate and *ataaya* with my research assistants and myself. I can only hope that this book does justice to their stories and experiences and, in some way, helps to address the many hurdles they face in their daily lives.

I found welcome space to develop this project into a book manuscript during the three years I spent at Northwestern University. Jim Mahoney, Will Reno, and Rachel Riedl offered notable support during this period as did the broader

African studies community. I thank participants in the Buffet Center's Comparative Historical Social Sciences workshop and attendees at the Program of African Studies' noon lunch talks for their constructive feedback as well as for providing a stimulating intellectual community during my time in Evanston.

When I joined the political science department at the University of California, Berkeley in 2018, I thought this book was nearly done, but the insights and feedback of my new colleagues led me to push deeper and further in my thinking in ways that have been especially productive. Particular recognition is owed here to Leo Arriola, Thad Dunning, Andrew Little, and Alison Post, though the department as a whole has my gratitude for the warm welcome I have received. I benefited enormously from a book workshop during my first year at Berkeley, where Pierre Englebert, Dominika Koter, and Ann Swidler provided detailed and generous comments. Paul Thissen, Justine Davis, Allison Grossman, and Melanie Phillips have also kindly read numerous parts of this project. I extend my appreciation as well to the other regular attendees of the African Studies Workshop in addition to participants in the 2020 UC-Africa Workshop, which offered one last opportunity to present this material as I wrapped up edits.

Various parts of this project have benefited from constructive feedback from, at some point or another, Ryan Briggs, Elliott Green, Robin Harding, Adam Harris, Mala Htun, Daniel de Kadt, Devra Moehler, Amy Poteete, Phil Roessler, Ryan Sheely, Prerna Singh, Richard Snyder, Jennifer Widner, and Joseph Woldense as well as participants in the 2018 Governance and Local Development (GLD) conference in Gothenburg, Sweden. The entire process of embarking on my career has been eased by the supportive mentorship of Lauren Morris Maclean and, deserving mention once again, Leo Arriola and Rachel Riedl. I would also like to thank Natalie Letsa, Kathleen Klaus, Jeff Paller, and Whitney Taylor for their friendship; it has been a true pleasure to bump into you all again and again around the world.

The field research for this book was made possible by the Houston J. Flourney and Boren Fellowships as well as grants from the Center for the Study of Inequality, Institute for African Development, and the Cornell University Graduate School. The Afrobarometer, Centre de Suivi Ecologique, the Senegalese Ministries of Education and Health as well as the PEPAM program all generously shared data with me. At Cambridge University Press, I thank the close reading of two anonymous reviewers as well as the guiding hand of Sara Doskow. Portions of this project have been published in *World Politics* as Martha Wilfahrt. 2018. "Precolonial Legacies and the Contemporary Politics of Public Goods Provision in Decentralized West Africa." *World Politics* 70 (2):239–274 and in *World Development* as Martha Wilfahrt. 2018. "The Politics of Local Government Performance: Elite Cohesion and Cross-Village Constraints in Decentralized Senegal." *World Development* 103:149–161.

Acknowledgments xiii

My family has been indispensable in my entire academic journey. My parents, Lori and Jeff, have offered nothing but encouragement, imparting in me from a young age the firm (if not borderline stubborn) belief that I can do whatever I set my mind to. I likewise thank my brother, Peter, and sister-in-law, Mandy Maring, as well as my in-laws in Zaandam, who have welcomed me (and my halting Dutch skills) with unparalleled warmth. Ankica Runac and Anabel Njoes have endured endless stories about the minutiae of academia with great cheer; their friendship means the world to me. Though he is not here to read this, my older brother, Andrew, left an incredible mark on my life and I miss him daily.

Like many, I will conclude by thanking my partner, Robert Braun. As with many academic couples, this project has been so discussed and debated – on Skype during long periods apart, during Saturday afternoon hikes, at cafes, and over dinner – that his influence on this book is impossible to categorize or count. But while I might prefer to remember the moments that sparked new ideas or solved sticky problems, this should not obscure the many moments of frustration that go into a project of this length. It is for the light you offer in those moments, Robert, for which I am most grateful of all.

This title is part of the Cambridge University Press *Flip it Open* Open Access Books program and has been "flipped" from a traditional book to an Open Access book through the program.

Flip it Open sells books through regular channels, treating them at the outset in the same way as any other book; they are part of our library collections for Cambridge Core, and sell as hardbacks and ebooks. The one crucial difference is that we make an upfront commitment that when each of these books meets a set revenue threshold we make them available to everyone Open Access via Cambridge Core.

This paperback edition has been released as part of our Open Access commitment and we would like to use this as an opportunity to thank the libraries and other buyers who have helped us flip this and the other titles in the program to Open Access.

To see the full list of libraries that we know have contributed to *Flip it Open*, as well as the other titles in the program please visit http://www.cambridge.org/fio-acknowledgements

Introduction

THE MILLET MILLS

In 2016, two local governments in rural Senegal had a total of seventeen millet mills to distribute. The first local government had been granted eleven mills by a national government program.[1] When choosing from among the many villages in the local government, Mamadou Dia, the former mayor who had brokered the program, carefully designated the mills for the villages of his political supporters and extended family.[2] Because the mills arrived after Dia's defeat in the 2014 local elections, however, his successor, Abdoulaye Ka, quickly put his own mark on the project. Upon taking office, Ka dissolved the women's committees that Dia had formed to manage the mills' profits and recreated them with more politically favorable members. In a political coup for himself, Ka was able to change one mill's destination to his own supporters because the recipient village had been ambiguously listed in official paperwork. As Dia grumbled to me later, Ka had really "played the situation."[3] As a result of these distributional choices, villages with less than 100 residents received mills while women in villages three times that size remained with no choice but to pound their families' daily millet by hand.

---

[1] Reforms in 2014 changed the nomenclature of the local state. The Rural Community President (*le président de la communauté rurale*, commonly called the "PCR") became the "mayor" and "rural communities" became "rural communes." Because the research was conducted pre and post reform, I opt to follow the post-reform language as it reflects the current appellation of the local state in Senegal today. I further employ local state, local government, and local council interchangeably to refer to the rural commune.
[2] I employ pseudonyms to protect the confidentiality of respondents who requested it.
[3] Interview, February 18, 2017. An example of the ambiguity that the incoming mayor made use of would be where a village was listed as "*Keur Abdou*" in a commune home to two villages named *Keur Abdou Wolof* and *Keur Abdou Peulh*, thus allowing him to choose between the two.

In the second case, the local government purchased six mills and delivered them to six different villages, none of which had a functioning mill previously. Recipients reported that their villages were chosen because their female residents spent endless hours each day pounding millet and because every year their villages paid the entirety of their local taxes. Neighboring villages did not contest the decision or its logic. Rather, despite the fact that the current mayor had won with a much narrower vote share than in the first case, local elites noted with pride that their community possessed a powerful sense of solidarity that guided such distributive decision-making. As the imam of the local government's capital village mused one evening, "the best politics are the politics where everyone gets their share."[4] Across the local government's many villages, no one had much to say about the affair.

The seventeen mills represent a fraction of the services delivered each year by local governments in rural Senegal. Since 1996, the country's democratically elected local governments have been tasked with delivering basic social service investments, ranging from building primary schools to organizing yearly youth soccer tournaments to purchasing millet mills. Yet as these illustrations suggest, local governance has produced stark differences in how goods are delivered and, by extension, who benefits from government largess. Why do some local governments deliver goods broadly across their populations while others target even the most basic of services to meet narrow political ends?

The answer to this question does not only concern Senegal. Similar scenes unfold across Africa – and the Global South more broadly – every year. Over the past quarter century, donors have urged most sub-Saharan African states to adopt similar governance reforms, rendering decentralization among "the most significant facets of state restructuring in Africa since independence."[5] As an institutional reform, decentralization has become the bearer of most good things desired by the international development community: it is argued to promote democracy and political participation, to increase the voices of women and minorities, and to improve efficiency and equity in basic service access while stimulating bottom-up development and economic growth in the process.[6]

The varied fates of the seventeen millet mills should give advocates of decentralization pause. The example of the first local government suggests clearly that the decentralization of public goods delivery leaves basic investments vulnerable to local political pressures. After all, local officials spoke frankly about using the mills for their own political ambitions; when asked how he decided which villages would receive the eleven mills he had to distribute, the former mayor Dia responded clearly "I chose the villages that are with me."[7] Dia's candor calls into question the promise that decentralization would

---

[4] Interview, February 8, 2017.   [5] Ndegwa and Levy (2003, 283).
[6] See for example, Nzouankeu (1994); Oxhorn et al. (2004); and Bardhan and Mookherjee (2006).
[7] Interview, February 18, 2017.

help enact the preferences of the local community, rendering government more accountable and responsive.[8] But such cases risk obscuring the second case, where the local government more or less did what scholars and donors would have hoped: they allocated scarce goods according to equity and need.

Herein lies the first of two questions motivating this book: why are some communities able to come together to improve their collective lot while others are not? I examine the distributional political logics adopted by local governments to advance a novel answer to this question: local decision-makers are better able to cooperate around basic service delivery when their formal jurisdictional boundaries overlap with informal social institutions, by which I mean norms of appropriate comportment in the public sphere demarcated by group boundaries. I refer to this spatial overlap as institutional congruence. When local government boundaries pool together villages that share preexisting social institutions, the preferences of local elites (such as local government officials, village chiefs, and other notables) shift toward group goals, dampening potentially explosive political situations, curtailing opportunism, and enabling elites to adopt longer-run time horizons. This is the dynamic that explains the six mills delivered by the second local government in 2016. The most significant lesson from the story of the seventeen millet mills is not one that fulfills our more pessimistic expectations about distributional politics therefore, but rather in the comparative banality of cases where such dynamics are absent.

If the social institutions that I argue are critical for reorienting elite interests are not evenly distributed across space, then why do some local governments possess robust cross-village norms while others do not? This is the book's second motivating question. If we want to understand why elites in the second local government did not pursue their own private gain, we must situate it in a much longer history than the tale of the millet mills alone. This local government falls in the heart of the precolonial state of Cayor, where petty disputes over a few millet mills cannot be allowed to undermine centuries of cohabitation and cooperation between villages. In areas that fall in the footprints of the country's precolonial polities, elite incentives are more prosocial toward their neighboring villages because they inherited robust cross-village social institutions that are repurposed and redeployed following institutional reform.

This book thus argues that historical structures of political order can remain politically consequential long after the formal institutions themselves have disappeared. Even if the precolonial past does not at first glance appear to have much of anything to do with contemporary local governance, the following chapters document how the advent of decentralization in the 1990s granted new venues for much older social repertoires, forcefully bringing the weight of the past into the sphere of formal politics. In brief, this book is about such

---

[8] For example, Wunsch (2000); though see Crook (2003) and others for concerns.

differences – between areas defined by institutional congruence, where local elite comportment is constrained by shared social institutions, and communities where such congruence is absent, between areas that were home to precolonial kingdoms and those that were not. These differences, I argue, drive profound variation in the politics of representation and redistribution at the grassroots in rural West Africa today.

REDISTRIBUTIVE DILEMMAS IN RURAL AFRICA

African governments have made dramatic investments in basic social services since the turn of the millennium. Even in the wake of the 2008 financial crisis, social spending increased countercyclically in many countries.[9] For its part, Senegal increased education spending from 3.2 percent of its gross domestic product in 2000, to 7.1 percent by 2015.[10] The material outcomes of these budgetary changes are highly visible as new clinics, roads, and schools pop up across the landscape.

The academic consequence of this expansion in public goods delivery has been a resurgent interest in distributive politics on the continent. Though research has long recognized the political calculations behind public policy and redistribution, publications on service delivery on the continent have increased nearly tenfold since the early 1990s.[11] The vast majority of this work, however, focuses on the political logics of the central state, meaning that we possess relatively less theoretical and empirical insight into local redistributive decision-making.[12] In general, local governance in Africa remains understudied compared to the experiences of other regions.[13] This is a notable oversight given the fact that African citizens report their most frequent government contact at the local level, echoing Wibbels' (2019, 15) observation that in much of the Global South local governments "are often the only governments that materially impact the lives of citizens."[14]

More insight into the nature of local distributional politics might be found in the proliferation of work on decentralization over the past quarter century. Yet this body of work tends to fall into a dichotomy between an overly macro-focus on the institutional environment of reform on the one hand and a micro-focus on community-specific outcomes on the other. The former focuses on failures of

---

[9] International Monetary Fund (2010).   [10] World Bank (2018).
[11] Bates' (1981) seminal study of postcolonial coalition-building strategies exemplifies this approach. Publication increases as reported by querying "public goods delivery" and Africa on https://app.dimensions.ai.
[12] For example, Jablonski (2014).   [13] Though see Gottlieb (2015).
[14] Twenty-five percent of respondents in Round 5 of the Afrobarometer reported having contacted their local councilors over the past year in contrast to only 12–14 percent who reported contacting their deputies or other government officials.

institutional design where the animating assumption is that the benefits of decentralization will be unleashed once the institutions are "right."[15] An alternative version of this macro-perspective emphasizes the politics surrounding state implementation of decentralization reforms, rendering differences in local government performance a function of the political ambitions of the central government, be it manifested through politicized implementation, uneven fiscal transfers, or other forms of favoritism.[16]

At the micro level, decentralization has largely been studied as a question of elite capture.[17] This literature, which focuses on how elites "control, shape, or manipulate decision-making processes or institutions in ways that serve their self-interests and priorities," suggests that when power is concentrated in the hands of a few, elites will collude, using their role as intermediaries to advance their own interests and divert resources to themselves.[18] In this book, I conceptualize local elites as holders of local social status within their villages, the base social unit in rural Senegal. This definition captures both customary authorities, such as village chiefs, and lineage-based status hierarchies, such as those holding notable or high-caste status, as well as religious leaders and individuals who obtain status via their association with the state, such as elected officials. Theories of elite capture have generated substantial pessimism about the fate of local redistribution, but they offer little theoretical leverage on why these dynamics would be more active in one local government, but not another.[19] If local elites systematically pursue their own interests at the expense of the collective good, then absent institutional safeguards, decentralization should produce equally poor development outcomes everywhere.

Taken together, neither the recent literature on distributive politics nor work on decentralization easily explains the varying distributional decisions adopted by Senegal's local governments that I document in the following chapters. As I show, we see variation in local government performance within a shared macro-institutional environment, indicating that we must look beyond questions of institutional design. My research also reveals that local political cleavages only rarely parallel national ones and are more clearly shaped by deep-seated social histories at the grassroots than the nature of political connections to the center, suggesting that distributional politics follow distinctly local political dynamics and are not reducible to the ambitions of the central government.

At the same time, my findings challenge the idea that local governance is reducible to the question of when local elites are able to control local positions

---

[15] A related version of this argues that decentralized governance may vary as the result of structural endowments, such as local human resources and capacity, though these appear to only weakly explain differences in decentralization's outcomes (Romeo 2003).
[16] Boone (2003a) and Lambright (2011).
[17] See Bardhan (2002) for a review. See also Crook (2003); Manor (2004); and Wunsch (2001).
[18] Labonte (2012, 91). [19] Mookherjee (2015).

of authority because this ignores a prior question of when local elites perceive themselves to have shared interests. Recent scholarly and policy-oriented attention to elites has often focused on identifying specific actors capable of moderating interventions or, alternatively, those whose authority must be checked.[20] I seek to trouble this emerging dichotomy of local elites as either a peril or a promise for development and democratization by focusing on the nature of intra-elite relationships as the variable of interest. By emphasizing elites as self-interested individuals, we have lost sight of the ways in which elite authority is interdependent and imbricated in broader social webs that are as, if not more, consequential than individual motivations.[21] In other words, even if elites may be able to capture local government positions everywhere, I do not predict this to generate universally good or bad outcomes because what matters is not their positions as elites alone but the broader social networks that shape the social and political strategies available to them.

In this way, I contribute to our understanding of local governance by drawing attention to the political negotiations that take place between local elites, shifting the unit of analysis downward from macro-level work focused on the central state and up from the micro-focus of work on elite capture, to look squarely at the local state itself. Because democratic decentralization pools numerous villages into one administrative unit, local elected officials are obliged to negotiate *across* villages when deciding how to distribute scarce projects and resources. Certainly, local elites seek to maintain and reinforce their social status *within* their villages, pursuing local government office in order to capture state resources as one means of doing this. Nonetheless, when local elites meet within the local state, we can neither assume that they share a common interest to collude nor that they are inherently rivalrous. Rather, their political incentives emerge from their social worlds and are intimately influenced by historical legacies that long pre-date the modern advent of decentralized governance. It is only by recognizing the social underpinnings of local political life, that I argue we can understand distributional politics following decentralization.

THE ARGUMENT

I advance a theory of institutional congruence to explain subnational variation in local government performance following decentralization. Specifically, I posit that local redistributive politics is a function of the degree of spatial overlap between the formal institutional extent of the local state, created and reformed from above, and local social institutions, by which I mean norms of appropriate behavior in the public sphere demarcated by group boundaries,

---

[20] For example, Cruz and Schneider (2017).
[21] Echoing a point recently raised by Baldwin and Raffler (2019).

inherited from the precolonial past. Despite the fact that West Africa's precolonial kingdoms are long defunct, I show that they left a legacy of robust, cross-village social institutions that continue to define local social life. When social institutions embed the vast majority of local elites from across a local government's many villages, elites are more likely to factor the interests of others into their own preferences. This is true even though today's local government boundaries are much smaller than the territorial extent of precolonial kingdoms; institutional congruence does not necessitate the perfect overlap of physical boundaries as long as local elites are mutually embedded within shared social institutions. Though comparable social institutions exist in historically acephalous zones, or those that lacked a centralized precolonial political authority, they remain delineated by village or clan boundaries and do not map onto the arena of the local state.

Why would such an overlap alter elite behavior? In cases of high congruence, the presence of shared social institutions encourages local actors to engage in more prosocial behavior toward group members. Here, a localized sense of community elongates time horizons and leads local elites to "encapsulate" the interests of their neighbors, enabling long-term cooperation.[22] In contrast, elites' political and social worlds are discordant in cases of low congruence, minimizing the risks that local elites face when they pursue individual interests and diminishing any rewards they may receive from acting with an eye toward the collective good.[23] This generates the expectation that representation and redistribution under decentralization will be broad and equalizing in cases of high congruence, but contentious and targeted in areas where it is low.

Social institutions shape the decision-making of local elites through two complementary mechanisms. The first mechanism is the presence of a shared social identity endowed by a precolonial state that ties local elites into a sense of shared fate. When actors invoke a shared basis of social identification, they delineate in- and out-group members, reinforcing the meaning of their mutual membership through shared narratives. As I document, the precolonial past forms a powerful identity that local actors can lay shared claim to, even in the face of other forms of diversity such as religion and ethnicity. The second mechanism arises from the social network ties among local elites. Communities that fall in the footprint of precolonial polities exhibit denser social ties across the many villages of the local state than in incongruent communities both because generations of cohabitation have fostered enduring ties around intermarriage and intervillage assistance, and because the ability to claim descent from the precolonial polity, no matter how romanticized, generates a mutually reinforcing justification for elite status across villages. Denser social network ties not only valorize shared social identities and social institutions, they also

---

[22] Hardin (2002, 4).   [23] See for example, Kollock (1998).

circulate information about actor behavior, enabling rewards and sanctions for those who uphold or transgress group norms.

Together, the identity and network mechanisms help explain both why social institutions have persisted to the present and why they continue to influence elite behavior: broad social identities create focal points for local action while dense social networks generate incentives to abide by locally understood social norms of behavior. Like all informal institutions, therefore, social institutions shape behavior through sanctions and rewards. What makes social institutions distinct is the degree to which actors internalize these expectations for both their own social comportment and that of their social relations.

In this way, I present a novel explanation for why local governments make strikingly different distributional choices when delivering basic public goods. Local elected officials face structurally distinct political *and* social incentives in cases like the second community with which this book opened, where the boundaries of the local state fall within the territory of the precolonial state of Cayor. Here, cross-village social institutions enable intra-elite cooperation by disincentivizing political conflict and fostering a sense of "we-ness."[24] Where such cross-village institutions are absent, however, as seen in the first case, politics pervades even the most basic of local government investments, skewing allocative decisions away from the neediest to the most politically useful or politically expedient.

The argument is not that areas home to precolonial states somehow produce more benevolent leaders, but rather that elites in these areas are particularly sensitive to perceived violations of local norms because they face distinct social risks in addition to those they face at the ballot box. In this way, social institutions simultaneously impose standards for political behavior and create broader webs of obligation for local elites, rendering the local politics of representation and redistribution endogenous to local social structure. Though shared identities and cross-village social networks are not necessarily unique to areas that were home to precolonial states, the presence of both mechanisms in these zones jointly reinforces the value of social institutions to elites from across a local government's many villages with powerful effects on actor behavior.

Why would the precolonial past generate such persistent social legacies? I locate the continued relevance of the precolonial era in the durability of rural social hierarchies throughout the West African Sahel, where social status is largely shaped by one's family lineage. Despite the onslaught of colonialism, the French colonial state stopped short of fundamentally altering village social hierarchies, meaning that most village chieftaincies and other markers of social status within villages have persisted by and large intact within families. Because the ability to claim descent from a zone's founding families bestows particular

---

[24] To adopt Singh's (2011) terminology.

social and political authority, local elites repeat and valorize local historical narratives justifying their right to local authority as a means to legitimate and shore up their own status. Precolonial identities are a particularly potent means to do so, but by invoking this historical right to authority, elites simultaneously validate the status of others making identical claims. The very act of claiming social status in these zones is therefore collective, linking local elites into broader cross-village networks of reciprocal recognition of elite status.

Social institutions that develop over generations of cohabitation thus come to mutually embed local elites in their behavioral stipulations by virtue of their ties to local status hierarchies. Yet in contrast to other prominent arguments about historical legacies, my theory stipulates that we should not expect the precolonial past to always matter for redistributive politics even if these social institutions are reproduced over time. Rather, it is only following decentralization reforms, when allocative authority is transferred downward, that the dynamics of institutional congruence should arise because it is only at this moment that social institutions map onto the scale at which distributional decisions are made.

POINTS OF DEPARTURE

My argument holds theoretical and empirical implications for four prominent debates in the study of the African state and political economy of development more broadly. In order, I detail below how the argument speaks to (a) the value of local narratives as a lens into actors' political strategies; (b) the social identities we prioritize in the study of African politics; (c) prospects for state-building on the continent; and (d) our understanding of how historical legacies shape contemporary development outcomes.

Local Narratives, Local Political Strategies

This book joins a growing interest in redistributive politics in developing countries. The motivating assumption of much of this work is that politicians are instrumental and vote-maximizing leading studies of service delivery in Africa to view public goods delivery as a function of the electoral calculi of politicians who target supporters along partisan or ethnic lines in an effort to earn votes.[25] I do not dispute the assumption that politicians pursue political power above all else. Like all politicians, the local elected officials I speak with in rural West Africa are sensitive to the demands of political competition. Rural politicians almost always run for reelection and cite delivering goods to voters as the way to get reelected. As one mayor cautioned, "never forget that tomorrow they will have to reelect you."[26]

---

[25] For example, Burgess et al. (2015); Franck and Rainer (2012); and Ejdemyr et al. (2017).
[26] Interview, Diourbel Region, February 15, 2016.

But focusing on short-term electoral motives alone risks leaving critical dimensions of local political behavior unexplained. During interviews, local politicians in rural Senegal voice broader and more interdependent preferences toward redistribution than those suggested by dominant theories of distributive politics. For example, they frequently detail at great length how they take into account prominent family lineages and social relations, balancing political decisions, such as who gets their name on electoral lists, across villages. One mayor in Fatick Region stressed the role of "social alliances" in his community, which he could not ignore because while such social ties may not always manifest themselves electorally, they were critical for local political success. In this case, the mayor's social relations and the obligations they engendered had led him to invest heavily in villages that had not voted for him and which he did not expect to do so in the future.[27]

While it is easy to dismiss these claims as face-saving stories told to an outsider, I suggest we should take them seriously as a lens into how local actors understand and interpret their political worlds. Listening to how local elites root their explanations of their political lives in the specific histories of their community helps us understand the beliefs they bring with them to their social and political interactions because such collective memory sheds unique light on the "history of play" between individuals.[28] To this end, the rhetoric that individuals deploy when explaining their behavior is a particularly powerful vantage point into the collective beliefs and norms that they use to formulate and justify their actions.[29] Narratives of local political life thus reveal what individuals view as "ordinary and right," generating a valuable form of data for understanding local action.[30] That the very telling and retelling of local narratives should be studied as an explicitly political act has recently been argued by Klaus (2020), who documents the ways in which narratives surrounding land ownership in rural Kenya delineate in- and out-group members to create or reaffirm the cultural meaning of land within communities. I suggest that a similar process is at play in rural Senegal: when local elites narrate their local political worlds, they reveal and reinforce their understandings of community membership and the rights and obligations this entails.[31]

Ultimately, it is less critical that the narratives I recount in the following chapters are strictly historically accurate because I am more interested in how actors believe their social worlds operate than in the absolute truth. Though I take care to cross-validate the degree to which narratives of local history and

---

[27] Interview, mayor, Fatick Region, May 16, 2013.   [28] Rothstein (2005, 157–160).
[29] Kowert and Legro (1996, 483–485).   [30] Patterson and Monroe (1998, 316).
[31] Writing on the local politics in the Sahel, anthropologist Sten Hagberg (2019, 15) remarks similarly on the importance of local idioms as a lens into local political dynamics. If being seen as "doing politics" (*faire la politique*) become shorthand for one who lies or pursues political power at the expense of the community, local actors prefer instead to be seen as honest and working toward a common good.

political life are *collective* across a local government and though I draw on multiple methodologies to test the ability of these narratives to explain redistributive patterns, I am indifferent to whether or not they document a community's "true" history. To the extent that the actors I interviewed recount their communities' histories from their social worlds, they shape how local social and political objectives are understood and, by extension, the appropriate policy to pursue them.

Accordingly, I theorize how elites pursue power *through* their social relations. When local elites share collective narratives about their community, they also share norms about appropriate political comportment, including not only what is expected of them but also what others will tolerate and what will enhance their reputation and their social and political influence. How elites negotiate, in other words, varies as a function of the social institutions they are mutually embedded in and not their narrow political interests alone. This is a less radical reimagining of political strategies that it may at first imply, but it does nuance considerably the assumption that elites can pursue purely electoral strategies. The reality of local politics in the developing world is that many rural elites live within the communities they serve, engaging in iterated, daily interactions with one another that extend their time horizons.[32] The effects of this become clear in the narratives of local political life heard in many Senegalese communities where key political actors – representatives, patrons, chiefs, and brokers alike – speak openly about how their social and political lives are entangled, limiting their ability to pursue individual or electoral gains alone explicitly because their political strategies are shaped by a broader set of political, economic, and social interests.[33] Listening to local narratives, I argue, offers an unparalleled lens into these dynamics.

Rethinking Forms of Identity Politics in Africa

By studying how local elites understand and negotiate their political worlds from the ground up, I am able to make two interventions in a long-standing interest in identity politics in Africa. I begin by pushing back at the assumption that ethnicity is the most obvious political cleavage for mobilizing political support in the region. Ethnicity has been granted a particular privilege by students of African politics, where it is viewed as a core source of political preferences and where ethnic ties are considered the prevalent channels of clientelism and service delivery.[34] From the advent of ethnic or hometown associations in the colonial era to elected politicians in the present, patrons with access to the state are conceptualized as conduits for services and

---

[32] Hicken (2011, 292–293).
[33] This has, of course, been studied in some depth by political anthropologists, particularly in the French tradition, though their findings are case and region-specific.
[34] Boone (2014, 317).

privileges that are channeled downward to co-ethnic clients.[35] In the aggregate, ethnic diversity is associated with slower economic growth and worse development outcomes.[36] Indeed, the benefit of ethnic homogeneity has been so widely accepted that much of the ensuing debate focuses on adjudicating between potential mechanisms.[37]

The influence of this literature is seen clearly in the recent explosion of research on service delivery in the region, which takes ethnic favoritism as a default hypothesis. But while African politicians are frequently assumed to find the most viable path to electoral victory in ethnic coalition building, the evidence for this tends to be strongest in Anglophone cases and some scholars have suggested that co-ethnicity may not yield the benefits that have long been ascribed to it.[38] Critically, even if ethnicity is a key political cleavage nationally, it may not operate similarly at a local level, a reality Nugent (2010, 50) identifies in The Gambia, where ethnicity's "salience remains weak in the internal politics of most rural communities" despite being politicized nationally.[39]

In questioning the dominance of ethnicity in the study of African politics, I do not deny that ethnicity is a relevant social category for Senegalese. Individuals describe themselves along ethnic lines and they invoke ethnic stereotypes and categories, but it has never mapped neatly onto national political cleavages.[40] In areas home to precolonial states, ethnicity is rarely mentioned by respondents other than in simple descriptive terms, though such claims do come out strongly in many historically acephalous, or stateless, areas of the country. In the following chapters, I test the ethnicity hypothesis in numerous ways, but like others before me I find little evidence that ethnicity is a useful predictor of Senegalese political cleavages or distributive politics in the country.[41] Instead, place-specific identities dominate local political life. Among these, a sense of descent from the precolonial past holds special currency, but throughout the country local histories of settlement order local claims to political resources. These identities may intersect with ethnicity, but they are not reducible to it.

---

[35] For example, Rothchild and Olorunsola (1983); Barkan et al. (1991); Azam (2001); and Koter (2013).

[36] Easterly and Levine (1997). See also the review in Kimenyi (2006).

[37] For example, Miguel and Gugerty (2005) and Habyarimana et al. (2007) on the role of shared norms or sanctioning mechanisms. On common preferences, see Alesina et al. (1999); Baldwin and Huber (2010); or Lieberman and McClendon (2013).

[38] Kramon and Posner (2013); Jablonski (2014); and Briggs (2014) offer evidence of ethnic coalition building. Recent challenges have come from Kasara (2007); Van de Walle (2007); Franck and Rainer (2012); Jackson (2013); and Gisselquist (2014).

[39] Boone (2014, 324) joins this critique in cautioning against the ecological fallacy of assuming that "the local is a microcosm of the national."

[40] For example, Diouf (1994). Others have suggested that *cousinage* or joking cousin relations might create cross-cutting cleavages (Galvan 2004 and Dunning and Harrison 2010).

[41] Notably Koter's (2016) comparison of Senegal and Benin.

This leads me to make a second, more novel intervention about the prevailing tendency to deduce politically relevant identities from observed political behavior.[42] Despite growing recognition that political identities rooted in the past can be consequential decades if not centuries later, I challenge the assumption that they are *always* politically relevant.[43] My argument, which documents how social identities can persist at the grassroots with minimal political effect only to forcefully reenter political life decades later, offers a framework for understanding why identities may generate distinct behavior at some moments of time but not at others.[44] We analytically limit ourselves when studying institutional change when we assume that identities are exogenous or static variables. In contrast, it is exactly in these moments that we might expect shifts in which identities individuals prioritize.[45] As I show, previously latent identities can become politically relevant once they become congruent with newly introduced formal institutions, revealing why the spatial interaction between identities and institutional boundaries deserves our explicit attention.

By taking seriously the social identities that rural Senegalese themselves utilize in conversation, I reinforce Cramer Walsh's argument that researchers should not ignore how individuals describe their own political identities since these are "touchstones for individuals' understandings of the political world" (2003, 176). If, as I argue, old identities can be politicized in the relatively short term following institutional reform, then assuming that rural Senegalese see themselves in ethnic terms, say as Wolofs or Serers, rather than as descendants of the Kingdom of Saloum, means we risk never understanding local politics at all. In this way, my findings caution against the tendency to discuss what we can most easily measure at the risk of ignoring consequential identities that are less amenable to quantification.

Revisiting the Question of State-Building in Rural Africa

Scholars have long diagnosed the ills of the African state. It is either too heavy-handed, suppressing a dynamic society or conversely it is too embedded within society itself, propping up its weak legitimacy by reinforcing blurred boundaries between the public and private realms.[46] Among our most foundational questions about the African state is why African leaders have been unable or unwilling to expand the authority of the state outward across their

---

[42] A classic example is Posner's (2004b) PREG measure.
[43] For example, Acharya et al. (2016).
[44] This claim finds a parallel in Wittenberg (2006, 13), who documents the persistence of mass political loyalties in Hungary despite the political upheaval of Communism, a phenomenon he attributes to the strength of local institutions which provide "focal points for mutual interaction" even under moments of extreme social duress.
[45] Echoing recent work by Singh and Vom Hau (2016).
[46] For example, Hyden (1980) and Azarya and Chazan (1987) on the former. Bayart (1993) and Chabal and Daloz (1999) articulate to the latter case.

territories. Why, nearly three generations of scholars have asked, have we failed to see the emergence of political bargains between the center and its citizens?

Recall that decentralization was proposed by many as a means to address these various "pathologies" by encouraging social-contracting. Accordingly, my argument generates a distinct set of implications for the fate of state-building on the continent. I present empirical evidence that precolonial histories position some communities to do better under decentralization than others in a way that is independent of institutional design or the political ambitions of the center. This means that forces often conceptualized as impediments to the state-building project – precolonial, indigenous social organizations – can actually entrench the state locally when the local state is sufficiently able to graft onto a preconceived understanding of community.

The more radical implication is that the very reforms intended to "fix" the African state risk heightening inequalities in state strength as some communities attach themselves to the local state, slowly building capacity and commitment to the democratic project, while elsewhere others disengage from local governments which they see as unresponsive and foreign. The argument holds mixed lessons, therefore, for long-standing questions about the relationship between state and society in the region. The state is ultimately stronger, I find, when it is embedded within or legitimated by society, but only in particular spatial constellations. Like Boone (2003b) or Herbst (2000) before me, I document great territorial unevenness driven by structural, historical legacies, but I root the source of this variation in purely local dynamics.

Critically, the production of these inequalities is ongoing, which would indicate that even if we hold the central state's relative strength or weakness constant in the short term, organic properties of social structures at the grassroots are capable of generating variable degrees of state-building subnationally. This refocuses our attention to the local level even when we want to understand the center because state-building ultimately takes place at a granular level within communities. In lieu of studying how the state looks downward, I emphasize how local actors negotiate reforms initiated by the center, integrating them into their own political worlds. This, in turn, has implications for national outcomes, from the nature of party strength to the distribution of economic opportunity.

Decompressing Historical Legacies

In recent years, it has become near gospel that "history matters" in the study of why contemporary development outcomes vary across and within countries.[47] Our renewed interest in historical legacies assumes a distinct temporality: the past influences future sequences of events by raising the costs of deviating from

---

[47] See for example, Akyeampong et al. (2014).

Points of Departure

a given pathway through the development of routines, beliefs, or networks, to name but a few common causes.[48] Yet despite the embrace of path dependence by students of political economy, the study of institutional legacies has become surprisingly apolitical and, in its own way, atemporal. This project offers a corrective on both fronts.

I illustrate this by referencing the most relevant debate to my own argument: the growing interest in the long-term legacies of precolonial centralization. This literature is dominated by a series of cross- and subnational studies that demonstrate how early experiences with state formation correlate with a number of contemporary outcomes, including greater economic growth, rule of law, and tendencies toward authoritarianism.[49] Much of this work relies on the assumption that a historical cause, once unleashed, persists to the present in a uniform fashion; for example, that group-specific attributes, like ethnic norms, explain why historically centralized regions perform better over the long term than others.[50] Michalopoulos and Papaioannou's (2015) prominent paper concludes in this vein that the robust correlation between precolonial centralization and better public goods access today is the result of "ethnic-specific attributes," which they argue raises an important question as to how "ethnic institutional and cultural traits shape economic performance." Arguments of this nature are not inherently at odds with my own: the persistence of cultural attributes could plausibly explain why some local governments perform better under decentralization than others. Problematically, however, these arguments assume that group attributes are homogenous across space, equally internalized by members, and persistent across time, and empirical claims that I test and find no evidence for in Chapters 4 and 6.

This literature bolsters my contention that precolonial history continues to matter in the present, but the explanations it offers stop short of helping us understand the "causal channels" through which historical factors course.[51] By estimating a cause and effect with decades, if not centuries, in between, scholars "compress" history and lose insight into how the temporal evolution of our independent and dependent variables alike indicates more and less plausible hypotheses.[52] One consequence is that historical legacies are only rarely tested against each other; yet as I show in Chapter 7, different legacies may face distinct prospects for persistence. Despite the powerful influence of the colonial

---

[48] Put otherwise, "historically evolved structures channel political battles in distinctive ways on a more enduring basis" (Thelen and Steinmo 1992, 2). See here Page (2006) and Wittenberg (2015).
[49] For example, Bockstette et al. (2002) and Hariri (2012).   [50] For example, Hjort (2010).
[51] Nunn (2009, 31).
[52] Grzymala-Busse (2011). See Austin (2008); Hopkins (2011); and Jerven (2011). Dell (2010) offers one of the few efforts to estimate the effect in history by looking at district-level education outcomes at three points in history, though with mixed support for her central argument.

state on subnational public goods access in the twentieth century, for instance, this effect has largely faded by the twenty-first.

This is particularly striking because we know that institutions, which are never distributionally neutral, are inherently subject to political contestation, rendering historical interactions all the more consequential, both empirically and theoretically.[53] Apart from Mahoney's (2010) study of colonialism in Latin America, which argues that the nature of precolonial political organization conditioned the forms of extractive regimes implemented by Spanish colonizers, much of this literature is strangely silent on the question of power at all. Like Mahoney, I focus on how the past generates distinct power dynamics over time, culminating in local elites' deployment of narratives of the precolonial past that I document in subsequent chapters. I go on to "decompress" history in order to examine empirically whether precolonial legacies have always impacted service delivery, only to find no evidence of institutional congruence until the exogenous shock of Senegal's 1996 reforms that devolved distributional authority to the local level. This demands a theory that is both rooted in precolonial political geography and that is logically consistent with the precolonial past only impacting the local level and only under certain formal institutional configurations. By looking at *when* the precolonial past can explain distributional patterns, I offer an explicitly temporal story: the long shadow of the precolonial past on contemporary development outcomes is at best a story of intermittent effects.

EMPIRICAL STRATEGY AND OVERVIEW OF THE BOOK

The remainder of this book elaborates upon my theoretical and empirical claims that the precolonial past intimately shapes the nature of contemporary local governance in rural West Africa. In the following chapters, I employ a comparative, subnational analysis of one country's experiences with formal institutional reform, leveraging the uneven geography of precolonial statehood to examine variation in my independent variable, the degree of institutional congruence following decentralization. Subnational research designs such as my own are particularly well-suited for uncovering the divergent consequences of political and economic reforms because they allow us to hold constant the nature of reform (in this case decentralization) as well as concerns about any number of unobservable characteristics that are expected to differ across but not within countries.[54] In the process, I am able to shed light on the "humanly important" variation that is unleashed by institutional reform, while avoiding the risk of theory-stretching by not assuming a priori that theories developed at the national level will translate neatly downward to subnational units.[55]

---

[53] As argued by Thelen (2004). [54] See here Snyder (2001) and Pepinsky (2018).
[55] Giraudy et al. (2019).

In contrast, I demonstrate that *where* a local government falls spatially within a country offers more leverage than prominent theories of public goods delivery developed at higher levels of governance, which prove to be poorly suited to explain the variation I document in the following chapters.

The risks of this strategy are twofold. First, there is the question of cumulation and generalizability.[56] My findings might tell us a lot about local governance in Senegal, but is the impact of precolonial centralization limited to Senegal alone? In seeking to keep national-level institutions constant within one case, I risk inadvertently selecting a country where something inherently unique is happening. To address this concern, I expand my dataset to look at all of West Africa in Chapter 8, where I find consistent and robust results across the subregion. Second, subnational studies can pose a trade-off between gains in internal validity and our ability to ask enduring questions in the field.[57] But this is not necessarily so. The big, meaty questions that have long defined the study of comparative politics, such as order, democracy, or inequality, are alive and well in the chapters of this book. As I document, only by taking seriously local dynamics of redistribution can we see the important subnational variation in development and democratic consolidation emerging across West Africa following the introduction of decentralization.

Why Senegal?

Senegal is not the only African state whose territory was home to a heterogenous political landscape in the precolonial era. Yet Senegal provides a unique opportunity to explore the long-run legacies of precolonial statehood on contemporary distributive politics because it offers clear leverage on both the independent and dependent variables. First, Senegal was home to a dynamic microstate system prior to French colonization. On the eve of the final French push to conquer Senegal in the early 1880s, slightly under half of Senegal's territory was under the control of a centralized political organization. Introduced in more detail in Chapter 2, the West African state system was populated by polities that were far more state-like than is often assumed, capable of enforcing property rights and of adapting to the changing whims of capitalist markets.[58] Importantly, Senegal's precolonial states were smaller and less capable of capturing the colonial or postcolonial political arena, in contrast to well-studied precolonial heavyweights, such as the Ashanti in Ghana or Buganda in Uganda.

Senegal also offers clean leverage on the central dependent variable - the nature of local social service delivery – as well as the question of representation in the local state, the secondary outcome of interest. Though Senegal began its decentralization process in 1972, earlier than many in the region, it was only in 1996 that local government councils became fully elected by the popular vote

---

[56] As argued by Pepinsky (2018), 196.   [57] Pepinsky (2018, 200).   [58] See Warner (1999).

and gained the right to independently allocate public services, most notably the placement of primary education and health facilities.⁵⁹ As a result, studying Senegal allows me to isolate the local logics of social service delivery that came with decentralization reforms in 1996 from those emanating from the central state in years prior. In essence, the 1996 reforms serve as an exogenous shock, revealing how local political dynamics are conditioned on antecedent conditions rooted in the precolonial past because, as will be shown, the effect of precolonial centralization only emerges when local actors are charged with making distributional decisions.

If anything, Senegal is a hard test for the argument that precolonial legacies persist to the present. Unlike the dominant outcome in British colonies, the French colonial administration's policies of direct rule resulted in more consistent dismantling of precolonial hierarchies and chieftaincies. This means that any legacies of the precolonial past have to persist through some informal mechanism not tied to the formal institutional structure of the state. Moreover, the fact that Senegal's decentralization project was top-down should bias against the risk that precolonial identities were instrumentally revived by politicians for the sake of obtaining subnational autonomy, such as has been seen with the creation of new states in Nigeria.⁶⁰ Together, these two factors suggest that the persistence of grassroots identities was far from overdetermined.

In choosing to investigate the question of how decentralization reforms interact with precolonial legacies in Senegal, I join a long tradition of looking to the country's dynamic spatial variation in political form. The iconic study for political scientists is Boone's (2003b) *Political Topographies of the African State*, where Senegal serves as a key case in Boone's argument that state-building efforts are shaped by the relationship between the center and the periphery. Whether rural areas become allies or rivals for the center is determined for Boone by two axes: the presence or absence of social hierarchy, which grants rural areas bargaining power, and the degree of economic autonomy, which generates or suppresses incentives to collaborate with the state. Recent work has expanded these insights to examine variation in the ability of local Senegalese leaders to serve as brokers under the long-dominant Socialist Party (*Parti socialiste* or PS) as well as under the Alliance for the Republic (*Alliance pour la république* or APR), in power at the time of writing.⁶¹ More recently, Honig (2017) suggests that the value of hierarchical customary authority extends to land markets as well, with chiefs' resistance to or facilitation of state efforts to control authority over land generating subnational variation in state-building.

Collectively, however, this scholarship has kept its focus on relations with the *center*. I shift focus to look solely within local governments, revealing

⁵⁹ Ouedraogo (2003). ⁶⁰ For example, Suberu (1991).
⁶¹ Beck (2008) and Gottlieb (2017).

divergent outcomes in otherwise quite similar local governments. For example, Beck (2008) argues persuasively that Senegal's Mouride Brotherhood, an influential Sufi, Islamic sect, possesses both high political and social autonomy, making them particularly influential political brokers with the central government. I show in the following chapters that predominantly Mouride communities that fall within the bounds of a precolonial state nonetheless engage in distinct redistributive strategies following decentralization compared to their counterparts in historically acephalous areas. One implication of my study for our understanding of Senegalese politics, therefore, is that the social structures that are consequential for center-periphery relations do not automatically correspond to those that are critical for determining the nature of political life at the local level.

Overview of the Book

I develop and test my theory through a nested empirical analysis that structures the following chapters. Specifically, I combine extensive qualitative data with quantitative tests of my theoretical predictions in order to iteratively develop, test, and refine my argument. I begin by detailing my theory of institutional congruence in Chapter 1. I argue that persistent forms of social cooperation at the grassroots are revitalized following institutional reform where communities have inherited robust social institutions stipulating appropriate social behavior from a precolonial polity. I elaborate on the theory's dual mechanisms of shared social identification and dense cross-village network ties to illustrate how institutional congruence helps local elites navigate a two-level political game introduced by decentralization: local elected officials face pressure within their villages on a first level that may be more or less compatible with their incentives at the second level of the local state itself, where they must negotiate with other elites from other villages. My theory of institutional congruence offers leverage on how local elites resolve this unique redistributive dilemma by arguing that shared social institutions stretch across the many villages of a local government, elites find it easier to negotiate at the second level of the local state because these social institutions reorient them toward group-based goals.

Chapters 2 and 3 lay out three historical building blocks that are critical for my theoretical argument. Chapter 2 presents the core antecedent condition under study. Here I introduce my measurement of precolonial statehood and specify why these states left enduring legacies even in the face of substantial upheaval during the colonial encounter by detailing the mechanisms of persistence: the nature of village-based social hierarchies. Chapter 3 goes on to introduce Senegal's decentralization reforms, the second historical condition for the argument, in depth, before turning to the third and final historical building block, the delimitation of Senegal's subnational boundaries during the colonial and postcolonial era. Employing archival and interview data, I demonstrate that decentralization and boundary delimitation were largely top-down processes, suggesting that the emergence of institutional congruence was not driven by endogenous, bottom-up demand.

Subsequent chapters document and explain the empirical variation in local governments' redistributive strategies through the use of five distinct data sources. Chapter 4 offers initial evidence for my core empirical claim that there is subnational divergence in the nature of local political life following decentralization. I draw on an original survey with more than 350 rural Senegalese political and traditional elites to develop insights into how local decision-makers themselves understand their sociopolitical worlds. The survey reveals remarkable diversity in how political cleavages are articulated across the country, but which nevertheless share structural similarities rooted in relative degrees of institutional congruence. From this data, I deduce the two mechanisms of group identities and social networks to explain how social institutions impact local politics under decentralization.

Chapter 5 employs an original, geocoded dataset of village-level primary education and basic health infrastructure across rural Senegal to test the effect of precolonial centralization on a village's likelihood of receiving a public goods investment between 2002 and 2012. I find robust evidence that falling within the territory of a precolonial state increases a village's chance of receiving local infrastructural investments from the local state. This result is robust to a number of alternative explanations and model specifications, affirming the argument that there is something different about how local governments deliver local public goods in formerly centralized areas, even when accounting for similar objective need.

While the quantitative dataset allows me to confirm that we are witnessing the emergence of subnational variation in patterns of public goods delivery, I return to the communities where this book opened in Chapter 6 to present model-testing case studies that help me explore the theory's mechanisms in the third stage of analysis. Specifically, I follow a "typical" or on-lier case selection strategy from the statistical analysis in Chapter 5 to select cases that are similar in as many respects as possible apart from their exposure to a precolonial polity.[62] By pairing oral histories, in-depth interviews, and network analysis of local elite social ties, I trace how the presence of a shared social identity and dense network ties shape redistributive preferences in a "typical" case of institutional congruence, while their absence generates more biased forms of redistribution elsewhere. Collectively, Chapters 4 through 6 suggest that the nature of local governance following decentralization varies meaningfully and systematically in line with my theory.

One of the central claims of this study is that the impact of informal social institutions is contingent on the formal institutional environment they operate within. This argument is explored in Chapter 7, which looks at the historical trajectory of basic public goods investments in Senegal from the onset of

[62] Following Lieberman (2005).

colonial rule in 1880 to the present. By extending my quantitative dataset backward in time to the onset of French colonial rule through archival data and ministerial reports, I "decompress" history by taking both spatial and temporal processes seriously. In so doing, I find that the impact of precolonial centralization only appears in force following the 1996 decentralization reforms that transferred authority over public goods placement to local governments. Chapter 7 makes two contributions to the broader project: first, it isolates the 1996 decentralization reforms as an exogenous shock that facilitated cross-village social institutions to emerge as a key driver of subnational distributional politics. Second, it offers me the opportunity to disprove the possibility that precolonial legacies interact with or reflect what are ultimately colonial legacies. This fourth stage of analysis shows that the colonial past did matter for access to social services, but that colonial effects have largely faded by the 2000s.

A final empirical chapter assesses the generalizability of my empirical findings. Chapter 8 scales outward from Senegal, using data from the Demographic and Health Surveys (DHS) and the Afrobarometer to establish that we observe similar patterns in public opinion and development outcomes across decentralized West Africa in areas that were home to precolonial states, indicating broad, empirical tractability for the argument. While my theory is built around the specific legacies of precolonial statehood, I secondly move beyond Africa to show the analytic leverage of the theory's twin mechanisms for Comparative Politics more broadly. The chapter concludes with a discussion of scope conditions for the argument. A conclusion to the book in its entirety follows.

1

A Theory of Institutional Congruence

How can we explain subnational variation in local government performance? This chapter develops a theory of institutional congruence to explain why local elites pursue divergent distributional strategies following decentralization reforms. The theory is motivated by a core empirical observation: when the boundaries of elites' political worlds overlap with their social ones, local governments become more representative and redistributive across villages. But when social and political boundaries are further apart, local governance is marked by internal divisions that leave the local state more susceptible to individual opportunism. This divergence informs the animating logic of my explanatory variable of institutional congruence, or the degree of spatial overlap between the boundaries of the local state and cross-village social institutions inherited from the precolonial past.

Social institutions, which I define as norms of appropriate behavior in the public sphere demarcated by group boundaries, are a critical concept for my argument and I offer a detailed discussion of them in this chapter. In the short term, social institutions generate highly regularized expectations of behavior for group members, but these norms themselves emerge and are institutionalized over a much longer time frame. What is critical to the theory is not the mere existence of social institutions, which can be found throughout the Senegalese countryside regardless of precolonial history, but rather their spatial implications in demarcating groups. Institutional congruence relies on dense social institutions that stretch *across* the many villages of the local state, embedding decision-makers in collective norms of comportment and leading them away from short-term opportunism. I specify two mechanisms to explain why the presence of cross-village social institutions is relevant for the decision calculi of local elites: first, social institutions are oriented around shared social identification, here collective descent from a precolonial state, and second, they are maintained and reinforced by social network ties. Together, these two mechanisms help ease political negations over allocative choices by encouraging elites to demonstrate prosocial behavior and abide by local social institutions.

The resulting theoretical prediction is that variation in institutional congruence drives variation in local government performance following decentralization. Local governments that fall within the territory of a precolonial state are expected to have denser cross-village social institutions that constrain elite behavior and broaden local government redistribution and representation. Local governments in historically acephalous, or stateless, areas lack the twin mechanisms to carry social institutions into the realm of local governance, leaving elite interests oriented toward sub-local government populations, be it a village, clan, caste, or ethnic group. It is the variable boundaries of elites' social solidarities, therefore, that lead them to make spatially distinct allocative decisions not easily explained by existing theories of distributional politics.

I lay out the theory in three steps. First, I introduce the cross-village redistributive dilemma that emerges under decentralized governance. I then conceptualize social institutions and detail the two mechanisms through which social institutions impact elite behavior. The chapter concludes with a short discussion on why bygone forms of political order, like precolonial states, generated enduring social institutions.

REDISTRIBUTIVE DILEMMAS OF DECENTRALIZATION

Decentralization presents both opportunities and challenges for local elected officials: public goods investments are valuable local patronage, but delivering them necessitates thorny political decisions. Together, local elected officials must decide how to distribute a finite stock of goods across competing claimants. More concretely, if the average local government in Senegal is home to fifty-one villages, each itself home to elites with personal preferences and ambitions for the distribution of local resources, how do elected officials collectively coordinate or collude over how to distribute scarce goods in the local state?

In recent years, political science has seen a growth of potential answers to this question.[1] The most prominent conclusion follows from the dominant rational choice framework, positing that politicians redistribute goods in order to maximize their individual political payoffs. This may manifest as targeting goods to core or swing voters or, to draw on a common argument from the African context, leaders may construct networks of support by distributing limited resources strategically along ethnic lines.[2] In line with this approach, recent research on the politics of public goods delivery in rural Africa tends to view contemporary redistributive dilemmas as largely identical from the national to the local level:

---

[1] Golden and Min (2013).   [2] For example, Azam (2001); Briggs (2014); and Jablonski (2014).

elites vie to deliver public goods strategically to different political constituencies to maintain support.[3] Local politicians are largely assumed to parallel their central state counterparts, governing with a constant eye to their own future political and material payoffs.[4] In turn, the results of these political calculations explain emerging and consolidating patterns of subnationa inequalities.

This literature rests on two assumptions: first, that the political logics of the central state apply constantly as we descend to lower levels of government; and second, that local politicians have substantial levels of social autonomy not only in relation to citizens but from other elites as well. Baldwin's (2013) work on the relationship between politicians and chiefs in Zambia exemplifies this approach. Per her argument, Zambia's Paramount Chiefs act as powerful vote brokers in rural areas because they are sufficiently embedded in their local communities to deliver votes while also standing to benefit personally from the resources that politicians deliver. As unelected officials, chiefs do not risk electoral sanction, but nor in Baldwin's theory do they risk a reputational one from citizens, granting them the space to act with self-interest vis-à-vis society. More recently, de Kadt and Larreguy (2018) have argued similarly that politicians can deploy traditional authorities strategically as vote brokers because traditional leaders stand to gain considerably, again with no apparent cost to the legitimacy or authority of either party.

Though I question the validity of both assumptions in the study of local governance, applying the theoretical insights derived from the behavior of the central state offers one lens into explaining the redistributive dilemmas that emerge following decentralization. Local elites may very well see their political interests as mirrors of those of the center, for example, and seek to maximize party gains. An alternative perspective is found in the rich literature on elite capture, which studies how participatory reforms are prone to capture by local elites, who may use their role as intermediaries to implement their own preferred policies, siphon resources, or, more simply, unilaterally enact policies they believe will help their communities.[5] By studying the micro-dynamics of bottom-up reforms such as decentralization, this body of work has voiced substantial skepticism about the ability of grassroots initiatives to be truly emancipatory for average citizens because the concentration of power in the hands of a narrow elite induces collusion. Departing from the macro-level literature on the central state, this literature explains the nature of elite capture by looking to the structure of local social relations, with the risks of elite capture most acute under high levels of inequality and in communities with strong social hierarchies.[6]

In this way, the fact that many African countries have seen a "resurgence" of traditional authorities following the dual reforms of decentralization and

---

[3] On national-level distribution, see Burgess et al. (2015). Examples of work, looking at subnational distribution, include Carlitz (2017) and Ejdemyr et al. (2017).
[4] Cheema and Rondinelli (2007, 7).   [5] Sheely (2015).   [6] Mookherjee (2015).

democratization has left rural African communities particularly prone to elite control, as customary elites have seized upon local governance as a means to regain authority they had lost or to enhance what authority they had.[7] This has led to opposing interpretations: traditional authorities either offer a legitimate source of social capital on which new, democratic regimes could be built or they hinder democratization because the "bonding" social capital they represent encourages consensus politics and marginalizes the voices of minorities.[8] As a result, the elite capture literature has remained skeptical of decentralization's ability to foster inclusive development, leading academic attention to shift toward theorizing how we might best check elite power, be it via institutional designs intended to minimize elite influence or, alternatively, by co-opting elites by gaining their buy-in for particular projects.[9]

At its core, however, the assumption that local elites undermine decentralization and development initiatives by pursuing their own individual self-interest mirrors my critique of the macro-perspective to the extent that both approaches ignore the question of when elites are more or less autonomous. The result is that at both macro and micro levels, political science's dominant lenses for explaining redistributive politics stop short of theorizing local elites as relational actors operating within social and political structures. If local politicians act with an eye to both self-interested and prosocial motives, then studying the former at the expense of the latter leaves us insufficiently equipped to study why elites make the choices they do and with what consequences for society.

I refocus the study of local redistributive politics by theorizing the unique redistributive dilemma faced by local elites when making allocative decisions within the local state. Decentralization in Senegal, as elsewhere, generated a new layer of government between the central state and the village, the lowest political unit in the country. Accordingly, local governments aggregate a number of villages, each home to their own social and political debates, into a newly autonomous administrative unit beneath the central state. By taking the local state as a distinct sphere of governance seriously, I join a small body of scholarship that seeks to theorize the specific political dynamics that arise at a local level.[10] I suggest that local actors' strategies reveal the dual political realities of decentralized governance: local elected officials must attempt to meet village-based expectations on one level while at the same time navigating the cross-village political environment of the local state.

In this way, the governance structure of decentralization effectively creates a two-level game with unique social and political demands at each level.[11]

---

[7] For example, Englebert (2002a); Lund (2006); and Kyed and Buur (2007).
[8] For example, Economic Commission for Africa (2007) versus Mamdani (1996) and Ribot and Oyono (2005).
[9] Respective examples would be Cruz and Schneider (2017) and Labonte (2012).
[10] For example, Paller (2019).   [11] Akin to Putnam (1988).

Local elected officials are pressured by village- or client-based expectations in the first level of the village. A local government councilor, for instance, may feel obliged to meet the demands of voters or neighbors in their village, perhaps to fulfill campaign promises, because they views them as clients, or, more simply, to be well-regarded by their families and neighbors. The councilor and their family members are also likely to benefit directly from any investments. But at the level of the local government, politicians must navigate a second political arena. Here, the competing demands of the many villages that comprise the local state mean that councilors must engage in negotiations over which villages receive scarce investments. What is rational for a councilor vis-à-vis their village, co-ethnics, or extended family is not therefore always their best choice in the arena of the local state, where a politician may face incentives to target swing voters for their party, or to show respect to a prominent village or extended kin. This raises the real risk that the individual incentives of any given councilor run counter to those of the collective or, alternatively, that in the pursuit of their first objective they risk upsetting important relations at the second level of the local state. This, I argue, is the unique distributive dilemma faced by local politicians under decentralization.

How elites resolve this dilemma generates the empirical variation under study in the following chapters. I focus on how local governments allocate social service investments and, as a secondary area of interest, who gains representation in the local state. Critically, if these two levels are at times more compatible while at others they are farther apart, we can generate predictions about when local elites are likely to arrive at broader or narrower redistributive equilibria. The theory of institutional congruence outlined in the next section does just this.

A THEORY OF INSTITUTIONAL CONGRUENCE

My central theoretical proposition stipulates that the nature of local political life, and hence local distributive politics, is a function of the degree of spatial overlap between the formal institutional boundaries of the local state and informal, social institutions inherited from the past. Where institutional congruence is high, the presence of social institutions that stretch across villages enables cooperation within the local state because social institutions imbue elites with more prosocial preferences toward group members. In brief, institutional congruence brings the two levels of demands faced by politicians – those emanating from their village or family and those that emerge from the political dynamics of the local state – more closely into alignment.

This is for two reasons. First, the presence of dense cross-village social institutions reorients elites toward group goals, say to help the neediest or to preserve community cohesion. This elongates elite time horizons, enabling cooperation in the short term on the promise of longer-term payoffs for individual actors. Because these norms and networks are legible to villagers, the majority of whom are embedded in the same local social institutions, the risk of village-based sanction is mitigated. This alone does not lead local elites to abandon their personal political ambitions or their desire to bring goods and resources to their own villages and families, but it does broaden the range of distributional decisions they view as desirable. Effectively, social institutions extend elites' perceptions of their social obligations beyond their immediate village or individual interest, expanding their prosocial preferences toward the boundaries of the local state itself.

At the same time that institutional congruence raises elite interests to the level of the local state, it also increases the costs of individual opportunism. Elites embedded in cross-village social institutions risk broad social sanction, which may range from public scorn or ridicule to losing one's spot on electoral lists, precisely because their social worlds more directly map onto their political ones. Under these conditions, social institutions set boundaries on village-based opportunism because local elites know that pursuing individual goals alone will be sanctioned both politically within the local government and socially within their wider social networks.

The theory thus predicts that local government redistribution should be broader across space in areas that were home to precolonial states because these areas face structurally distinct redistributive dilemmas following decentralization. In these communities, institutional congruence encourages elites to demonstrate a preference for long-term interactions with the group over short-term individual- or village-based gains and to collectively abstain from predation by stipulating that such behavior is inappropriate.[12] Even if actors retain a desire to deliver to their "core" constituents, overlap between cross-village social institutions and the jurisdictional boundaries of the local state endows them with concurrent preferences informed by their social relations at the second level of play, the local government. In contrast, where institutional congruence is low, elites find their social and political worlds less intertwined, facilitating their pursuit of narrow opportunism.

Two points merit clarification. First, all societies possess identities, social networks, and informal social norms that regulate members' behavior.[13] What is critical for my theory is that these dynamics map onto the formal institutional bounds of local decision-making in cases of high congruence. Social institutions exist everywhere, therefore, but on the eve of decentralization only some communities had inherited social institutions stretching across the numerous villages of the local state. At stake is the relative congruence between formal institutions and informal, social ones, not the presence or absence of such institutions in the first place.

Second, the theoretical framework that I develop in this book contributes to our understanding of when informal institutions can improve development

---

[12] Raub and Weesie (1990).   [13] Ellickson (1991) and Munshi and Rosenzweig (2008).

outcomes, while at other times they impede or pervert them.[14] In locating the argument in the degree of relative overlap between formal and informal institutions, however, the argument does not necessitate an exact spatial overlap between the boundaries of precolonial states and contemporary local governments. In contrast, West African precolonial kingdoms were far larger than the boundaries of today's subnational units. Even when the boundaries of a decentralized jurisdictional unit overlap with only a small part of what was once a precolonial kingdom, this should be sufficient to embed local political life within longer-term social dynamics.[15] Institutional congruence can therefore emerge under the less demanding condition that social institutions inherited from the precolonial past embed the majority of villages within any given local government. The critical component is not the nature or size of the precolonial political unit but rather the legacy of shared social institutions these defunct political structures left behind, a point I return to at the end of the chapter.

Conceptualizing Social Institutions

I have briefly defined social institutions as norms of appropriate behavior in the public sphere that are demarcated by group boundaries. Like all institutions, social institutions structure action for group members by rewarding behavior deemed socially desirable while imposing costly sanctions on poorly viewed behavior. They are institutionalized to the extent that individuals have highly regularized expectations for the behavior of both fellow community members as well as themselves.[16]

Social institutions rely intimately on understandings of group boundaries, which we can break down into two components: categories and networks. These dual aspects invoke the concept of *catnet* pioneered by White (2008 [1965]) and Tilly (1978).[17] Here the presence of local identities that "classif[y] people in a way that plausibly corresponds to their concrete experience of social ties to others" generates categories that are embedded within interpersonal

---

[14] For example, Hyden (1980); Collins (2004); and Mattingly (2016).
[15] Naturally, individuals' social ties extend beyond the boundaries of the local state. This is illustrated in the answer that one village chief in Louga Region, home to the precolonial state of Cayor, gave when asked whether he would change his local government boundaries. He would add a few villages that had close ties with his neighbors, the chief stated, but "I could not remove any" (Interview, February 20, 2016). It is not necessary that a local government encompasses the entirety of a social network therefore, but rather that local elites see the villages in the local government as part of a shared network, however much more broadly that might spread.
[16] My use of the term is distinct from an older use of the term as organizations formed by individuals coming together for a shared purpose. For example, Lipset (1959) argued that social institutions – as churches or social clubs – could help sustain democratic systems.
[17] Weber (1978 [1922], 390) similarly observed that shared memory of community origin can generate powerful identities that are shaped by persistent social relationships.

network ties.[18] This serves to render these identities, what Gould (1995) refers to as a sense of "groupness," particularly salient. Of course, individuals have and always will identify with many categories. "Groupness," however, depends on primacy and stability in social relations that cannot be assumed from merely possessing an identity. Rather, collectively held identities only motivate behavior when they establish both who group members are and who has "lived" social connections with whom. A key implication of this is that group identities are particularly mobilizing at the local level, while also opening up the possibility that highly localized understandings of sociopolitical cleavages drive political behavior.

Consequently, social institutions inhere in social relationships and are intimately tied to actors' identities as a member of a given public, via their social network ties and their identification with a group. This means that social institutions shape and constrain behavior by stipulating how things should work for members of a given group explicitly because the act of belonging prescribes certain behavioral strategies.[19] I conceptualize social institutions as more than "individuals' obligations and incentives for maintaining them," as recently defined by Lust and Rakner (2018), therefore, because they cannot be understood as a property of individuals.[20] Rather, as norms demarcated by group boundaries, they are animated through social relations, meaningful only to the extent that they shape actor preferences and expectations for their social interactions.[21] In so doing, social institutions "truncate players' strategy space" by conditionally shaping actors' beliefs and strategies.[22] Individuals believe that others expect them to behave a certain way and, in turn, that others will behave similarly.[23]

Social institutions are particularly potent in shaping local political life both because they are enforced through social interactions and because they are internalized by actors. Social scientists have disproportionately focused their attention on the former; we know that norms inform actor behavior because they lead individuals to anticipate the reactions of others, for example, what will earn esteem and what will earn scorn.[24] Though these dynamics certainly matter, the materialist approach of much of our scholarship on informal institutions risks overemphasizing the fear of punishment in explaining individual compliance. In contrast, I seek to broaden the incentives that motivate actors by taking into account altruistic or other-regarding behavior for those within their social networks. Social institutions induce compliance because they build on

---

[18] Gould (1995, 18–19).   [19] See discussion in Kowert and Legro (1996).
[20] In contrast, my definition is closer to Hechter's (1990), who defines social institutions as "some regularity in collective behavior," though he includes conventions in his account.
[21] Akin to Katzenstein's (1996) conceptualization of norms as "collective social facts."
[22] Platteau (2000, 291).   [23] Goldstein and Keohane (1993, 18) and Bicchieri (2006, 15).
[24] As Elster (1989, 99) writes, "for norms to be social, they must be both shared and partly sustained by approval and disapproval."

"reservoirs of authority," long histories of social cooperation that add weight to the meaning individuals place on their own behavior.[25] To the extent that social institutions are internalized by actors, they persist because individuals seek to behave honorably in accordance with what they deem appropriate or good. This means that social institutions can influence behavior even absent a palpable threat of sanction; individuals may behave in accordance with such social norms because they are internally motivated to do so.[26]

Two social institutions feature prominently in the empirical chapters.[27] First, norms of conflict avoidance among group members check the escalation of intra-elite splits. Across historically centralized areas, rural Senegalese elites consistently speak of the dangers of letting political "squabbles" escalate, detailing how they circumscribe conflicts before they can impact local social relations.[28] This comes out clearly in an idiomatic Wolof expression invoked in the region of the precolonial kingdom of Cayor, which – to paraphrase – states that problems should be discussed "first in the room, then in the household, then in the compound and then under *l'arbre à palabre*," a reference to the location where elders meet in the afternoons to converse, often found in the center of a village. The saying signals an aversion to the escalation of conflict or behavior that could reveal social disharmony by stipulating a series of social mechanisms to limit a conflict's spread. This is a social institution: it proscribes a specific action (the resolution of conflict as discretely as possible), it is social to the extent that it is rooted in a clear group (here locally understood as descendants of "Cayor"), and it is institutionalized because its behavioral consequences are regularized and expected.[29]

Second, communities that were home to precolonial states share strong social institutions around principles of balance and equity. This is illustrated well with the politics of local electoral list construction. Local party leaders in historically centralized areas are quick to clarify that they are obliged to put individuals from a large number of lineages and villages on their party's list or risk being seen as biased or unfair, undermining not only their electoral prospects but their broader reputations. Similarly, one village chief explained his local government's allocative strategy: we "let others take something at their turn" because by so "doing a favour," we ensure that projects will flow to all villages and, over time, everyone will get their share.[30] As an investment in social relations that may generate returns in the long term, local elites are

---

[25] Hall and Lamont (2013, 51). [26] Dasgupta (1988).
[27] In rural Senegal, social institutions are rarely justified explicitly. Rather they are assumed to be self-evident, often articulated through adages or offhand comments. On the ground, individuals often describe various local social institutions in cultural terms, or as community *values*. I retain the language of institutions because social institutions remain firmly rooted in shared expectations about behavior or local "logics of appropriateness" for group members.
[28] Interview, mayor, Fatick Region, May 10, 2013. [29] See Coleman (1990a).
[30] Interview, Kaffrine Region, February 8, 2016.

A Theory of Institutional Congruence

willing to balance resources and benefits across villages whom they see as falling within shared group boundaries both because they believe it as the fundamentally appropriate course of action and because they view it as an assurance of returns for their own villages in the future.

It is important to clarify that even when they are broadly based, social institutions should not be read as implying an absence of conflict. Conflict in West African societies is often masked as villagers adopt a "front" of solidarity.[31] The political disagreements – from the mundane to the scandalous – which were widely reported in historically acephalous areas may indicate that similar controversy exists unseen in historically centralized zones. Indeed, I found disagreement to be as prevalent in areas of rural Senegal that were home to precolonial states as in areas that were not. Rural Senegalese everywhere remember and note their displeasure and conflicts with others. Yet strong group norms can lead individuals with otherwise disparate interests to adjust behavior and opt for civil negotiations that protect social relations.[32] Social institutions, I suggest, help explain why communities actively *constrain* political conflicts from upsetting community social relations, but that does not mean there is an absence of conflict in the first place.

Why Social Institutions Influence Elite Behavior

Social institutions shape elite behavior via two mechanisms. First, social institutions are rooted in a category of shared social identification, which imbues social institutions with meaning and orients them in the minds of actors. Second, they are tied to actors' social networks, which allocate sanctions and rewards for abiding by stipulated behavior and, in so doing, reproduce the value of social institutions for the group. These mechanisms interact in powerful ways and both are integral in generating institutional congruence. Together, a shared sense of group identification and dense social networks among elites carry social institutions into the realm of local politics, reorienting elite behavior toward group-level goals at the second level of the local state.

The Social Identity Mechanism

Social identities can provide a vehicle for cooperation because shared identification with a group creates "commonsense notions" about political and social life that structure individuals' political preferences and strategies. As an illustration, take a comment given to me by one local government councilor in Senegal. When asked to describe his relations with other villages in his local government, he dismissively responded, "we are all *ceddos* here," a reference to

---

[31] An absence of conflict should not be accepted at face value, as Bierschenk and Olivier de Sardan (2003, 161) argue, because preserving reputation in dense social networks is a necessary act since "one's adversary in a moment may be needed in another situation."
[32] Ellickson (1991).

the warrior slave caste influential in the region's precolonial kingdom.[33] In reality, it is highly unlikely that all citizens in his community descend from the *ceddo*, but by taking the category as self-evident, the councilor reveals how durable and localized understandings of identity persist in the region and are granted new prominence under decentralization. Local interpretations of political life of this nature shed light on how actors understand their sociopolitical obligations because such narratives reveal and reinforce the demarcation of social boundaries, but also the value and relevance of group membership itself.

Of course, there is no shortage of social identities and cleavages within any given community. What allows an identity rooted in a shared descent from a precolonial past to emerge as such a powerful driver of elite behavior? Across rural West Africa, social identities are often mobilized around local histories of settlement and descent.[34] These can verge on the mythical, but they are recounted with great pride, such as one village chief in Fatick Region tale of his maternal ancestor, a revered hunter who had ruled over more than ten lineages as a provincial titleholder under the King of Ndoffene in the precolonial state of Sine.[35] Much like Laitin's (1986) study of the role of Yoruba ancestral cities in Nigeria, I suggest that shared identification with a precolonial kingdom generates "commonsense frameworks" that limit the ability of politicians to mobilize other identities for political gain. If the dominant framework for social identification is rooted in descent from a precolonial state, one's social and political rights, as well as one's obligations, are intimately tied to these shared claims to group membership.[36]

In this way, shared social identification reinforces the logic of local social relations and provides a focal point for community cohesion. The power of such localized identities can hold even in the presence of other sources of diversity. By way of illustration, we can return to Laitin, who emphasizes that ancestral cities remain as the hegemonic identity for the Yoruba despite the presence of other politicized identities, such as religion.[37] Identifying as *ceddo* is likewise not a new identity nor does it exclude the local councilor from embracing his other identities, such as being a Wolof or a Muslim. It gains potent political viability, however, once it is redefined within the territorial space of the local state as the most "natural" identification for the community as a whole. Social identities are not absent in historically acephalous zones, but they stop short of becoming hegemonic within the local state. While village chiefs proudly recount their past throughout rural Senegal, the depth of that history – and the degree to which it extends beyond any given

---

[33] Interview, Tivaouane Department, May 14, 2013.   [34] For example, Hilgers (2011).
[35] Interview, village chief, Fatick Region, May 7, 2013.   [36] Laitin (1986, 159, 177).
[37] Echoing language heard in rural Senegal, Yoruba deny the idea that there is a meaningful religious cleavage, stating to the contrast that "we are all one family" (1986, 136).

A Theory of Institutional Congruence

village – varies significantly, meaning that social identities more often than not serve to delimit group divisions within the local state.[38]

This suggests that social institutions shape political outcomes most strongly when they are tied to widely recognized and locally internalized identities. Comparing the postcolonial performance of Indian states, Singh (2015a, 2015b) similarly documents how states that have strong subnational identities outperform those that lack them. Singh chronicles how politicians in some Indian states actively nurtured the development of subnational identities for political ends only to find themselves subsequently constrained by their earlier political strategy. Once subnational identities are internalized by the population, elites are obligated to meet citizen demands for further welfare investments.[39] Ultimately, Singh draws a similar conclusion: states are more likely to invest in citizen welfare when there is "a match between the political-administrative unit that has jurisdiction over social policy and the locus of collective identification."[40]

Locally hegemonic identities of this nature translate into measurable political behavior by reorienting preferences toward group goals. To the extent that individuals' attachment to their group identities can explain otherwise "irrational" behavior by altering their preferences, we know that self-interested actors do not always define their self-interest narrowly.[41] Rather, possessing a local collective identity can establish claims to community resources that change how local elites order their priorities. This produces what Collins (2006) refers to as "goal congruence" as identification with a group valorizes group goals while also raising the cost of individual opportunism. To wit, one rural Senegalese politician clarified that it was impossible to ignore demands on the local state by autochthonous residents "in their ancestral villages" because they held an unquestionable right to community membership.[42] While they may not have all voted for him, the politician's recognition that they held a shared community identity, tied to an idea of descent from the community's past, altered his political behavior.

More forcefully, shared group membership generates a distinct sense of common purpose. This is exemplified most clearly in the pervasive language of "social cohesion" and the concern over intra-elite splits.[43] Despite the right to discipline councilors who miss three meetings in a row, for example, a mayor in the territory of the former Saloum Kingdom noted, "we don't do it, because

---

[38] For example, one mayor explained how he had run for office in order to defend his ethnic group, which he perceived as being in competition with other ethnicities in the community, a clear reference to the late-colonial arrival of Wolof peanut farmers. Upon winning office, his co-ethnics were clearly favored, revealing that while group identities matter here as well, in acephalous areas, they serve to demarcate groups *within* the state, fracturing the second level of play (Interview, Tambacounda Region, March 19, 2013).
[39] Singh (2015a, chapter 3).   [40] Singh (2015a, 5).   [41] Akerlof and Kranton (2000).
[42] Interview, councilor, Kaolack Region, May 4, 2013.
[43] See Schaffer (1998) on Senegalese norms of social cohesion.

it's not good for social cohesion."[44] The mayor spoke at length of his displeasure with the poor attendance of some councilors, but group-oriented preferences outweighed his individual inclination to sanction.

Indeed, shared group membership has been found to foster a sense of common goals, to lead individuals to act in the interest of the group, and to increase sharing among in-group members.[45] Lab experiments revealed that individuals strongly prefer in-group members – even in cases of randomly assigned group membership – and not only are individuals more likely to opt for social-welfare-enhancing choices when paired with fellow in-group members, they are also more charitable to fellow group members who receive lower payoffs.[46] Outside of behavioral economics and social psychology, political scientists have repeatedly shown that within-group members are better able to overcome collective action dilemmas, be it via shared norms, rules, or preferences to reach better outcomes.[47] The creation of new formal institutions can create or emphasize existing social ties by virtue of how institutional boundaries can demonstrate shared commonalities. In this way, decentralization and other similar reforms are capable of "rais[ing] the ceiling of participant identity" by facilitating collective action at a higher level than would previously have been possible based on informal, daily interactions alone.[48]

The Social Network Mechanism

Social identities reorient actor preferences toward group goals and imbue them with meaning. How group boundaries are understood is intimately tied to the social networks that these identities are embedded within. Individuals have been widely shown to be more likely to cooperate with those they share social connections with, and such ties can help them overcome ethnic or other demographic divisions.[49] This is the second mechanism animating institutional congruence: dense social network ties carry social institutions into the political preferences of decision-makers.

Critically, what differs is not what bestows social status within villages. Rural African social relations are largely determined by family lineage structures, such as the ability to claim descent from the zone's founding families. This renders elite status highly path-dependent, meaning that *who* comprises the local elite of any given village is relatively consistent. What does differ is the structure of relationships between elites *across* villages. Because social networks are relatively sticky in the short run, local elites face circumscribed choices as to

---

[44] Interview, Kaffrine Region, April 24, 2013.
[45] Brewer (1979); Tajfel and Turner (1986); Transue (2007); Shayo (2009); and Grossman and Baldassarri (2012).
[46] Fowler and Kam (2007); Chen and Li (2009); and Goette et al. (2006).
[47] Bates (1983); Ostrom (1990); Miguel and Gugerty (2005); Habyarimana et al. (2007); and Singh (2011).
[48] Gould (1991, 21-22).   [49] Glaeser et al. (2000); Dionne (2015); and Leonard et al. (2010).

whether or not to invest in their network ties. This is in part because their own claims to authority and resources often depend on reinforcing the value of the network as a whole. In this way, social networks are themselves "historically embedded."[50] Networks promote cooperation, in other words, not only because they enable trust or friendship but also because they are durable.[51] Critically, network structure is as consequential as an individual's ties to it since it is only in the aggregate that these ties collectively allow for mutually beneficial outcomes.[52] For this reason, understanding elite behavior demands that we take into account "the shape of these [social] networks, whether cohesive or fragmented; the interdependencies they created ... the opportunities for action, reaction, maneuvers and adjustments."[53]

My theory stipulates that when elites share dense social ties that extend throughout the local government, they behave differently. Social networks have been shown to generate positive social properties by enabling cooperation, evidenced in the literature on social capital.[54] The literature on social distance shows that individuals are more generous and prosocial to members of their social networks in anticipation of reciprocal exchanges.[55] While we know that one's behavior is sharply influenced by one's social relations, therefore, I theorize that the nature of cross-village social ties matters for how local elites approach local distributional politics because of three specific effects on local political action: (a) they circulate information about group goals and group boundaries; (b) this informational dimension produces rewards and costs of individual behavior; and (c) they reinforce the internalization of social institutions.[56]

NETWORKS CIRCULATE INFORMATION. Social relations shape the flow of information. In dense networks, local elites are not only more likely to know each other socially, they are also more likely to communicate and observe each other's preferences and needs. Reflecting this, a village chief in Diourbel Region reported finding his local government fair and transparent in its distribution choices. "We know the neediest villages, we know that some need priority ... all of the villages are old here, and we all know each other," he argued. In his local government, he concluded, "all the villages are united and engaged."[57] Answers of this nature are common in historically centralized areas. When asked how he would evaluate the introduction of democratic decentralization, a village chief in Louga Region, himself an ethnic minority in the zone, commented similarly, "in this zone at least, it has succeeded because many villages are related, and we know each other. When we see each other, we all discuss, we find a coherence ... our ties prevent conflicts."[58] In this way, social network

---

[50] Granovetter (1985, 486).   [51] Axelrod (2006, 182).
[52] Coleman (1988); Putnam (1993); and Gould (1991).   [53] Barkey (2008, 17).
[54] Putnam (1993) and Woolcock (2010).   [55] Leider et al. (2009) and Apicella et al. (2012).
[56] Granovetter (1985) and Raub and Weesie (1990).   [57] Interview, February 15, 2016.
[58] Interview, February 20, 2016.

ties communicate and reinforce the value of group goals, while at the same time reducing perceptions of local politics as a zero-sum game by first spreading information about relative needs.

In contrast, weak networks impede the flow of information and amplify the costs of sociopolitical exclusion. This can be relatively permanent in the medium term, for example, a newcomer village with no connections to its neighbors has few means to demand local representation. But it can also arise from short-term fluctuations in political fortunes. One village chief who was a political ally of his local government's former mayor told me that while he used to be well-informed, he really did not know what the current administration was doing because no one from his village or those he had social ties with currently held seats on the local council.[59] Critically, the difference is not that formal rules are better understood in historically centralized areas. I find little meaningful difference in village chiefs' knowledge about the legal structure of decentralization.[60] Rather, network ties may matter most for circulating *informal* sources of information, such as norms of comportment, discourse about the boundaries of local political cleavages, and gossip about poorly and well-performing elites. If a narrow cleavage dominates local politics, the ability of others to monitor the behavior of elites and to at the least try to sanction opportunistic behavior is inhibited, even if those actors are aware of the formal rules of the local state.

NETWORKS GENERATE EXTERNAL COSTS AND REWARDS. By circulating information about elite behavior, networks enable citizens and elites alike to sanction poorly viewed behavior and to reward behavior that is deemed good. The ability of social networks to generate external costs and rewards extends elites' time horizons. This leads actors away from exploiting partners because the short-run gains cannot compensate for the long-run costs that a damaged reputation incurs.[61] "In this way, mutual abstention from attempts to exploit partners, based on conditional cooperation, can become individually profitable," write Raub and Weesie (1990, 647). Elites in dense networks are more likely to forgo defection that might produce short-term rents, such as embezzling funds for a local development project, if they think that their reputation will suffer.

Networks also highlight the reputational benefits of well-viewed behavior. The fact that individuals desire social status and prestige and that "local status

---

[59] Interview, Kaffrine Region, February 18, 2017.
[60] In an original survey of local elites introduced in Chapter 4, respondents can almost all correctly identify who is in charge of *état-civile* paperwork (97 percent can do so across the country) and they are equally likely to correctly identify the local government as being in charge of primary education and health. There is likewise no ambiguity as to who one should contact in the case of a land-related dispute: 61 percent of respondents in historically acephalous areas cite the rural council or mayor, as do 64 percent of respondents in historically centralized areas.
[61] Greif (2006).

has a price and can be traded for material things that have value" is increasingly recognized in political science.[62] These insights have long been at the core of work on social networks in rural Africa.[63] Experimental and survey data tell us as well that individuals are willing to sacrifice their own consumption to improve their status, that they will seek relative and absolute status rewards as ends in and of themselves, and that they engage in more prosocial behavior when their actions are public or their identity revealed.[64] To the extent that social status generates both material and social benefits, local elites in rural West Africa are hesitant to violate local social norms that could undermine their position in the community.[65]

Local officials both acutely observe and are observed by the community they serve, leading one councilor to explain "this isn't like Dakar ... our politicians *live* in the same community."[66] These pressures are particularly demanding in communities where actors' social, economic, and private worlds are closely connected.[67] As one mayor in Senegal's south wryly commented, "of course the [central] state doesn't care ... they are far from the population. At the local level, we are always seen – at baptisms, at weddings, at the market..."[68] This echoes neatly the description that one local mayor in Burkina Faso gives of his work:

you must be humble, very social, help the community and always be available. There is no time to sleep here because someone can come wake you up at one in the morning to ask for money or your help. You must always have your door open from midnight to the morning. It is not easy. You always have to sacrifice yourself for others. (Barry and Hagberg 2019, 29)

Consequently, while the creation of local governments created a new venue within which elites could pursue their interests, it also created new constraints

---

[62] Notably, McClendon's (2018) recent work on the role of envy and status in political life, though also Cowen and Sutter (1997); Tsai (2007); and Paller (2014). From other disciplines, this argument also draws on Akerlof (1997); Loch et al. (2001); Besley and Ghatak (2008); and Frank (1985, 10).

[63] Berry (1985) and Hyden (2006).

[64] Ball and Eckel (1998, 162); Weiss and Fershtman (1998, 802); Heffetz and Frank (2010, 20–21); and Huberman et al. (2004). From a different perspective, Kahan (2003, 71) suggests a *logic of reciprocity*, whereby individuals contribute to public goods provisions when they feel others are helping because they are also motivated by honor, altruism, etc. In contrast, when they feel others are not helping, they are less likely to help out of hurt pride or anger even when their own material interest is held constant.

[65] On the benefits of social status, see Goode (1978); Hawkes et al. (1993); and Weiss and Fershtman (1998, 802).

[66] Interview, February 13, 2017.

[67] Although close ties with other elites can lead to collusion in non-electoral settings, Grossman and Baldassarri (2012) find that democratically elected leaders are more responsive to the welfare needs of constituents. Similar effects of elections have been found in Liberia (Baldwin 2015).

[68] Interview, Kolda Region, April 11, 2013.

on elite behavior via local behavioral norms embedded within elite social relations. The devolution of local development projects, the annual distribution of seed and fertilizer from the central government, the resolution of particularly sticky land disputes, etc. have all gained new institutional fora under decentralization, but because they are close to home and by extension close to friends and family, elites risk wide-ranging social sanctions if they are perceived as too self-interested in these transactions. As one village chief mused, "whether [local officials] do good or bad, they do it to themselves."[69] When elites' social networks are narrow, limited perhaps to their own village, they can more easily pursue their individual- or village-based interests because they act toward the first level of the village alone. In networks that are fragmented or weak, information about reputations and behavior is less likely to circulate widely, undermining the effectiveness of social sanctioning.[70]

NETWORKS REINFORCE THE INTERNALIZATION OF SOCIAL INSTITUTIONS. I have argued that local elites in rural Senegal feel the weight of history, embedded in long histories of social cooperation. Social networks not only shape behavior by producing positive and negative external sanctions but also because they are deeply internalized. This helps explain why rural Senegalese inhabiting the former territories of precolonial kingdoms speak of "social cohesion" as an apparent and evident reality. To illustrate, I draw on a casual conversation between my research assistant, myself, and an elderly villager who stopped by to inquire after my research assistants and I's stay in a local government in Louga Region in 2017. The elderly villager was happy to hear that we found the community hospitable and welcoming. Things are peaceful here, he commented, noting that Mr. Diouf, a local household head whose horse cart we had hired that day, must have told us this as well. The prime virtue of the area, he continued, is that everyone knows and cares about each other, unlike in the country's bustling capital of Dakar, and because the community had "social cohesion" after years of cohabitation, which kept things peaceful. "If Diouf [the horse cart driver] told you something, and you were to later tell it to someone else, that person would certainly tell you that if it was Diouf who told you, then certainly Diouf has told you everything," he explained. We all know each other, the villager concluded, and that is the community's strength.[71] Embedded within this anecdote is the very logic that animates why social institutions are so powerful: the elderly villager takes for granted that his community is cohesive, that this is rooted in their shared history, cueing the identity mechanism, and their social relations, cueing the role of network ties. This is viewed as naturally producing trust, peace, and reciprocal generosity in the community. In other words, people behave in

---

[69] Interview, Saint-Louis Region, February 16, 2013. [70] Platteau and Abraham (2002, 108).
[71] Fieldnotes, Kebemer Department, February 7, 2017.

accordance with local social institutions because they assume that to do so is good, proper, and natural.

Norms can be effective without external sanctions, whether positive or negative. Individuals regularly sanction their own behavior for purely internal reasons, what Olson (1965) dubs "social" costs and benefits, such as guilt, shame, or self-esteem.[72] If individuals value behavior that accords with a social institution, they comply because it is "intrinsically rewarding" or, conversely, because their deviance would be internally punishing.[73] This is not to deny the material trade-offs that individuals face when opting to follow social prescriptions of this kind, yet individuals often act to avoid a guilty conscience even in settings where they risk few external costs.[74] In her work on social norms, Bicchieri (2006, 23) emphasizes the tendency of people to rely on norms as heuristics that guide their behavior, resulting in far more compliance than that expected by the average social scientist. People comply because they fear punishment, but also because they have a "desire to please" or because they simply believe that a norm is well-founded.

Because social institutions are self-enforcing within groups, one's social networks stipulate the norms we internalize. What we see others do (or not do) informs what we think is correct and how we think we should behave as group members.[75] This has numerous effects on social behavior: individuals trust that others will behave appropriately, it encourages reciprocity, and, critically, it can limit the necessity for negative sanctions because the internalization of social norms makes such behavior less likely precisely because of internal sanctions like guilt and shame.[76]

Elites living in dense communities have ample opportunity to internalize the preferences of community members, facilitating their willingness to cooperate and to act altruistically toward fellow community members. While some who truly prefer short-term gains continue to abide by local social institutions because they fear social sanction, others may do so because they simply think it is the correct course of action. For many, these two influences are likely conflated. Where social institutions are splintered within the local state, elites do not see the majority as capable of generating external, reputational sanctions, nor do they face internal rewards for behaving "well" because their political worlds only weakly overlap with their social ones. If someone believes that not all community members are equally deserving, they are unlikely to feel shame or guilt for not sacrificing their most immediate individual preference for the needs of others.

---

[72] Elster (1989, 131) and Coleman (1990b, 243).   [73] Horne (2001, 4) and Opp (1979, 792).
[74] For example, Axelrod (1986, 1104) observes that experimental participants justify their decisions to be more equitable than narrow theories of rational choice would predict with responses such as "you have to live with yourself."
[75] Axelrod (1986, 1105).   [76] See here Platteau (2000, 300).

How Cross-village Social Institutions Generate Institutional Congruence

Decentralization creates a new layer of governance between the central state and the village, each home to its own enduring hierarchies and sociopolitical dynamics. I have argued that this effectively produces a two-level game as local elites must balance between the social and political pressures emanating from their villages while at the same time responding to the demands of cross-village political negotiations at the level of the local state itself. Understanding variation in local government performance necessitates theorizing how local elites resolve this unique redistributive dilemma.

The theory of institutional congruence outlined here offers one such lens: local elites find it easier to negotiate across villages at the second level when the formal jurisdictional boundaries of the local state encompass shared, cross-village social institutions inherited from precolonial states. Specifically, this endows local elites with more prosocial preferences by reorienting them toward group-based goals informed by a shared sense of social identification and reinforced through social network effects. The creation of new local administrative units thus unintentionally netted social institutions stretching across the many villages of the local state in some cases, easing elite negotiations within the local state. Where local government boundaries pool villages with dispersed social institutions, negotiations at the second level are more contentious and prone to capture by individual- or village-based opportunism.

The argument is displayed visually in Figure 1.1, which offers a schematic representation of how divergent precolonial political geographies generate distinct predictions for redistribution following the introduction of decentralization reforms. Taking each circle as a village scaled to population size, Figure 1.1 illustrates how divergent precolonial political structures (Figure 1.1a) generate distinct distributive outcomes (Figure 1.1d). Specifically, the delimitation of local government borders (Figure 1.1b) captures villages with a shared history under a precolonial state under high congruence, while pooling villages with no shared historical identification in areas of low congruence. This generates a shared social identity that is reinforced by dense social ties among elites across villages in cases of high congruence (Figure 1.1c). The theory's prediction can be seen in (Figure 1.1d): public goods should be distributed more evenly across space in areas of high congruence, while a few large villages prove able to capture the local state in contexts of low congruence.[77]

At its core, this argument echoes an enduring idea that social context can determine the nature of formal institutional politics. The most prominent corollary in political science – whereby strikingly different development outcomes are found within the same country as a result of a long-gone past – is

---

[77] This is schematized in Figure 1.1 as a function of population, though as my empirics show in Chapters 4 and 6, the political cleavages in historically acephalous areas remain diverse.

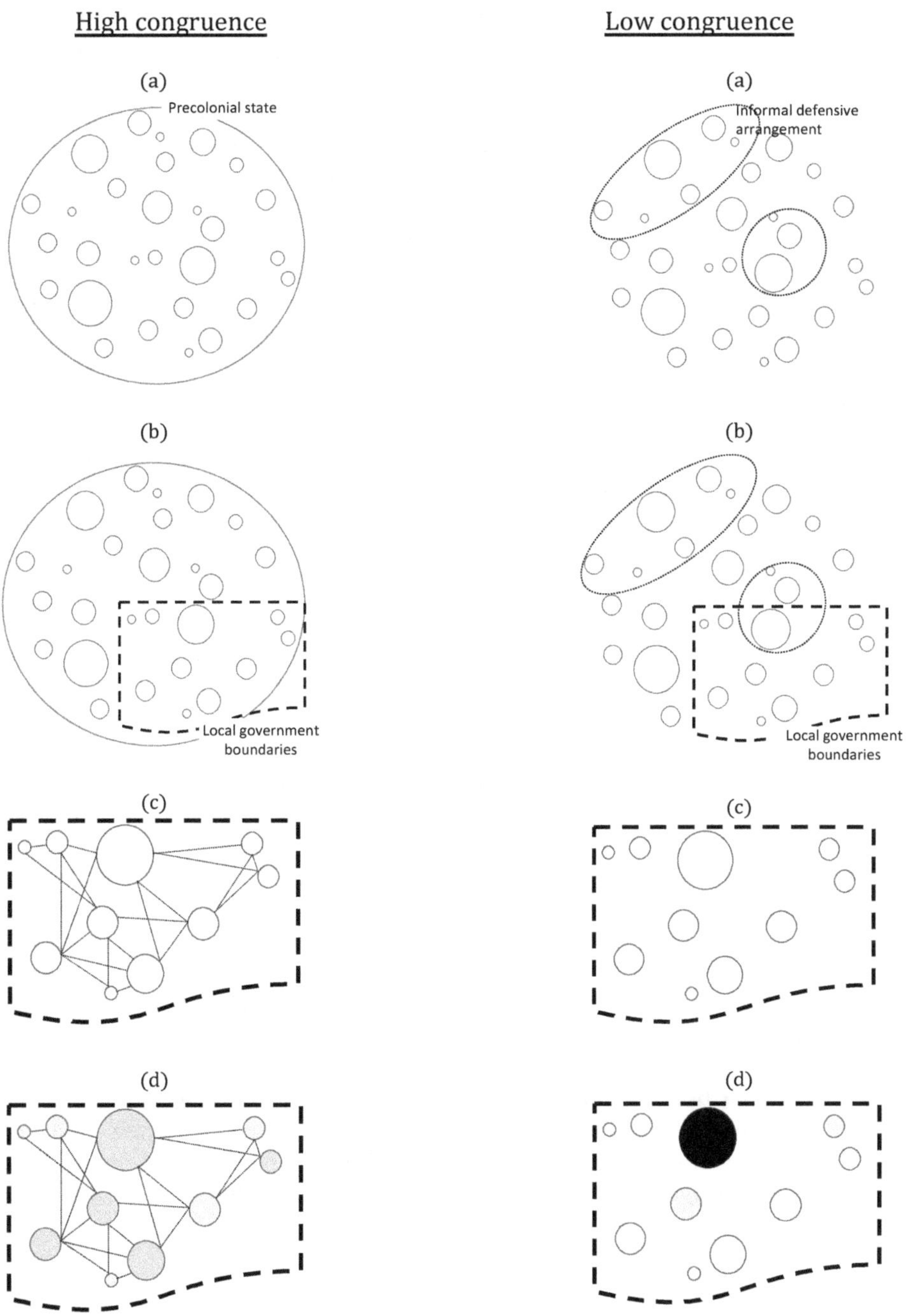

A Theory of Institutional Congruence 41

FIGURE 1.1 Redistribution across political geographies – high congruence and low congruence: (a) precolonial political space, (b) decentralization, (c) social ties, and (d) distributive pattern

Putnam's (1993) monumental study of divergent civic traditions in Italy, in which he documents that communities with robust, horizontal social ties inherited from the past perform better following Italy's devolution of power to regional governments. My argument builds on Putnam as well as a small yet high-profile body of work that likewise finds the social dilemmas inherent in governance are eased when formal and informal institutions overlap. This has been shown to create the basis for better self-government, heightening accountability, and improving economic development at different levels of government – from the village to the state – and in very different cultural and institutional contexts – from authoritarian China to Native American reservations in the United States.[78]

Much of this work highlights cognitive mechanisms rooted in relatively durable prescriptive norms.[79] Many, like Tsai's (2007) well-known work on solidary groups in China or Englebert's (2002b) work on African postcolonial regime, link these norms to leader incentives. According to Tsai, rural Chinese local officials pursue moral standing in the community by meeting societal expectations when the villages they administer are home to embedding and encompassing solidary groups, while for Englebert postcolonial African leaders are rewarded for choosing developmental policies and investing in state-building when the postcolonial state overlaps significantly with precolonial political structures. In other words, the postcolonial African state performs better when it has high degrees of horizontal legitimacy or high agreement over what constitutes the polity. Outcomes are worse when the state remains exogenously grafted onto society.

I seek to advance a more universal claim that brings this small and relatively dispersed body of work together: social institutions create distinct redistributive coalitions when they are congruent with the spatial boundaries of governance. Two core commonalities of this work are important in making this assertion. First, this work shows that an overarching basis of solidarity can facilitate governance even in the face of social diversity.[80] Institutional congruence does not demand cultural or ethnic homogeneity, in other words, but some shared category of identification must both be present and salient. Understanding how individuals identify locally is important because "who we perceive ourselves to be influences our sense of obligation and responsibility to others."[81] Second, though not always explicitly theorized and/or measured, these arguments all assume in one way or another that actors are enmeshed in social networks that valorize and reinforce the cognitive properties in question. This reinforces the argument that actor's behavior is not reducible to opportunistic

---

[78] For example, Englebert (2002b); Cornell and Kalt (1995); and Tsai (2007). See Chapter 8 for a more detailed discussion.
[79] Simpser et al. (2018, 428).   [80] For example, Dippel (2014). See also Singh (2015a).
[81] Cramer Walsh (2003, 183).

individual incentives alone, but instead that individuals' preferences are inherently relational.

The experience of rural Senegalese governments that I document reveals more flexibility in when and how institutional congruence is likely to emerge. I suggest that this is not tied to the existence of specific physical institutions, such as the ancestral temples that help maintain village solidary groups in Tsai's study of rural China, or about forms of associational life, as argued by Putnam. My evidence indicates that institutional congruence can emerge out of relatively diffuse stories of a shared past and even under relatively hierarchical social relations. It can emerge across a range of regime types and even in the wake of short-term reform where formal institutions remain far from any indigenous understanding of governance. At the same time, by refocusing the question of institutional congruence onto the dynamics of spatial overlap, I seek to avoid the deterministic bent of earlier work by political scientists such as Eckstein (1966) or Inglehart (1990), who argued that democratic stability demands a congruence between specific cultural norms and formal, democratic institutions.[82] As the empirical chapters illustrate, the Senegalese case does not suggest that some communities are endowed with prodemocratic norms that are absent elsewhere, but more minimally that the perceived webs of mutual obligation generated by social institutions must map onto the scale of decision-making.

THE LONG-RUN EFFECTS OF PRECOLONIAL POLITICAL ORDER ON PROSPECTS FOR CONGRUENCE

I root the origins of the social institutions in long-defunct precolonial polities. A growing body of evidence demonstrates the ways in which historical political structures can leave behind enduring legacies, be it through formal institutions or cultural beliefs, such as trust and cooperation.[83] Because Senegal's precolonial political hierarchies were dismantled under French colonial rule, the legacy I identify is not carried through formal institutional structures. My argument, that institutionalized norms persisted among local elites, who continued to valorize and reinforce regularized expectations of proper comportment for their communities, suggests that the long-run effects of precolonial polities course instead through sociocultural channels.

---

[82] For Eckstein (1966, 241, 192), democratic stability emerged when patterns of governance and social authority were highly congruent, dynamics that he identified as being particularly critical in the realms of elite recruitment, competition, and political socialization. I show that the social dynamics of congruence are not tied to the nature of norms at all; villages across rural Senegal value conflict avoidance. What matters is the spatial extent of how social institutions map onto the formal boundaries of decision-making, meaning that any idea of cultural match is insufficient.

[83] Examples include, respectfully, Acemoglu et al. (2001) and Becker et al. (2014).

As I introduce in detail in the next chapter, Senegal's precolonial states were robust political organizations with clearly demarcated elite hierarchies. Like all states, the polities that populated West Africa prior to European colonization were run by dominant elite coalitions, wherein elites gained lucrative positions in a kingdom's clientelist organization in exchange for sacrificing their right to engage in short-term predation on others in the polity. In this way, Senegambian states were "natural states": elites forwent competition and deferred to each other's rights and resources.[84] The importance of intra-elite cooperation in these states is further seen in the fact that decision-making was not absolute in most of the region's precolonial polities but rather mediated through highly structured intra-elite relations. In the trading state of Gajaaga, for example, a royal assembly was held after the annual harvest, with all branches of the ruling Bacili clan meeting to negotiate the state's finances as well as to make major decisions, such as those about war or state expansion.[85] Such interactions were heavily prescribed; holders of elite status in the West African Sahel were held to a moral code, with an honorable man expected to display values of honesty, generosity and to strive to uphold the social and moral ideals of his community.[86] Although I ultimately remain agnostic about the exact origins of the social institutions under study in this book, institutionalized norms of intra-elite comportment such as those I identify here lay at the foundation of precolonial West African political order.

My suggestion that intra-elite norms originating in the distant past remain salient today builds on recent findings that norms can persist even after the political system that generated them has disappeared.[87] Of course, norms often persist because they are tied to formal institutions, such as the chieftaincy, but they can persist just as powerfully because of intergenerational socialization. Indeed, many of Africa's precolonial states fostered imagined communities. De Juan and Koos (2019) show this for the precolonial Bushi Kingdom in the eastern Democratic Republic of the Congo. They document an enduring impact of past processes of social integration – such as the sense of group loyalty fostered by precolonial polities like the Bushi – on prosocial behavior among the Bushi's descendants today. In many ways, I offer a parallel argument: precolonial kingdoms engendered enduring legacies via the social norms they left behind. In the present, intra-elite norms of appropriate comportment shape redistributive strategies and, similar to what De Juan and Koos show for the Bushi, these norms have persisted because of continuing shared identification with the precolonial past.

More specifically, I root the perseverance of social institutions in the persistence of rural social hierarchies. I detail the ways in which rural social hierarchies have been reproduced over time, reinforcing cross-village social institutions

---

[84] This is North et al.'s (2009, 15–18, 255) definition of a natural state. [85] Bathily (1989, 197).
[86] See Ly (1967) on the Wolof and Peulh. [87] See Lowes et al. (2017) and Dell et al. (2018).

in the process, in the next chapter, but my basic contention is that because social status in the West African Sahel remains strongly tied to histories of settlement, shared claims to descent from a precolonial kingdom constitutes a powerful form of local capital for local actors. Laying claim to descent from a precolonial kingdom provides local elites with a portable identity that not only justifies their own claims to local social status but also that of their relatives and friends by enabling hierarchical claim-making to local authority. The relative continuity in local social organization in the face of a weak and remote colonial state only further assisted in the survival of local mythologies of precolonial preeminence and authority.

In this way, the continued value of shared identification with the precolonial state as well as the continued relevance of local social networks collectively reinforce the narratives communities tell about themselves and the values they believe they should uphold as members thereof. Social order is often rooted in exactly such an idea of shared past, aligning assumptions about what constitutes a legitimate exercise of social or political authority.[88] As long as local histories inform who can claim local social status, the social institutions that have been passed down should remain relevant. In turn, as long as claims to local elite status remain interdependent across villages, we should see the possibility of institutional congruence.

It merits abundant clarification that I seek to emphasize how social institutions are the product of *active* social processes. I consciously depart from the tendency to flatten political dynamics that enable norms to persist over time among some scholars.[89] Social institutions are only reproduced to the extent that they are valorized in everyday social interactions by both excluding and enabling certain behaviors.[90] I locate the legacy of precolonial political order in cross-village sociopolitical relations and not in an inherited "stock" of an attribute, like trust. This serves as a point of caution against romanticizing shared narratives of a bygone political order because the group identities and social networks they rest upon reflect power as much as they do solidarity, to paraphrase Meagher (2005, 225). It is the explicitly distributive nature of social institutions, which rest upon and replicate "hierarchal forms of domination" that leads to their reproduction.[91]

CONCLUSION

This chapter presented a theory of institutional congruence to explain variation in the local politics of representation and redistribution under decentralization. By conceptualizing local governance as a two-level game, where local elites

---

[88] Connerton (1989). [89] For example, Nunn and Wantchekon (2011). [90] Nee (1998, 9).
[91] Mahoney (2010, 19).

have to balance between village- and family-based interests on the first level while also negotiating across villages within the local state at the second, I highlight the unique dilemmas facing rural elites under decentralization. Divergent outcomes can be traced to persistent social institutions at the grassroots, which stipulate and regulate appropriate social behavior, and which have been repurposed following institutional reform. When local governments inherit robust social institutions that stretch across villages, elites face distinct political incentives because their social and political worlds overlap. This constrains opportunism by imposing both reputational costs and internal rewards via the network mechanism at the same time that the identity mechanism valorizes group goals within the local state.

Consequently, when formal and informal institutions are congruent, shared social institutions imbue the majority, if not all, elites with more prosocial preferences toward the group, enabling spatially broader redistributive politics because the local state itself captures elites' boundaries of solidarity. This raises the costs borne by elites for acting toward their village-based interests alone. In contrast, when the overlap between formal and informal institutions is low, the absence of cross-village social norms weakens checks on individual opportunism, rendering local political negotiations a zero-sum endeavor between villages. In this way, decentralization – like any formal institutional reform – did not descend onto blank political terrain, but merely put old identities, conflicts, and debates into new relief, unintentionally generating significant and consequential differences in the capacity of elites to cooperate within the local state.

The next two chapters provide a historical platform for the argument's viability in Senegal, introducing the region's dynamic precolonial state system that interacts with contemporary decentralization reforms to generate variation in institutional congruence. Chapters 4 through 8 turn to empirical tests of my theory's predictions.

2

Bringing Old States Back In
Senegal's Precolonial Polities

Even though Africa's precolonial states ceased to exist as political units long ago – their kings co-opted and their bureaucracies dismantled by the colonial state – the country's precolonial history remains prominent in the national imagination. The names of precolonial kingdoms still circulate widely: Senegalese speak of traveling to *Fouta* (short for Fouta Toro) rather than Kanel or Podor Department, they shop at *Baol Décor*, and in the footprints of the country's ethnically Wolof kingdoms, mayors are as frequently referred to as *bour*, the precolonial title for king, as they are "the mayor." These references reflect not only regional pride but the palpable nature of precolonial legacies in contemporary Senegal, legacies that I argue actively inform and constrain behavior under democratic decentralization today.

This chapter introduces the first of three historical building blocks for the argument. Specifically, I present two empirical propositions below. First, I locate the source of historical divergence at the heart of my argument by detailing the histories of Senegal's precolonial polities as well as the political forms that were present in what we might call "stateless" – though certainly not anarchical – areas, to document the historical antecedent to my independent variable of institutional congruence. I then introduce my criteria for identifying what qualifies as a "state" as well as my strategy for measuring their geographic footprints. The second proposition relates to the question of why precolonial legacies persist to the present. I begin by introducing three prominent reasons that we may in fact predict the *opposite* of my argument. Precolonial legacies may have been erased by (a) French colonial rule, particularly French aspirations of direct rule; (b) religious conversion and the emergence of influential Sufi Islamic brotherhoods; and (c) migration induced by the introduction of cash crops. I argue that none of these overturned the key mechanism of persistence linking the precolonial past to contemporary local politics: the nature of village-based social hierarchies. The second and third building blocks,

47

Senegal's decentralization reforms and the top-down process of boundary demarcation that unintentionally netted precolonial identities within new jurisdictional boundaries, are presented in the following chapter.

SENEGAL'S PRECOLONIAL POLITICAL GEOGRAPHY

This book's core empirical argument is that local governance following Senegal's decentralization reforms is intimately shaped by the region's dynamic state system in the precolonial era. Africa's savannah belt was home to a series of complex polities that rose and fell between the fourteenth and nineteenth centuries. These states possessed well-defined territorial administrations and projected powerful national identities.[1] They collected revenue, adapted to capitalist markets, managed far-flung intermediaries, enforced property rights, and established clear rules for succession while maintaining checks on any given leader's power, all reflecting defined, state-like attributes.[2] The distinction between the patchwork of states that dominated the region prior to French conquest and the political organization of "uncentralized" areas is the first historical foundation of my argument.

Precolonial Kingdoms

When Portuguese ships first began exploring the West African coast in the late fifteenth century, Senegambia was home to more than a dozen small states that had formed in the ruins of the Malian Empire in the 1300s. In Senegal, the immediate inheritor of the Malian Empire was the Djoloff Empire, ruled by a powerful ethnically Wolof aristocracy based in the center of present-day Senegal. Like most states that formed in the West African Sahel, the Djoloff Empire consolidated power by acting as a gateway to the trans-Saharan trade. Beginning in the sixteenth century, the rise of the Atlantic slave trade reoriented local economies toward European traders along the coast. This proved costly to the Djoloff's interior base, as the lure of new coastal- and river-based trade with Europeans prompted considerable unrest within the empire's constituent provinces. Soon, ambitious political leaders sought independence and the lucrative ability to control their own profits from the growing Atlantic trade.[3] By 1566, the empire had largely collapsed as the Djoloff's vassals stopped paying tribute – an effective declaration of independence.[4] Though the Djoloff Kingdom persisted with much more limited territorial control, it never regained its prior levels of regional hegemony.

Like all states in Senegambia at the time, the Djoloff and its various inheritors were run by an ethnically defined aristocracy. Some of the Wolof kingdoms, such as Cayor and Baol, were able to capitalize on their seaports to

---

[1] Warner (1999).   [2] Colson (1969, 37).   [3] Monteil (1966, 122).   [4] Searing (2002, 14).

enrich themselves, becoming regional economic powerhouses. Others, such as Walo in the northwest, faced continual internal and external pressures as raids from Maure populations to the north amplified internal weaknesses created by endemic conflict between the three ruling Wolof lineages. Although the kingdom received some support following the establishment of the French trading post at Saint-Louis, Walo was beset by civil war and largely ceased to exert meaningful political authority over its territory by the mid-nineteenth century.[5] Also gaining independence from the Djoloff in the late sixteenth century was the southern vassal of Saloum, which became the region's second kingdom run by an ethnically Serer aristocracy along with its neighbor Sine, which had formed in the mid-fourteenth century.[6]

To the northeast, stretched out along the northern arc of the Senegal River, lay Fouta Toro, an ethnically Peulh Islamic theocracy. Fouta Toro was a regional "breadbasket," and an early site of French commercial interest, exporting salt, gum arabic, slaves, and gold sourced from the southeast from the late fifteenth century onward.[7] Unlike its neighbors that had formed on the vestiges of the Malian Empire (~1200–1400s), states like Fouta Toro or Walo illustrate the presence of bottom-up pressures to centralize in the area, both having been founded in fertile floodplains that lay in close proximity to the Saharan trade. Fouta Toro was also an early adopter of Islam.[8] In 1690, a second Peulh Kingdom, Boundou, rapidly consolidated power to the south, as the economic link between the Gambian and Senegal River basins, subduing the zone's heterogeneous population in the process.[9] In the decades before colonization, the Upper Casamance saw the emergence of Fouladou, when Molo Egue Bande, also a Peulh, overthrew the declining Mandingue aristocracy of the federated state of Kaabu in 1867, though Fouladou was never to consolidate to the same degree as its counterparts to the north.[10]

A number of minor polities populated the landscape as well. Between Fouta Toro and Boundou were the small, Soninke trading states of Gajaaga and, weaker and less organized, Guidimakha, located at the confluence of the Senegal and Faleme Rivers.[11] The Gambian River Basin saw a number of small, ethnically Mandingue states – such as Rip, Pakala, Niani, or Ouli – peak in the seventeenth and eighteenth centuries during the height of the slave trade before entering a period of decline, beset by internal rivalries, pressure from neighbors, Islamic jihads, and the Atlantic trade's abolition.[12]

---

[5] Barry (1985, 64) and Suret-Canale and Barry (1976, 464).　　[6] Sarr (1986–1987).
[7] Clark and Phillips (1994, 142–143).　　[8] Curtin (1975, 7–8).
[9] Clark and Phillips (1994, 142–143); Gomez (1992); and Clark (1996).
[10] Girard (1964); Ngaïdé (2012); and Innes (1976). The true extent of Fouladou's territorial control at the end of the century remains contested (see Fanchette 1999).
[11] Gomez (1992, 19).　　[12] Quinn (1972) and Van Hoven (1995).

Senegal's political geography in the century leading to colonization was thus a dynamic and shifting one, as political entrepreneurs sought to capitalize on changing economic and social realities. But despite their variation, these polities shared three commonalities. First, though all states were controlled by an ethnically homogenous political aristocracy, significant ethnic minorities were present everywhere. Minorities often held specific rights, such as the distinct tax collected by Cayor's fourth minister from Peulh herders.[13] The Wolof-dominated state of Baol was home to a number of Serer provinces in its western stretches, while Saloum was "pluriethnic" with important Wolof and Peulh minorities.[14] Even the population of Fouta Toro, strongly associated with the Peulh, is estimated to have been 10 percent Wolof, Soninke, and Maure by the mid-nineteenth century.[15] This diversity reflects a broader regularity in precolonial Africa. As observed by the historian Elizabeth Colson (1969, 31),

> political and ethnic boundaries rarely coincided in precolonial Africa. Human ambitions were too pressing to allow people to remain static over long periods. States expanded when they were sufficiently powerful to do so. Communities competed with one another to attract settlers and thereby gain supporters ... Men moved to find better land or more favorable opportunities in their craft ...

Second, in all cases, social and political life was structured around social caste. With the exception of the acephalous Diola in the southern Casamance, Senegal's major ethnic groups are all caste-based with three social groups: an aristocracy, freemen, and slaves.[16] Under the caste system, an individual's profession, marriage choice, and place of residence were circumscribed by the caste they inherited from their parents.[17] Slaves could be owned by the aristocracy and casted individuals alike. While many slaves worked domestically, the Wolof and Serer kingdoms were notable for their powerful warrior slave castes (*ceddo*), who protected the royal court, collected taxes, and served as a standing army in many parts of the country.[18]

Finally, the political structures of these states were all based on elective monarchies, with kings selected from among a set of eligible families. Both Fouta Toro and Saloum had federated systems, comprised of provinces that retained substantial autonomy; in the former, province-based electors served to protect their own localized interests as a check on any lineage or province from

---

[13] Ba (1976, 173).   [14] Becker et al. (1999, 49).   [15] Robinson (1975, 5).

[16] This varies slightly by ethnic group. The Serer had a less rigid caste system than other states north of The Gambia (Searing 2002, 8). All non-casted ethnic groups fall in acephalous areas (Koter 2016, 70).

[17] Castes are assigned by profession to artisans and griots (praise singers). Blacksmiths, weavers, carvers, and other artisans were considered to work with unclean materials (in the case of griots, words were the perceived danger). Unlike slaves, many casted groups retained important positions in the community; griots attached to aristocratic families, for example, kept the oral history of the lineage (Clark and Phillips 1994, 85–87).

[18] Diouf (1990) and Getz (2004).

consolidating power.[19] The Bourba (king) Djoloff consulted with a council of seven titleholders on questions of great importance for the kingdom, including the declaration of war.[20] Political authority, in other words, was far from absolute as the need to negotiate among a broader set of stakeholders "meant that power was in effect collegial," reflecting the institutional checks on political leaders that defined all of the region's polities.[21] Each was administered through hierarchical organizations that extended from the king down to the village. In Sine, for example, the king was represented directly in each village by a *sakh-sakh*, who served as judge and tax collector.[22]

Acephalous Polities

Of course, political order was not absent outside of what I define as a state. I label as acephalous any society that did not have a unified political hierarchy beyond the village level.[23] Originally categorized as the inverse of statehood in influential early work by anthropologists, acephalous societies do not lack political structure, but rather take horizontal (as opposed to vertical) forms of organization, such as segmentary lineages or confederacies.[24] As a term, acephalous embraces an admittedly broad category of societies that risks equivocation. The key distinction I wish to make, however, is that historically centralized areas were home to political institutions that were maintained by an elite stratum of society and which were enforced across villages through a political hierarchy. In contrast, though acephalous societies were often equally complex, their complexity was not oriented around a set of overarching political institutions that integrated diverse populations across space.

The Diola in the Casamance (present-day Ziguinchor Region) remain the most invoked example of an acephalous ethnic group in Senegal, though many smaller acephalous groups existed. Among the Diola, village chiefs were elected by all household heads, who sought the bravest and most respected man in the village for the role.[25] A chief's power was not absolute, however, and no unifying hierarchy existed between villages. As Méguelle (2012, 80) cites the French explorer Hecquard (1850), "the chiefs have very little influence and cannot take any important deliberation without assembling the village elders." Even though villages at times recognized mutual religious leaders, political organization remained fractured. By way of illustration, Pakao (in current-day Sedhiou Region) was home to a small group of villages that were unified around a powerful marabout or Muslim religious guide. Despite their shared

---

[19] Robinson (1975, 19, 27).   [20] Monteil (1966, 604).
[21] Klein (1968b, 21) and Beattie (1959).   [22] Klein (1968b, 16).
[23] We might otherwise refer to these as decentralized societies, but I opt for acephalous to avoid confusion with decentralization as a contemporary political reform.
[24] Classically, Fortes and Evans-Pritchard (1940); see also Kaberry (1957).
[25] See the accounts of Pélissier (1966); Boone (2003b); and Beck (2008).

religious adherence, the principle of independence across villages was "central to the social ethic." Villages rarely intermarried and high levels of suspicion existed between them.[26] The explorer Hecquard also visited Pakao, observing in 1855 that "each village forms a sort of republic, governed by an imam, directing religion, and by a chief in charge of dispensing justice."[27] Balans (1975) describes Niominka, a territory straddling Sine and the present-day Gambia along the Atlantic oceans, similarly.

At times, villages maintained informal protection arrangements. The Mandingue-dominated Bambuk, for example, a territory along the Senegalese–Malian border, was comprised of villages grouped under loose, protective confederations.[28] The Bassari, Konigui, and Bedik peoples of southeastern Senegal, all acephalous, conversely developed strategies for self-protection that included settling in isolated, hilltop villages.[29] Other regions, such as much of present-day Kaffrine Region and western Tambacounda Region, were sparsely inhabited forests by a small number of largely isolated villages or, in the Ferlo desert, pastoralist populations organized largely by clan.

Historically acephalous zones of Senegal were thus equally if not more variable in political form than their centralized counterparts. They also were important economic actors in their own right; despite lacking a centralized political apparatus, the Casamance River delta was home to an active economy in the centuries preceding colonization, trading wax and slaves with Portuguese and French traders.[30] Importantly, with the exception of the Diola, many of the region's major ethnic groups inhabited both centralized and acephalous political systems. The Toucouleur Peulh inhabited the kingdom of Fouta Toro, while the closely related pastoralist Peulh inhabited the Ferlo desert. Similarly, Mandingue populations resided in the microstates within the Gambian River basin, but they also expanded into acephalous stretches of present-day Tambacounda Region. This point, that all of the country's significant ethnic groups can likewise be located both within and outside of Senegal's precolonial states, is an important one, indicating that political centralization is not reducible to ethnic group traits.

MEASURING PRECOLONIAL STATES

The above discussion indicates a spectrum of political forms with varying degrees of centralization. When should we consider a polity sufficiently centralized to engender the legacy theorized in this project? I employ four criteria to assess precolonial statehood, following North et al.'s (2009, 5–9) definition of a natural state, these are (a) a limited organizational form, notably an elite tied together through personal relations and a political hierarchy built around

---

[26] Schaffer and Cooper (1980, 45).   [27] Quoted in Schaffer and Cooper (1980, 44).
[28] Clark and Phillips (1994, 74).   [29] Kywels and Ferry (2006).   [30] Mark (1985).

patron–client relationships. Political rule in the Djoloff, in central Senegal, for instance, was assured by a well-defined set of elites who together formed an advisory council to the King.[31] (b) A system for taxing trade. Many of West Africa's states profited off of the slave trade, taxing caravans as well as European traders.[32] Drawing on Hawthorne's discussion of features specific to African precolonial states, I add (c) regularized tribute systems from clients.[33] In West Africa, yearly tributes took specific forms in each state, such as a locally administered payment for the right to farmland claimed by the royal court in Boundou.[34] In Saloum, the Buur (king) received the following: each village farmed a field for the royal household, with one animal per herd and one-tenth of the millet crop going to the Buur as well.[35] Lastly, (d) some form of local representation to regulate social and economic life has to be present. This included direct appointments from the royal court or, more commonly, a system whereby a local chief or religious figure was delegated to enforce the king's orders and laws. Because precolonial states rose and fell over time, I measure the existence of these attributes in fifty-year intervals between 1500 and 1880 to create an inventory of the polities that we can describe as "states" in the precolonial period.

By this definition, on the eve of the final French push to conquer Senegal in the early 1880s, slightly under half of Senegal's territory was under the control of a centralized political organization. Yet generating a list of polities that meet my definition of statehood leaves a critical question unanswered: how can we estimate their spatial extent? Although certain regions of the country are associated with certain kingdoms, Baol with Diourbel Region is a case in point, this is not always the case and remains an empirical contention to be confirmed.

Certainly, early traders along the coast or explorers, such as Henry Barth or Parfait-Louis Monteil, made maps of some of Senegal's precolonial states in the 1800s, but the accuracy of their representations should give us pause for thought. Most explorers only passed through small segments of a given state and early maps follow what Branch (2014) describes as the boundary-focused character of the European state, leading to neatly bounded polygons that are questionable measures of felt state presence. These concerns are compounded by the fact that many precolonial states in the interior, such as Boundou, largely escaped the attention of early traders and explorers or were poorly understood as territorial political units.

Accordingly, I develop an alternative estimation strategy to capture the territorial footprints of Senegal's precolonial polities. The principal insight of this method is that of Herbst (2000), who argued that precolonial power was projected concentrically outward from nodes of power. Drawing on secondary and archival material for all of Senegal's polities that meet my criteria of

---

[31] Monteil (1966, 603–604).   [32] For example, see Gomez (1992, 64) on Boundou.
[33] Hawthorne (2013, 77).   [34] Clark (1996, 8).   [35] Klein (1968b, 20).

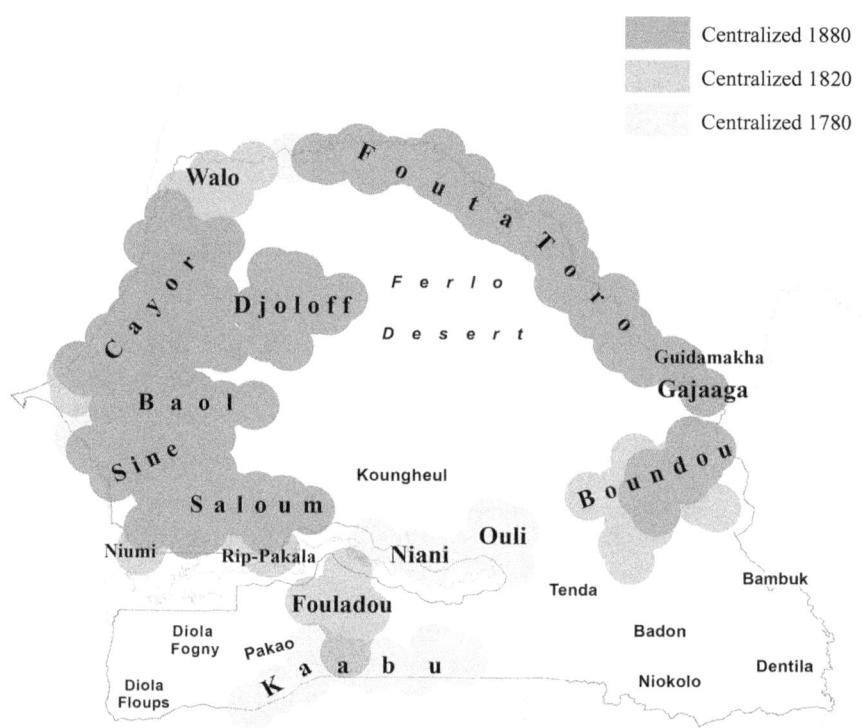

FIGURE 2.1 Precolonial polities and historically acephalous regions

statehood, I code the key political, social, and economic centers of each state. Georeferencing these locations to a spatial dataset of Senegalese localities today, I am able to estimate the spatial extent of the country's precolonial polities by generating buffers around these core nodes of power.

This approach generates the map of Senegal's precolonial states between 1500 and 1880 as seen in Figure 2.1. The map, which displays both my estimates of the general locations of precolonial states and the approximate location of historically acephalous, or stateless, regions that had commonly used names, shows spatial estimates with 20-kilometer buffers. I use 20 kilometers as a baseline because it is a reasonable daily travel distance for an individual on foot. That travelers were unlikely to cover much more territory than this is supported by Lasnet et al.'s (1900, 285) observation in the late 1880s that camels employed to transport cargo in the regions of the Djoloff, Cayor, and Baol could travel no more than 25–30 kilometers a day.[36]

---

[36] As noted in Chapter 5, my results are robust to expanding these buffers upward to 30 kilometers.

This distance also best approximates the more reliable boundaries found on early colonial maps. My coding process is detailed in more depth in Chapter 5.

WHY DO PRECOLONIAL IDENTITIES PERSIST?

Students of African history have long debated whether colonialism was a fundamental moment of social transformation or whether preexisting social and political dynamics mediated or persisted through the colonial encounter.[37] My argument – that legacies of the precolonial era persist at the grassroots – falls clearly within this second perspective. But if precolonial Senegambian states generated the seeds for historical divergence as I argue, then I must explain why these legacies were not eliminated by the rupture of the colonial encounter.

The remainder of this chapter addresses this issue. I begin by reviewing the three most prominent reasons that we would expect the *erasure* of precolonial legacies: the nature of French conquest, which introduced policies of association and direct rule that dismantled precolonial political hierarchies, the spread of new forms of religious practice, notably Sufi Islam, and migration following the introduction of the cash crop economy. I then turn to examine why social institutions emerging out of defunct precolonial states have persisted by specifying the mechanism of reproduction: the persistence of rural social hierarchies. Throughout the West African Sahel, local elite status is largely tied to genealogical descent from the families that first settled or ruled a territory. As a consequence, village status hierarchies reproduce local historical narratives because these narratives explicitly bolster elites' claims to local authority. Although similar place-based status claims exist in acephalous areas, these are only sometimes mutually reinforcing across villages, generating village-specific narratives that are incapable of generating congruence with the local state.

Social Shocks Predicting Erasure

The colonial encounter was a period of substantial social and political change: old power structures were dismantled and new ones constructed. New economic imperatives emerged at the same time that legal systems changed and technological inventions transformed landscapes. In many ways, therefore, my claim that precolonial legacies persist over a century after these polities were dismantled is a puzzle. After all, Senegal has seen substantial changes in the interim, including most obviously the onset of French colonial rule which dramatically altered the country's social, political, and administrative structure.

---

[37] See for example, Young (1994) or Mamdani (1996) compared to Ballantyne (2010) or Reid (2011).

In reality, French influence was felt in the subregion as early as the 1600s, most notably through the economic demand for slaves, gum arabic, and peanuts generated by French traders based in a series of trading posts along the Atlantic coast and, later, the Senegal River. A tentative effort to conquer the interior by General Faidherbe in the mid-1850s proved costly and resulted in a quick retreat.[38] The French did not seriously pursue territorial expansion again until the late 1800s, but once they did, the process of conquest went quickly. Beginning with the reestablishment of the protectorate of Cayor in 1883, most of Senegal north of the British Gambian territories was under nominal French control by 1890.[39] Up until this point, existing states had retained control over their territory and actively negotiated with the French.[40] As late as 1880, for instance, the French were forced to make a series of concessions to Abdoul Bokar, the king of Fouta Toro, in order to complete a telegraph line linking Saint-Louis, France's long-standing coastal commercial base to Kayes in present-day Mali. The king's refusal to allow the French to complete a section between French forts at Salde and Bakel resulted in five years of diplomatic negotiations and, ultimately, French retreat in 1881.[41] This should not obscure the militarization of French conquest, however. France forcibly subdued polities across West Africa. The most famous example in Senegal was with Lat Dior, the last *Damel* (king) of Cayor, who took up arms against the French in response to France's seizure of his territory for the construction of a railroad linking the French coastal trading centers of Saint-Louis to Dakar. Dior's forces were ultimately defeated and Dior himself was forcibly replaced by the French.[42]

In the ensuing years, the French made their final conquests in the area. In 1888 they replaced the Almamy of Boundou, a sign that they no longer depended on alliances with autonomous rulers, and in 1890 French troops entered and quickly occupied the Djoloff and Fouta Toro, bringing the last two semiautonomous areas under direct control.[43] Following the pacification of the Casamance in 1900, France had effectively claimed control of the territory we now know as Senegal. The economic motives that led France to secure the coastline in earlier decades saw no parallel in the late 1800s as it was well-known by the second half of the nineteenth century that the West African Sahel held little economic value.[44] Instead, it was largely the French Navy that roused domestic interest and drove inland expansion in the latter part of the nineteenth century. In particular, a number of emerging African political leaders produced useful fodder for French metropolitan newspapers, which documented the French Navy's pursuit of leaders like El Hadji Omar Tall or Samori Touré.

---

[38] Fage (1969, 163–167); Robinson (1975, 168); and Searing (2002, 35).
[39] Getz (2004, 137, 147). [40] Ajayi (1998, 3, 271). [41] Robinson (1975, 126–138).
[42] The railroad was motivated by both economic and political objectives: the French wanted to open the Wolof countryside for peanut production at the same time that they wanted to consolidate their control over Cayor, the strongest state in the region (Pheffer 1985, 33).
[43] Robinson (1975, 149–151). [44] Roberts (1963, 304) and Crowder (1968, 55).

Rather than a clear plan for conquest, therefore, French expansion in the Sahel produced a series of "deepening entanglements" that led the French onward.[45] French conquest, in other words, was far from overdetermined.

The widespread changes that followed have become the focus of a recent body of scholarship estimating the long-run effects of colonial occupation. This work views colonialism as a critical juncture that generated profound differences in contemporary development outcomes both across and within countries. The colonial era introduced new institutions, new forms of human capital, and new avenues for economic accumulation, all potential fundamental causes for present-day disparities.[46] I test these potential alternative explanations empirically in Chapter 7, but I focus here on three substantial shocks to local social life that came with French colonization and which were most likely to have erased precolonial legacies.

Colonization: "Association" and Direct Rule

French rule in Senegal exemplified extreme poles of the country's colonial aspirations. Influenced by enlightenment philosophy, France's stated aspiration was for their colonial subjects to assimilate into French culture and become French citizens. This assumption of an evolutionary progress toward French civilizational ideals resulted in the substantial legal recognition granted to residents of Senegal's four coastal urban centers (Saint-Louis, Dakar, Gorée Island, and Rufisque) – known as the *quatre communes* or "four communes" – in 1848. France had maintained these coastal trading posts since the seventeenth century, and each was home to French traders and a sizable *métis* population. In this way, the four communes saw the purest practice of the French colonial ideology of assimilation as residents were granted specific citizenship rights, including representation in France's *Chambre des Députés*, the right to local municipal councils, and access to the French education system.[47] The contrast with rural areas was sharp. Here the colonial administration sought more pragmatic, short-term strategies.[48] The first two decades of colonization were thus defined by a bifurcated administrative structure with the interior placed under a system of protectorate that more closely resembled the classic dichotomized view of British indirect rule while the direct rule commonly associated with the French was limited to the four communes.[49]

As the colonial state gained strength, it became evident that the ideals of assimilation were too burdensome for the thin colonial state to apply beyond the four communes. As a consequence, French thinking evolved toward a *politique d'association* as an intermediate approach. Association did not

---

[45] See Ajayi (1998). [46] See for example, De Juan and Pierskalla (2017).
[47] Diouf (1998, 676) and Crowder (1964, 202).
[48] Rural Senegalese were subject to the *indigénat* penal system and forced labor requirements, for example, far from the legal rights held by their urban compatriots (Hesseling 1985, 134).
[49] Idowu (1968, 248).

abandon the core tenets of assimilation – African subjects were still expected to be socialized into French culture through a centralized administration – but the timeline was extended and the scale of state intervention reduced.[50] Colonial schools were scarce, for example, but they nonetheless taught a French curriculum. By 1920, the colony had been unified politically under a colonial council, wherein residents of the four communes were represented by elected representatives while rural subjects were represented via their *chef de canton*, or canton chiefs, appointed by the French as district-level intermediaries.[51] This disjuncture only ended in 1956 when France passed the *Loi Cadre*, which made all colonial subjects French citizens in an effort to construct a "modern Africa." At no point, however, was the ultimate authority of colonial officers questioned. Even as territorial assemblies were constructed following the Second World War, African representatives could not amend colonial budgets and had minimal policy influence.[52]

The influence of France's pragmatic policy orientation is perhaps seen most clearly in the role of traditional authorities. Early efforts to locate and appoint aristocrats favorable to French rule quickly registered a number of failures, leading the colonial state to shift away from ruling via indigenous hierarchies.[53] With the exception of the Bour Sine, who ruled until he passed away in 1969, the French had eliminated all precolonial monarchs by the early 1900s. The experience of Boundou's Almamate, which was officially dismantled in 1905, was common: the state saw its territory split into two with French-appointed canton chiefs from the kingdom's ruling lineage put in charge of each.[54] By the interwar period, the French were neglecting customary rights in favor of more politically expedient selection criteria for even canton chiefs.[55] While the French worked with and tolerated traditional authorities throughout the colonial period, this was a matter of expediency rather than a normative commitment and there was a firm guardrail of expected loyalty to French interests.

As a result, the ultimate symbol of the French colonial administration in rural areas became the French *commandent du cercle* and his indigenous

---

[50] Crowder (1964, 203) and Idowu (1968).
[51] Legally, there were no recognized intermediaries in rural areas until the First World War. It was only after this that canton and village chieftaincies were institutionalized (Hesseling 1985, 146–147).
[52] Chafer (2001, 170).
[53] Searing (2002, 107). In Baol, for example, the failure of French colonial officers to understand the rules of succession – assuming that a king's son was his natural heir – ignored the true nature of hereditary claims. The French accordingly put in place a former king's son by his concubine, a maternal line that would at most have earned the son a provincial chiefdomship (Searing 2002, 114.).
[54] Gomez (1992, 173). Note that while the French used easily identifiable aristocracies when present, they often violated traditional rules of succession.
[55] Hesseling (1985, 147).

counterpart, the canton chief. The French came to see the canton chiefs as a form of professional bureaucrat, trained if possible, in the *Ecoles des Chefs* in Saint-Louis. Ultimately, to the extent that the role of a canton chief was to collect taxes and organize *corvée* labor, it should be of little surprise that canton chiefs grew increasingly unpopular as "the traditional state had been incorporated into the French bureaucratic state."[56] Writing in 1946, the French administrator Delavignette also observed a growing animosity to canton chiefs: "the spirit of indigenous power has left the big chiefs [*chef de canton*] and sought refuge in the lower chiefs [village chiefs], who are less touched by our actions."[57] The result of France's consistently ambiguous attitudes toward traditional authority meant that public confidence in colonial chiefs declined over time as they became divorced from any precolonial understanding of legitimacy.[58]

To summarize, French colonial policies of *assimilation* and its applied policies of *association* were predicated on an evolutionary progress away from indigenous tradition and cultural practice. The French colonial state dismantled precolonial political hierarchies and established a new administrative apparatus that emphasized a uniform stratum of higher-level chiefs, undermining in the process notions of traditional legitimacy even when aristocratic lineages were employed. From the level of urban elites to rural authorities, therefore, French colonization prioritized a Cartesian administrative hierarchy that should bias *against* the persistence of robust precolonial political hierarchies, which we might think of as an important conduit for the legacies that I document in this book.

Religious Conversion and the Spread of Islam

A second historical factor that we might expect to undermine the persistence of precolonial legacies is the expansion of new forms of religious practice, most notably via the rise of the Sufi Brotherhoods that dominate Senegalese Islamic practice. Islam has been practiced in West Africa since the eleventh century and was adopted relatively early in some precolonial states like Fouta Toro. Nonetheless, the vast majority of the Senegalese peasantry did not begin practicing Islam until the onset of colonial rule.[59] As precolonial systems of authority buckled under French advance, a number of charismatic religious leaders sought to fill the leadership void that was emerging across the rural countryside; "everyone was seeking protection, land, and new opportunity, and this is precisely what the Sufi clerics offered," Boone (2003b, 52) writes of the era.[60] While doing great violence to precolonial political and social institutions, the gradual consolidation of French hegemony produced relative peace in the

---

[56] Klein (1968b, 204).   [57] Delavignette (1947, 146).   [58] Hesseling (1985, 148–149).
[59] See discussion in Klein (1972).   [60] Markovitz (1970) and Searing (2002).

region, increased trade, and opened new lines of communication that enabled Islam to spread rapidly.[61] New forms of religious practice also provided new forms of social mobility for peasants as slaves found they could shed their status or young men saw new avenues of social advancement.[62]

The most studied long-run effect of this is the "Senegalese Exception," a reference to the unique alliance between the country's Islamic brotherhood and the colonial and postcolonial state.[63] The most prominent of these are the Mourides, whose spiritual leader and founder, Amadou Bemba, was initially seen as a threat to French interests in eastern Baol, where Bemba was settled. Despite the fact that the French twice exiled Bemba in an effort to counter his influence, over time the Mourides and French settled into a "pragmatic" alliance. French concerns about Islam as a counterbalance to their authority were largely assuaged by the start of the First World War as the colonial state came to understand that Bemba's ability to organize his followers in large-scale farming schemes was a means to boost groundnut production in the region, culminating in a policy of effective "noninterference."[64] As the Mourides encouraged and actively assisted followers to settle new villages and devote themselves not only to their religion but also cash crop production, both parties came to learn that they could use the other to advance their own goals.[65] Mouride influence quickly spread outward from the Mouride Brotherhood's de facto capital of Touba as Bemba's followers expanded into new zones. Today, many of these early sites of settlement are among the Brotherhood's most sacred.[66]

Of course, the Mourides were not the only religious movement during this period. Other Sufi sects were also spreading, notably the Tidjanes and Layennes. Here as well, French thinking pivoted dramatically in the early years of colonial rule. The French initially viewed the Tidjane sect as fanatical because prominent nineteenth-century jihadists, like Omar Tall, were adherents. Yet the Tidjane's charismatic leader, Malick Sy, adopted an explicitly pro-French attitude; in 1912, for example, Sy called upon all Tidjanes to support French authority.[67] Catholic missions also played a role in religious conversion during this period, though it was a more geographically concentrated one.[68] The only areas where missions were truly active in Senegal was on the *Petit Côte* south of Dakar, home to the precolonial kingdom of Sine, and in the Casamance, where the Catholic church had made early inroads, strategically

---

[61] Clark (1999, 155).
[62] See for example, the arguments of Mark (1978) and Bayart (1993, 119).
[63] Cruise O'Brien (1971) and Villalón (1995).
[64] See Harrison (1988, 166–169) and Boone (2003b, 52).   [65] Clark (1999, 158, 150).
[66] Searing (2002, 242).   [67] Harrison (1988) and Searing (2002, 131).
[68] French West Africa had relatively few missionaries compared to British colonies, in large part because France declared a separation of Church and state in 1905 which restricted access (Crowder 1968, 283).

focusing on these two areas because their populations, the majority of whom were animist, were seen as more likely converts than the Muslim populations that dominated the coastline north of Dakar.[69]

The mass religious conversion of the 20th century generated new social identities that have not only spiritual but also political and economic consequences for citizens. This might suggest that religious identities are more salient forms of social identification at the local level than the precolonial identities I focus on here. To the extent that Sufi religious leaders are endowed with "saint"-like properties, they have become powerful organizing symbols in Senegalese social and political life that could provide powerful counterweights to precolonial structures.[70] Senegalese peasants devoutly follow religious leaders – indeed their hierarchical structures have long formed the backbone of the state's most reliable clientelist networks – raising the question of why claims to descent from a precolonial past would hold currency in the face of these alternative structures.

Migration

The third factor that may predict an erasure of precolonial legacies is the substantial migration induced by colonial efforts to boost cash crop production. At many moments, this intersected with the spread of the Mouride Brotherhood as discussed above. The colonial state allocated vast tracts of land to Sufi religious leaders, encouraging eastward settlement from densely populated precolonial states like Cayor, Baol, and Saloum in a process that created a tight relationship between Islamic conversion and an expanding peanut economy.[71] This led to significant demographic shifts. The availability of open land and the leadership of new religious leaders generated a notably sharp population increase in present-day Kaffrine Region during the colonial era.[72] Migrants also came from outside of Senegal, most prominently via the importation of seasonal migrant workers, or *navetanes*, who came to work in the country's peanut basin from Mali and Burkina Faso as well as eastern Senegal. Over time, many navetanes settled permanently in Senegal, most notably in the region of the precolonial state of Saloum (contemporary Kaolack and Kaffrine Regions).[73] Earlier parallels can be found in Mandjak and Mandingue populations from what is now Guinea-Bissau who settled in the Casamance. These flows were not negligible; David (1980) estimates that the Mandjaks were producing two-thirds of the peanut crop in the Casamance in the first decades of independence.

---

[69] Indeed, missionaries were often hostile to the French colonial reliance on Muslim elite, believing that their own efforts alone could form a Catholic base capable of preventing the further spread of Islam (Foster 2013, 15, 46).
[70] Cruise O'Brien (1975).   [71] Pélissier (1966).   [72] Faye (2016).   [73] See David (1980).

Other causes of migration existed as well. In addition to the rapid rural to urban migration that Senegal has seen over the past half century, state policies in the early postcolonial era continued to encourage resettlement in underpopulated areas, notably during the *Terres Neuves* projects in the 1970s, which encouraged Serer peasants from Fatick and Diourbel Regions to resettle in Kaffrine and Tambacounda.[74] Elsewhere, these dynamics took specific forms, such as the colonial and postcolonial states' efforts to settle pastoral populations. The construction of permanent water points and increased regulations on things like vaccinating livestock, encouraged Peulh pastoralists to create new, permanent villages around traditional migratory routes.[75] Regional political dynamics also influenced population movement. Kedougou and Tambacounda Regions (as well as Dakar) have seen a number of in-migrants from Guinea, as families fled the postcolonial regime of Sekou Toure in the 1960s.

Because in-migration has not affected all regions equally, we might expect these flows to mitigate precolonial legacies where descendants of precolonial polities cohabitate with in-migrants. For my theory and measurement to be correct, the legacy of the precolonial states must be *spatially* dependent over time. Yet if populations that were exposed to a precolonial state migrate, this may suggest that they will carry with them attributes that facilitate governance today. Inversely, if areas that were home to precolonial states see substantial in-migration, this could dilute the strength of precolonial legacies. As I argue in the next section, the mechanism of persistence is not a portable, cultural attribute, however, but rather is rooted in village-based social hierarchies that both rest on and reinforce the value of territorial claims. Where communities that had fallen under a precolonial state saw substantial in-migration, my theory's mechanisms – social identities and social networks – should only be destabilized if in-migrants set up extensive parallel social hierarchies, but not if they are integrated into preexisting village social structures which effectively subsume them to cross-village social institutions.

Figure 2.2 offers a visual display of the geographic spread of the three factors reviewed above and their intersection with the territories of precolonial states. Early colonial centers concentrated along major trade routes, including the Senegalese river in the north, the railroads, and peanut-producing zones. In-migration flowed along the railway lines, particularly into Saloum, but also into the Casamance and southeastern Senegal. Finally, although the entire country saw mass conversion to Islam during this period, Figure 2.2 indicates the territory associated with the Mouride pioneers, which settled large tracts of sparsely inhabited forest that lay on the eastern edges of the country's large Wolof kingdoms.

---

[74] Garenne and Lombard (1991).   [75] Touré (1990).

Why Do Precolonial Identities Persist?

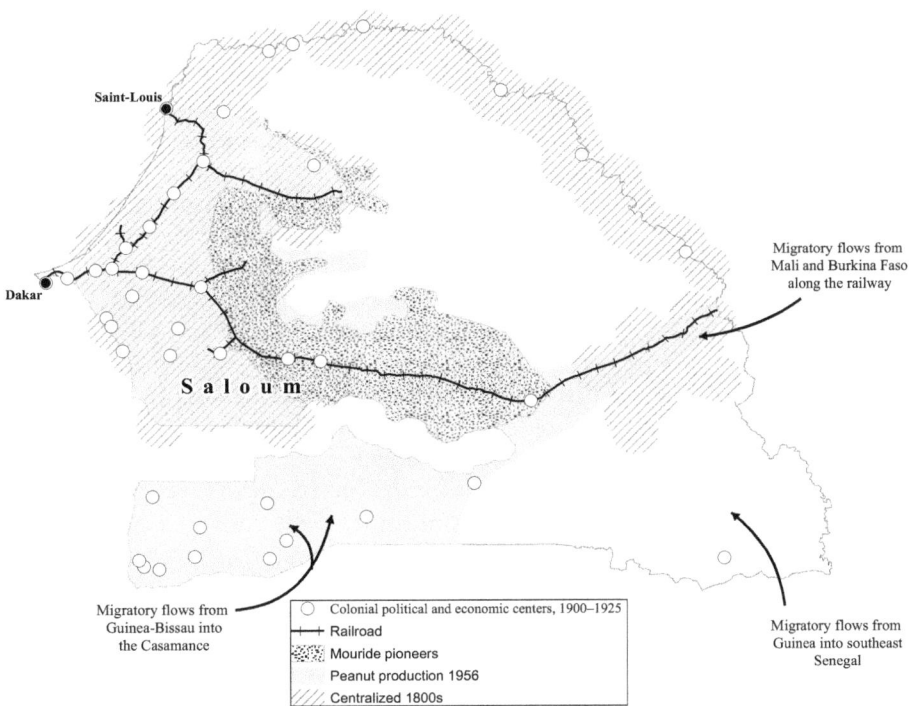

FIGURE 2.2 Colonial-era dynamics predicting erasure of precolonial legacies

The Mechanism of Persistence: Village Social Hierarchies

Given the social upheavals of colonialism, conversion to Islam, and migration documented above, why do I think that precolonial legacies have been able to persist to the present? Precolonial forms of political order may have rested on institutionalized norms of intra-elite comportment, but these norms could have easily been dismantled with the arrival of the French colonial state. In the final section of this chapter, I elaborate on my contention that cross-village social institutions inherited from the precolonial past have persisted over time. Specifically, I argue that the precolonial past remains a unifying focus of local political narratives in areas that were home to precolonial polities because these narratives justify rural social hierarchies. As the "fundamental social unit of the region," villages in the West African Sahel are home to enduring internal sociopolitical hierarchies that define elite status.[76] I cast a broad net to define local elites as anyone holding local social status within a village, or, put otherwise, anyone who exerts some authority in village-based hierarchies.

[76] Searing (2002, 6).

Typically, this includes village chiefs, notables, religious leaders, elected officials, and their families. These individuals inherit social authority that extends into political, social, and sometimes, though certainly not always, economic life.[77]

Throughout much of the West African Sahel, lineages obtain social status through historical patterns of settlement. This grants substantial sociopolitical rights to individuals who descend from a village's founding families. Even 100 years later, these families remain tied together as the "first founders."[78] Lineage and genealogy have long served as key markers in rural social hierarchies, with lineage heads "reproduc[ing] a social, not individual identity, with obligations and rights attached" that structures local social life.[79] Village chiefs, for example, are almost always chosen from among the descendants of the village's founders with the title transmitting from father to son or to the oldest male in the family. This is an old pattern; even in the precolonial era, village chiefs were often chosen from the oldest branch of the founding lineage.[80] In many villages, the local imam comes from the lineage of the second family to arrive in a village.[81] Prominent families in some of the country's oldest settlements trace their social status back for generations, illustrating how markers of social status are highly persistent over time.[82] Indeed, lineage structures served as the animating locus of local political allegiance in many precolonial states, with the clan or family serving as a mechanism by which to maintain and adjudicate local authority.[83]

To the present, narratives of shared settlement or, in its strongest form, narratives of shared descent from a precolonial state, provide a portable identity that local actors can invoke to justify their own claims to social status as well as that of their relatives and friends. Across rural Senegal, therefore, social status is animated by identities based in histories of settlement that enable hierarchical claim-making to authority as questions of "first-comers" versus "later-comers," ethnicity or caste come to define social hierarchies and rights to local resources. Among these, the ability to trace descent from a precolonial kingdom via one's lineage comes to constitute an undeniable claim of community membership. As local lineages make shared and mutually reinforcing

---

[77] My definition thus includes holders of customary authority as well as individuals who obtain social status via their association with state or economic spheres of opportunity though as my empirical material shows these often overlap. In this way, a distinct feature in many rural Sahelian communities is the absence of a consistent class division. While some village chiefs or councilors are wealthier than their neighbors, most are only marginally so at best.

[78] See Galvan (2004) for a discussion of this among the Serer.   [79] Juul (1999, 211–212).

[80] See Diouf (1990, 67) on Cayor.   [81] For example, Juul (1999).

[82] Boone (2003b, 47). Indeed, many villages are spatially organized into lineage-based quarters or neighborhoods that reflect patterns of settlement (Tamari 1991, 231).

[83] See Kane (1987) on Fouta Toro, for example. Bathily (1989) notes that in states like Gajaaga the clan itself was the mechanism of state power, more important than who actually held the title of *tunka*, or king.

Why Do Precolonial Identities Persist?

TABLE 2.1 *Descriptive data on persistence of village social hierarchies*

Respondent type	N	% related to village founder	% chiefs inherited from family	% with family members in authority positions	% related to current chief
Chiefs	380	81.8	86.8	75.8	
Elected Officials	123	67.5		75.6	57.7

claims to a precolonial past, actors reproduce the power of narratives of the precolonial past over time.[84]

Elites in historically acephalous areas likewise root their claims to local status in local histories of settlement, of course. To illustrate, one mayor in Kaffrine rooted his decision to enter local politics in his family's history of "traditionally tak[ing] part in things." His uncle had founded his village and his father had been a canton chief and then the *chef d'arrondissement* following independence.[85] Elsewhere, such as the Casamance, local narratives are more likely to detail historical rivalries between villages than they are to recount historical alliances. The difference is not that histories of settlement only influence elite status in historically centralized areas, but that these claims remain fragmented across villages in historically acephalous areas as historical narratives of settlement remain village-based. Acephalous histories have similarly long afterlives, therefore, but their form is quite distinct.

I substantiate this claim by presenting descriptive data from more than 500 interviews I conducted with rural elites over the course of six years. Table 2.1 displays the percentages of these respondents who reported family ties to other elites in their local government. These numbers parallel claims found in the secondary literature and my own qualitative data. More than 80 percent of village chiefs are related to their village's founder and directly inherited their position from a family member. Seventy-five percent of all interviewees reported that another family member currently or recently had held another position of authority, such as serving as a religious guide, village chief, or local government councilor. Table 2.1 not only provides evidence for robust elite control of local positions of authority but also reflects a broader trend documented by scholars of West Africa: rural social relations are structured by sticky, lineage-based attributes.

A second test of this can be had by looking at villages, whose names contain a patronym. Many villages in the West African Sahel are named after their founder, for example, the village Sinthiang Bourang Ly implies that someone named Bourang Ly founded the village, with Sinthiang acting as a placeholder

---

[84] Similar to Walther (2012). [85] Interview, February 8, 2016.

(here "home of"). Across the country, certain patronyms have known adaptations, the last name Tall is adopted to Pallene, Diaw into Ndiawene, or Diop into Ndiobene. Taking the 2011 *Repertoire des Villages*, which lists all official villages and their current chiefs, I code whether or not villages that contain such a name marker had a chief with the associated last name in 2011.[86] Of the approximately 3,000 villages with a patronym or a known derivative of a patronymic in their name, 69 percent are headed by a village chief of that same name today. In historically centralized areas, this rises to 71 percent compared to 63 percent in historically acephalous zones.[87]

On the ground, individuals recount the stories of how their family settled an area or their genealogical descent from an area's first founders with great pride. Similar to most work on the persistence of cultural norms over time, I recognize the role that intergenerational transmission of values and behavior plays in the reproduction of social institutions and local historical narratives.[88] This is more plausible than some might initially assume. To begin with, Africa's precolonial states projected national identities to which their subjects ascribed.[89] Serer populations in the precolonial state of Baol assimilated into the state's majority Muslim, Wolof identification, for example.[90] Wright (1999, 419) notes similarly of the Niumi, which lay along the Gambian River basin: "like it or not, villagers were part of Niumi. Most knew who the royal families were, and some knew a good bit of Niumi's history, which they had heard from bards reciting the glories of Niumi's royal lineages."

A second factor that has ensured the persistence of narratives about the precolonial past is found in the role of griots, or traditional praise singers. As a distinct social caste, griots hold reciprocal socioeconomic ties to prominent families within casted ethnic groups of West Africa. Griots function as "oral historians," memorizing and reciting a family or community's history, ensuring the intergenerational transmission of local mythologies and histories of settlement.[91] These histories are, of course, constructed. As Leyti (1981, 8) wryly notes, among griots "noble traditions of the family know neither flaws, nor weaknesses, nor even setbacks." Nonetheless, griots play a critical role in keeping popular history alive, with each generation memorizing and adding to a family's lore. Because griots recite these tales at weddings, funerals, and

---

[86] I eliminate villages that have an ethnic marker that is distinct from the ethnic group associated with the village name because this frequently indicates that in-migrants settled next to an existing, non-co-ethnic village. For instance, it is common to find two villages such as Keur Malick Diaw Wolof and Keur Malick Diaw Peulh in the same area. This generally implies that Keur Malick Diaw Wolof is the original village (Diaw being a Wolof last name) and that Fulani in-migrants either passed through Keur Malick Diaw when first arriving in a community or settled on land allocated to them by Keur Malick Diaw Wolof. To code Keur Malick Diaw Peulh as a village founded by the Diaw family would then be inaccurate.

[87] This difference is statistically significant at the $p < 0.000$ level.

[88] Tabellini (2008) and Acharya et al. (2016).   [89] Warner (1999, 238).

[90] Searing (2002, 9).   [91] Galvan (2004, 41).

Why Do Precolonial Identities Persist? 67

other major ceremonies, these stories are performed publicly. The value of descent from a precolonial state not only comes through private, intragenerational socialization, therefore, but is amplified in explicitly public spaces in ways that create interlocking narratives across lineages and generations.

Why Village Social Hierarchies Survived Colonial-Era Shocks
My claim that rural elite status in historically centralized areas has largely persisted over time will strike some as particularly puzzling given that the French colonial state actively dismantled precolonial political hierarchies. Two reasons explain why areas home to precolonial states saw their village social hierarchies girded against the challenges of colonial rule, new forms of religious authority, and, when relevant, in-migration.

First, where legible political structures existed, they facilitated France's desire for "a cheap, efficient administration" in the years immediately following conquest by offering the French the chance to make opportunistic alliances with existing monarchies.[92] Even though France quickly abandoned their reliance on indigenous leaders as noted above, this buffered village social hierarchies in historically centralized areas against the tumult of the era.[93]

This is seen perhaps most clearly by looking at the marked social upheaval in historically acephalous areas during this period. Population movements driven by the wars and social upheaval of the nineteenth century created competing political claims that undermined the ability of village chiefs and lineage heads to solidify power and assert the advantages that come with having established "first comer" status. Writing on Mali's Bougouni Region, laying to the immediate east of the Senegalese border, Peterson (2004, 124) notes that the French faced a chronic authority problem in the region, with one officer reporting in 1926 that over one-third of villages in the region had no designated chief due to fights between local lineages. The autochthonous Mandingue population in Koungheul was beset by deep divisions as a result of the Soninke–Marabout wars of the mid-1800s, for example, a situation only amplified with the in-migration of Wolofs during the early colonial era.[94]

The result was that acephalous zones presented a unique administrative challenge to colonial administrators.[95] In some cases, villages revolted over the mere idea of appointing an official village chief. In the Casamance, which mounted the longest resistance to French rule, the French signed treaties with village chiefs without recognizing that many chiefs were religious rather than

---

[92] Searing (2002, 66); Klein (1968b, 290); and Roberts (1963, 304–306).
[93] Searing (1993, 107).
[94] Klein (1968b, 211). Kedougou Region is characterized similarly. Following substantial population movement in the years leading up to French conquest, the onset of colonial rule saw Bedik, Bassari, and Diahanké minorities who had long inhabited the area joined by Mandingue and Peulh in-migrants, generating new claims to land and authority (Aubert 1923).
[95] Cohen (1971, 76) and Bayart (1993, 120).

political or administrative figures and commanded little real authority within the village.⁹⁶ In contrast, the relative stability of historically centralized areas helped preserve village-level social hierarchies even as broader precolonial state structures were dismantled. Because village chiefs remained largely removed from French political interference – provided they met French demands for labor and taxation – village-level political structures were relatively more legible to the nascent colonial state in historically centralized areas, facilitating continuity in local social hierarchies.

Second, village-based social hierarchies in a region's home to precolonial states proved more adaptable to the challenges posed by in-migration and religious conversion because they could effectively graft these changes onto existing social hierarchies. Although religious conversion took place across the countryside as Sufi religious leaders filled emerging gaps in social authority, historically centralized areas saw elites effectively "reconstruct the old social order on a new religious base."⁹⁷ In Diourbel, the Mourides became so influential, for example, that they functionally incorporated the social and political elite of the precolonial state of Baol.⁹⁸ With the exception of casted villages, village imams throughout the country are always of freeborn status, illustrating how conversion did not eliminate – but rather often reinforced – traditional social hierarchies.⁹⁹ Though Islamic conversion did allow those of a lower social status, notably slaves, to find new patrons in religious leaders, Searing (2002, 224) speculates that many slaveborn populations migrated *away* from the rigid hierarchies that defined historically centralized areas as a way to both shed their status and obtain access to land.

West Africa was historically home to flexible practices for integrating migrants, such as *cousinage*, "adoption," or clientelism, whereby the logic of "wealth in people" as opposed to wealth in land created a pressing need for elites to welcome and integrate valuable labor into the polity.¹⁰⁰ The massive churning of migration that took place in the colonial and early postcolonial period challenged this logic more in acephalous areas, which saw particular pressures from in-migrants as the lack of established social hierarchies undermined the land claims of autochthons.¹⁰¹ The tendency of the French to appoint outsiders as canton chiefs in these areas, often employing former soldiers or interpreters, effectively assigned local indigenous political authority to someone

---

⁹⁶ Pélissier (1966, 678) and Klein (1968b, 175). The Diola "village did not exist as a collectivity," Méguelle (2012, 117, 119) writes. "Social life as mostly limited to clans and family concessions," and while the French designation of "villages" met an administrative objective, it never mapped onto any real political community. The administrative difficulty the French faces was described in a 1902 Political Report, the people of the Casamance "are refractory to all progress and in a social state neighboring on anarchy," with villages refusing to pay taxes or recognizing village authority (Senegal et Dependances 1902).
⁹⁷ Cruise O'Brien (1971, 15).   ⁹⁸ Searing (2002).   ⁹⁹ See Venema (1978, 124) on the Wolof.
¹⁰⁰ Geschiere (2009); Hilgers (2011); and Bayart et al. (2001).   ¹⁰¹ Klein (1972, 439).

with a thin understanding of local history and, critically, with minimal social pressures through which individuals could press their claims.[102]

Adopting in-migrants into local social structures was more viable in areas that were home to precolonial polities. Pélissier, who wrote at length on the social organization of the Senegalese peasantry in the mid-twentieth century, observed that in-migration in the Saloum had not in fact undermined or challenged the land rights or social status of autochthonous elites. Rather, he describes the Saloum as "cosmopolitan," writing that not a single village was ethnically homogenous in Kaolack's Langham Canton mid-century.[103] The integration of in-migrants into the Saloum's existing social structures by village chiefs who lent land and hired laborers suggests that the migration patterns induced by the introduction of the colonial cash crop economy were met in these zones with older repertoires of behavior. Qualitative interview data suggest that this pattern has broader traction. To take one representative example, in Kebemer Department, which falls in the heartland of the precolonial state of Cayor, one former mayor recounted how the community's minority Peulh population had come to settle permanently in the area: the Peulh had passed through the area for generations, but it was under the first colonial canton chief that they were given empty land to settle on. Today, the mayor noted, the Peulh village was quite large and an important part of the community after over a century of cohabitation.[104]

As shown in subsequent chapters, sociopolitical dynamics around religious belief and migration continue to reverberate in contemporary local governance across the country, but they do so with a particular sharpness in historically acephalous areas. In areas that were home to precolonial states, I find that they have neither prevented the persistence of powerful shared narratives about the precolonial past nor do they offer robust leverage on contemporary local government performance. Precolonial political hierarchies were dismantled, but the nature of who could claim local social status and village-based hierarchies remained largely unchanged in these areas even if things were more fluid elsewhere.[105] In other words, factors that might predict erasure were effectively grafted onto existing social hierarchies, meaning that social institutions that had developed to regulate intra-elite conflict in the precolonial period have by and large persisted in historically centralized areas. Local elites' claims to local

---

[102] Boone (2003b, 107). The French themselves realized the dangers of appointing canton chiefs who had no ties to the region they were about to rule, though Klein (1968b, 209) argues that French use of imported chiefs was more successful "in stateless areas and in areas where the community was new."

[103] This, Pélissier (1966, 452–456) argues, was the result of in-migrants who need to quickly learn the Wolof language in order to work, the unifying effects of Islam, and the fact that everyone – autochthon and allochthon – was deeply implicated in the peanut economy.

[104] Interview, Louga Region, February 12, 2017.

[105] Crowder (1968, 7). As Gellar (2005, 31) describes, "noble families continued to support retainers and show largess to social inferiors, though on a more limited scale."

authority remain rooted in the same villages and lineages that existed before the onset of French rule. Consequently, elites seek to preserve their status by reinforcing historical narratives of shared descent from a precolonial kingdom that justify their social position and which remain locally hegemonic, leading them to reinforce their social ties with other elites who make comparable claims across villages.

The Costs of Elite Persistence

One of the most persistent critiques of decentralization emerges from exactly the social dynamics I describe above: efforts to empower local communities provide a venue for social and economic elites to pursue their own political and material interests.[106] By appropriating resources or monopolizing decision-making, the pervasiveness of such elite capture undermines the benefits of reform for average citizens because those already at the top of the social hierarchy dominate new avenues for economic, political, and social advancement.[107]

My research confirms this core insight: local elites disproportionately occupy local elected office and continue to dominate in local positions of authority, reflecting what Dasgupta and Beard (2007) dub "elite control." Because social status is by and large durable over time both within families and over an individual's lifespan, elite status has persisted despite recent waves of socio-economic transformation. Thus while the introduction of Western education and new forms of associational life have generated new avenues for building authority across the country, most of these positions continue to be filled by "good" families, as individuals parlay social status ascribed to them at birth into other forms of prestige later in life. A common manifestation of this is found in Patterson's (2003) account of the village of Ndoulo, where the president of the women's cooperative is also the wife of the village chief.

The consequences for local political life are pervasive. Elite status shapes not only who is accorded influence ("if you are from a respected family, then each time you speak you are listened to," one village chief summed up) but also one's propensity to enter local political life.[108] For example, one highly educated mayor in Diourbel had formed a development-focused youth association before becoming involved in politics. It didn't hurt, he added, that he was the descendant of a historically royal family.[109] Even following reforms intended to open the political playing field, such as gender parity laws introduced in 2014, high-status families still dominate.[110] As one councilor in Louga Region explained, she had been placed on the electoral lists because she was the daughter-in-law of the village chief, though she had been chosen from among all the women of

---

[106] Bardhan and Mookherjee (2006). [107] Ribot (1999) and Mattingly (2016).
[108] Interview, village chief, Kaffrine Region, April 23, 2013.   [109] Interview, February 15, 2016.
[110] In principle, village chiefs should not serve as councilors though in some cases they do run and are elected. Approximately 15 percent of my interviewees serve both roles, for example. Many more chiefs had served as councilors in the past before taking over the duties of the chieftaincy.

the family because she alone had gone to school.[111] Local elected officials often report having run for office because of their family's social status rather than any particular political platform or skill. A rural development agent with years of experience working with local councils observed that many elites he had met did not even seem interested in local policies, but ran because they thought they ought to – and indeed that they deserved to – as holders of elite social positions.[112]

The most obvious cost of this elision is that those born into low-status families often face undue obstacles when pursuing civic and political opportunities. Within villages, social exclusion tends to revolve around questions of caste or autochthony, with notables or autochthons still controlling access to most agricultural land.[113] As a consequence, individuals from low-caste families are significantly less likely to obtain high-status positions in the community. This rarely results in complete exclusion, but rather the maintenance of an uneven playing field. Casted villages or quarters are often allocated a small number of places on electoral lists, for example, meaning that they are "represented" in a tokenized way, even if they face considerable resistance in participating equally in local political and social life. Migrants similarly tend to see reduced social and political rights in their communities. The long-run significance of colonial and postcolonial patterns of migration is acutely reflected in the rise of autochthony claims in contemporary West African political discourse. To the extent that "first-comers" are those who rendered a locality habitable, subsequent waves of migration add layers of "late-comers" or even "latest-comers" with differential degrees of rights to a community or land.[114] Even co-ethnics might compete over who has more authority in a community if they represent unrelated waves of settlement.

This is perhaps best seen in the example of village creation. The value of obtaining the status of an official village is both material and symbolic: the status offers residents of hamlets or informal settlements "their part" of

---

[111] Interview, February 8, 2017.
[112] Interview, Chef de CADL, Goudiry Department, March 27, 2013.
[113] Tamari (1991) and Koter (2016, 63–64). The fact that this does seem to matter more in some communities has implications for expectations about the role of *cousinage*, or joking cousin relations, in preventing the escalation of ethnic conflict (e.g. Dunning and Harrison 2010). The rules of *cousinage* are consistent across the country, leaving open the question of why it is cited as a moderator of ethnic or caste tension in some regions of the country while apparently failing to do so in others despite the presence of the same ethnic groups and caste categories which form the basis for joking relationships.
[114] For example, Ece (2009) documents how villages founded by populations evicted in the 1970s from Niokolo-Koba National Park, located in Senegal's southeast, continue to be considered "foreigners" within their local government, despite the fact that their original villages have been located within the local government's boundaries. Such disputes had increased following the 1996 decentralization reforms.

projects and aid, which is otherwise biased toward official villages.[115] In historically acephalous areas, many bemoaned the tendency of intra-village feuds and in-migration to lead to a rapid proliferation of villages. "Oh just anyone can create a village here," said one exasperated local development agent in Tambacounda Region.[116] A frustrated subprefect in the area agreed, commenting that he had witnessed many family disagreements lead one party to decamp and form a new village a short distance away during his current posting. He went on to draw an explicit contrast with his previous post in Matam Region, home to the precolonial state of Fouta Toro, where such behavior would have been unthinkable.[117] The tendency toward exit is not uncommon in the Sahel, but it is in sharp contrast to the dominance of loyalty as a strategy in areas where social institutions around consensus and saving face dominate.[118] Notably less village creation has taken place in areas that were home to centralized states, where in-migrants tend to be integrated into specific quarters of existing villages or to settle in hamlets on the periphery.[119] Indeed, approximately 83 percent of villages in areas that were home to precolonial states are listed in the colony's 1958 village census versus only 65 percent in historically stateless areas. The question remains contentious throughout the country, however, and interviewees in historically centralized areas indicate that appeals for official recognition and their subsequent denial by local elites had created tense political situations in the past. This serves as a visible policy area where the politics of institutional congruence have a profoundly undemocratic impact.

CONCLUSION

This chapter has introduced the first of three empirical building blocks of my argument, the historical antecedent: the political geography of precolonial Senegal was home to stark differences in the organizational form of political systems, with some communities ruled by precolonial kingdoms while others remained acephalous, or stateless. Because social status in rural West Africa is largely tied to historical settlement patterns, the nature of an area's precolonial political organization shapes the degree to which local elites make interdependent claims to local authority today. Though there are many reasons that may predict the erasure of these identities, most notably French policies of

---

[115] This dynamic is described by Juul (1999) in her study of Barkedji, Senegal. The ease of obtaining official village status varies, though in principle any hamlet could appeal a denial by the part of the local council to the central state.
[116] Interview, CADL agent, Goudiry Department, March 27, 2013.
[117] Interview, March 22, 2013. [118] Bierschenk and Olivier de Sardan (2003).
[119] Two exceptions are the present-day areas of the Saloum (Kaolack Region) and the Djoloff (Linguere Department) which have seen substantial in-migration. These are discussed as specific cases in Chapter 4.

Conclusion

association and direct rule, the spread of Islam, and patterns of migration during the colonial and postcolonial periods, I argue that none of these fundamentally undermined the village-based social hierarchies that reproduce local social status over time. In areas that fell under a precolonial state, elites are more likely to be able to claim descent from lineages dating to the precolonial kingdom to justify their social status in ways that are mutually reinforcing. The consequence is that such shared narratives of descent from the precolonial past are glorified and repeated, as elites collectively reinforce the value of social identities rooted in the distant past. This, in turn, obligates elites to reciprocally recognize the status of others who can likewise trace their genealogy to a shared past, reinforcing the perceived legitimacy of social ties among elites. At the same time, historical narratives justifying local social hierarchies are inherently exclusionary with serious consequences for those who can access and hold various positions in a community.

3

The Politics of Decentralization in Senegal

The previous chapter introduced the historical driver of my argument about why we are seeing the emergence of disparate local redistributive strategies in rural Senegal: variation in exposure to precolonial statehood. Core to my argument, however, is the idea that these precolonial legacies interact in unforeseen ways with subsequent institutional reform. Accordingly, this chapter takes up the task of laying out the two remaining historical foundations of my argument. I begin by introducing Senegal's system of decentralized local governance, which intersects with the country's precolonial political geography to generate institutional congruence or incongruence. The second half of the chapter explores the third empirical building block that relates to the unit of analysis itself: how were the boundaries of Senegal's local governments drawn? If what is critical is how elites relate to each other across villages, then the argument risks being endogenous to the very social relations that benefit local governance today if some communities were able to self-select into a local state with their friends and family. Drawing on archival and interview data, I find scant evidence that boundaries were systematically driven by bottom-up social dynamics. In contrast, the material suggests that decentralization reforms were implemented from above, in some cases netting villages with shared social institutions of cooperation and reciprocity into new administrative units, while in others grouping together villages with no meaningful shared history. Taken together, this historical detail enables me to explain why Senegal's decentralization scheme structures distinct cross-village social dilemmas across the country.

THE STRUCTURE OF GOVERNANCE IN POSTCOLONIAL SENEGAL

Centralizing Tendencies in the Senegalese State

Senegal gained independence from France in 1960. The newly independent nation inherited a highly centralized colonial state and, under the leadership of the country's first president Leopold Sedar Senghor, the government pursued nation-building and economic development through a statist and socialist model. This had three consequences for the decentralization reforms that were to follow. First, it centralized power around the executive and within the ruling Socialist Party (*Parti socialiste* or PS). This concentrated political competition from the national to the local level within the party itself, as political disagreement manifested in party factions or "clans." The drafting of a new constitution in 1963 further consolidated the "winner-take-all electoral regime" and rendered even prestigious ministerial posts mere "high-level functionaries."[1]

Senghor's "amalgam" party apparatus was largely built on relations of convenience rather than a serious adherence to socialist ideology.[2] The second defining feature of the postcolonial regime was the patronage ties Senghor reinforced with local brokers as Senegal became a clientelist regime par excellence. As Boone (1992, 98) writes, "power relations in the rural areas that were rooted in long-established social hierarchies and relations of production constituted the regime's most solid and reliable bases of political power." This largely continued a pattern set in the colonial era, when Sufi marabouts and other traditional leaders built and maintained their authority by cultivating relationships with elites in Dakar.[3] Even as the regime centralized, therefore, it did so *via* local brokers, most famously the Mouride Brotherhood, introduced in the previous chapter.

In an early challenge to the regime, Senegal saw a constitutional crisis in 1962 that was marked by a falling-out between Senghor and his Prime Minister, Mamadou Dia, largely attributed to Dia's more radical vision of reform than that held by Senghor, who was wary of directly challenging the regime's clientelist network. Part of Senghor's disagreement with Dia was over the regime's ambitious rural outreach program, *animation rurale*, which aimed to bring the peasantry into the modern economy by improving their access to modern agricultural practices and social services.[4] While making inroads in the regions of Casamance and Fleuve (present-day Saint-Louis and Matam Regions), the program met resistance in the heartland of the country's peanut basin, where local brokers and religious authorities saw the program as a challenge to their authority. Senghor's solution was to imprison Dia and eliminate the position of prime minister, a political maneuver his regime was able to weather precisely because he maintained the support of the Mouride leadership

---

[1] Beck (2008, 54–55). Politics were liberalized – though not fully democratized – under Senghor's appointed successor, Abdou Diouf. Diouf sought both "continuity and change" with his predecessor: he maintained the state's clientelist base, for example, but he also lifted Senghor's ban on opposition parties and called elections in 1983 (Hesseling 1985, 288). This did not amount to extensive regime liberalization, however, to the extent that the PS unilaterally wrote the electoral code, ensuring its own survival in the process (Beck 2008, 59).

[2] Boone (1992, 94–95).   [3] Diop and Codesria (1993, 236).   [4] Zuccarelli (1965, 41).

throughout.[5] In turn, animation rurale shifted toward less radical goals, emphasizing agricultural production over social reform.[6]

Cumulatively, this centralization of power and the subverting of the regime's stated development goals to the exigencies of its clientelist relations produced a third consequence: the crisis of *le malaise payson* that beset the country in the early 1970s. Despite the fact that the state had already begun to back away from the ambitious – and costly – expenditures associated with animation rurale, Senghor's patronage system was under pressure.[7] Groundnut production, the state's primary export commodity, fell short of projected growth, inhibiting Senghor's ability to generate the necessary revenue to keep the centralized clientelist system running smoothly. Despite the young state's vast ambitions, the cooperatives established by animation rurale had neither transformed the lives of rural producers nor produced rapid economic growth. In sharp contrast, peasants had used these services opportunistically at best.[8] As the promised benefits of the socialist regime floundered, rural producers became increasingly vocal in their dissatisfaction.[9]

Decentralization in Three Acts

Senghor responded to this crisis in 1972 by announcing the creation of a new administrative unit below the *arrondissement*: the rural community (*le communauté rurale*). Diouf (1993, 237) quotes Jean Collins, the Ministry of the Interior at the time:

> over the past several years it has become clear that the rural population has not really been involved in our administrative structures ... That means that only a tiny minority of the population participates. It is just as clear that if administrative activities are to be carried out with genuine efficiency, they have to be based on the active, responsible involvement of the population. After all, they are in the best position to assess their own needs.

Now known as *Acte I*, the creation of local governments made Senegal an unwitting trailblazer for decentralization in the region. Designed to improve the ability of state officials to respond to local needs and unrest while simultaneously appeasing PS brokers by deconcentrating the power that Senghor had amassed in the presidency, the government rolled out 320 local governments over a ten-year period between 1974 and 1984, beginning in the peanut basin where the rural citizenry was most vocally unhappy.[10] Each local government was comprised of numerous villages, collectively run by locally elected rural councils (*le conseil rural*). Although local elections began in 1978, one-third of seats were allocated to state agents, while the remaining two-thirds were elected

---

[5] Beck (2008, 11–12).   [6] Gellar et al. (1980, 27).   [7] Gellar et al. (1980, 86).
[8] Diop and Codesria (1993, 240).   [9] Boone (1992, 94–95, 169–170) and Diouf (1993, 238).
[10] Boone (1992, 180) and Dickovick (2011, 54).

The Structure of Governance in Postcolonial Senegal

from the single party lists assembled by local PS party branches. At the head of the local government council sits the influential Rural Council President (*le président du conseil rural*) – today known as the mayor – along with two vice presidents.

Acte I granted local authorities the right to prioritize local needs, but because rural communities were subject to the *tutelle* of the central state and hence not autonomous actors, actual decision-making remained with the central-state-appointed subprefect (*sous-préfet*), based in the next highest administrative unit, the arrondissement. This effectively ensured central government control of rural development initiatives. What Acte I did offer was the transfer of authority over land allocation to local councils. Land had been moved out of the customary domain and to the central state with the 1964 *Loi sur le domain national*, but the 1972 decentralization law transferred authority over allocating uninhabited or unused land for farming or herding to the rural council, quickly making it the most significant source of power for local councils.[11]

In 1996, Senegal's second president, Abdou Diouf, announced *Acte II* of the country's decentralization reforms and transferred substantial new fiscal and developmental authorities to local governments. Diouf's reforms built on the country's first phase of decentralization, but profoundly shifted the nature of local governance by introducing three major changes. First, all council seats became subject to popular vote, though the country remained dominated by the PS until the election of President Abdoulaye Wade with the *Parti démocratique Sénégalais* (PDS) in 2000. As a result, a number of parties contested and were elected in the 2002 local elections.[12] Local elections had originally been based on proportionality, but Acte II introduced a mixed proportionality–plurality model. To the present, half of local council seats are allocated proportionally, while the other half goes to the majority winner, thus that even if the second place party obtains 49 percent of votes, they hold at most 24 percent of seats. Not surprisingly, this results in considerable premium being placed on obtaining a majority and, once earned, the ruling party has substantial say in decision-making.[13] Councilors are elected from party lists with the entire local government functioning as a multimember district. Following the popular vote,

---

[11] In reality, village chiefs, who head the lowest administrative unit in the country often continue to informally distribute parcels of land within villages. While village chiefs have a right to participate in any land deliberations by the local government, they have no official role in these deliberations.

[12] Vengroff and Ndiaye (1998). Wade replaced all local councils with *delegations speciale*, three-member councils appointed by the state in 2001 to rout out remaining PS support at the grassroots before holding new elections in 2002. Donors attempted to sanction the regime by suspending new financing for local governments, limiting the activity of local governments during this time (Dickovick 2011, 152–154).

[13] This also results in considerable turnover, as the failure to reelect the winning party effectively means that the majority of councilors lose their seats.

the mayor and his two adjoints are elected indirectly by their fellow councilors at the first meeting of a local council's new term.

These changes to the council's political dynamics are particularly consequential in view of the second major policy change in 1996: Acte II enlarged the local council's authority to nine policy areas, including the responsibility to prioritize and implement the construction of high-demand basic social services, such as classroom and clinic construction.[14] Consequently, local councils have full legal autonomy within the decentralized sectors.[15] Today, most local governments are not active in all nine of the domains, though all local councils run activities in health, education, and many implement programs in the areas of youth and culture in addition to distributing and adjudicating issues surrounding land access.

The central government appoints a local government secretary, or *Assistant Communitaire*, to each local government to help with paperwork, but we should be careful to not overestimate the planning capacity of local governments, which suffer from weak tax receipts, poor training, and meager transfers from the central government in proportion to their devolved areas of authority. Still, even though local officials like to quip that the central state transferred "the nine biggest problems in the country, with none of the means," local governments are able to engage in a number of yearly activities, such as providing school supplies at the start of each school year, building new classroom blocks or health clinics. Combined with resources that may enter a community through donors, this can result in a number of "small" improvements over a five-year term.[16]

The third major change introduced by Acte II was the transfer of fiscal resources to local governments, including the local government's ability to collect a series of taxes. Most councils only collect the rural tax (*la taxe rurale*, still referred to in many areas by the colonial nomenclature, *l'impot*) and, less frequently, taxes on local market stalls or parking.[17] Many local governments collect almost nothing in a given year, but even those who do raise the rural tax

---

[14] The full list of competences devolved to local governments is (a) management of land usage (private and public), (b) natural resource management, (c) health and social action, (d) youth, sports, and leisure, (e) culture, (f) education and professional formation, (g) urban planning, (h) urbanism and housing, and (i) planning/development strategy.

[15] The central state plays a consultative role by providing technical and planning services.

[16] Donors are expected to work through and consult with the local council when determining where to run projects. Once a donor approaches the local council, some local governments are able to implement a project without delays, while others are besieged by in-fighting, unable to retain and implement projects as documented by Kaag (2003).

[17] Local governments also receive a portion of fines collected by central state agents in their area, part of receipts from the *état-civile* (birth, death, and marriage certificates), and any taxes paid during the delimitation of fields or village parcels. Other taxes, such as those on public lighting, garbage collection, spectacles, and advertising are almost never collected by local councils, though they can be lucrative for urban communes.

have to rely on other financial sources to actually implement projects.[18] The key revenue source of local governments is then by default central government transfers, which cover operating costs and a few development investments per year. The central transfer, the *Fonds de Dotation de la Décentralisation* (FDD) averaged between $22,000 and $28,000 in 2013, for example.[19] Together, this means that Acte II granted local councils expenditure autonomy for investments in capital or maintenance, while key patronage activities, such as staffing rural administrations, remain firmly within the control of the central state.[20]

The arrival of Acte II – with its new resources and autonomy – dramatically altered the incentives facing local elites, reorienting their behavior toward the local state. The ability to target villages with a school or clinic is an unparalleled source of local patronage, thus that even if financing is insufficient, it is nonetheless non-negligible. And while local governments make varied investments, such as building a football pitch for a youth league or buying millet mills to alleviate women's labor, their most significant accomplishments in a given term are almost always the construction of major infrastructure.[21] Demand for new public goods, like new schools, additional classrooms or clinics, should not be underestimated. Requests such as one chief's in Kaolack Region, that the local council "should build us a school so that we have our own and so that our children do not have to walk two kilometers to the school ..." are heard throughout the countryside.[22]

Still, Acte II was far from a perfect reform and local politicians articulate lengthy reclamations from the state; local governments need more funding, more technical assistance, more training, and more central state support. When President Macky Sall introduced a new set of decentralization reforms, *Acte III*, in December of 2013 – intended to harmonize decentralization and encourage localized direction of economic and social development – local politicians anticipated long-awaited improvements to their working conditions.

The most immediate outcome of Acte III was the elimination of disparities between decentralized political units. The country was home to urban and rural *communes* under Actes I and II, but Acte III brought *communalisation integral*, creating urban and rural communes alike, a long-desired goal among rural politicians. Still, uncertainty around the changes generated substantial skepticism. "I think Macky Sall enacted Acte III just so he could leave his own

---

[18] Tax receipts in and of themselves being insufficient for most communities to finance their development investments (Interview, adjoint subprefect, Nioro Department, April 30, 2013).
[19] This includes the salaries of the mayor and his adjoints (~8,400$ per year combined in 2014). Some communities get significantly more than this, such as Touba Mosquee, the seat of the influential Mouride Brotherhood whose population hovers around 560,000 inhabitants, far above the average of 28,000. Touba received 120,000$ in FDD transfers in 2013.
[20] As summarized by Dickovick (2011).   [21] Venema (1996, 10).
[22] Interview, Kaolack Region, May 1, 2013.

footprint on decentralization in Senegal," remarked one local development agent cynically, given that "Senghor created it, Diouf undertook Acte II, even Wade made his mark ..."[23] In the short term, Acte III generated substantial confusion over financing, resulting in a common lament that President Sall enacted the reforms "too fast" and with insufficient attention to the financial resources available to local governments.[24] "All we felt here was a change in name," one adjoint mayor commented in 2016, noting that federal government transfers had remained the same while citizens' expectations about the role of the local state continued to expand. "We cannot wait for the texts while the population is there waiting ... we cannot just cross our arms and wait on Dakar," he surmised.[25]

These changes in Senegal's administrative hierarchy over time are summarized visually in Table 3.1. Note that the changes brought by Acte III of decentralization in 2014 do not fundamentally change the structure of local government, but rather the nomenclature alone.

As introduced in Chapter 1, I conceptualize the introduction of elected, decentralized governments as creating a form of a two-level game. This is illustrated well in Table 3.1. Local elites who pursue elected office face two levels of play: their local governments are comprised of numerous villages, within which they seek and retain clients, promising local government goods in exchange. Yet at the second level of the local state itself, local elected officials find themselves facing a second political arena. Here, elected officials must adjudicate between the competing demands of the many villages that comprise the local state, generating distinct negotiations over which villages receive which investments. Evidence of this dilemma can be found elsewhere in the region. Koné and Hagberg (2019, 44), for example, observe how the legitimacy of a local government candidate in Mali's decentralized system rests on two levels: candidates cannot be seen as neglecting their extended family and social network on the one hand, but on the other they cannot risk completely favoring them either, generating a precarious balancing act for local candidates. This means that a local elected official's preferences vis-à-vis their home village, their co-ethnics, or their extended family are not always the best choice for their political party or allies in the arena of the local state. Senegal's decentralization reforms have delivered valuable patronage for local politicians to distribute across the villages of the local state, but by asking village-based elites to compete at the level of a newly created local state, the devolution of authority

---

[23] Interview, Kaffrine Region, February 9, 2016. This refers to the allocation of a car to each local government by President Wade in 2006, meant to alleviate the burden of having to travel to far-flung villages. A local city hall (*le maison communitaire*) was also constructed for each local government in the mid-2000s, although their construction was still underway in local governments created in the 2009 redistricting as of 2017.
[24] Interview, mayor, Kaffrine Region, February 8, 2016.
[25] Interview, first adjoint mayor, Diourbel Region, February 15, 2016.

TABLE 3.1 *Administrative hierarchies over time, with relevant officials in italics*

2014 Democratic Decentralization, Acte III	Central State *(President)*	State of Senegal	Region *(Governor)*	Department *(Prefet)*	Arrondissement *(Sous-Prefet)*	Rural Commune *(Mayor and Councilors)*	Village *(Chief)*
1996 Democratic Decentralization, Acte II	Central State *(President)*	State of Senegal	Region *(Governor)*	Department *(Prefet)*	Arrondissement *(Sous-Prefet)*	Rural Community *(PCR and Councilors)*	Village *(Chief)*
1972 Decentralization, Acte I	Central State *(President)*	State of Senegal	Region *(Governor)*	Department *(Prefet)*	Arrondissement *(Sous-Prefet)*	Rural Community *(PCR and Councilors)*	Village *(Chief)*

(*continued*)

TABLE 3.1 (continued)

	Central State				
1960		State of Senegal (*President*)	Region (*Governor*)	Department (*Prefet*)	Arrondissement (*Sous-Prefet; Chef d'arrondissement*)	Village (*Chief*)
1900–1959	Colonial State	Colony of Senegal (*Governor*)		Cercle (*Commandant*)	Canton (*Chef de Canton*)	Village (*Chief*)
pre-1880	Precolonial Political Systems	Precolonial States (*Kings*)		Provinces (*Sub-Kings, Provincial Chiefs*)		Village (*Chief*)
		Acephalous Areas			[Small-Scale Chiefs]	Village (*Misc authorities*)

to democratically elected local governments has generated unique redistributive dilemmas that, as the following chapters show, are resolved in structurally distinct ways across the country.

Central–Local Relations under Decentralization

To the extent that Senegalese politics was long defined by a centralized administration with extensive clientelist relations to rural brokers, how has the increased responsibilization of local governments impacted central–local relations? Certainly, national politics loom large across the country and rural Senegalese eagerly debate shifting party alliances and the fates of favored politicians. Nonetheless, the general impression across rural Senegal is that the central state uses rural areas opportunistically. This is not lost on local actors. For example, it is widely acknowledged that the redistricting of many localities prior to the 2009 elections was motivated by central state ambitions. "The redistricting was only political," sighed one community secretary whose local government had been placed under a special delegation following the elevation of one of the local government's larger villages to the statute of an urban commune. Because the mayor was from the opposition, she continued, the regime of former President Wade had rewarded a partisan ally in the now urban commune, punishing opposition politicians based in the former local government's remaining villages.[26]

This does not make rural actors mere passive recipients of state action, however, and the relationship between the central and local state is far from top-down. In contrast, even if many individuals cynically remark that national parties use local elections as de facto mid-term barometers of their popularity, local electoral fortunes are heavily influenced by local political dynamics.[27] Spots on local electoral lists are widely ascribed as going to those with local "electoral weight." As one chief described, it helps a candidate if they are well-known and have a history of doing good work in the community because this inspires "confidence."[28] This means that rather than national parties endowing any given local actor with electoral power by virtue of offering their party affiliation, local politicians who have "mass" behind them are highly valuable allies that national parties seek out. As a mayor in Dagana Department remarked, "locally, it's the person that counts" not the party.[29] This renders partisan attachments fleeting; when asked about local partisanship, one chief summarized pithily what many spoke of across the country, "we follow our leader [the mayor] and right now he is with the APR."[30]

---

[26] Interview, February 21, 2013.   [27] As described by Alvergne and Latouche (2010, 474).
[28] Interview, Kaffrine Region, February 9, 2016.
[29] Interview, Saint-Louis Region, July 21, 2013.
[30] Interview, Kaffrine Region, February 8, 2016.

One consequence is that Senegalese politicians prioritize winning by large margins, rather than pursuing a minimum winning coalition.[31] Indeed, it is far more common for local party leaders to speak of the need to "massify" their parties than to narrowly target certain segments of the electorate. As one community secretary wryly commented, "politics is all about who has the people behind him."[32] This means that party affiliation and coalitions at the local level are in many ways a function of the availability of prominent local politicians. Take, for instance, one subprefect's prognosis for the 2014 local elections: the mayor of the local government I had visited in his arrondissement was, in his opinion, "strong enough" to run with the APR alone. But elsewhere in his district, he commented, incumbents were weaker and would need the help of the broader presidential coalition, *Benno Bokk Yakkar*. Indeed, he observed, the dynamic would be much the same as in other local elections he had observed since 1996: "everyone needs to consolidate their base to have a chance ... they need local party militants" and this, he continued was largely a function of a politician's own "strengths" and not their party.[33]

The 1996 reforms were a dramatic shift from the early centralizing tendency of Senghor's regime, therefore, but despite the extent that local governments have become important sites of political contestation, they remain in their own unique local venues. In contrast and substantiated in the qualitative data marshaled in the following chapters, local politics is animated by distinct logics that call into question the idea that the central government and national level parties "telecommand" the local state.

DRAWING BOUNDARIES IN THE COUNTRYSIDE

Chapter 2 established that rural Senegal is home to durable social hierarchies rooted in histories of village settlement. This raises the possibility that local governments in historically centralized and acephalous areas never faced comparable redistributive dilemmas at all. Is variation in local governance endogenous to the ability of historically centralized communities to select into a meaningful administrative unit in the first place?

Political scientists have only rarely theorized the spatial origins of territorial units, despite the fact that borders may in many cases be a result of the very political processes we study.[34] What attention has been paid to this question has focused on the nature and repercussions of Africa's national boundaries.[35] Less attention has been paid to subnational boundary-making, however, despite Posner's (2004a) well-known conclusion that the legacies of colonial boundary-making are as much domestic in nature as they are international

---

[31] This is not specific to Senegal; see for example, Koné and Hagberg (2019) on Mali.
[32] Interview, Saint-Louis Region, February 22, 2013.
[33] Interview, Kaolack Region, May 3, 2013.   [34] Soifer (2019, 99).
[35] For example, Michalopoulos and Papaioannou (2016).

because subnational administrative boundaries put social and cultural identities into particular relief. In South Africa, for example, the fact that local jurisdictional boundaries lay arbitrarily on top of the territory of traditional authorities has generated substantial contention.[36] My argument asks us to think seriously about the question of boundary delimitation specifically because the politics that boundaries enable or obscure hold profound consequences for citizens.

Below, I trace the history of subnational boundary delimitation from the colonial period to the present through archival documents and interviews. Of course, it is implausible that subnational boundaries are as-if random but examining the history of boundary creation does suggest that there is no clear path by which precolonial provinces or territories have either persisted or been reinvented following decentralization. In sharp contrast, redistricting has almost exclusively been done as a means to obtain the objectives of the colonial or postcolonial central state, such as rendering the population more legible or political coalition building. I find minimal evidence that they systematically incorporated local preferences, reducing concerns that local government boundaries were systematically structured by bottom-up preferences of local elites.

Colonial Boundary-Making

The early years of colonialism were marked by French efforts to create usable administrative units for the colonial project.[37] In 1895, the French administration divided Senegal into *cercles* and, three years later, they created *cantons*, the base unit of French colonial governance, within each cercle. Cantons were intended to mirror France's own *départements*, "neat logical units with approximately the same size and population," but in reality, administrators were quite practical, at times co-opting precolonial provinces and cantons as described to them by customary authorities, while at others creating units around principles of ethnic homogeneity or by relying on geographic markers.[38]

General William Ponty's 1909 *Politique de Race* was the first significant articulation of France's policy toward their new colonial subjects, arguing that France should create similarly sized cantons of homogenous religion or ethnicity and abandon precolonial structures, which he viewed as "arbitrary groups created by the tyranny of local chiefs."[39] In large part, this was the consequence of French skepticism of indigenous African authority, meaning that even if early years saw the French seeking out reliable "aristocratic"

---

[36] Anath Pur (2007, 416).
[37] French efforts to annex territory following Faidherbe's advances in the mid-1800s had created a small number of *cercles*, under the command of military commanders, but these were unclearly demarcated stretches of lands.
[38] Klein (1968a, 199); Becker (2007, 146); and Zuccarelli (1965, 2).   [39] Zuccarelli (1965, 10).

intermediaries, this initial reliance on precolonial understandings of territories quickly eroded as Cartesian principles seeped in.[40] This generated strange hybrids in the short term. Administrators proposed two provinces, all comprised of five to six cantons, for each of the precolonial kingdoms of Baol, Saloum, and Sine, for example. In other cases, they stressed administrative ease, citing a need to balance the population evenly across units and to avoid unmanageable territorial expanses.[41] Plans to merge a series of cantons in the former kingdom of Sine in 1925 were met with outrage unforeseen by the French, who assumed that everyone being Serer and loyal to the Bour (king) of Sine would make their consolidations acceptable.[42]

Different strategies had to be employed altogether in historically acephalous areas, where colonial administrative units often had no geographic or political significance.[43] Borders in Senegal Oriental (present-day Tambacounda and Kedougou Regions) long remained imprecise, relying on natural features, such as rivers, or straight lines to delineate cantons.[44] Ten cantons were created in Bignona, but only in Tendouck Arrondissement did any of them reflect any degree of ethnic homogeneity.[45] In the Fouladou in the Haute-Casamance (Kolda Region), the French sought meaningful indigenous political organization, but the administration fundamentally misunderstood the loose ties between ruling families and ended up creating eleven cantons that failed to correspond either to precolonial understandings of territory or to produce the political acquiescence they desired.[46]

As the colonial state bureaucratized, the administration continually sought to improve their territorial organization.[47] To take the year 1924 as an illustration, the French made the following changes in that year: the canton of Nioro Rip was reattached to Wack and Rip and Pakalla-Mandakh was reattached to Ndoukoumane in Saloum. Twelve new cantons were created in Casamance and while Sandock Diagagniao was merged into Sao-Ndimack in Tivaouane, La and Ndoulo were split in Baol.[48] Redistricting was done to meet a myriad of objections. The broad demographic changes induced by colonialism – notably the rapid conversion to the Mouride Brotherhood as well as the expansion of the colonial economy – spurred territorial changes driven by economic motivations.[49] By way

---

[40] Cohen (1971, 75–77) and Boone (2003b, 50).
[41] L'Administrateur de Cercle de Thies (July 17, 1897); Senegal (1898).
[42] Commandent de Cercle de Sine-Saloum (August 3, 1923).   [43] Boone (2003b, 106).
[44] Becker (2007). For example, the boundary between the *cercles* of Tambacounda and Kaolack was still being negotiated in a contestation over a series of small villages as late as 1937. In a lengthy correspondence, only one claim is made about the contested villages' attachment to any historical political unit, and even then an administrator denied the value of historical claims made in the "tales of old notables" (Commandent de Cercle de Sine-Saloum, August 3, 1923).
[45] Pélissier (1966, 646, 647 n. 2).   [46] Fanchette (1999, 40–41).   [47] Crowder (1968, 191).
[48] Zuccarelli (1965).
[49] Most commonly as the result of the Mouride expansion which had dramatically changed the ethnic composition of areas that had seen an influx of Wolof and Serer Mouride settlers. These changes, one colonial administrator wrote in 1924, demanded a territorial reorganization. The

of illustration, the canton of Meringahem was reassigned to Louga *cercle* in 1928 due to its population's reorientation toward Louga's economic centers for the sale of their peanut crops; "administrative divisions should correspond as exactly as possible to the economic regions created by the implementation of colonial rule," justified the French *Chef de Cercle*.[50] Diplomatic objectives were also pursued – a proposal in 1953 to merge the cantons of Kadiamoutayes-Ouest and Kadiamoutayes-Sud-Est (originally split as "a matter of personal satisfaction ... and subsequent administrative instigations, but not one of real political or economic interest") was rejected due to the perceived need to amplify France's administrative presence along the colony's southern border, where the two cantons lay.[51] Alternatively, the sheer inability to locate reliable intermediaries resulted in the merging of numerous cantons at various points of time, particularly in historically acephalous areas.[52]

By the end of the colonial era, Senegal was home to only a handful of cantons that still resembled the provinces of precolonial states. Most colonial units had been dramatically altered by decisions both large and small.[53] That few canton chiefs ruled over meaningful territorial divisions reflected the fact that precolonial polities had effectively "been incorporated into the French bureaucratic state" by the onset of the First World War. By 1935, the colonial state had abandoned any formal demand that the canton corresponds to indigenous history, defining it simply as "a group of villages and the territories that depend on them."[54] The result of this nearly constant tinkering with administrative borders was that the canton "ceased to have, in effect, an ethnolinguistic or historical base necessary to be more than a simple territorial subdivision."[55]

Efforts to map these changes are stymied by the imprecision of French colonial maps or, more accurately, their nonexistence before the 1920s. Such ambitions are further impeded by the fact that the French had at best an approximate idea of where many villages were physically located in early decades, meaning they were inconsistently allocated to the correct colonial canton in early censuses. One way to estimate the degree of change is to engage in a simpler endeavor of counting the frequency of changes to subnational units. To do so, I turn to the *Journal Officiel du Senegal*, which recorded all

---

canton of La was not firmly "in French hands," he continued, and its current management was complicated by the fact that it was not a unified territorial or ethnic unit (L'Administrateur en Chef Commandant le cercle du Baol, May 14, 1924).

[50] Administrator Chef Commandent de Cercle de Louga (October 29, 1927).

[51] Geay (May 21, 1953).

[52] For example, discussions to merge Pakala and Mandack to Ndoucoumane. These cantons were on the edges of the Saloum Kingdom and had been severely affected by the Soninke–Marabout wars of the mid-1850s. The administration repeatedly struggled with the area, at times splitting and at others rejoining the cantons (Commandant de Cercle de Sine-Saloum, August 3, 1923).

[53] As noted by Boone (2003b, 50).

[54] Crowder (1968, 191); Klein (1968a, 204); and Zuccarelli (1965, 14).

[55] Zuccarelli (1965, 12–13).

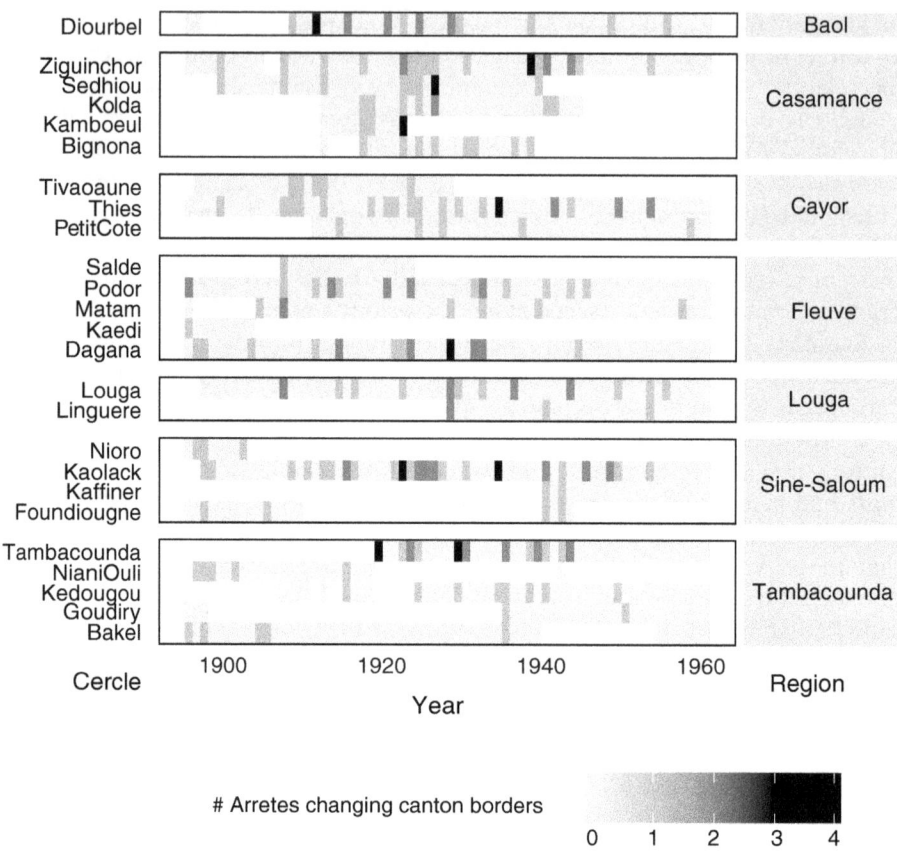

FIGURE 3.1 Colonial changes to cantons by cercle and region, 1895–1960

administrative changes in the colony. Figure 3.1 displays the frequency of territorial changes to canton borders within each cercle over time. Note that cercles, grouped by colonial regions on the right-hand y-axis, themselves come in and out of existence during this period. The figure demonstrates that all cercles and regions saw redistricting at least once. Changes to canton borders were particularly prominent in the 1920s and some regions, such as Dagana, witnessed numerous changes while others, such as Bakel or the Petite-Cote, home to Dakar, remained more consistent.[56] There is no apparent correlation between the frequency of changes and a cercle having had most of its territory

---

[56] In Fouta Toro, the colonial administration largely kept precolonial province names, but this should not mask notable boundary changes. For example, the cantons of Irlabes and Ebiabes

Delimiting the Postcolonial State

Following independence in 1960, the postcolonial Senegalese state took its own turn at restructuring the state as a vehicle to promote state-led development, turning cantons into arrondissements and, in 1964, creating departments, similar in size to colonial cercles, nested in regions.[58] Though a few arrondissements persisted untouched, many aggregated two or three colonial cantons. Alternatively, others split existing cantons to create new administrative units altogether. On average, cantons were split into 2.5 arrondissements and, in turn, today's average arrondissement includes territory from three to four cantons.[59] Like their colonial predecessors, the postcolonial state sought to balance the population across arrondissements and to generate economic complementarities by creating administrative units based around central economic infrastructure.[60] The cost of this strategy was significant variability in surface area and population density across administrative units. This eliminated "any fiction of a territory based on historical tradition," and, accordingly, the state renamed all administrative units after their *chef-lieu*, or capital city or village, to signal this break.[61]

Numerous changes took place in the first years of independence. At times, they were practical, such as the decision to move the capital of Adeane arrondissement to the village of Niaguis after Adeane-village was deemed too remote. Similarly, a new arrondissement was created in Bakel because citizens were traveling to neighboring Mali for social services rather than the more distant headquarters of their arrondissement.[62] At others, they were political. As the postcolonial regime sought to consolidate a reliable political foundation in the countryside, they proved willing to negotiate with key vote brokers, notably Sufi religious leaders.[63] The state redrew the border between Thienaba and Pout arrondissements in this vein, moving a handful of villages to the former, for example, to improve the villagers' access to their marabout, a resident of Thienaba-village.[64]

---

were merged in 1922, the canton of Ferlo was created and Dimar was split into Dimar Oriental and Dimar Occidental (Zuccarelli 1965, 13).

[57] The correlation between the total number of changes a cercle saw throughout the colonial period and that cercle having been home to a precolonial state in the late 1800s is 0.09.

[58] Diouf (1993, 235–237) and Zuccarelli (1965, 45).

[59] The average number of cantons in an arrondissement are 3.91 and 3.58 for centralized and uncentralized areas of the country, respectively. Note that these numbers are based on maps that have been digitized and georeferenced by the author and likely contain some margin of error.

[60] Zuccarelli (1965, 52) and CNAM-SERESA (1960, II-2 2-3).   [61] Zuccarelli (1965, 50–51).

[62] Zuccarelli (1965, 53–54).   [63] As described by Boone (1992, 98).

[64] Zuccarelli (1965, 53).

Decentralization brought the need to further divide the country. This process is crucial to subsequent outcomes of such reforms. To the extent that local elites – who seek to distribute goods to their own villages or clients as a means to reinforce their social status – strive to capture local policymaking as I have argued, the dynamics of *which* villages comprise the local government is central to understanding local redistributive politics. If local elites could coordinate around the delineation of their local governments, it is possible that something about their relative ability to do so drives the outcome variables under study here. When local government boundaries are created via a bottom-up, consultative process, such was the case during Mali's decentralization reforms, then contemporary government performance could be the product of the capacity of some communities to organize and demand their own local government.

As stated in the 1972 law introducing decentralization (article 1 of law 72–75 *Relative aux Communautes Rurales*), a local government, or rural community, would be "a number of villages belonging to the same territory, united by a solidarity resulting from their neighborship, having common interests and able to find the resources necessary for their development." The degree to which these ideas of solidarity and neighborliness came into play is questionable, however. To the extent that the 1972 decentralization reform was designed to meet the central state's political objectives, the boundaries established by the 1972 reform by and large left the previously lowest level administrative unit, the arrondissement, intact, simply dividing it into three to four local governments.[65] Rather than seeking out meaningful political entities, the state stuck to eminently rationalist strategies, crafting an administrative structure that divided each region into three departments, each department into three arrondissements – themselves the product of a late colonial bureaucratic desire for uniform administrative divisions – and each arrondissement into three local governments. Local governments were created according to a "principle of centrality" as the government employed technical criteria to identify villages that served as economic poles, such as weekly markets, peasant cooperatives, or health centers, for local government capitals.[66] Over half of the villages identified as local economic poles in response to a 1962 government request for the name of influential villages in Senegal Oriental (contemporary Tambacounda and Kedougou regions) are either urban communes or local governments capitals today, for instance.[67]

Beyond this, the government was concerned with ensuring demographic balance and, more ambiguously, "economic potential."[68] The stated goal of

---

[65] Vengroff and Magala (2001).
[66] Interview, Charles Becker, Dakar, February 6, 2016. Here, locally influential figures were at times able to divert the pole to their home village; a reality particularly true for influential religious figures.
[67] Chef d'Arrondissement de Goudiry (September 8, 1962).
[68] Interview, development planner, Dakar, February 3, 2016.

having 5,000 inhabitants as a minimum threshold for economic viability led to exceedingly large territorial units in areas of the country with low population density. The government did commission a series of studies undertaken by the *Direction de l'aménagement du territoire* (DAT) to identify potential ways to divide the country into viable socioeconomic units. These included sociological criteria, though these rarely won out in the end.[69] In Koungheul, DAT technicians faced low population densities that problematized their ability to create "economically viable" units, conceptualized thinly as a locality's ability to raise sufficient revenues from the rural tax, without risking under-administration and weakened popular participation. The DAT proposed two solutions: they could firstly delimit local governments around potential "villages-centres," those with the historical importance, population, proximity to infrastructure, and transport. This would create local governments where every village would be within 15 kilometers of a center, but it relied on the hope that future population growth would make the units economically viable. Alternatively, they could delimit six local governments that were much larger and more diverse, but able to muster sufficient tax revenue in the present. The latter option won the day.[70]

Thus, while the central state aspired to create administrative units composed of villages that shared attributes like neighborly solidarity, this goal had to be reconciled with other, more tangible objectives, such as grouping villages that together would have "the resources necessary for their development."[71] Despite paying lip service to the value of consulting with local populations, in many cases, the state simply delimited local governments solely by rational "demographic criteria or on the number of villages grouped together, without any meaningful historical or socioeconomic reference," or to the lived dimensions of territory.[72]

There is little evidence that local political cleavages systematically influenced boundaries delimitation.[73] Writing on Kolda Region, Fanchette (2011, 234–235) notes that local governments lack "any historical legitimacy," resulting in rural communities that are "too large, heterogeneous and traversed by multiple political conflicts." In many areas, local government boundaries are seen as inimical to development. This generated complaints from central state officials assigned to rural areas, such as one adjoint subprefect who noted bitterly that government functionaries in Dakar had simply devised boundaries

---

[69] Darbon (1988, 93, 171).   [70] Blundo (1998b, 118).   [71] Diop (2006a, 102–103).
[72] Interview, decentralization consultant, Dakar, February 6, 2016; Diop (2006a, 153).
[73] This was verified in interviews conducted in 2016. One councilor explained that his local government borders, as drawn by the central state in 1976, were the same as those created by the French, though the colonial canton had no clear historical meaning that he was aware of. The 1976 reforms did shift the local government seat to a more central location along a main road as the colonial canton seat, though historically prominent, had declined significantly in size (Interview, Louga Region, February 19, 2016).

they thought would meet the state's political needs at the cost of local considerations. "The populations do not question the boundaries because the administration made them," he sighed.[74] Faced with endemic political divisions induced by local government boundaries, "democracy can do nothing" in many communities, surmised one technical advisor in Dakar.[75]

Still, this is not always the case. One village chief in Louga Region described his local government as a "homogenous and solidary unity," echoing almost directly the language of early planners. In this case, the local government boundaries reflected one-half of a colonial canton that had been split into two.[76] At the other extreme however, the delimitation of decentralized political units has been "explosive" as villages with long histories of rivalrous relations find themselves within the same local government. This has repeatedly resulted in weakened local government institutions beset by in-fighting as local factions gained a new and influential venue within which to adjudicate longstanding disputes.[77]

More recently, Senegal undertook significant administrative redistricting in 2009, creating fifty new local governments, and in 2011–2012, thirteen more. This leads to a total of 384 local governments at the time of research with the addition of 126 urban communes (including Dakar's urban communes). Numerous explanations have been put forward for these changes. The government claimed it was trying to bring the administration closer to the citizenry by creating smaller administrative units, but the general consensus is that the regime of President Wade was acting with a direct eye on the 2009 local elections. In reality, local governments that were divided had, on average, more villages (76 versus 56) and larger surface areas (110,437 hectares versus 58,784). Historically, acephalous areas were more likely to have an administrative division, with 33 percent of local governments seeing some boundary change compared to only 16 percent in formerly centralized regions (significant at $p < 0.001$).

It is not a secret that these changes were driven by the political motives of the central state. A government bureaucrat at the *Direction des Collectivites Locales* laughed when I asked about new commune creation, pulling out a file full of such requests. Most would go nowhere, he argued, because they were so clearly political – written by members of the opposition or disgruntled villages' chiefs – even if petitioners framed them in terms of local development. Still, a few that were more serious would be sent to the Ministry of the Interior for

---

[74] Interview, Tambacounda Region, March 22, 2013. [75] Interview, February 2, 2016.
[76] Interview, February 19, 2016.
[77] Darbon (1988, 172). Village rivalries exist throughout the country, not simply in acephalous zones. But while Darbon (1988) notes that this can shut down local government work in the acephalous Casamance, Diop (2006a) argues that this generates the inverse outcome in historically centralized Fouta Toro where villages want to maintain similar levels of development as their rivals.

review though the outcome was often contingent on central government preferences.[78] This claim is supported by the story one mayor shared of having written to the Minister of Local Authorities in the mid-2000s to petition for a division of his local government, which covered a vast expanse that made it difficult to serve the nearly 100 villages within its boundaries. He was shocked, he recounted, when a presidential *décret* arrived at his desk with a list delineating which villages would stay in his local government and which would be removed to form a new collectivity. "I thought they would come and consult with the population," he mused, but instead the whole process was "antidemocratic," resulting in villages only a few kilometers from his local government's capital being attached to the new local government, whose own seat was nearly 10 kilometers to the south.[79] Indeed, numerous individuals working in rural areas noted the sloppiness with which recent divisions had been conducted in Dakar. In one community in southeastern Senegal, a village was officially listed as belonging to a neighboring local government even though it was more than 10 kilometers from the border. This meant that citizens of the village had to travel to their "official" local government for all paperwork for over a year while the local administration attempted to remedy the situation.[80]

Looking across archival documents, secondary literature, and interviews, I find scant evidence that areas home to precolonial states were routinely able to self-constitute their local governments. Though boundaries are rarely, if ever, plausibly as-if random, we can be more or less confident that they are not endogenous to the processes under study. The delimitation of subnational boundaries throughout the colonial and postcolonial eras prioritized the practical and political ambitions of the central government and I find no evidence of a systematic relationship between the ability of elites to influence the process of local government boundary delineation and precolonial political geography in archival and interview data.

CONCLUSION

This chapter made two historical claims that build on the introduction to Senegal's dynamic precolonial political geography offered in Chapter 2. The decentralization reforms introduced in 1996 dramatically altered the nature of local public goods delivery at the same time that it introduced new incentives and rewards for politicians. These reforms intersected with the divergent grassroots legacies of precolonial statehood to structure distinct cross-village

---

[78] Interview, Dakar, November 5, 2013.
[79] Interview, Kaffrine Region, February 8, 2016. His request, he went on to say, had had nothing to do with the division that followed. Instead, the new local government was a gift of sorts to a loyal PDS politician from the new commune's capital village, who was, not surprisingly, promptly elected as that commune's mayor in 2009.
[80] Interview, Kedougou Region, April 2, 2013.

redistributive dilemmas across the country. It is precisely because democratic decentralization opens up the possibility that local elected officials will draw from a number of villages, that local decision-makers are obliged to negotiate *across* villages when deciding how to distribute scarce projects and resources.

This also reveals the importance of my final historical claim: how did any given local government come to be comprised of the villages that constitute it? By tracing the history of subnational boundary creation from the colonial period to the present with a range of archival and interview data, I mitigate the concern that local government boundaries are endogenous to local social networks. In contrast, redistricting was repeatedly undertaken with an eye to the multitude of changing objectives of colonial and postcolonial states. This raises an important reminder that space is not neutral, and we should not assume that the boundaries we reflexively use are necessarily exogenous to the processes we study.

It was only with the 1996 decentralization reforms, therefore, that social legacies of Senegal's precolonial past interacted with the bounds of decision-making, facilitating institutional congruence in some communities and incongruence in others. I map out these diverging political dynamics in the next chapter.

4

Political Narratives across Rural Senegal

Across rural Senegal, local actors lament that their local governments suffer from weak resources and insufficient support from the central state. National political parties are only fleetingly engaged, leaving local officials alone with innumerable demands from constituents as villages petition for large investments like schools and with citizens passing constantly to seek assistance with medical bills or funeral expenses. Yet despite their shared challenges, data from an original survey with more than 300 rural Senegalese political and customary elites reveal striking subnational divergence in how local actors experience decentralized local governance. For some, decentralization is a boon, with the local state capturing a meaningful community that works well together. But for others, local governance has heightened political competition between neighboring villages and failed to deliver on its promises.

In this chapter I document this empirical variation to build the contours of my theory. I introduce the survey in the next section before drawing on open-ended questions to outline the dominant narrative arcs offered by respondents about their local political lives. In areas that were home to centralized polities prior to the onset of French colonial rule, local elites describe their local governments as unified and meaningful political entities. More precisely, they describe the properties of institutional congruence: respondents speak of powerful local social institutions that map onto the local state, leading elites to report feeling obligated to alter their political behavior. These attributes are absent in areas of incongruence, where interviewees describe splintered social relations among local elites that increase competition for control over the local government and the resources that come with it. Embedded within these narratives are the theory's two mechanisms: the role of shared group identification and dense social networks are cited at length in historically centralized zones but are largely absent in local governments without histories of precolonial statehood.

The survey's sampling design further allows me to examine two of the social shocks that might predict the erasure of precolonial identities that were introduced in Chapter 2. What happens, I ask, in communities that have seen substantial immigration or mass religious conversion, particularly in those local governments home to powerful religious figures? The survey data suggest that institutional congruence is relatively flexible, able to adopt in-migrants and new forms of religious practice to the extent that the twin mechanisms of cross-village social networks and shared group identification are preserved. Elsewhere, the arrival of such challenges enflames disputes over redistribution and representation. Still, these are not absolute truths and the survey demonstrates how institutional congruence can be attenuated by social shocks at the margins.

The chapter ends with a presentation of the survey's quantifiable measures. Across a number of questions, I find consistent patterns to those emerging out of the qualitative data: respondents in congruent local governments are more positive about their local government's performance and are less likely to allege unequal treatment, suggesting that narratives of local political life map onto reported experiences with local governance.

ORIGINAL SURVEY DATA

This chapter uses data collected from an original survey of Senegalese village chiefs and local elected officials conducted between February and July of 2013.[1] Formatted as highly structured interviews, the survey asked respondents questions about the history of their village and local government, their level of social service access, their evaluations of the economy and the local and central government as well as a host of personal details. Because the questions ranged from standardized to open-ended formats, the data are amenable to a qualitative and quantitative analysis.

I supplement the survey with interviews conducted with central state officials appointed to rural areas, notably the subprefect (the lowest central state administrator) as well as local development agents, both posted to the arrondissement, and officials at the *Agence Régionale du Développement*, or regional development agency.[2] Finally, I spoke with the local government secretary in order to collect data on local government activity. Secretaries are often best

---

[1] All interviews were conducted by either the author or a research assistant in the language of the respondent's choice. When respondents preferred a language other than French, research assistants translated for the author. Because some interviewees expressed interest in remaining anonymous, the interconnected nature of my interviews leads me to anonymize all interviews out of caution for protecting respondent privacy. Respondents are identified by their title, the department the interview was conducted in, and the interview's date.

[2] These interviews were completed subject to availability. Because central state officials travel with more frequency, it was not uncommon for one of these three officials to be unavailable.

Original Survey Data

positioned to verify local government statistics, such as the number of meetings held in the previous year, because they are charged with keeping logs of this information. In the frequent occurrence where the mayor is illiterate, the secretary often has the clearest documentation of the local government's recent procedures and activities.

In total, the survey covers fifty-six rural communities, sampled from Senegal's forty-two departments. The survey's central objective was to illuminate what, if any, empirical variation existed in experiences with local governance along the key axis of historical variation: precolonial statehood. To sample the antecedent independent variable, I purposefully chose fourteen departments that were balanced between areas that were historically centralized or acephalous as well as zones that had an intermittent history of precolonial statehood.[3] I further sought to ensure variation in exposure to migration patterns and geographic location. For example, all of Kedougou Region was acephalous and it is located far from Dakar while some departments within Tambacounda and Kolda Regions, also far removed from Senegal's capital, were exposed to precolonial polities. Certainly, these factors are not invariant by department and some departments were chosen specifically because they are home to both historically acephalous areas *and* smaller states; here again, Tambacounda and Kolda Departments are good examples. Absent exact data on migration, I likewise approximated regions known to have experienced in-migration, such as the peanut basin or Guinean in-migration to the southeast, while cognizant that not all local governments within those units were equally affected.

A map of surveyed regions can be found in Figure 4.1.

Within departments, I employed a random selection strategy to choose local governments. Specifically, I randomly selected two arrondissements from within each department and, in turn, two local governments in each arrondissement.[4] This helps attenuate the concern that outliers on the independent (precolonial statehood) or dependent (local government performance) variables were intentionally chosen. In reality, I had relatively little information on selected units before visiting given the relative absence of publicly available data on local governments and local social characteristics. To date, I am unaware of any standardized metric of local government performance. In many

---

[3] Sampling excluded the region of Cap-Vert, which is dominated by Dakar, the national capital.
[4] Random selection was done as follows: each eligible unit was assigned a number, following alphabetical order. A random number generator then selected one or two numbers within the eligible range. To illustrate, if I were to have conducted the survey in Foundiougne Department (Fatick Region), the random number generator would have chosen two numbers between one and three, corresponding to Djilor, Niodior, and Toubacouta arrondissements, respectively. One exception is that Bignona was dropped as a potential department in Ziguinchor Region given ongoing insecurity in the region.

FIGURE 4.1 Map of surveyed departments

cases, even the names of local mayors were not available until I contacted the relevant subprefect.

Within each local government, the mayor (or in two cases when the mayor was unavailable, his adjoint) was interviewed in addition to one or two local government councilors and four village chiefs, again all chosen randomly.[5] Chiefs were randomly sampled by assigning a number to each official village and using a random number generator to draw four numbers. In the event that the chief was unavailable (due to illness, travel, or, at times, old age), the next closest village was chosen.[6] Councilors were almost exclusively selected by again choosing a village randomly and asking if a councilor lived in that village

---

[5] In one community, neither the mayor nor an adjoint was available. A few sampled communities were under a "special delegation" as the result of administrative redistricting (this is not correlated with precolonial centralization). A special delegation dissolves the local council, which is replaced by a committee of three individuals – appointed by the state – until the next local elections are held. In this situation, only the President of the Special Delegation was interviewed. In four of the five communities where this is the case, the current President of the Special Delegation was the elected mayor in the 2009 elections.

[6] An exception to this was if a village had a "delegated" chief, for example, a chief's brother or nephew who fulfills the duties of the chiefship while the named chief is away (often working in Dakar or another urban center). In these cases, the delegate was interviewed.

or, if not, a neighboring one. In cases where multiple councilors lived in a village, we interviewed the councilor whose house we encountered first.[7]

Descriptive data on interviewees, disaggregated by department, can be found in Table 4.1.

Are These Narratives Accurate?

Much of the material presented in this chapter (as well as in Chapter 6) comes from open-ended survey questions or interviews with rural elites. The data I derive from these interviews are at times quantified, but I suggest that it is equally valuable as a lens into local political narratives. Taking the narratives individuals voice about their political experiences seriously emphasizes how individuals reason toward certain conclusions or reinforce certain beliefs or identities.[8] When local elites reinforce a narrative that local politics is either harmonious or disharmonious, they not only reflect on their political worlds but also reinforce the value of these narratives at the same time. Comments such as those by one village chief in the east of the country, "here politics takes a single form: it's the interest of the elected officials and their party," both reflect and reify alienation from political life.[9] Similarly, when respondents invoke a sense of shared identity or cohesion across the local government – for example, "We have different political parties, but we live in conviviality. We are almost all related" – they valorized a powerful sense of common fate.[10]

This poses a risk: how do we know that the tales spun about the past actually matter, let alone whether they are accurate or not? I recognize that the stories people recount about their communities or the past may be untrue. At the same time, however, I question whether the past is a "limitless symbolic resource."[11] In rural Senegal, historical narratives often appear bounded by cultural norms that set a framework for how the past is "remembered" in any given community. In no interview did elites claim a precolonial history when they fell outside the generally understood boundaries of the country's precolonial politics, suggesting a limit to any opportunistic claim-making to a precolonial past, even when it would be relatively easy to do so to an outsider, such as myself. Still, this threat directly informs my multi-method strategy: employing quantitative

---

[7] In a few cases, a councilor was present at the local government office when we made our first introductions and was subsequently interviewed. This was most common because the local government secretary took it upon themselves to introduce us to a councilor who "happened to be there that day." I have little reason to think that this introduced systematic bias. These councilors were not more likely to be educated and in only one case were they from the chef-lieu. Councilors commonly stop by the local government office when they have business with the local government or when they travel to the chef-lieu to visit friends or attend a market. Indeed, in most communities, a number of councilors circulate through the town hall on any given day.

[8] See also Kendhammer (2016).   [9] Interview, Tambacounda Region, March 22, 2013.

[10] Interview, councilor, Fatick Region, May 11, 2013.   [11] Appadurai (1981, 202).

TABLE 4.1 *Descriptive statistics for local elite survey respondents, by department*

Department	Inst. congruence	In-migration	Respondent type	N	Avg. age	Modal educ. level	Percent related to village founder (%)	Percent chiefs inherited from family (%)	Percent with family members in authority positions (%)	Percent related to chief (%)	Average years chief/# Mandates
Dagana	Low	Low	Chiefs	13	60.3	Koranic	76.9	85.6	69.2		13.7
			Elected Officials	9	55	Koranic	33		55.6	22.2	2.17
Fatick	High	Low	Chiefs	16	69.1	None	50	81.2	68.8		23.3
			Elected Officials	8	52.4	High School	0		50	50	1.5
Goudiry	Mixed	High	Chiefs	14	60	Koranic	100	100	71.4		10
			Elected Officials	10	53.9	Koranic	30		50	30	1.5
Kaffrine	Mixed	High	Chiefs	16	51.4	Koranic	81.3	87.5	50		11
			Elected Officials	8	63.4	Koranic	42.9		62.5	50	2.5
Kaolack	High	High	Chiefs	15	58.5	Koranic	86.7	100	66.7		19.2
			Elected Officials	9	59.2	Koranic	66.7		88.9	88.9	2
Kebemer	High	Low	Chiefs	13	73.2	Koranic	92.3	100	76.9		14.8
			Elected Officials	11	60.9	Koranic	66.7		90.9	81.8	1.43
Kedougou	Low	High	Chiefs	16	65.1	Koranic	50	65.3	52.5		14.1
			Elected Officials	8	48.6	High School	33.3		50	50	1.63
Kolda	Mixed	Medium	Chiefs	16	61.8	None	40.3	100	76		16.38
			Elected Officials	8	49.6	Koranic/Some Primary	12.5		87.5	62	1.25

Linguere	Mixed	Medium	Chiefs	16	65	Koranic	81.2	92.8	68.8		16.16
			Elected Officials	6	54.7	Koranic	100		83.3	83.3	1.66
Nioro de Rip	High	High	Chiefs	16	67.4	Koranic	75	100	81.3		10.83
			Elected Officials	8	53.8	Koranic	57.1		75	75	1.88
Podor	High	Low	Chiefs	17	58.9	Koranic	88.2	94.1	76.5		9.79
			Elected Officials	8	53.1	High School	50		100	100	1.88
Tambacounda	Mixed	High	Chiefs	14	60.1	Koranic	78.6	85.7	62.3		13.78
			Elected Officials	10	61.7	High School	22.2		80	80	2.25
Tivaouane	High	Low	Chiefs	16	67.2	Koranic	75	100	62.5		11.48
			Elected Officials	7	56	University	60		85.7	85.7	2.14
Ziguinchor	Low	Low	Chiefs	15	56	Middle School	33.3	60	86.7		9.49
			Elected Officials	9	52.4	High School	12.5		77.8	66.7	1.63

and archival data as well as network analysis (see Chapter 6) allows me to cross-validate the patterns described to me by interviewees.

Ultimately, however, the truth matters less than the process of creating and recreating communal memories that are taken as truth. As the Italian historian Portelli (1991, 50–52) explains, listening to people's retelling of the past reveals that "what is really important is that memory is not a passive depository of facts, but an active process of creation of meanings." This does not mean that our informants are not credible, but rather that the narratives they recount are as reflective of the symbols and beliefs that inform how they understand their past as they are of concrete sequences of events.[12]

When rural Senegalese work through what it means to be a descendant of Sine or Fouta Toro, therefore, they at once provide an explanation for the boundaries that define a group while simultaneously making the identity collective by stipulating how individuals fit into this shared narrative.[13] A precolonial state may define an identity's scope while also stipulating how they can assert their belonging, be it through tales of their grandfathers' adventures, their family name, or the land they farm. These tales and memories may be inflated, but they nonetheless serve a critical role in the persistence of shared identities and collective norms alike. Indeed, I find remarkable consistency in the narratives told by elites both within any given local government and within the broad dichotomy I draw between historically centralized and historically acephalous zones. In this way, I suggest that listening to narratives of local political life offers us insight into key processes of norm creation and maintenance and the ways in which individuals reinforce the importance of local identities and shared histories in their daily lives.

NARRATING LOCAL POLITICS IN DECENTRALIZED SENEGAL

I begin my analysis of the survey data by distilling two dominant representations of local politics from the surveys: regions where respondents invoke narratives of cohesive and territorially bound identities and areas where local governance is described as divisive, beset by politically rivalrous claims to the local state.

Narratives of Local Governance across Senegal's Precolonial Geography

Respondents in local governments that fall in the footprints of Senegal's precolonial states spoke about their local governments in distinctive ways that reveal two clear themes. The first is an idea of a common descent or shared heritage, even though these are at times partially imagined. For example, many respondents in Podor Department scoffed when asked to enumerate other local

---

[12] See also White (2000, 30).   [13] See here Tilly (2006).

elites they were related to, responding simply that "we are all family here." An equally common version of this is seen in the boastful comment of one village chief that there was no conflict in his community because "we are a single family." Such responses should not lead us to immediately conclude that areas home to precolonial states are simply inhabited by one, large lineage. Like many who made such claims of familial ties, this specific village chief reported few immediate family relations with other chiefs or elected officials in his community.[14]

This practice of adopting a broad rhetoric of kinship with community members even absent identifiable shared bloodlines is common in the West African Sahel as a means to reinforce community solidarity between lineages and settlements.[15] Communities often have strong narratives of shared descent based on family or clan, that may reflect friendship, "host" relations with in-migrants or cross-ethnic or cross-caste relations. As one community secretary in Senegal's Wolof heartland described, the local government she worked for was cohesive and efficient. This, she explained, was because "almost everyone is related," adding "there are many Sow, Mbaye, Ndoye in the rural community." Typically, Mbaye and Ndoye are Wolof surnames, reflecting the ethnic dominance of the Wolof in the zone. Sow, however, is an ethnically Peulh last name. By including it as one of the "related" families in the community, the secretary reinforces the historical inclusion of Peulh minorities in her area.[16] Many historically centralized communities report such long-standing ties between non-co-ethnics, "I have almost no boundaries, they are all my family except for the Peulhs and they are my friends," remarked a councilor in the Saloum.[17]

The second theme emphasizes the value of social cohesion or the prioritization of preserving peaceful social relations. Respondents in historically centralized areas explicitly linked a collective commitment to maintaining social cohesion to the performance of their local governments. Political "colorings" or divisions were repeatedly suggested to be at odds with the historical ties that bound villages together. As a result, one councilor explained, "we put the common interest before politics here."[18] This is not to deny social conflict, which is as prevalent in historically centralized areas as anywhere else. What differs, the survey data suggest, is the priority elites place on resolving conflicts with minimal social upset. Thus, for example, in Podor Department, which occupies the eastern stretches of the territory of the former precolonial state of Fouta Toro, long-standing sources of socioeconomic tensions related to caste and social hierarchy persist to the present. Still, one subprefect in Podor

---

[14] Interview, village chief, Thies Region, May 15, 2013.
[15] For example, see Koné and Hagberg (2019, 45).
[16] Interview, Louga Region, March 6, 2013.
[17] Interview, councilor, Kaffrine Region, April 22, 2013.
[18] Interview, Thies Region, May 16, 2013.

noted that elites in the communities he administered managed a "grand diplomacy" to avoid any issues escalating.[19]

I argue that these are narratives of institutional congruence. Here, local histories are deployed to justify social institutions, particularly those around norms of social cohesion and conflict resolution, in ways that offer leverage on the reported behavior of elites. The presence of shared social institutions that are congruent with the local state generates pressure to be broadly representative and redistributive across the local government. Elsewhere in Podor Department, a local government mayor reported that his administration worked carefully with all village chiefs within his jurisdiction explicitly because everyone knew each other and claimed a shared descent from the region's founders. Village chiefs in his community broadly corroborated this, noting that most villages had a councilor elected to the council, explicitly invoking their shared identity as shaping the right for everyone to gain equal representation.[20]

In stark contrast to their centralized counterparts, interviewees in historically acephalous zones did not speak of social cohesion in the local government.[21] Local political narratives were more likely to center around social divisions *between* villages or political parties, with less extreme versions best described as narratives of dispersion, communities of numerous parts that didn't sum up to a whole. This is reflected in the lack of a robust, unifying identity around any given community's past.[22] What is distinct about these zones is not that they lack rich local histories, but that these histories do not encompass the local state as a whole. Respondents were more likely to narrate their history around the foundation of their individual village facilitating what Arcand and Bassole (2007) have dubbed "village capture," whereby each village is seen as being out for themselves.[23] This was lamented upon even by elected officials themselves; one mayor in Kolda Region, for example, observed that budget meetings in his government were hindered by the politicking of councilors who only "wear the shirt of their village."[24]

Alternatively, some local governments were dominated by a specific clan or lineage spread over a handful of villages. In one local government, for example, the mayor was the descendant of the former canton chief. His family remained prominent in the area and a number of his extended family members were

---

[19] Interview, February 11, 2013.
[20] Interviews, mayor, February 13, 2013 and village chiefs, February 12–14, 2013.
[21] Though certainly in many cases there is social cohesion *within* the village.
[22] For example, when asked about what the political system had been like before the arrival of the French, one mayor in Ziguinchor answered hesitantly, "it was the Diola Confederacy, but I never really knew what that was." (Interview, July 8, 2013).
[23] This takes numerous forms, of course. In some local governments, a few large villages vie for control or, elsewhere, a subset of villages has historically dominated local political life and settled into an uneasy alliance.
[24] Interview, Kolda Region, April 11, 2013.

elected on the council. A central government official posted to the zone described the family as a "fortress," adding that he had recently had to intervene during a local government meeting to ensure that all councilors were allowed to speak following the efforts of one representative from the "ruling" family to restrict who could comment during local council sessions. They "reign there," the state agent concluded, and there wasn't much the administration could do.[25] Indeed, some of the most intractable political fights seemed to arise when a small network of local elites, often based in a handful of key economic and political centers, dominated local politics. In contrast to narratives of cohesion and shared descent, the local histories recounted in acephalous zones were notably *incongruent* with local government boundaries.

The specific form that local political cleavages take displays remarkable diversity, therefore, but regardless of their content, respondents linked them clearly to local government performance. It was in historically acephalous areas that local government officials reported trouble meeting the quorum because of political divisions, with councilors knowingly choosing not to attend.[26] At times, these divisions were along lines of ethnicity or caste. One casted mayor in Tambacounda was obliged to pay for a car to go pick up all councilors of a higher caste – who would not otherwise pay to travel to a meeting led by a "casté" – if he wanted to meet the required quorum for local council meetings.[27] In Ziguinchor Region, many respondents lamented that the population could not overcome minor arguments to unite around anything. Even before the 1996 reforms, Darbon (1988, 173) chronicled the intervillage tensions within some of the local governments in the region. In Mlomp, Oukout, and Oussouye, for example, historically rivalrous villages had been pooled into the local government weakening the ability of the newly formed local government to function properly. As one councilor in the Casamance explained, the Diola's lack of hierarchical authority meant that while there was (and always had been) independence and equality between villages, this came at a cost: "it's not like the North ... [people here] all have arguments with each other and this means that they get less [services]" because mayors and parliamentarians alike felt little sense of obligation to their neighbors and constituents.[28]

The political divisions recounted in historically acephalous areas were thus directly cited as impacting public goods delivery. One local government, under the rule of a special delegation following an administrative redistricting, was so internally divided along ethnic lines that even the special delegation was "blocked" and had been unable to execute any development project for more

---

[25] Interview, adjoint subprefect, Tambacounda Department, March 22, 2013.
[26] This was noted as a problem in two-thirds of rural communities in acephalous areas.
[27] The influence of caste was noted extensively in these areas, with some villages refusing to vote or send their children to school because either their assigned voting booth or the nearest school was in a casted village.
[28] Interview, July 8, 2013.

than seven months. The community secretary noted that projects, some of which the funding had already been delivered for, were at a standstill because of the political deadlock.[29] Complete blockage such as this is rare, but the perception dominated in acephalous regions that the only way to get something from or "have a say" in the local council was to have family or ethnic ties to a local councilor or, alternatively, to be a political ally of the ruling party.[30] "It is not a good political life here, because if you are not in power you are not represented at all," one village chief surmised.[31]

Why Social Institutions Influence Local Governance

Across historically centralized areas, local elites directly and indirectly described a central role for cross-village social institutions. As defined in Chapter 1, social institutions are norms of appropriate behavior in the public sphere demarcated by group boundaries. They are at once inherently relational – encompassing a relevant network of actors – while also necessarily tied to an identity category that imbues social institutions with meaning. This makes social institutions particularly motivating because they both externally and internally shape actor behavior: externally they offer social sanctions and rewards and circulate information about comportment, but they are also internalized by actors, leading them to think that abiding by any given social institution is an appropriate course of action.

The qualitative components of my survey reveal two key social institutions that embed elites across villages in cases of institutional congruence. First, elites observe norms of conflict avoidance. In Fatick Region, home to the precolonial state of Sine, respondents were particularly proud of their local social harmony, noting that local social institutions prevented political conflict or divisions between Muslims and Christians. "For us in [local government] our politics is limited to trying to solve our problems ... we all know each other and that is why nobody dares create political conflicts," explained one village chief.[32] Comments such as one community secretary's in Louga Region, that during elections "everyone has their corner, but afterwards, that is put aside" for the sake of local development were repeated throughout areas that were home to precolonial states.[33]

The second social institution is a norm of balancing voice and resources across villages. This is illustrated well in descriptions of the process of drafting

---

[29] Interview, community secretary, Saint-Louis Region, February 21, 2013.
[30] Interview, village chief, Saint-Louis Region, February 14, 2013. Interestingly, despite many individuals invoking partisanship as an important political cleavage, 74 percent of respondents in historically acephalous regions reported holding a party identification, slightly (and insignificantly) below the 78 percent who identified with a party in congruent areas.
[31] Interview, village chief, Saint-Louis Region, February 21, 2013.
[32] Interview, village chief, Fatick Region, May 10, 2013.   [33] Interview, March 1, 2013.

electoral lists. One mayor was quick to clarify that in his position as a local party leader, he had to be careful to put individuals from a large number of lineages and villages on the list or risk being seen as biased or unfair, which would violate local norms.[34] This was described elsewhere as a geographical balancing act across villages or as a social one across lineages.[35] Of course, politicians everywhere desire to stay in power and cite delivering goods as the way to do this. Yet it was only in historically centralized regions that politicians proudly claimed to help those who had not voted for them.

Social institutions working behind the scenes shaped the behavior of local politicians and other rural elites. Mayors often lamented a lack of engagement by the majority of local councilors they served with, but they were also quick to note that they valued protecting the reputations of others in the local public sphere more than voicing their dissatisfaction. "You can sanction the act, but not the person," observed one mayor, explaining that if a chief tried to build something, such as a granary, without passing by the local government council, the council would reject their request to grant the land parcel rather than critiquing the action outright.[36] Decisions to alter one's behavior to protect social relations such as these reflect how local social ties stipulate costs while also reinforcing internalized social institutions, here around the value of preserving social harmony.

For many elites in historically centralized areas, the power of local social institutions was directly related to their understanding that their local government was an interdependent community with a shared fate, reflecting the two mechanisms that animate my theory. The presence of dense social ties and a strong sense of common identity were frequently cited as helping prevent deadlock from local political competition and as enabling the local council to find agreement. For example, one local government secretary told me that local social ties prevented "squabbles" with opposition party members from escalating, or, according to a mayor in Louga, that it kept politicians from conflating personal and political desires.[37] Indeed, political conflict was spoken of as a direct threat to long-standing social relations. Elected officials in historically centralized areas described this as a balancing act rather than a battle: we have to gain party militants to win, said one mayor in Thies Region, but this cannot be allowed to escalate because we "are all kin."[38] These patterns were not only

---

[34] Interview, mayor, Saint-Louis Region, July 22, 2013.
[35] Interview, mayor, Thies Region, July 24, 2013.   [36] Interview, Louga Region, March 5, 2013.
[37] Interviews, community secretary, Fatick Region, May 10, 2013 and mayor, Louga Region, March 6, 2013.
[38] Interview, Kaolack Region, May 31, 2015. In Fouta, in the North, where social hierarchies are considered to be the most rigid in the country, the recognition that historical alliances and factions among the various clans and subclans populating the region was a point of concern for local administrators. Political conflict in Fouta, one councilor explained, "was [previously] always linked to [family/clan] alliances." But holding such grudges was not viable for elected officials such as himself who were tasked with representing all the local government's villages.

evoked by local elites. Even central state officials posted in these areas observed that dense social ties led congruent communities to find "amiable solutions" more often than not.[39]

If the defining feature of local politics in areas that were home to precolonial states is the presence of cross-village social institutions animated by a shared social identity and dense social ties, then their absence goes a long way to explaining the political contention on display in historically acephalous zones. There was little, if any, reference to balancing goods and voice across communities in these areas. In many local governments, partisanship emerged as a vehicle for targeting services, in large part because it offered the most effective means of obtaining a majority or forming a sufficiently large voting block across otherwise disconnected social networks. The comments of two community secretaries illustrate this: "politics is all about who has the people behind him," stated one, while his counterpart to the south had resigned himself to the fact that "politicians are only politicians ... the interest of the party dominates."[40]

Not surprisingly, evaluations of local government performance varied roughly in line with those who considered their relations or allegiances to be in or out of local power. One subprefect in such a zone complained that village chiefs often came to him with questions rather than approaching their elected officials, noting pessimistically that elected officials would need to learn that they would need the local chiefs if they ever wanted to accomplish anything.[41] Respondents frequently noted that councilors in these regions only think of their own village, seeing the village as a more important entity than the local government as a whole, leading elites to orient projects toward their own villages as a result. Chiefs with no family ties to the local government were often simply disengaged, stating that they relied on themselves or villagers who had migrated to Dakar or beyond to help them. Decentralization hasn't improved anything "because the rural community has the power now and if you are not on their side, you will not receive anything, even rice," complained one chief.[42] This further impeded the circulation of information about needs across villages. To take one example, a village chief in Kaffrine Region speculated that while the local state hadn't helped his own village, "perhaps they had in the others," though he remained unsure since he did not speak to many other village chiefs.[43]

Moreover, he continued, "here we are all related" (Interview, Saint-Louis Region, February 12, 2013).

[39] As one subprefect observed, "no one wants to send their relatives to the sub-prefect or the police" (Interview, Kaolack Region, May 3, 2013).
[40] Interviews, Saint-Louis Region, March 11, 2013 and Ziguinchor Region, July 1, 2013.
[41] Interview, Ziguinchor Region, July 5, 2013.   [42] Interview, Kolda Region, April 10, 2013.
[43] Interview, April 23, 2013.

This is not to say that no sense of collective identity emerged during interviews in acephalous areas of the country, merely that collective identities were incongruent with the local state, encompassing only part of the local government's population in these areas. Respondents could clarify these lines of demarcation in great depth: one village chief provided a long list of all of the villages that he perceived as particularly advantaged in the local government by virtue of their shared history of arrival in the zone and ability to mobilize and dominate local politics.[44] Alternatively, minority ethnicities spoke of themselves as victims by virtue of their collective minority status (e.g. one Peulh councilor clarified, "the Wolofs [are more powerful] because the notables are from that ethnicity").[45] In sharp contrast to their counterparts in historically centralized areas, respondents in historically acephalous zones noted splintered social networks within the local state, they did not espouse shared identities and politicians were reported to engage in far more opportunistic behavior.

Politicians in historically centralized areas also referred with great frequency to their social ties when explaining their political choices. This reflects in many ways the circulation of information across social networks. One community secretary described his local government's broad family ties as the "cement" of the community; there are numerous social benefits, he explained, of "old men taking their horse carts from [village A] to [village B] to chat with their friends for the day before heading back home at night."[46] Village chiefs also reported frequent contact with councilors in the area to discuss both personal and political issues. Many village chiefs pointed out how close they lived to the councilors from their village and reported that these same councilors (or those from immediately neighboring villages) informed them of what happened in the local government council.[47] Together, these factors led village chiefs in historically centralized areas to report strong relations with their local governments (e.g. "they are very accessible and they help us all the time"), often speaking of them with pride.[48]

To substantiate the claim that there are subnational differences in the density of elite ties across villages, Figure 4.2 shows difference of means tests from more than 330 local elites interviewed in the 2013 survey, distinguishing between those residing in local governments that were home to a precolonial state, where I expect institutional congruence, and respondents in historically acephalous areas, where I expect incongruence. I asked each respondent whether they were related to other elites in their local government as well as a short list of central state officials. I distinguish between *family* and *friendship* ties for local elites, with family ties measuring both immediate (parents, in-laws, siblings,

---

[44] Interview, village chief, Kolda Region, April 6, 2013.
[45] Interview, Saint-Louis Region, March 19, 2013.
[46] Interview, Louga Department, February 17, 2016.
[47] Interview, village chief, Thies Region, May 14, 2013.
[48] Interview, village chief, Louga Region, March 7, 2013.

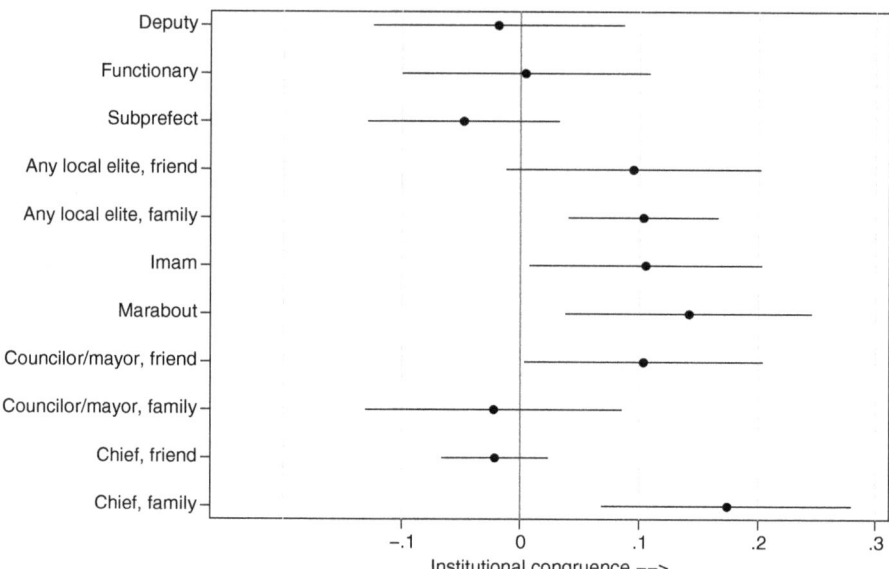

FIGURE 4.2 Difference in means in elite social ties

uncles, first cousins) as well as extended (second cousins, '*la grande famille*') family relations. Respondents in centralized areas are significantly more likely to report at least one family tie to another elite (chief, elected official, imam, or marabout) in their local government and, at the 10 percent significance level, to report a friendship tie with another elite as well. These relations are broken down by type of elite.[49] In general, respondents in congruent local governments have more social ties with other local elites, though there is no difference in having a family tie with at least one elected official or considering a village chief to be a friend.

I adopt a more liberal definition for relations to central state elites to include reported relations of neighbors (e.g. someone from the village who now works in Dakar) or those that an individual reports having worked with in the past. This is both because the types of social ties are repeatedly invoked by respondents as meaningful connections to the center and because they are simply more common. Only eleven respondents, or 3 percent of my total sample, reported a family connection to their deputy. The data suggest that there is neither a meaningful difference in reported connections with central government bureaucrats (*functionaries*), *deputies* in the National Assembly nor the local

---

[49] Relationship types for Imams and Marabouts are pooled for brevity, but the result holds when distinguishing between friend and family, with the exception of friendship ties with imams, where there is no significant difference.

subprefect. This suggests that historical experiences with precolonial centralization have not predisposed some areas of the country to systematically have better social conduits to central state favoritism.

Exceptions to the Theory

Collectively, this evidence accords with my theory. Respondents in historically centralized areas speak of their local governments as encompassing a meaningful community (cueing the identity mechanism) that shapes local leaders' behavior by virtue of their dense social ties (cueing the network mechanism). Some or all of these parts break down in historically acephalous areas.

Though my theory is structural, it is not deterministic and the analysis above presents dominant, but not uniform responses. Historically acephalous areas do see forms of cooperation, with local elites making concessions to each other. One mayor in Kedougou Region explained at length the efforts he had taken to ease tensions with vocal critics in his local government's capital village, intimating the political and social costs he would incur if he violated the delicate balance he was trying to establish with them.[50] Similarly, local governments marked by institutional congruence should not lead us to ignore cases where political disagreement does arise. Even in areas where local governance was broadly seen as positive, these narratives were not always universally voiced and non-confirming opinions are heard across the country. A minority of village chiefs in congruent areas complained of not receiving enough from their local government. What sets these complaints apart from those voiced in areas of incongruence is that inequality claims in historically centralized areas were predominately made on an ad hoc basis and were voiced by exactly those the theory would predict would have the least claim on local government resources: those with weak ties to dominant local political narratives, such as in-migrants or casted individuals.

In only a few cases did this appear to be actually driven by neglect on the part of the local state, in contrast to historically acephalous areas where having received nothing from the state was more common. For example, one village chief in Podor Department argued that his local government did not treat his village fairly. The chief, whose family was Wolof and had migrated to the area in the late 1880s, explained that his village which had only become officially recognized fifty years before and, though it had received a health hut and a primary school, an ongoing dispute over land within the community led him to conclude that although the idea of local governance was good, his local government "took sides too often." "Decentralization is a bad system," another village chief in Fatick with no social ties to his neighbors said, "because it favors the politics or the strongest of those with family

---

[50] Interview, April 5, 2013.

relations in the council."⁵¹ In both cases, these chiefs felt excluded because they were "outsiders" whose claims were taken less seriously because of this status (despite the fact that both villages had been founded prior to Senegal gaining independence). Though neither village could claim that they had never received goods from their local council, they felt less included in an abstract, representative sense because their own settlement in the area did not fit into the dominant historical narrative of descent from the precolonial state. This reflects the central role of social network ties to the theory; under institutional congruence, local elites are more broadly representative, but the limits of this may be found at the network's edges.

In villages with ties to dominant social networks, but who had not received much from their local government, respondents were much more likely to justify this inaction. Noting that his local government had not done anything for his village, one chief was quick to defend that "they don't interfere either. If I go there with a problem they are patient towards me and are very attentive."⁵² Other chiefs speculated that they might get more if they had a councilor in their village, but that they never get one because their villages are too small to get someone a place on the party lists⁵³ or, more simply, that their villages have been diminished in size and statute and hence "we aren't considered much anymore."⁵⁴ Excuse making such as this is a sharp contrast to chiefs in equally small villages in acephalous areas, who never made such justifications for why they were relatively (at least in their view) underserved. Moreover, such complaints – even though at times seemingly warranted – are far rarer in the territories of precolonial kingdoms. Much more common are responses such as one chief's that "the collective work is better" under democratic decentralization, directly calling on a sense of a common mission that was noticeably absent elsewhere in the country.⁵⁵

THE MEDIATING EFFECTS OF SOCIAL SHOCKS

I have argued that distinct narratives of local political life are heard across rural Senegal, with a central cleavage being whether or not local elites view their local government as congruent with meaningful, cross-village social institutions. When they do, they invoke both a shared category – a social identity rooted in the precolonial past – and a dense network of social relations across villages. Together, these two mechanisms alter elite preferences and constrain elite

---

⁵¹ Interview, village chief, May 7, 2013.
⁵² Interview, village chief, Louga Region, March 7, 2013.
⁵³ Interview, village chief, Thies Region, May 16, 2013.
⁵⁴ Interview, village chief, Thies Region, May 15, 2013. In this case, the village chief claimed that the village had been much respected in the past and that it dated back to the time of Cayor Empire, but the village's population had dwindled over the past half-century.
⁵⁵ Interview, village chief, Fatick Region, May 7, 2013.

behavior by imbuing elites with more prosocial preferences to the group. As introduced in Chapter 2, however, a series of major social shocks may have altered the composition of local elites and their social networks during the colonial and postcolonial periods. Could the politics of institutional congruence presented above obscure or be altered by these intervening forces? The sampling design of my survey takes into account two of the three factors introduced in Chapter 2: in-migration and religious conversion.[56] I address each in turn.

In-Migration

Attentive to demographic changes over the past century, I sampled local governments in areas that both had and had not seen substantial in-migration. As described above, interviews in historically acephalous zones suggest political narratives of social division; these tendencies are amplified in acephalous zones that had seen substantial in-migration over the past century. When in-migrants create new villages, they also create new claims to local social and political space that often parallel but only rarely integrate with those of the host population, effectively proliferating the social networks and identities present in a locality.

In general, historically acephalous areas that had seen in-migration displayed some of the most intense political competition and a bimodal distribution of attitudes toward the local government: the local council was representative and redistributive for those with ties to the current power-holders or it was biased and negligent for those without such connections. Though the nature of social cleavages varied – at times understood locally as falling along the lines of ethnicity, caste, autochthony, or partisanship – politics was decidedly zero-sum. Local politics, one subprefect in such a region described, is a "continual battle. Everyone is involved in the political terrain and they all want to occupy it."[57] Indeed, the majority of interviewees in regions marked by substantial in-migration noted severe political blockage in the local council, preventing projects from being administered, taxes from being raised, and allowing mayors to flagrantly embezzle local funds.

One consequence was that political competition often fell along lines of how perceived rights to community resources were ordered following in-migration. In one local government in Tambacounda Region, twenty out of thirty-six councilors were elected from the capital village, the local government's second largest village and among its youngest, having been founded by migrants along the colonial-era railway. The local government's largest village was far older and had a long-standing rivalry with the capital over the latter's perceived

---

[56] The third, French colonial policies, is assumed to have a constant effect across survey zones given that no sampling was done in the four communes or other areas that obtained urban status in the colonial period. The impact of exposure to the colonial state is explored in depth in Chapter 7.
[57] Interview, Kaffrine Region, April 26, 2013.

favoritism by the colonial state. This simmering conflict had been inflamed during the 2009 local elections when the mayor had allegedly changed the local electoral lists after party officials had signed off on it. Because the mayor submitted an altered copy to the subprefect, a large number of candidates from the older, larger village had been removed in favor of those from the mayor's own native village, the local government capital. The cascading political scandals created by his actions substantiate my contention that such communities lack cross-village norms of conflict avoidance. Here, the mayor was able to pursue his village's political interests at the expense of broader social relations in a way that is far more difficult in historically centralized areas.

Arguably the most pernicious outcome for long-run development in historically acephalous areas that had seen substantial in-migration was disengagement from the state altogether. While elsewhere in the country many chiefs complained that all they had received from their local government was "one pen and one notebook" per child prior to the start of the school year or the occasional sack of rice, in some local governments numerous non-autochthonous village chiefs reported having been cut out of even these most basic deliveries. "The rural community is useless for us," one village chief concluded.[58] These communities were also home to the only villages where multiple village chiefs stated that they had never met their mayor: "we only know the name" said one chief in Tambacounda.[59]

Interviewees in historically centralized areas of the country indicated that in-migration had left a more muted impact on local political discourse. I illustrate this with evidence from the former kingdom of Saloum. Although not the only precolonial state to see in-migration, Saloum arguably saw the most rapid influx of migrants in the first decades of colonialism via the *navetanes*, or seasonal migrant workers coming from the West African interior. While originally arriving as temporary migrant workers during the peanut harvest, many migrants eventually settled in the area permanently.[60] As discussed in Chapter 2, in-migrants to the Saloum are considered to have been integrated into existing social structures, in line with long-standing practices of fictive kinship in the region.[61] This accords with my own interviews. Despite the Saloum's ethnic diversity, ethnicity was only mentioned by one village chief as a meaningful cleavage in the region. This is surprising given the fact that ethnic fractionalization (measured through a Herfindahl index) in the Saloum ranged between the high 30s and the 50s, reflecting more ethnic diversity than the national average of 63.8.[62] Because migrants were often integrated into existing villages, few villages in the zone are ethnically homogenous, which, as

---

[58] Interview, Tambacounda Region, March 28, 2013.
[59] Interview, village chief, Tambacounda Region, March 26, 2013.
[60] David (1980, 34, 59–61, 108).   [61] As argued by Pélissier (1966).
[62] Interview, village chief, Kaolack Region, May 2, 2013. One other chief did make a veiled ethnic comment, noting that no one in the community had the economic means to help out his village in

one subprefect posted to the region observed, meant that any attempts to mobilize ethnic or caste tensions would be hard-pressed to find support.[63]

Still, it must be acknowledged that interviewees in historically centralized areas that had seen in-migration were more likely to report disharmony in local political life than those that had not. But while social and political tensions do appear to be heightened in these zones, social institutions were nonetheless involved to regulate the behavior of autochthons and in-migrants alike. Tensions in these zones were almost always qualified as being resolved in the end without escalating competition among villages. "They can have a big fight," one village chief observed of the local councilors in his diverse local government in the Saloum, "but two days later you see them together again."[64]

While in-migration may attenuate the core properties of institutional congruence, therefore, it does not easily overturn these dynamics provided that dominant social institutions survived the colonial era. Institutional congruence can be eroded when the theory's twin mechanisms weaken sufficiently to render social institutions incongruent with the boundaries of the local state, however. Take one subprefect's characterization of local political life in the territory of the precolonial state of Boundou, which had seen significant depopulation in the late 1800s. The kingdom's territory had over time seen significant new settlement, most notably from many in-migrants from present-day Guinea. This challenged the ability of Boundou's remaining descendants to claim the political power they believed themselves entitled to. Many of these elites were indignant that local government projects went to the newer migrant villages, a complaint voiced with particular acuity toward those of Guinean-descent, despite the fact that they were co-ethnics and that many of the villages in question were much larger and had clear objective need. The old elites whose grandparents had lived under the Boundou were committed to the idea that they deserve priority by virtue of their historical claims in the region. The result, the local subprefect bemoaned, was that sociological factors such as village age and caste became bound up in understandings of deservingness, creating divisive politics that pervaded all local development initiatives.[65] Despite the persistence of a shared identity rooted in the precolonial past as well as tight social networks among Boundou's descendants, in-migration had diluted the density of these identities and networks, meaning that the local state was not imbued with the sense of collective purpose that defines congruent areas.

---

times of need: "the Wolofs, they don't help anyone," he concluded (Interview, village chief, Kaolack Region, April 29, 2013).
[63] Interview, Kaolack Region, May 3, 2013.
[64] Interview, village chief, Kaolack Region, April 30, 2013.
[65] Interview, Tambacounda Region, March 28, 2013.

Religious Conversion

If in-migration risks proliferating group identities and social networks, what happens when the defining base of a group identity fundamentally changes? This is a possible outcome of mass religious conversion. Indeed, the early 1900s saw widespread conversion following the expansion of Sufi Muslim brotherhoods, most notably with the rise of the Mouride or Tidjane Brotherhoods, and far less frequently, with the arrival of Catholic missionaries. Yet even in the face of these new forms of religious practice, my interviews and survey data do not suggest that conversion fundamentally altered social ties or replaced locally hegemonic identities. In contrast, in many areas, social networks and shared identities transcended religious identities, suggesting that religious conversion did not fundamentally upset or alter local cross-village social institutions. One Catholic mayor in a majority Muslim local government in Thies spoke openly of his status as a religious minority. "At first," he recounted, "I had to work to make inroads with the local marabouts, but now we attend each other's religious festivals. We have the same population, their followers are my constituency, and we both work for local development."[66]

There is one notable situation that generates an exception. In communities where powerful religious guides become actively involved in local politics, either by running for office themselves or by putting in place candidates who are widely understood to be their proxies, the establishment of a distinct form of political hierarchy despite ostensibly competitive elections obviates the ability of social institutions to coordinate local action because the religious guide himself dictates (or attempts to dictate) local governance. This decidedly less democratic dynamic is illustrated in two local communities surveyed in 2013.[67]

In Louga Region's Darou Mousty Arrondissement, four out of seven rural communities are run by powerful maraboutic families that descend from Cheikh Amadou Bemba, the founder and spiritual leader of the Mouride Brotherhood. Since the capital villages of all of these communities were founded by Bemba's descendants during the colonial era, these families have begun claiming their "right" to run their local governments. I surveyed one of these local governments where a prominent marabout had run for and been elected mayor in 2002. "As mayor, I am more respected before the Senegalese administration than if I was just a marabout" he explained, "so I decided that things would go better here if I was mayor as well." He went on to describe his *talibes*, or religious followers, as his political base (they "sweep the way for me"), noting that his dual mandates uniquely positioned him to provide things

---

[66] Interview, May 29, 2013.
[67] Arguably the best case of this would be the Mouride's holy city of Touba, which is legally a rural local government despite having the population of a large-sized city and being run by religious leaders.

to the community.[68] To a large degree, his statement is correct. The local government had seen significant improvements in the time since he took office.[69] While only two villages had potable water in 2002, for example, 95 percent had it by 2013.

Though in the territory of Cayor, in this case, the presence of a religious hierarchy in local governance circumvented preexisting social ties as the marabout's religious, social, and now political authority subjected the local government less to shared social institutions than to the marabout-mayor's own vision. To local residents, this was seen as less autocratic in practice than it may first appear to many readers. More than 95 percent of local government citizens adhered to the marabout and described this as a natural elision of authority. Still, not everyone approved. The only village chief interviewed in the local government who was not the mayor's follower, for example, claimed that Peulh villages such as his own were left to themselves even though they had inhabited the area long before the arrival of the Mourides.[70]

For followers however, the local government was doing good work. One councilor defined himself as a "councilor of the marabout," having been unknowingly enrolled on the electoral lists by the marabout.[71] Indeed, 38 percent of councilors on the 2002–2009 council and 22 percent in 2009–2014 were from the chef-lieu, which, home to only 11 percent of the commune's population, was the marabout's religious base. In such cases, therefore, social institutions do little to shape local governance because alternative structures dominate.

Elsewhere, prominent religious leaders had less uniform adherence, generating what we might characterize as a distinct form of institutional incongruence. I illustrate this with a local government near the Gambian border whose capital village was also home to an influential Mouride marabout. The chef-lieu had been founded around the Second World War by a descendant of the Mbacke family in Touba, much later than the rest of the villages in the area who largely dated their foundation to the era of the precolonial state of Rip. Approximately 60 percent of the population were followers of the Tidjane Brotherhood, meaning that the marabout's followers – both local converts as well as those who had in-migrated with his grandfather – were concentrated in the local government capital village.

As in the first example, the marabout's influence on local politics was striking. The marabout regularly made party electoral lists himself, resulting

---

[68] Interview, mayor, Louga Region, March 5, 2013.
[69] The ability of the mayor to extract projects from the central government is not surprising given the long-standing relationship between the central state and the brotherhood. The area had long been favored; the chef-lieu – only founded in 1948 – received a borehole in 1960 and a school two years later. A health post arrived much later in 1999 and all three of Senegal's presidents had visited the village as of 2003.
[70] Interview, village chief, Louga Region, March 4, 2013.
[71] Interview, councilor, Louga Region, March 4, 2013.

in the local government capital receiving a disproportionate number of council seats. "The autonomy of the [council's] decisions is not always assured, especially in the management of community goods," a 2003 planning document notes, and the mayor "fails to make the distinction between himself as *talibe* and President [mayor]." This was no longer the case in 2013, when the previous mayor, who had served two terms, had been replaced with a more dynamic individual with a background in local development. The new mayor claimed a good working relationship with the marabout, but was not personally a follower, citing his independence as a positive feature in his ability to make improvements in the local government.[72] Yet the capital village retained a disproportionate number of councilors (35 percent of the total compared to a population share of 18 percent) and it remained unusually well-doted in public goods.[73]

This "notable favoritism" was commented on at length. One chief concluded that he could not appreciate decentralization because "we have the power of the marabout and this is a defeat for [the mayor]." Noting that many villagers were having trouble getting land titles delivered by the local government, he alleged that when the marabout asked on behalf of a follower, the process went fast, while for other villagers it remained painfully slow.[74] These same facts were evoked positively by those with ties to the marabout, one village chief who was a *talibe* and extended family member noted that "it is the marabout who matters here," before adding negatively "even if the mayor is trying to change that."[75]

Both cases illustrate how the presence of a prominent marabout in a community can undermine the properties of institutional congruence when it prioritizes a distinct social identity and social network – adherence to the marabout. Still, this is the exception. The vast majority of local governments surveyed were Sufi-dominated and many were home to villages with influential religious leaders, yet congruence remained possible. What matters is whether those leaders are able to dominate the local government, at which point we see the influence of local social institutions inherited from the precolonial past undermined.

ELITE ASSESSMENTS OF LOCAL GOVERNMENT PERFORMANCE

Taken together, the qualitative data presented above indicate that the politics of representation and redistribution in local governments is a function of (a) whether a local government's boundaries are congruent with cross-village

---

[72] Interview, mayor, Kaolack Region, April 30, 2013.
[73] The marabout, a 2011 planning document notes, "retains a stranglehold" on the management of the chef-lieu's borehole, unlike the other two which are managed by a users' association.
[74] Interview, village chief, Kaolack Region, April 29, 2013.
[75] Interview, village chief, Kaolack Region, April 29, 2013.

social institutions inherited from the precolonial past and, subsequently, (b) whether or not the area saw a diversification of social identities and networks due to in-migration in the colonial or postcolonial period. In the last section of this chapter, I turn to quantifiable components of the 2013 survey, using questions asked of all respondents to evaluate these patterns more systematically. I break respondents into three categories: first, those residing in local governments in historically centralized areas, which I expect to display properties of institutional congruence; second, those residing in historically acephalous areas where I expect incongruence; and finally those where in-migration generated or amplified incongruence.[76]

Perceptions of Government Performance

I begin by evaluating individual perceptions of local government performance. Figure 4.3 shows the distribution of responses to two sets of questions designed to capture evaluations of the performance of the current local council. The histogram represents responses to the question, "in your opinion, is the local government here in [*local government name*] going in the right or the wrong direction?" The kernel density line laid over the histogram reflects an aggregated score of responses to a series of questions asking respondents to evaluate their local government's efforts in specific issue areas, including primary education, health, clean water, bringing in new projects, finding financing, responding to citizen demands, facilitating participation in local government issues, and being equitable. For both, responses are more favorable as one moves to the left and they are broadly consistent across questions, though respondents in congruent local governments are more critical of their local governments when asked about specific issue areas.

Collectively, respondents are cautiously encouraging their local governments, with very few respondents reporting that the government is doing "very good" or going "completely in the right direction." Support is strongest in areas of high congruence, where 70 percent of respondents evaluate their local government positively. In contrast, attitudes are more bimodal in incongruent areas that have seen significant in-migration, following the patterns in the qualitative data. Here, 53 percent of respondents are positive while nearly 47 percent are negative. Areas of low congruence are slightly more even, but nearly 40 percent of respondents still view their local government's performance poorly. Cumulatively, this shows that there is a 10–20 percent increase in negative evaluations in local governments that do not meet my definition of institutional congruence.

---

[76] In view of the qualitative evidence and the relatively small number of communities interviewed that were historically centralized but saw significant in-migration, I keep all congruent communities in one group, though my results do not change if I remove those that saw substantial in-migration.

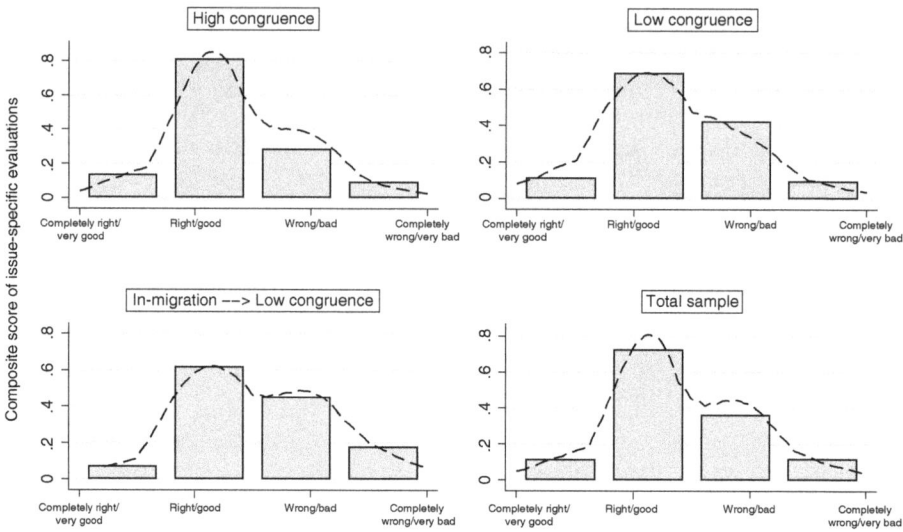

FIGURE 4.3 Evaluations of local government performance

Of course, social desirability bias or respondents who are hesitant to critique friends and family members could drive the positive direction of evaluations. Yet this appears to not be the case. The upward bias in positive evaluations by family members is much stronger in areas of low congruence, where the correlation between having a family member in elected office and a positive evaluation is 0.181, compared to 0.023 for areas of high congruence, suggesting that in the latter case evaluations are less affected by social relations. I display this visually in Figure 4.4, which reproduces the bar charts in Figure 4.3, but distinguishes between responses by those with elected family members in their local government (dark gray) and those without (light gray). This means that any gap between dark and light gray bars represents bias for or against the local state by family members.

In general, family members are more likely to report that their local government is going in the "right" direction. This bump is smaller in areas of high congruence compared to incongruent local governments, however, and it is only in areas characterized by low congruence that family members are more likely to say that things are going "completely right." While family members are generally more positive, difference of means tests suggest that it is only in cases of low congruence that family members are statistically more likely to report a positive opinion.[77] To the extent that the histograms in Figure 4.3 are

---

[77] On a four-point scale, the average score in areas of high congruence is 2.72 and 2.75 for those with and without family ties. In areas of low congruence, there is a significant difference at the 5 percent level between those with family connections on the local council and those without

Elite Assessments of Local Government Performance   121

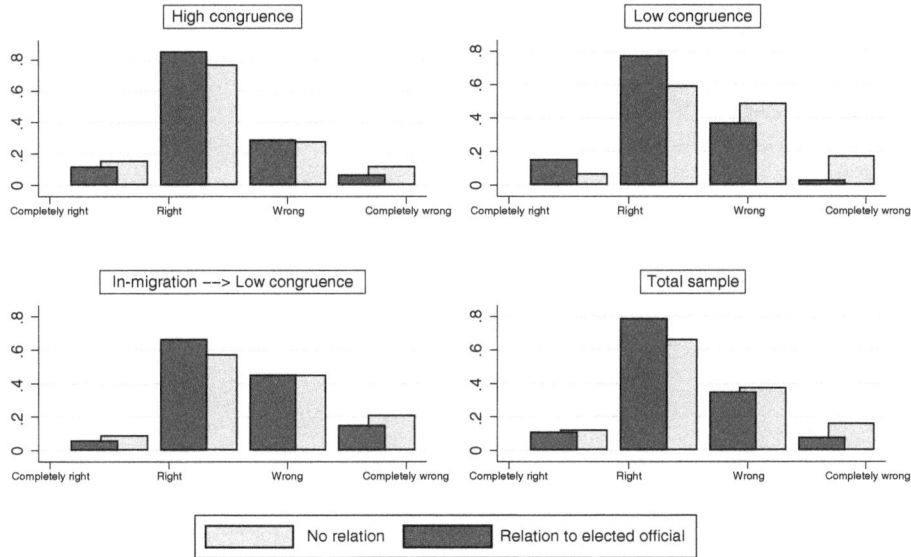

FIGURE 4.4 Evaluations of local government performance by family relation

driven, at least in part, by a desire to positively evaluate personal relatives or friends, this bias is primarily found in incongruent local governments, further reinforcing the story emerging out of qualitative data that suggests strong in- and out-group dynamics in such communities.

Perceptions of Government Responsibilities

The quantitative data also suggest that respondents have distinct conceptualizations of the local state's obligations vis-à-vis the citizenry.[78] I asked respondents to tell me what they thought the three central responsibilities of their local government were, coding responses into one of five categories. Some respondents discussed *universalistic* obligations: local government should provide universalistic benefits or policies for the entire community. For example, responses that the local government should "expand the healthcare network in the local government" or "provide security" fall into this category because they are indicative of an obligation to provide broad coverage. Conversely, an answer

---

with averages of 2.74 and 2.47, respectively. These numbers are 2.46 and 2.45 for cases of in-migration, also insignificant.

[78] Note that the average level of education for elected officials, often cited in Dakar as an important factor in local government performance, does not significantly vary between congruent and incongruent zones, nor are respondents more or less likely to report having received any kind of training on local governance from the central state or donors.

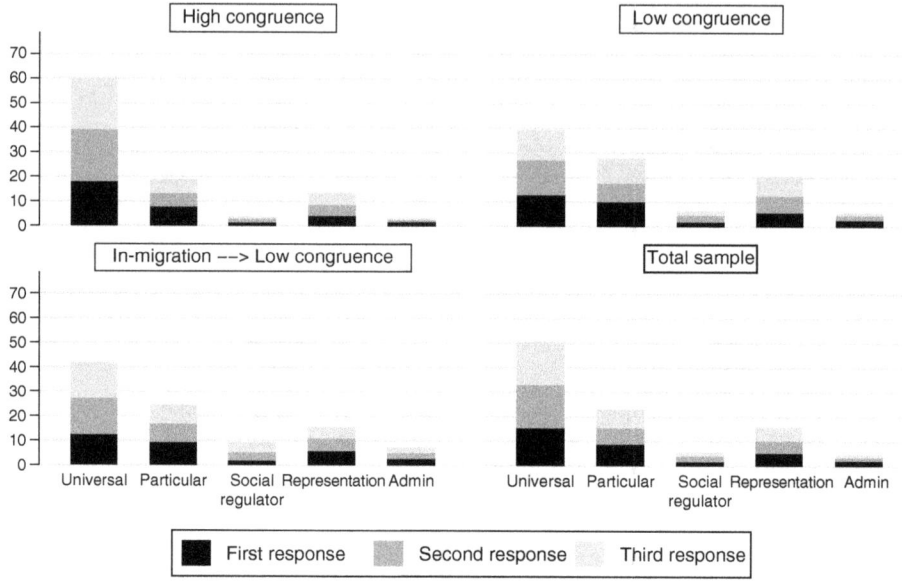

FIGURE 4.5 Local government responsibilities (% responses)

is *particularistic* if the answer implies that the local government should do something targeted to the respondent, for example, to "build a health hut in the village" or provide fertilizer, food relief, or other individualistic benefits. Third, some respondents indicated that the local government should solve problems between community members or otherwise act as a *social regulator*. It was also often suggested that local governments had a responsibility of *representation*. These answers suggested that the local council should represent the population's interests to the central state and/or donors and to respond to their desires in a general sense (i.e. "listen to the population"). Finally, some respondents listed *administrative* responsibilities, such as providing *état-civil* papers and collecting local taxes.

These responses are visualized in Figure 4.5. Most respondents invoke universalistic roles, representing 50 percent of total answers across all three questions. Still, respondents in high-congruence local governments list universalistic obligations in more than 60 percent of their answers, compared to roughly 40 percent in incongruent local governments, a 20 percent difference. In areas of low congruence, by contrast, respondents were more likely to note particularistic benefits, though here the difference is less sharp at only 5–10 percentage points. Interestingly, 10 percent of answers in areas of low congruence following in-migration indicated that local governments should play a role as a social regulator, double the rate at which respondents indicated this category elsewhere.

Perceptions of Equality

I thirdly evaluate whether or not perceptions of equality in treatment by the local government expressed in interviews can be systematically explained by the mechanisms highlighted in my theory. Table 4.2 reports odds ratios for a series of logit models that takes as the dependent variable a measure of whether or not a respondent made a reference to unequal treatment by their local government during the course of the interview. This is coded zero (no allegations of unequal treatment by the local government) or one (one or more comments that there is targeted inequality). Simply stating that the respondent's village had not received anything was insufficient to be coded as an inequality claim, rather there had to be a specific statement that the local council played favorites, either generically or by naming which villages or communities were treated better or worse by the local government. Models include a series of controls for the logged population size of the respondent's village, whether the respondent reported having received any training about local governance or development, their age, their reported meeting attendance during the previous year, and dummy variables if a respondent was a village chief or, similarly, a councilor.[79]

The results support the general contention that perceptions of inequality are impacted by network ties and the availability of different forms of identities in the local government. Being a co-partisan or co-ethnic as well as having family ties to other elites or living in a village with a number of councilors all reduce the likelihood that a respondent made an allegation of inequality. Having some form of a social tie to other elites therefore decreases the probability that a respondent views the local government as treating citizens unequally. Model 5 reports that in-migrants are more likely to allege bias. Finally, in line with my central theoretical predictions, respondents in congruent local governments, proxied here by exposure to precolonial statehood, are less likely to find their local governments unequal in Model 6, one of the few effects that remains significant in a pooled model (Model 7).

Assessing the Role of Local Government Resources

I conclude with a brief discussion of the possibility that the differences I have identified are driven by variable levels of local government resources. Respondent evaluations of their local governments may be influenced by the ability of their local elected officials to finance local projects, be it through donors, central government transfers, or local taxation. In reality, most donor financing is allocated to ministries or is channeled to local governments via state-sponsored programs; few local governments have individual relationships

---

[79] Neither the average number of mandates that councilors have served (with a mean of 1.8) nor the average number of local council meetings in the previous year (five to six) significantly varies by precolonial political geography.

TABLE 4.2 Odds ratios of perceived inequality in the local council

	(1)	(2)	(3)	(4)	(5)	(6)	(7)
Elite Family Ties	0.746* (0.131)						0.941 (0.178)
Co-ethnic		0.556** (0.126)					0.895 (0.274)
Co-partisan			0.506** (0.148)				0.481** (0.173)
# Councilors				0.934* (0.035)			0.949 (0.036)
In-Migrant					1.478** (0.222)		1.165 (0.293)
Institutional Congruence						0.540** (0.151)	0.441** (0.143)
Constant	6.57 (7.82)	7.574 (9.216)	12.61 (16.37)	3.026 (3.994)	3.042 (3.833)	7.171 (8.268)	8.77 (14.98)
Controls	Y	Y	Y	Y	Y	Y	Y
Pseudo-R^2	0.157	0.159	0.165	0.156	0.166	0.164	0.198
N	332	332	332	302	332	332	302

* $p < 0.1$, ** $p < 0.05$. Results from logit models with robust, clustered standard errors by local government in parentheses. Control variables include logged population of respondent village, reported rural council meeting attendance in previous year, whether or not the respondent reported having received any training sessions about their role in the rural council and/or local development, their age, and dummy variables for councilors and village chiefs.

with donors, though some have established sister-city relationships with cities in France or Belgium. Local governments in historically stateless areas are actually more likely to report donor activity, with an average of 3.2 versus 2.4 active NGOs for congruent local governments, though the presence of bilateral partners (such as USAID) is comparable.[80] The local state relies most heavily on central government transfers, the most important of which is the *Fonds de Dotation de la Decentralisation* (FDD).[81] Average transfers between 2009 and 2012 are higher in historically centralized areas, at $23,927 versus $22,773, but the bias is in the opposite direction in per capita terms at $2.18 per capita in historically acephalous areas versus $1.59 in historically centralized areas.[82] I test the influence of average FDD transfers more robustly in the quantitative dataset presented in the next chapter.

Alternatively, if local governments that fall in the footprints of precolonial states are more efficient at collecting local taxes, respondents may be more enthusiastic about the local state as a function of nascent state-society bargains. Although the role of taxation has played a prominent role in studies of service delivery elsewhere in the world, a generally low tax incidence and a lack of publicly available data have limited investigations into this question in sub-Saharan Africa. National data on local tax revenue are not available, but informal data collected from local government secretaries suggest that areas of high congruence are more likely to collect local taxes, notably, the rural tax (*la taxe rurale*), which is set at about $2 per resident, with exemptions for the elderly, children under fourteen, women with more than eight children, active military service or disability. Historically centralized areas report an average collection rate of 56.3 percent of their tax rolls compared to only 16 percent elsewhere. In the survey data, there is no clear association between whether or not a village chief reports raising taxes and receiving goods, nor is there an association between rural communities that have higher tax collection rates and those that do not in terms of goods delivery. Certainly, if fully collected, the rural tax would facilitate government functioning. But even a 100 percent collection rate would only amount to around $4,000 in a medium-sized local government, far from enough to engage in significant development initiatives, such as the visible infrastructure projects I measure in the next chapter.

One way around the issue of missing fiscal data is to examine reported payments by citizens. I proxy compliance with tax payments by turning to data from Rounds 4 and 6 of the Afrobarometer which both asked respondents a

---

[80] A significant part of the higher NGO activity in uncentralized areas is driven by the Casamance, but there remains a significant difference if Ziguinchor Region is excluded, bringing the average number of NGOs in uncentralized areas to 2.9.

[81] Thirty-six percent of chiefs surveyed in historically centralized areas were familiar with the main central government transfers of the FDD and FECL compared to 23 percent elsewhere; both significantly different at the 0.05 level.

[82] Both are significant at $p < 0.01$.

series of questions about taxation. While respondents in local governments that fall within the territory of a precolonial state are more likely to report paying the rural tax at 64 versus 50 percent, attitudes about the legitimacy of taxation do not differ. Respondents in historically centralized areas are no more likely to report that a good citizen should pay taxes and that it was wrong to not pay taxes or to report that they had refused to pay taxes in the past year. This would suggest that while tax collection does appear to be higher in congruent local governments, this does not reflect differences in underlying attitudes about the legitimacy of tax collection on the part of the state.

In contrast, the ability of congruent local governments to raise more taxes more likely reflects their improved capacity to work with chiefs. Eighty-seven percent of chiefs in historically centralized areas report collecting the rural tax as opposed to only 47 percent elsewhere in the country. That this is a function of local government initiative is reflected in the fact that 42 percent of chiefs in historically centralized areas reported discussing collecting taxes with an elected official in the past year as opposed to an average of 22 percent elsewhere, further demonstrating that historically centralized areas see heightened informational flows between elites.

CONCLUSION

This chapter presented data from an original survey to identify distinct differences in how local elites describe their political worlds between areas of the country where I expect institutional congruence and those where I expect incongruence. In so doing, the chapter establishes an empirical baseline for my argument: respondents in areas of institutional congruence view democratic decentralization more favorably and are disproportionately more likely to cite the responsiveness and benefits of contact with their local governments as the reasons they appreciate the reforms. They also evaluate the work of their local government councils more positively, they view their local governments as responsible for delivering universalistic benefits, and they are less likely to upwardly bias their evaluations when they are related to elected officials.

This chapter has stressed the importance of *how* individuals talk about and conceptualize their local governments. The qualitative evidence supports the argument that experiences with local governance are influenced by shared narratives about a community's past. Though narratives of political life are distinctly *local*, taking a comparative lens across local governments allows me to identify *types* despite the inherent specificity at play in each local government. At base, debates about local belonging and who has the right to speak for the community (and *what* community) remain a key defining feature in rural political dynamics. Who feels represented and who gains access to social services are contingent on how these claims structurally manifest themselves among local elites. Certainly, this chapter has confirmed the expectations of many that distributional politics in rural Africa are informed by

Conclusion

ethnic, partisan, and other ascriptive political identities, but at best this explains only *some* cases. Elsewhere, the structural overlap between formal and informal social institutions aligns to produce what are seen as fairer and more responsive local administrations. Rather than dismissing local politics as inherently detrimental to decentralization reforms, therefore, I argue that we must look them squarely in the face or risk misunderstanding how local political practice generates new forms of inequality and exclusion.[83] How these different forms of local politics map onto actual delivery of public goods is explored in the next chapter.

---

[83] Echoing Alvergne and Latouche (2010, 467).

5

Delivering Schools and Clinics in Rural Senegal

Local elites across rural Senegal paint starkly different pictures of their experiences with local governance, but these narratives may reflect perceived but not actual bias. My theory, supported by the original survey data introduced in the preceding chapter, suggests that precolonial political legacies shape the nature of local governance by virtue of the social institutions these states left behind. This generates the predication that areas home to precolonial states, where I expect institutional congruence, should exhibit broader redistributive tendencies across the population than areas that were historically stateless.

In this chapter, I test this proposition by looking at the actual placement of two of the most consequential public goods for individual well-being under local government authority: the construction of new clinics and new primary schools. I find that common expectations from the literature, which has disproportionately focused on questions of ethnic favoritism and electoral politics, cannot explain patterns in the delivery of these public goods. Rather, the evidence provides support for the central argument of this book: the contemporary politics of public goods delivery in rural Senegal vary subnationally following the contours of precolonial political geography. In areas that were home to centralized polities in 1880, I find consistent evidence that local governments are delivering core investments to more villages than their counterparts in areas that were acephalous, or which lacked hierarchical governance on the eve of colonization.

This finding contributes to a growing body of evidence that regions home to Africa's precolonial states have, on average, better development outcomes.[1] Here, I shift focus to examine how different historical experiences create distinct forms of distributive politics at the local level today. I argue that the key empirical

---

[1] For example, Michalopoulos and Papaioannou (2015).

question is not about overall levels of access or how many services are built, but rather how local governments allocate public goods across the population. In order to test my expectation that local governments defined by institutional congruence are delivering public goods *differently* than other parts of the country, this chapter employs an original, georeferenced dataset of village-level basic primary education infrastructure between 2002 and 2012 and of basic health infrastructure between 2009 and 2012. The dataset covers all of Senegal's approximately 14,300 rural villages allowing me to measure which villages gain access to these new public services in the 2000s and which do not, while controlling for a range of local and structural factors. The dataset was assembled by combining multiple sources, including ministry-level data on school and clinic locations and original coding of the location of precolonial states, first introduced in Chapter 2. This process is discussed in detail below.

I begin by reviewing dominant theoretical expectations of redistributive politics in developing countries before moving on to detail the nature of local public goods delivery in rural Senegal. A series of empirical tests demonstrate that historical patterns of precolonial statehood offer the most leverage in explaining patterns of local public goods placement at the village level in Senegal between 2002 and 2012. I then turn to location-allocation models to evaluate the comparative efficiency of school and clinic placement and to create a metric for assessing a development-maximizing ideal point in potential social service locations. Finally, placebo tests demonstrate that this pattern does not hold for services delivered by the central government. Cumulatively, these findings suggest that in an era of rapid expansion of basic public services, the political distribution of public goods by Senegal's rural councils is spatially contingent on deeply embedded historical structures, even when taking into account similar objective needs. Cumulatively, the chapter provides further evidence for my claim that the effect of precolonial centralization is driven by decidedly ongoing political dynamics.

EXPLAINING ACCESS TO BASIC SERVICES IN SENEGAL'S COUNTRYSIDE

This chapter tests the central empirical predication of my theory: redistributive politics are a function of the relative degree of overlap between informal social institutions and the formal institutional boundaries of the local state. I look to the construction of primary school and basic health infrastructure in the 2000s to evaluate this claim. These sectors are critical for long-run socioeconomic development, but they function in the shorter term as an unparalleled source of patronage for local politicians. As in much of sub-Saharan Africa, governments still struggle to deliver a set of basic social services to citizens, meaning that community-targeted and community-specific physical infrastructure of this nature represents the most significant and often the most visible local government activity in rural areas. These services are both highly valued by local populations and feasible for local governments to deliver, making the ability to target a village with a school or clinic invaluable for those seeking to build political support in their communities.

Although experiences vary greatly, all local government decisions are in principle made in open, public meetings. Citizen input is intended to inform local development strategies via elected representatives attending these meetings as well as through local government planning documents (*plans locals de development* or PLDs) which lay out a local government's development objectives for a five-year period and which are made in consultation with the local population. In reality, however, PLDs are produced inconsistently and read like a "wish list" of all of a local government's needs instead of offering an implementable strategy with technical guidance.[2] As a result, it is common for local actors to report that PLDs are not enacted "as they should be"; they only rarely lay out a sequential plan for making investments or for weighing needs against each other and, as a consequence, their catch-all nature grants substantial leeway to local actors wishing to pursue their own individual agenda.

It is no secret on the ground that local preferences – both those articulated in planning documents and those working their way in via political pressure – inform choices about local investments. Recent years have seen scholars turn their attention to these dynamics in recognition of the fact that who benefits from state largess reveals a lot about the state's political intentions and loyalties. The growing interest in the politics of public goods delivery in Africa and the Global South more broadly has tended to take one of two approaches to explain how and when citizens gain access to new social services: it is either driven by the top-down strategies of elites or, conversely, it results from a more bottom-up process, with some communities or individuals theorized to be better or worse positioned to petition for or coproduce services.

I introduce the most prominent versions of these arguments below, going on to test their ability to explain rural public goods delivery in Senegal in the remainder of the chapter. Although I do not dispute that these dynamics matter in *some* communities, I show that they do not explain distributional politics writ large. In contrast, I find that falling within the territory of a precolonial state offers more leverage on the patterns of spatial distributions adopted by Senegal's decentralized local governments.

Top-Down Theories of Public Goods Delivery

Electoral Motivations

The most prominent top-down lens into public goods delivery takes as its guiding assumption that the expansion of access to public goods generates

---

[2] See Williams (2010).

electoral payoffs. A clear example is found in Harding and Stasavage (2013), who find that African governments that abolish primary school fees gain an electoral payoff in large part because it is an easy distributive policy for citizens to verify. More broadly, work building on debates over core versus swing voters has found that politicians target goods to incumbent strongholds – or core voters – as a means to reinforce patron–client ties with voters.[3] Arguments that politicians target swing voters are rarer, though Masaki (2018) documents how Zambian politicians are limited in their ability to precisely identify swing voters, leading them to target aid projects to opposition strongholds in an effort to lure opposition votes. In turn, studies of African electorates suggest that these strategies are not misplaced: African voters weigh government performance heavily when deciding between candidates and parties, making their vote choices more mutable than is commonly assumed, far from "captured" by narrow clientelist relations.[4]

Though we have seen a rise in work on partisanship on the continent following the growing regularization of multiparty elections, these dynamics are also frequently understood as following the contours of ethnic cleavages. In this variant of Cox and McCubbin's (1986) core voter theory, co-ethnics constitute a "core" constituency for leaders and empirical research has shown that being a co-ethnic of the executive can improve one's access to a range of government programs across the continent.[5] The power of ethnic identities as conduits of patronage has been granted a particular prestige in the study of African politics, but as I show below, these factors do not appear to explain the actual distribution of public goods, nuancing the assumption that ethnicity is always the most important political cleavage in African political life. Of course, this null effect is in part driven by the relative lack of ethnic politicization in Senegal and other Sahelian states. Franck and Rainer (2012) find ethnicity to be a weaker predictor of favoritism in public goods delivery in Francophone West Africa and, while ethnicity remains a relevant social category for Senegalese, it has never become a national-level political cleavage.[6]

Central Government Relations
Alternatively, public goods delivery may be driven by more relational top-down factors. If some local communities have better connections to the central government, for example, they may find themselves better able to gain favors from the state. This is the argument articulated by Boone (2003b), who contends that subnational differences in the ability of the central state to locate rural allies endogenously determines power relations between the center and periphery in West Africa. A systematic difference in the propensity of local elites to have ties to the central state could explain subnational differences in local public goods

---

[3] For example, Burgess et al. (2015); Briggs (2014); and Jablonski (2014).
[4] Bratton (2012); Weghorst and Lindberg (2013); and Harding (2015).
[5] For example, Kramon and Posner (2013); Burgess et al. (2015); and Ejdemyr et al. (2017).
[6] Diouf (1994) and Koter (2013).

delivery. Elites who spend more time in Dakar or have other ties to those in power might have an easier time pulling in other, unmeasured resources, such as advice from development agents or favors from friends, for example.

I am unable to test this specific version of an argument that central government ties shape local redistribution systematically in the large-N dataset introduced in the next section, but we can gain some insight by returning to the 2013 survey of local elites. Among my survey respondents, only respondents in Thies Region, which lies immediately outside of Dakar, were significantly more likely to travel regularly to Dakar or to live part-time in the capital. Elsewhere, mayors reported traveling to Dakar three to four times a year on average and there was likewise no difference in a respondent's likelihood of having been educated in Dakar, Saint-Louis, or Europe, another possible source of valuable contacts.[7] Nor, as was shown in Figure 4.2, are elites interviewed in 2013 more likely to have a family or friendship relation to their Deputy in the National Assembly or a central government bureaucrat.[8]

A more tractable manifestation of central government favoritism is found in central government transfers, which comprise the bulk of local government budgets. The most important is the *Fonds de Dotation de la Decentralisation* (FDD), which in principle is informed by population size and need. Though the FDD is at times clearly political (state ministers who serve a dual mandate as mayor, for example, often receive greatly inflated transfers), most local governments receive one of four or five set amounts according to their population size. As noted in Chapter 4, these transfers are actually biased *away* from historically centralized areas in per capita numbers, with the mean amount transferred per capita at $1.86 in historically uncentralized areas compared to $1.50 for centralized zones.

Bottom-Up Theories of Public Goods Delivery

Ethnicity Homogeneity

Co-ethnicity may serve as a proxy for core voters, but it is also argued to have bottom-up properties that are consequential for local goods delivery. More homogenous communities may find it easier to overcome local collective action

---

[7] Of course, another manifestation of this could be through one's allegiance to the national ruling coalition. Of those surveyed in 2013, roughly 45 percent of those claiming a partisan affiliation reported having been in contact with their party hierarchy over the past year but note that 2012 was an election year and over 90 percent of those who reported contact said it was to discuss the elections. Approximately half of the elected officials interviewed had received help developing an electoral platform or some form of training from their party. These numbers are consistent across the country.

[8] To the contrary, most local elites are quite skeptical of their deputies' commitment to their community's well-being. Deputies were dismissed as not listening to the population, for being absent from the local political terrain or, as one councilor smirked, because "when they are chosen, it is not for their competency" (Interview, Saint-Louis Region, July 29, 2013).

dilemmas to either petition the state for or coproduce public goods.[9] This would suggest that it is not identities bestowed by the precolonial past but rather ascriptive identities of ethnicity that enable or impede the resolution of local collective actions on the part of community members. The predominant role of ethnic identities often remains as our default expectation for African politics, but my own discussions with local elites suggest that these identities are less durable than are often assumed. In many communities, local political cleavages actually emerge *within* ethnic groups, such as between different castes or between long-time residents and newcomer co-ethnics. In parts of Kolda Region, for example, the "Peulh Fulani" were repeatedly claimed to be favored over the "Peulh Firdu," reflecting sub-ethnic disagreements based on putative regions of origins of different clans.[10]

Though I test the ability of ethnic homogeneity to explain patterns of public goods delivery as well as co-ethnicity with the executive, I present findings consistent with my expectation that far older identities offer more explanatory leverage following decentralization. Still, I recognize that my argument that a shared identity enables cooperative behavior will remind many of Habyarimana et al.'s (2007) finding that co-ethnics may be better able to coordinate around public goods provisions because they share strategies, such as social sanctioning or the presence of shared norms, to overcome collective action dilemmas. Are precolonial identities simply doing the same work here? I argue that identities inherited from the precolonial past are distinct for two reasons. First, though not predicated on face-to-face recognition of all community members, social institutions work because they are tied to dense social networks that enable individuals to circulate reputations and reputational sanctions more immediately than the diffuse networks that define many ethnic groups, suggesting that a more immediate social proximity drives action than that tested by Habyarimana et al. Second, although we might imagine that shared ethnic identification generates social institutions, the possession of a shared identity alone is insufficient to engender institutional congruence. What is key is not a collective identity, but the social institutions that they carry with them develop over a longer term.

In this way, my argument speaks to a broader challenge to the reigning hegemony of ethnicity in African political life. Taking seriously the identities that actors on the ground ascribe to themselves suggests that the availability of alternative collective identities, such as descent from a precolonial state, is equally, if not more, motivating for local actors. This means that the most consequential political identities in local African political life may be those that are hard to observe from on high and may be uniquely distinct from national political dynamics.

---

[9] Miguel and Gugerty (2005) and Habyarimana et al. (2007).
[10] For example, when asked whether he knew any councilors, one Peulh Firdu chief in this area shook his head before saying it was the "Peulh Fulani that rule here, not us" (Interview, village chief, Kolda Region, April 10, 2013).

Associational Life

A final bottom-up explanation explains local government performance by looking at horizontal networks of social capital. This approach, classically articulated by Putnam (1993), shifts gears away from identity categories like ethnicity toward associational life, which is argued to build trust and increase the capacity for collective action in a community. In line with this logic, we may expect that local governments home to more dense networks of civic associations will see better distributional outcomes by virtue of the social capital these associations produce. The distribution of public goods, in other words, is less the result of politicians' own strategies than it is endogenous to the ability of communities with high social capital to demand and coproduce services. This argument informed one of the core tenets of democratic decentralization reforms which sought to create local governments that were responsive to local needs and would be monitored by local populations and civic groups. I test two observable implications of the social capital approach in this chapter, looking first to the density of civic associations in Senegal's rural villages and, second, the question of social trust, which for many theorists of social capital, is a key mechanism by which associational life influences local governance. As my models show below, however, there is no evidence that either bottom-up explanation offers systematic leverage in explaining which villages receive new investments from their local government.

DATA AND MEASUREMENT

The rest of this chapter tests my theory's ability to explain actual village-level public goods delivery in decentralized rural Senegal by examining the placement of basic social services between 2002 and 2012 using an original dataset of the approximately 14,300 rural villages in Senegal. In the process, I examine the relative explanatory power of the prominent alternative hypotheses introduced above.

The dataset measures two infrastructure investments made by local Senegalese governments: new primary schools and new health clinics (*postes* or *cases*). By looking across different types of public goods, I mitigate concerns that different public goods would be driven by distinct logics and, because all rural communities build some mix of this infrastructure in the period under study, it allows me to focus on the most comparable and visible investments made by Senegal's local councils.[11] The dataset was built upon GIS data

---

[11] For example, Kramon and Posner (2013). As noted earlier, local governments do make other, smaller investments, such as financing yearly youth football tournaments, for which complete data is unavailable. A more complete assessment of this nature is found in the case studies presented in Chapter 6.

provided by the *Centre de Suivi Ecologique* in Dakar. Data on school placement were provided by the Senegalese Ministry of Education, and clinic data by the Senegalese Ministry of Health. This is complemented with data from the 2000 and 2009 rounds of the *Enquête villages sur l'accès aux services sociaux de base*, conducted by the Senegalese National Agency for Statistics and Demography (ANSD). To merge across datasets, I georeference basic infrastructure and control variables to their villages using Blasnik's (2010) method for matching fuzzy text: village names are matched within each local government and all non-exact matches were reviewed by hand. The sources for each variable are noted in Table 5.1.

Dependent Variables

I employ three dependent variables to assess my theory's ability to explain patterns of public goods delivery. These binary measures – *Primary Schools* (observed in two time periods) and *Health Clinics* – take the value of one if a village receives new access during the period under analysis and zero if not. In total, my dataset counts 2,331 primary schools as having been built in rural Senegal between 2002 and 2012. This number reflects a substantial push to improve primary education in the country, driven in part by renewed donor attention and the Millennium Development Goals, which, initiated in 2000, aimed to achieve universal primary education under Goal 2 by 2015. Similarly, between 2009 and 2014, 417 health huts (*case de santé*) and 173 health posts (*poste de santé*) were constructed in the 292 local governments for which data are available.

Because many local public goods are built with the intention that they will serve a set of villages, I use the Senegalese national standards for "access" to construct dependent variables of goods delivery. These are set at 3 kilometers for primary schools and 5 kilometers for basic health, meaning that anyone within that distance is considered "covered" by the state. This does not prohibit construction within these norms – a village whose nearest primary school is 2.5 kilometers away may certainly merit their own – but it does offer a guideline for estimating who has reasonable access to services in rural areas. Consequently, distance measures are constructed by calculating the distance each village in a local government must travel to reach the nearest primary school or clinic. Villages that had no access in the baseline year are coded as having been delivered a good if a new service is built in the access radius. Villages that were already within these standards are only coded as receiving a new investment when a facility is built *closer* than their previous point of access, meaning that a village within 1 kilometer of a school in the baseline year receiving a new school 3 kilometers away would not capture a meaningful investment and hence would be coded as having no change in access.

TABLE 5.1 *Descriptive statistics of large-N dataset*

	Variable	N	Mean	Range	Source
Independent Variables	Institutional Congruence, 2002	14,504	0.591	0–1	Author Coded
	Institutional Congruence, 2009	14,504	0.591	0–1	Author Coded
Dependent Variables	New School Access, 2002–2009	14,504	0.212	0–1	Senegalese Ministry of Education
	New School Access, 2009–2012	14,504	0.172	0–1	Senegalese Ministry of Education
	New Clinic Access, 2009–2012	11,409	0.157	0–1	Senegalese Ministry of Health
Controls: Local Need	Ln Village Pop	14,497	5.498	0.693–12.676	*Repetoire officiale du villages* 2011, Gouv. du Senegal
	Population Density, 3 km	14,398	1,395.7	2–342,315	Author Coded
	Population Density, 5 km	14,398	2,620	2–349,155	Author Coded
	D School 2002, sqrt	14,411	35.83	0–275.3	Author Coded from Ministry of Education data
	D School 2009, sqrt	14,414	28.71	0–273.3	Author Coded from Ministry of Education data
	D Clinic 2009, sqrt	14,488	49.95	0–203.8	Author Coded from Ministry of Health data

Controls: Local Demand	Local economic activity, 2000	14,489	1.872	0–8	ANSD *Enquête Villages* 2002, 2009
	Local economic activity, 2009	14,490	2.615	0–8	ANSD *Enquête Villages* 2002, 2009
	% Villages Schools, 2002	14,365	30.273	4.48–100	Author Coded from Ministry of Education data
	% Villages Schools, 2009	14,322	38.79	0–100	Author Coded from Ministry of Education data
	% Villages Clinics, 2009	14,499	13.1	0–100	Author Coded from Ministry of Education data
	Regional Wealth	14,459	−0.043	−1.49 to 2.41	Author Coded from DHS data
	% Villages Mouride, 2002	14,459	4.6	0–83.3	Author Coded
	% Villages Mouride, 2009	14,459	4.5	0–73.3	Author Coded
Controls: Ease of Access	LG Capital 2002	14,459	0.022	0–1	Author Coded
	LG Capital 2009	14,459	0.026	0–1	Author Coded
	Ln D Road	14,366	0.581	−2.30 to 3.58	Author Coded
	Ln D Admin Center/Market	14,488	1.80	−1.79 to 4.10	Author Coded
Controls: Geographic	Ln D Waterway	14,488	10.16	0–12.51	Author Coded
	Village Elevation	14,363	39.94	0–461	USGS Global Elevation Grids (75 arc seconds)
	Soil Suitability	14,494	7.23	0–42	Hengl et al. 2017
	Latitude	14,488	14.33	12.34–16.66	Centre de Suivi Ecologique
	Longitude	14,488	−15.42	−17.44 to 11.37	Centre de Suivi Ecologique

Independent Variables

As introduced in Chapter 2, I define a precolonial state as a political entity that meets four criteria: (a) a limited organizational form, notably a political hierarchy built around patron–client relationships; (b) a system for taxing trade; (c) regularized tribute systems from clients; and (d) some form of localized representation to regulate social and economic life, such as judges or tax collectors.[12]

While this generates a universe of eligible states, identifying their spatial extent is a separate empirical question. Although approximate borders of precolonial states can be found in early European maps, these maps offer unreliable estimates across sources and are heavily biased toward states located along the coastline, which were subject to more frequent exploratory missions. Importantly, they also reflect the efforts of Europeans to map precolonial Africa into European conceptualizations of political space, with states defined as neat polygons.[13] These concerns lead me to opt to measure precolonial statehood as emanating outward from precolonial power centers, following Herbst's (2000) argument that precolonial power was projected concentrically outward from nodes of power.[14] Adopting this logic, I consult historical studies of each precolonial state to assemble a list of capitals and other important sites for each precolonial polity that meets my criteria for statehood.[15] This includes major market villages, the seats of provincial titleholders, important religious centers, and other sites of historical note. Given the rotating nature of power among families in Senegambian precolonial states, for example, I georeference any village that was headed by a family that was eligible to produce kings or that were electors to this system. This allows me to be sensitive to what were often spatially diffuse concentrations of power in the subregion before the onset of colonial rule.

This produces a set of core nodes of power for each state, which in turn I georeference using the same GIS database of Senegalese villages upon which my social service data are based. I cross-validated these locations using maps produced in the first two decades of colonial rule in case villages have changed names or moved. I then construct 20-kilometer buffers around each of these villages to identify all contemporary villages that fall within this range of a

---

[12] North et al. (2009, 5–9) and Hawthorne (2013, 77). [13] Branch (2014).
[14] While many studies measure precolonial centralization following Murdock (1981) as a property of ethnic groups, Murdock's measure does not capture *political* institutions, but rather *cultural* attributes that do not inherently equate with polities. This is particularly relevant in the Senegambian context because many ethnic groups fall within both centralized and uncentralized zones. Coding centralization as an ethnic attribute would overly inflate or deflate the extent of exposure to a precolonial polity. Moreover, all of the precolonial states that fell within the boundaries of contemporary Senegal had explicit provisions for minority ethnic subjects (see discussion in Chapter 2).
[15] Coding details can be found at http://marthawilfahrt.weebly.com/senegals-precolonial-states.html

precolonial center of power. Twenty-kilometer buffers best approximate the boundaries in early colonial maps, but increasing the buffer size to a more generous 25- or 30-kilometer radius generates comparable results.[16] Because I am interested in the relative congruence between a precolonial state and villages within any given local government, villages receive a score of one if they fall within the buffer of a precolonial state that covers the majority of villages in their local government. Villages that are not congruent with the dominant precolonial state or which fall in local governments with acephalous histories are coded as zero.

To account for the rise and fall of states over time, coding is done for eight points in time between the first and second half of each century between 1500 and 1880, when the French begin fully moving into the interior of the country. I penalize more distant experiences with centralization under the assumption that longer intervals between the onset of colonial rule and precolonial statehood are more likely to have eroded the strength of precolonial identities and/or networks rooted in these histories. Accordingly, I apply a discount rate to any given village's centralization score, thus that the full score is taken for 1880, the score for 1820 is divided by half, 1780 by a third, and so forth. I then standardize the average score of the eight periods of assessment to range from zero to one to generate the central independent variable, *Institutional Congruence 20 km*. This measurement process is displayed in Figure 5.1.

Control Variables

I include four series of control variables in my analyses of new school or clinic placement. The first set captures local needs. Logged village population and population density, calculated as the total population falling within 3 (schools) and 5 (clinics) kilometer grid squares around a village, measure the number of potential beneficiaries of a new facility.[17] Because some villages had better access to social services in the baseline year, the square root of the distance to the nearest school or clinic as well as the percent of villages in a local government that had their own school/clinic in the baseline year are also included. Together, these variables capture initial levels of access under the assumption that worse access indicates greater need for new services.

A key assumption of this project is that rural Senegalese have similar preferences for public goods across space. I include a count measure of the number of facilities built by each local government during each time period as this might reflect local preference. Local demand may also be higher in wealthier areas of the country, who could be better positioned to demand or coproduce services.

---

[16] See Table A5.4 in Appendix.
[17] Results are robust to using the local government population density.

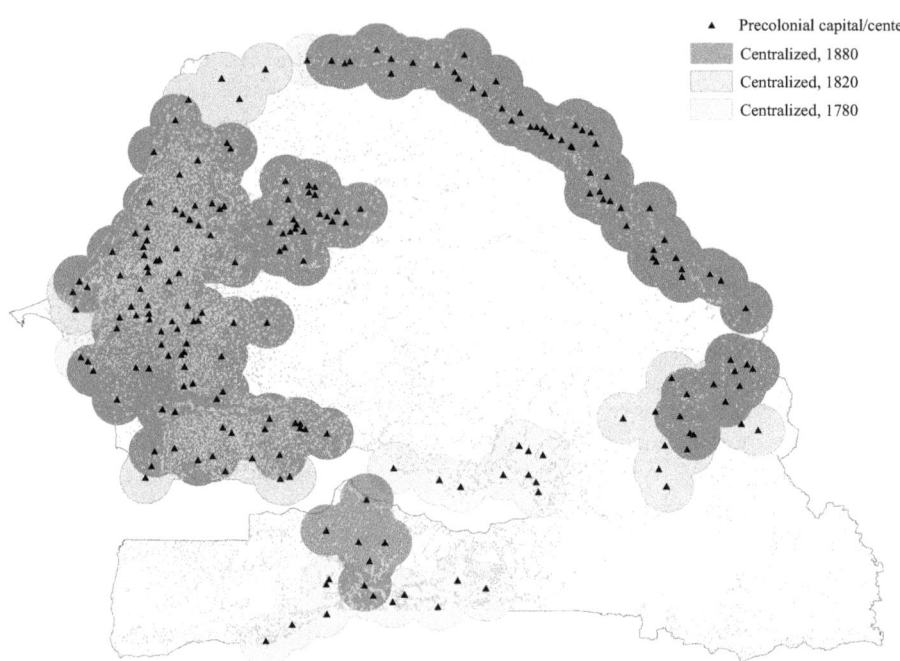

FIGURE 5.1 Precolonial capitals and discount rate illustration

At the village level, I include a measure of local economic activity in the baseline year, an additive measure of the presence of a boutique, market, artisanal workshop (i.e. metalworking), or facilities for transforming raw products (i.e. charcoal).[18] It is also possible that public goods construction is endogenous to an area's relative wealth, but given the absence of subnational income data, I proxy this by drawing on data from the 2010 and 1997 Demographic and Health Surveys to construct average *arrondissement*-level indices of household belongings to account for relative differences in wealth.[19] Of course, some families may prefer to send their children to Islamic schools in lieu of a secular education. I lastly control for the percent of villages in a local government whose names include common markers of affiliation with Senegal's Islamic brotherhoods, for instance, "Touba," "Darou," or "Mbacke," as a proxy for

---

[18] Unfortunately, data from the ANSD do not cover all official villages. Because the approximately 1,200 villages missing in the first period and 2,100 in the second are disproportionately small, dropping them from models could potentially bias results. Consequently, I assign the local government average to villages with missing data. Results are consistent using the arrondissement-level average or when villages with missing data are dropped.

[19] This measure is comparable to the DHS surveys own "rural wealth index," but it removes any possessions that are dependent on social services, notably electricity. The resulting index is composed of house material quality and a basket of possessions, such as a bike, cell phone, etc.

spatial variation in preferences for Islamic education.[20] Fixed effects models further indicate that any such local government-specific unobservables do not appear to drive the results.

In an additional set of models, I control for structural factors that may shape distributional strategies in the short term, such as the ease of access or proximity to decision-makers. This third set of controls includes a measure of a village's logged distance to the nearest road as well as its logged distance to the nearest administrative center or weekly market. This follows Herbst's argument that the African state has faced a reoccurring dilemma from the precolonial era to the present of how to project power over space. We may expect that villages farther from local centers of power and arteries of communication are harder to reach and service. These models additionally include a dummy variable that takes a value of one if the village is the local government capital or *chef-lieu* where local state power should be strongest.

Finally, a fourth set of geographic controls account for the possibility that longer-run geographic conditions favored both the formation of precolonial states and contemporary economic development. These include a village's elevation, its logged distance to the nearest navigable waterway (river or coastline), and its soil suitability (measured by its captation rate at 15 cm).[21] I also include a village's latitude, longitude, as well as their interaction term.

Descriptive statistics can be found in Table 5.1. Descriptive data for alternative explanations and robustness checks introduced below can be found in Table A.1 in the Appendix.

Alternative Explanations

The large-N dataset simultaneously allows me to test a number of the alternative explanations introduced above. As documented qualitatively in Chapter 4, evidence for many of these factors emerge in local governments in historically acephalous areas, hence I do not deny that these dynamics may explain the distributional strategy of some local governments, though I remain agnostic as to what dynamics emerge where. I do not expect them to explain outcomes as a whole nor to be more consequential than institutional congruence, however.

---

[20] Accordingly, I assume that Touba's role as the seat of the Mouride religious brotherhood merits its exclusion from the analysis. With 530,000 residents, Touba's population is closer to Senegal's secondary cities than other rural communities, but given the political status of Mouride leaders, the locality remains "rural." The area's piety means that only 9 percent of primary school-aged children were enrolled in public schools in 2012, far below the national average (50.6 percent). Results hold if included, but given improvement in model fit, I exclude Touba from the sample given its exceptionalism.

[21] Soil suitability data are from Hengl et al. (2017).

I begin with "top-down" explanations that focus on the strategic interests of politicians, parties, and the central state. To account for the possibility that the relative competitiveness of any given village might shape who is more or less likely to receive an investment, I match each village to the nearest voting booth in their local government for both the 2002 and 2009 local elections.[22] I use the percent of votes for the winning party at the nearest voting booth as well as a measure of the gap between the first and second place parties as a measure of swing votes. Because each village is assigned the results of its nearest voting booth, I interact a voting booth's vote gap with the logged population of the villages assigned to that location (*Vote GapxPop*); two neighboring villages sharing a polling location might both be home to swing voters, for example, but the attractiveness of targeting them with a public good is conditional on their population size. To measure core voters, I similarly interact the percent of votes for the winning party with village-level logged population (% *WinningxPop*). Since we might think of the effects of political competition accruing at the local government level rather than between villages, models are also run with a dummy variable that takes the value of one if the ruling local council is aligned with the incumbent, national political party (*PDS*).

Of course, focusing on local governments as the key actors in providing services risks ignoring the possibility that the central government is shaping differential outcomes through the unequal targeting of resources. To account for this risk, I include three measures of favoritism from the center. The first two capture unequal transfers. A measure of the percent change in the teacher/student ratio between the baseline and outcome years for each region (*Teachers/Students*) proxies for unequal transfer of resources from the central state because the allocation of teachers remains the purview of the Ministry of Education. For the second period, models include the average dollar per capita transfer from the central to local state between 2009 and 2012 via the FDD. Average FDD transfers ($ *Transfers*) thus directly captures any inequalities in central government transfers. On its own, these transfers do not appear to be biased toward formally centralized areas, as discussed in the section "Top-Down Theories of Public Goods Delivery." In view of arguments that the executive favors co-ethnics, I test whether President Wade was more favorable to dominantly *Wolof* communities.[23]

Finally, I address the two bottom-up mechanisms introduced earlier. Given the prevalence of claims about ethnic heterogeneity's dampening effect on public goods provision, I examine the effect of ethnolinguistic fractionalization (*ELF*).

---

[22] A similar matching procedure for voting booths was done as with social service infrastructure – matching villages to their GIS coordinates and then to the nearest voting booth within their local government, assigning the value of that bureau's results. Note that in 2002, thirty-eight villages from five rural communities are dropped due to missing electoral data. In 2009, this number is approximately 600 villages in 11 rural communities.

[23] I was unable to obtain village-level ethnicity data.

Data and Measurement

Given significant gaps in data on local ethnic composition, I measure this by averaging the ethnic fractionalization of local governments for which data are available across the next highest administrative level, the arrondissement. Once again, there is no effect, reflecting the relatively low level of ethnic politicization in Senegal.[24] Because horizontal social capital has been shown to improve subnational governance outcomes, improving the organizational capacity of villages to petition the local state, I similarly examine whether the differences between centralized and acephalous areas of Senegal can be explained by differential stocks of local social capital. I estimate whether a count measure of the number of civic associations in each village offers any leverage on local public goods delivery (*Civic Assns*). This is coded from the ANSD's *Enquête village* and includes the presence of village development associations, women's groups, local sports or youth groups, village political party branches, and economic interest groups.[25]

One variation of the social capital argument is that it is not civic associations but rather stocks of social trust that improve development outcomes. As a final test, I turn to recent arguments by Nunn and Wantchekon (2011) who find that precolonial exposure to the slave trade inhibits local community performance today because it eroded social trust. The impact of the Atlantic slave trade on West Africa is widely debated. Certainly, the slave trade at times strengthened existing states and weakened segmentary societies, increasing insecurity by undermining the "social glue" that had held communities together.[26] If areas that were acephalous prior to colonization were more likely to be raided for slaves and if this systematically reduces trust within communities today, it could explain poor performance as well as the weaker social ties observed in earlier chapters.

Estimation Strategy

I analyze the data with multilevel logit models that cluster at the local government level. Multilevel modeling allows me to capture variation in infrastructure provision between villages as well as variation between local governments. Since placement decisions are made at the local government level, hierarchical models offer efficiency gains in the standard errors because village-level observations within any given community are not independent of one another – a local government that has the resources to build two health clinics, for example, faces a choice between villages that violate assumptions of conditional independence. Additionally, significant variation in the number of villages

---

[24] Franck and Rainer (2012).
[25] The measure thus excludes associations dependent on a preexisting public good, that is, school associations. Given data gaps, this variable uses the same procedure as with local economic activity (see Footnote 22).
[26] Fage (1969); Whatley (2014); and Hubbell (2001, 38).

within local governments, ranging from 3 to 195 problematizes the common approach of clustering standard errors by local government. To capture potential unobserved heterogeneity within administrative units, I rerun the hierarchical models with local government fixed effects to estimate whether institutional congruence can explain within-unit variation. Because of Senegal's 2009 administrative redistricting (see discussion in Chapter 3), models are run for two electoral cycles: 2002–2009 and 2009–2012 with all relevant variables calculated to the adjusted boundaries.

Following Bell and Jones (2015) and Gelman and Hill (2008), all multilevel models include a centered mean score of precolonial centralization at the local government level. This is done in order to remove unobservable characteristics at higher levels that may correlate with level one predictors and the dependent variable, thereby violating the assumption that the random intercept is uncorrelated with other variables. This approach directly models this potential source of bias as a response.[27]

THE DELIVERY OF PRIMARY SCHOOLS AND BASIC HEALTH, 2002–2012

Main Results

My core statistical analyses are presented in Figure 5.2.[28] Together, the results suggest a robust effect of institutional congruence on the likelihood a village gains access to a new primary school or a new health post or hut during the 2000s. Panel (a) shows that the results of models include controls for local need and local demand. They suggest that villages that fall within the boundaries of a precolonial state are more likely to receive schools in both time periods. Depending on model specification, the marginal effect of centralization on new schools suggests that villages in areas that were always centralized in the 500 years prior to colonization are 11–12 percent more likely to receive a school, holding other variables at their means in the first time period and approximately 8 percent in the second. Across models, the odds of a village within a centralized area receiving access to a new primary school are over twice more likely than areas that were always acephalous. Finally, the last reported model estimate in Panel (a) indicates that villages in congruent areas are also more likely to receive access to new health facilities. Specifically, villages in congruent local governments are approximately 11 percent more likely to receive access to a health facility.

The addition of a host of geographic controls in Panel (b) does not fundamentally alter the results. Fixed effects models, displayed in Panel (c) further indicate that institutional congruence is important even within local governments: when the majority, but not all, of a local government's territory was covered by a

---

[27] All results are consistent with the exclusion of the centered mean as well.
[28] Full model results are available in Table A.2 in the Appendix.

Delivery of Primary Schools and Basic Health

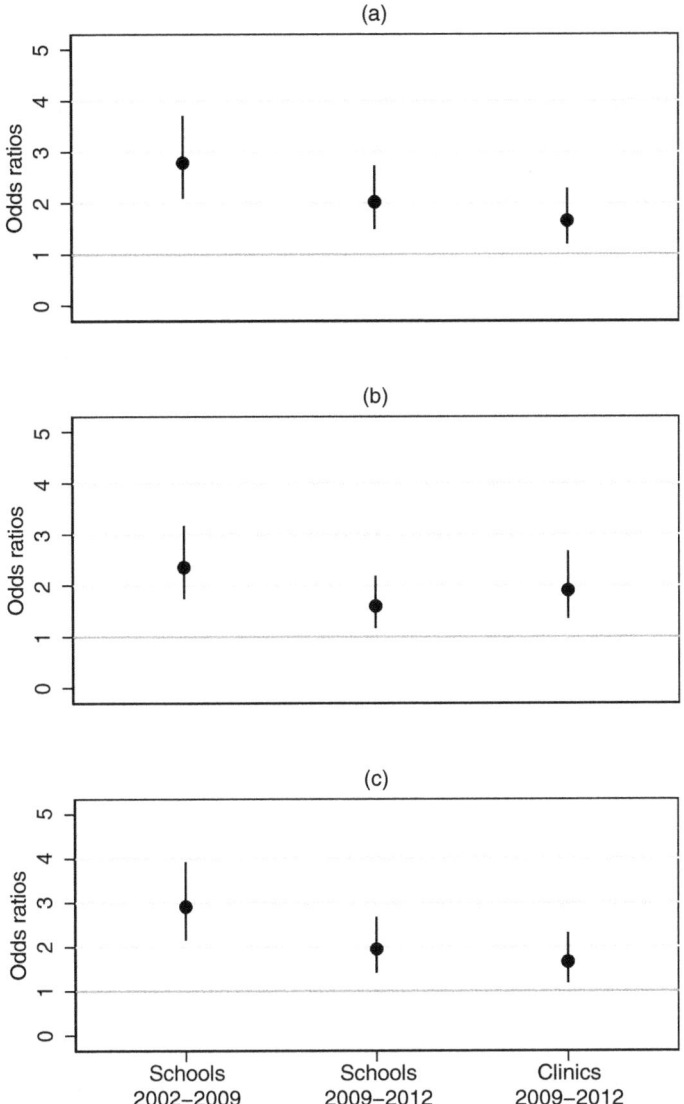

Note: Panel (a) includes controls for local need and local demand. Panel (b) adds a set of controls measuring ease of social service access in the baseline year as well as a set of geographic controls. Panel (c) presents results from models with local government fixed effects that omit all local government-level controls.

FIGURE 5.2 Effect of institutional congruence on village access to new social services: (a) main results, (b) with geographic controls, and (c) fixed effects models

precolonial state, villages that fall within the boundary of a precolonial state are more likely to receive public goods access than those that fall outside of the estimated boundaries. Together the results in Figure 5.2 suggest that local governments in centralized areas are improving access to basic public goods for their villages more than in areas of the country that were never centralized, or which had mixed histories with precolonial rule. Expanding my measure of precolonial statehood outward to 25- and 30-kilometer buffers or reducing the definition of access for new public goods to more conservative values produces consistent results, as seen in Tables A.3 and A.4 in the Appendix.

Most importantly, this is despite the fact that local governments who have a largely acephalous history were building more schools per capita in both time periods. Difference of means tests show that acephalous local governments built an average of 2.8 schools per 10,000 residents versus 2 in centralized areas between 2002 and 2009 (significantly different at $p < 0.001$) and 2 versus 1.9 between 2009 and 2012 (insignificant). In absolute numbers, there is only a significant difference in the first time period (5.7 versus 4.5 schools on average per local government) with a reverse finding in the second (2.5 versus 3.3 schools). Similar figures exist for clinic delivery: acephalous areas provided an average of 2 new health facilities per 10,000 residents between 2009 and 2012 compared to 1.9 in historically centralized areas, again an insignificant difference.[29] This suggests that this is not a question of volition or ability to provide social services, but rather of placement and distributional choice.

Alternative Explanations

How does the seemingly robust effect of precolonial centralization compare to preexisting explanations of public goods delivery? Figure 5.3 presents the results of an additional set of models that test whether common alternative hypotheses explain the patterns identified in Figure 5.2. Results are displayed by public good and time period. Across the board, these models suggest little systematic influence of common hypotheses derived from the literature. Thus while local political party activity is quite robust, with 76.5 percent of rural elites surveyed (and 97 percent of elected officials) for this project reporting feeling close to a political party and local councils have an average of 2.4 parties seated, I find little systematic evidence that electoral dynamics drive redistribution.[30] Although the interaction between village population and the gap between the first and second place parties does appear to be positively correlated with a village's access to a new school in the first time period – indicating favoritism to core voters – there is no similar effect in the second time period or

---

[29] In absolute numbers, this is an average of 1.6 versus 1.65 facilities.
[30] Competition declined nationally in 2009, when nearly 66 percent of local councils were aligned with the government in Dakar, up from 57.5 percent in 2002. This should not obscure however one of the most pervasive features of Senegalese politics: the tendency for elites to switch political parties frequently. Of those with a reported party identification in 2013, only 31 percent reported having always belonging to that party and approximately 65 percent of those who had switched parties had done so most recently right before, during, or after the 2012 Presidential and Legislative elections.

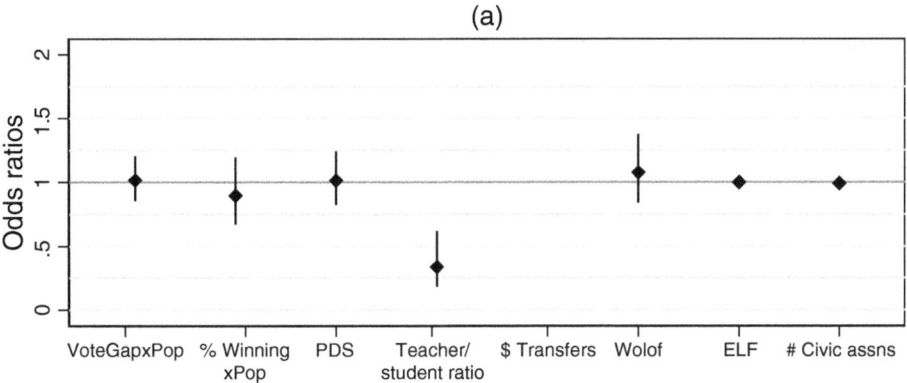
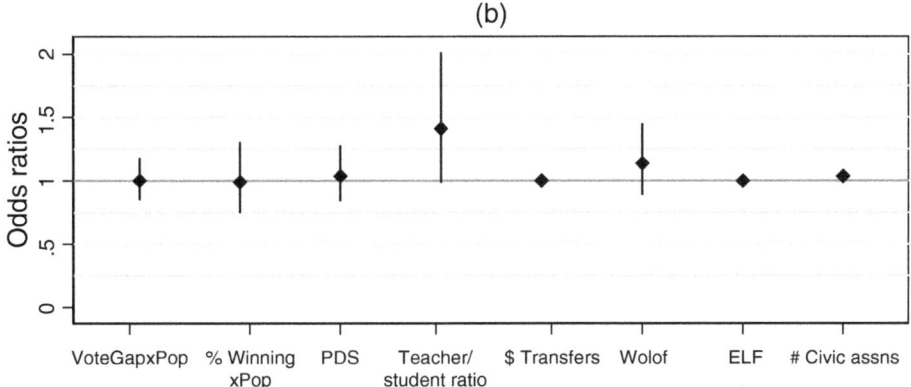
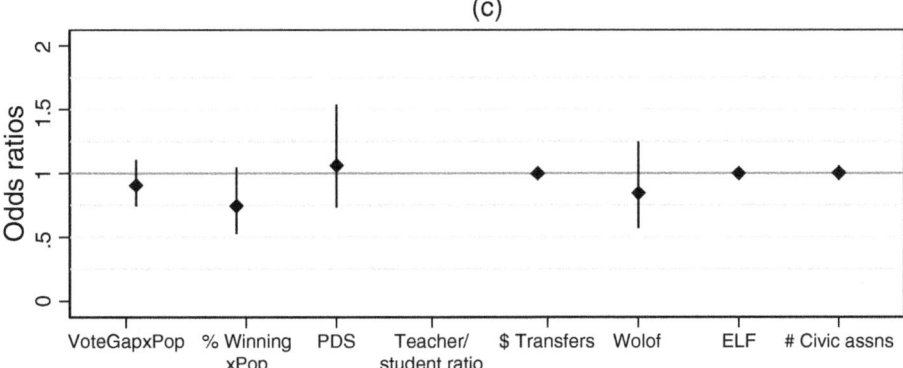

FIGURE 5.3 Effect of alternative explanations on village access to new social services: (a) new schools 2002–2009, (b) new schools 2009–2012, and (c) new clinics 2009–2012

in relation to other basic services. Moreover, a corresponding effect is not found when looking at the percent of votes going to the winning party, another measure of core voters.

At no point does the role of the central state appear to influence village-level redistribution, as measured by central state alignment or the favorable distribution of resources. There is no apparent benefit of residing in a local government that is predominantly Wolof, suggesting little favoritism toward co-ethnics of President Abdoulaye Wade who was in power during the years under study. Finally, theorized bottom-up drivers, an area's ethnic homogeneity, and the number of village civic associations do not appear to enable villages to obtain more access. Neither finding is entirely surprising. As noted above, though ethnicity is a salient social identity for Senegalese, it is not the only one and may obscure other relevant social divisions, such as caste or migration patterns.

Civil society organizations are active throughout rural Senegal, but remain weak democracy promoters, often quickly imbricated in local social hierarchies and power relations.[31] Despite a push to create social capital via civil society, the evidence presented here does not indicate that it systematically improves the ability of any given community or group to extract goods from their local governments. Critically, as reported in the full model results in Tables A.5a and A.5b in the Appendix, institutional congruence retains a positive and significant effect throughout.

Of course, we can imagine factors beyond associational life that might allow communities in areas that were home to precolonial states to be better able to monitor their local governments and hold them accountable. Additional evidence for this is found in data from Rounds 4 and 5 of the Afrobarometer. Forty-eight percent of respondents in acephalous areas versus 45 percent in centralized areas correctly identify "voters" as being responsible for making sure the local council does their job, an insignificant difference. Among respondents of my own survey, what does appear to differ – in line with the network mechanism – is that respondents are significantly more likely to report being able to monitor (50 versus 35 percent) or to sanction or reprimand elected officials when they disagreed with them (62 versus 51 percent) when they have family ties to elected officials. Similarly, friends and family members are significantly more likely to think that they can persuade the mayor to help them with something or see things their way than those with no affective ties.

One variation of the social capital argument is that it is not civic associations but rather stocks of social trust that improve development outcomes. Articulated most famously by Putnam (1993), a most recent prominent version of this argument comes from Nunn and Wantchekon (2011), who find that historical exposure to the slave trade results in lower levels of social trust today. Figure 5.4 presents three empirical tests to evaluate whether there are

---

[31] Patterson (1998).

Delivery of Primary Schools and Basic Health

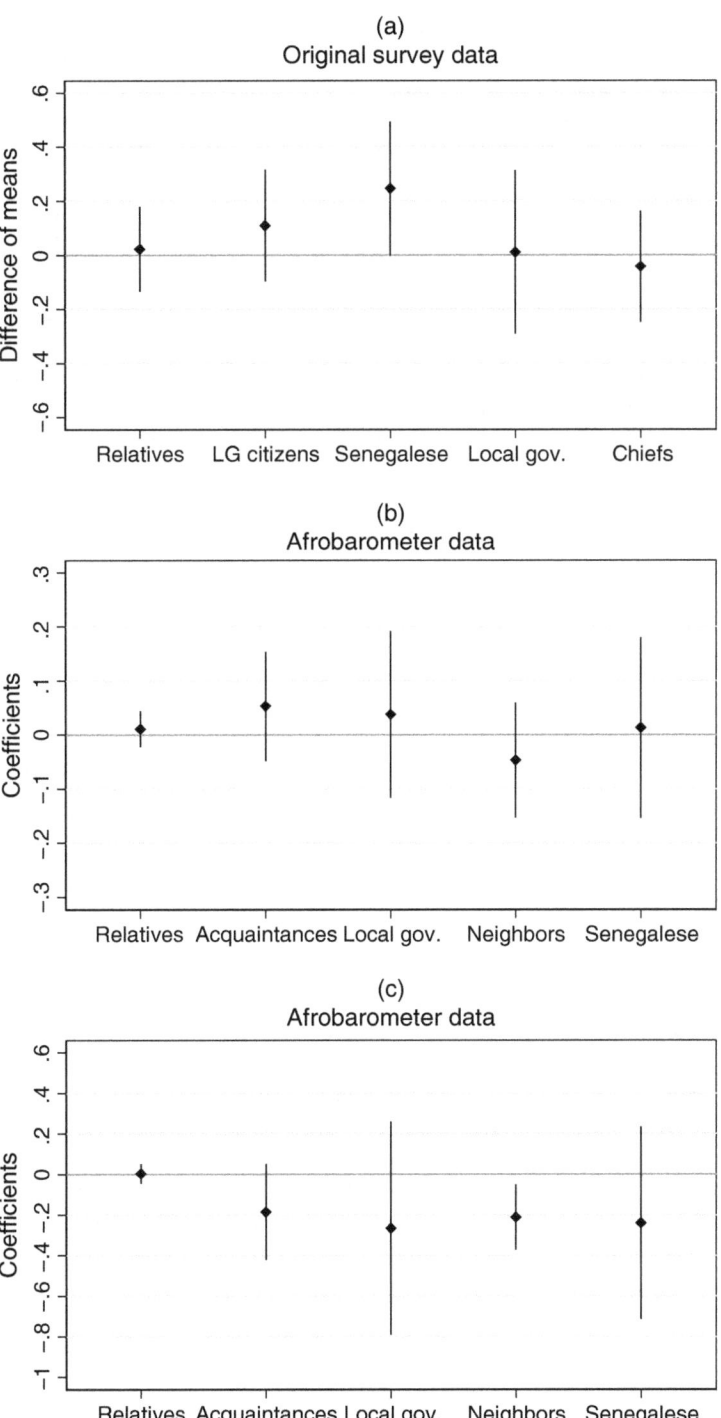

FIGURE 5.4 Trust estimates: (a) difference of means by institutional congruence, (b) slave exports per area (Nunn & Wantchenkon replication), and (c) institutional congruence

differential stocks of intra-community trust within congruent and incongruent local governments.[32] First, Panel (a) reports the differences in means of reported trust in a number of local figures among those I surveyed in 2013. Precolonial centralization does not appear to systematically explain these differences. Panel (b) replicates the models of Nunn and Wantchekon (2011) using Rounds 4 and 5 of the Afrobarometer. If Nunn and Wantchekon are correct, then the positive effects of areas that were home to precolonial states could be driven by higher levels of intra-community trust because they were less exposed to the slave trade. I find no evidence for this using Nunn and Wantchekon's preferred measure of exposure to the slave trade, measured as $\ln(1 + $ ethnic group exports/area of ethnic group). Nor does trust meaningfully vary among Afrobarometer respondents using my own measure of institutional congruence, presented in Panel (c). In fact, the only statistically significant difference appears to be that respondents in areas home to precolonial states are actually less trusting of neighbors, the inverse of the expected finding. Together, Figure 5.4 suggests that we do not see systematically lower levels of trust in historically acephalous areas, suggesting that differences in local stocks of trust are unlikely to be driving the variation I observe in Figure 5.2.

Relative Placement Efficiency

Central to my argument is the claim that local governments in historically centralized areas engage in spatially distinct patterns of redistribution. I have already established that the results of Figure 5.2 are not driven by historically centralized areas simply delivering more new facilities. This raises the question: do local government councils engage in spatially different patterns of distribution? Expectations of government favoritism abound, but despite growing interest in how public goods delivery is politically targeted, empirical research relies on the idea of an ideal allocative decision that is never actually modeled.[33] To get around this problem and to develop a metric for the relative efficiency of placement, I make use of location-allocation models, often employed by businesses and public agencies to help identify the most efficient location for public services, warehouses, stores, etc., taking into account the locations of existing facilities, potential new sites, and the spatial spread of demand.

The central empirical strategy behind location-allocation models is to compare between the model predicted, efficiency-maximizing location(s), and the location(s) actually chosen by any given local government. I run two forms of these models. First, local governments may seek to *maximize coverage*, calculating an ideal location for building a school/clinic thus that the percent of the local government's population that lives within 3/5 kilometers of a school or

---

[32] Full results can be found in Table A.6 in the Appendix.   [33] Golden and Min (2013).

Delivery of Primary Schools and Basic Health

clinic is maximized, taking into account existing facilities. Second, they may prefer to *maximize attendance*, calculating the capacity of existing schools (measured with students per classroom) and the locations of existing clinics. These models predict the best location if the goal is to increase the total number of residents "attending" a facility, discounting attendance by distance under the assumption that individuals prefer and hence are more likely to use public goods closer to their homes. For each local government, the models are run so as to identify as many locations as were actually built during the time period. The total number of students or villagers that would have been covered by the "ideal" location is then compared to the actual number covered by the built facilities by a local government.

I illustrate the logic behind these models visually using the example of Ndoyene, a local government in Louga Region, in Figure 5.5.

Figure 5.6 presents the results of these analyses, using the difference in students who could have been covered by new schools/clinics if a local government always chose the "ideal" location and those actually covered by the facility as built.[34] I construct the dependent variable by aggregating the difference at the local government level; a value of zero on the dependent variable indicates that a local government built at the ideal location(s). Negative coefficients therefore reflect more efficient choices as the number of students who *could* have been covered, but were not, decreases. Figure 5.6a reveals no significant relationship between precolonial centralization and building social services that maximize attendance. Precolonial centralization is however associated across the board with building schools and clinics in locations that increase the number of covered citizens. These areas are providing services to ensure that more villages gain access, building closer to the "ideal" locations. This is evidenced by the coefficient moving toward zero, which again represents the ideal choice. In other words, local governments in areas that were home to precolonial states on average improve coverage for 160 to more than 600 more citizens than their acephalous counterparts even controlling for baseline levels of access. These models offer a novel test of the argument that there are subnational differences in the politics of local public goods delivery in rural Senegal while confirming the argument that precolonial centralization is associated with broader spatial distribution today.

Placebo Tests

To further demonstrate that these patterns are explained by local-level rather than central state dynamics, Figure 5.7 shows the results of a series of placebo tests, using the placement of secondary schools in both time periods and the delivery of electrification and improved roads in the first.[35] These investments

---

[34] Model results can be found in Table A.7 in the Appendix.
[35] See Table A.8 in the Appendix for full results.

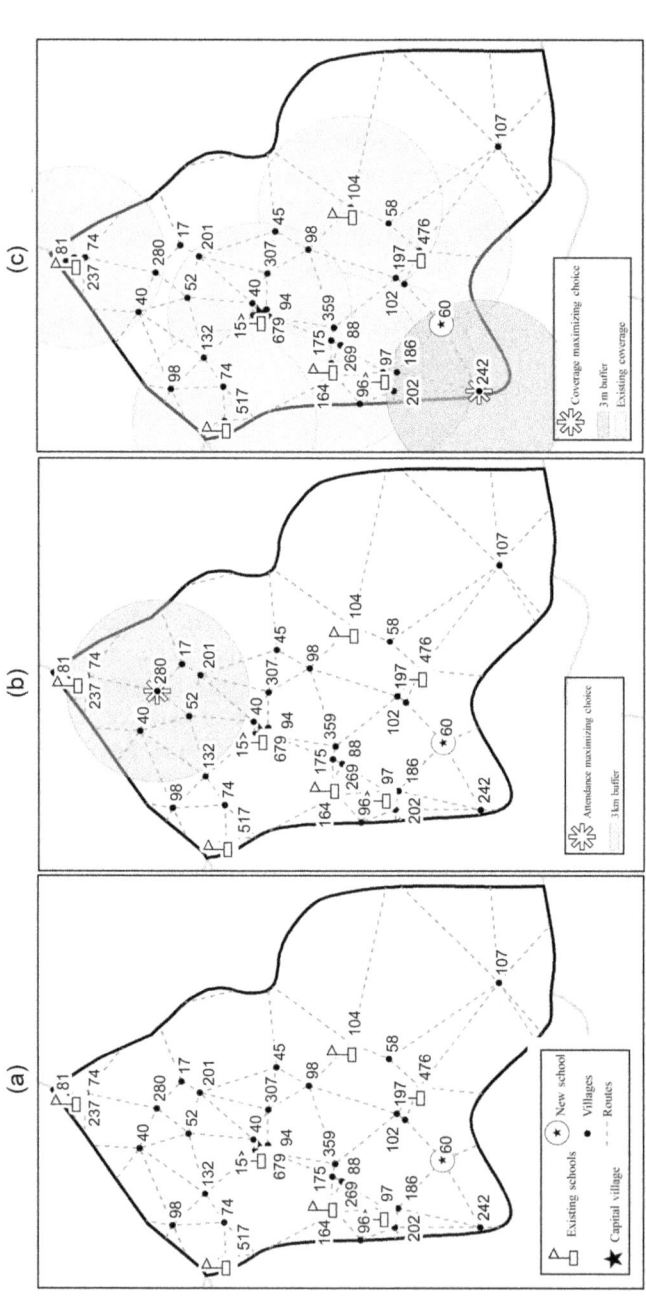

FIGURE 5.5 Illustration of location-allocation models: (a) Ndoyene (Louga Region), (b) Maximize Attendance Model, and (c) Maximize Coverage Model

Delivery of Primary Schools and Basic Health

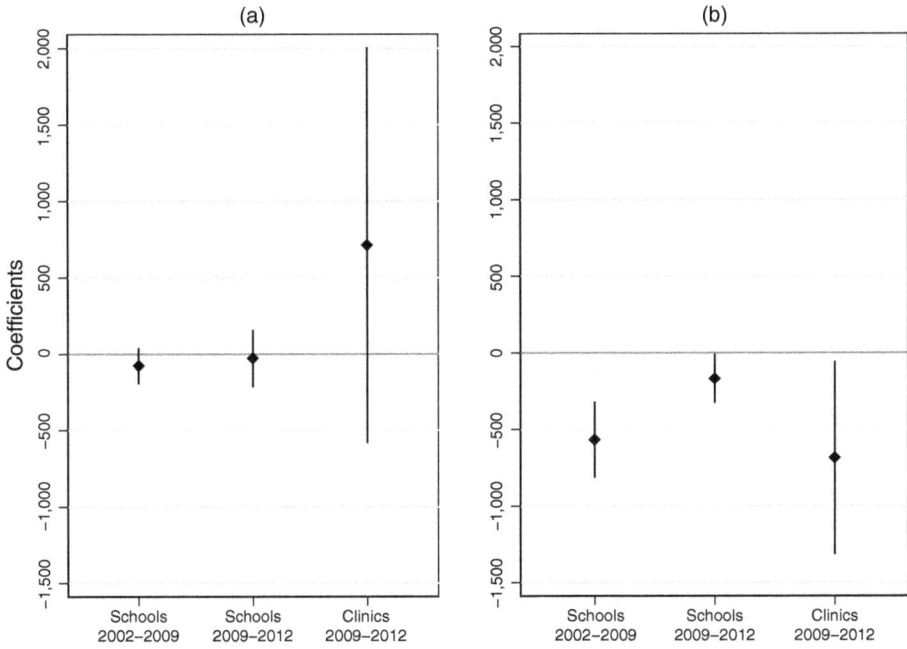

FIGURE 5.6 Effect of institutional congruence on location-allocation choices: (a) Maximize Attendance Models and (b) Maximize Coverage Models

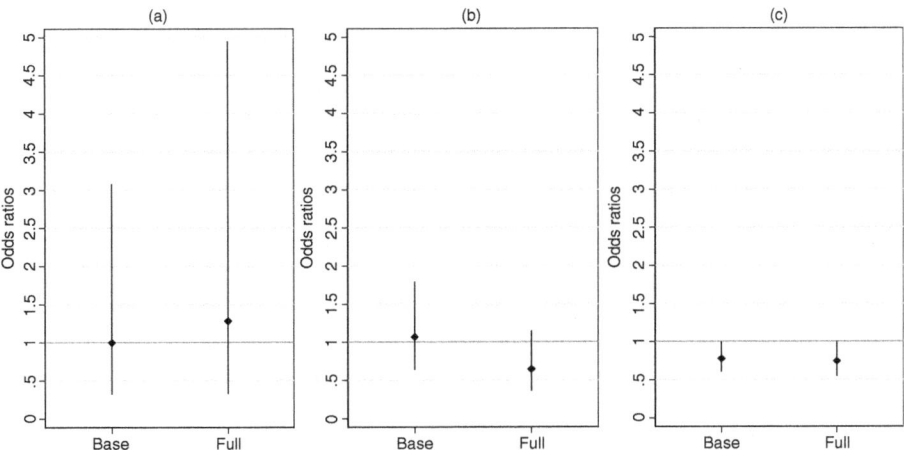

FIGURE 5.7 Placebo models – effect of institutional congruence on central-state-allocated goods: (a) new high schools, (b) electrification, and (c) new roads

are all exclusively provided by the central state and are far beyond the means – financial or technical – of local governments. Secondary schools make for a particularly useful placebo test because many unmeasurable factors that we may think drive placement – such as local demand and interest in Western education – should be similar for both primary and secondary schools. At the same time, electrification and improved roads are two of the most high-demand goods in rural Africa. The results indicate that precolonial centralization has no significant explanatory power over a village's likelihood of receiving any of these investments. If anything, historically acephalous areas appear to be more likely to receive investments in local road networks. This confirms the insights from the above analysis that precolonial centralization only influences public goods placement at the local level and is not a factor in decisions made in Dakar.

CONCLUSION

The findings presented in this chapter suggest that local governments that are congruent with the boundaries of a precolonial state engage in spatially distinct patterns of public goods delivery. Congruent local governments are more likely to ensure that more villages gain access to new services. Conversely, I find acephalous areas serve fewer villages than they could otherwise be doing. This difference is all the more puzzling given that there is not a great difference in the absolute number or per capita rate of schools or health centers being constructed in one area versus another during the same time period.

By locating the precise site of investments, this chapter has tested numerous theories of public goods delivery at a much more fine-grained level than has previously been done in the literature, allowing me to show that what differs is how local governments distribute public goods spatially within their borders. This lends support to the key observable implication of my theory: where I expect institutional congruence, for example, in areas that fall in the boundaries of a precolonial polity, local governments appear to deliver public goods in a spatially distinct manner. In contrast, dominant explanations in the study of redistributive politics offer little to no traction in explaining the investment patterns of Senegal's decentralized governments. This accords with the insights of my own original survey data presented in Chapter 4. More consequentially, it suggests not only that there are emerging differences in how public goods are delivered, but that subnational inequalities in access to services in rural Senegal are actually increasing under decentralization.

To address the concern that the results identified in this chapter may be the result of long-run, accumulating inequalities, I trace the evolution of public goods delivery from the onset of colonial rule to the present in Chapter 7, finding that the effects identified here only emerged following the 1996 decentralization reforms that devolved meaningful authority over local public goods delivery to the local level. The next chapter, however, presents three in-depth case studies of local governance to explore the mechanisms behind the theory.

6

Congruence and Incongruence in Action

The mayor is having a party. A retired bureaucrat, his cohort's *amicale*, or social club, is holding its quarterly meeting and it is his turn to host. The mayor's guests are among the West African state of Senegal's first generation of postcolonial civil servants and, now retired, they have scattered, some remaining in the country's urban centers while others, like the mayor, have returned to their natal villages. They pass the day recounting old tales and praising their host on a squeaky PA system, pausing only to share copious plates of rice and mutton. The mayor's compound also teems with extended family members, neighbors, local government councilors, village chiefs, and one visiting researcher, me. Looming large among the local guests is the village chief of the local government's *chef-lieu*, or capital village, a few kilometers to the south. Circulating in a grand white boubou, the chief plays the role of a second host, welcoming guests in between long, reciprocal exchanges of compliments with the mayor. Anyone with a passing familiarity of the local political terrain knows that the two are allies. If the chief can be credited with helping the mayor win the 2014 local elections, then the mayor is currently repaying him by bolstering the former's claim to his village's chieftaincy in the face of a challenger. Though not without criticism, theirs is no doubt a mutually lucrative alliance.

Herein lies the crux of the two political conflicts animating the local government in early 2017: the mayor narrowly won a first term in 2014, but his predecessor remains in the local council's opposition, either playing the role of gadfly or opposition party leader depending on one's perspective. Meanwhile, in the local government's capital village, the village chief's politically prominent extended family is beset by internal divisions over which branch of the family can rightfully claim the chieftaincy. Neither conflict is hidden for those who are in the know, but if one is not, the mayor's party – and the community more broadly – appears peaceful and harmonious. On all fronts, one local government councilor concludes that things proceed "like normal."[1] Indeed, there has never been – nor will there likely be in the near future – a grand political explosion. Rather, these conflicts simmer under the surface, beneath cordial greetings, and carefully protected reputations, kept in check by social norms that prioritize consensus and community stability.

This presents a puzzle to dominant theories of redistributive politics. After all, why would one of the most outspoken members of the opposition party vehemently argue that it was his duty to support the current mayor, for "without our support, it will be hard for the mayor to do any good in the community. So, we support him because we know this is the only way the community will go forward"?[2] I argue that such statements are not puzzling once we take into account the fact that the mayor's party is taking place in the heart of the Cayor. This chapter deploys two case studies to refine our understanding of how and why communities reach different redistributive solutions under decentralization, comparing the mayor's historically centralized local government – "Kebemer" – with an otherwise similar but historically acephalous local government – "Koungheul" – located a few hundred kilometers to the southeast. These model-testing case studies allow me to probe the theory's mechanisms with more precision than is afforded in the survey data or quantitative analysis presented thus far. At the same time, by spending an extended amount of time in each community, I was able to collect a more complete inventory of local government projects than that examined in Chapter 5, facilitating additional tests on the theory's observable implications.

Following a discussion of the case selection strategy and methodological overview, I introduce the cases of Kebemer and Koungheul, detailing how the mechanisms of shared local identities and dense social network ties among elites are present in Kebemer, but absent in Koungheul. The consequence is that shared social institutions net almost all of Kebemer's elites into reciprocal, cross-village webs of obligation that alter the behavior of politicians by encouraging them to adapt more prosocial attitudes toward the group. In contrast, politicians in Koungheul report being far less constrained in their behavior, rendering local government redistribution targeted and representation uneven.

I then introduce an "off-the-line" case of "Koumpentoum," which has a mixed history of precolonial centralization. Despite falling within the territory of the kingdom of Niani, the political fortunes of which declined dramatically at the start of the nineteenth century, Koumpentoum illustrates that institutional congruence is dependent on the social reproduction of social institutions over time. Because current residents descend from lineages that arrived after the onset of colonial rule, Koumpentoum's current population was never exposed to the state of Niani. As a result, the local government lacks cross-village social institutions, rendering it more similar to acephalous Koungheul

---

[1] Interview, Louga Region, February 12, 2017. [2] Interview, Louga Region, February 13, 2017.

Case Selection and Methodology

than centralized Kebemer. The chapter concludes with a short discussion of alternative explanations.

CASE SELECTION AND METHODOLOGY

I employ a paired case analysis to develop insight into the theory's mechanisms. To do so requires selecting cases that are similar in as many respects as possible apart from their exposure to a precolonial polity. I follow a "typical" or on-lier case selection strategy from the analysis of the village-level infrastructure investments made in the 2000s presented in the previous chapter.[3] Following Lieberman (2005), I sought two well-predicted cases to help refine my understanding of the mechanisms animating my theory, ideally ones that displayed extreme scores on the independent variable, which can be a useful method for discovering potential confounders.[4] I further sought an "off-the-line case" where I would *expect* congruence yet where exposure to a precolonial state does not appear to impact local governance today. To do so, I zoom in on the experience of precolonial states that had collapsed prior to French colonization.

To arrive at my final selection, I deliberately winnowed the pool in four ways. I first eliminated all cases I had already visited for the survey conducted in 2013. The choice was secondly constrained by my desire to visit a third local government, one that fell in the territory of a precolonial state that did not persist into the late 1880s. Together, these first two criteria left a relatively limited pool. Because we might hypothesize that different ethnic groups possess distinct norms that could influence local governance, I prioritized ethnic match as a third criterion. Lastly, I sought cases that were comparable on other factors likely to be influential, such as geographic zone, economic activity, and the level of social service access at the onset of the 1996 decentralization reforms.

Combined, this means that the three chosen cases were the most comparable cases within these parameters. The selected cases are similar on key political dimensions as well: their partisan alignment with the central state has been in lockstep since 1996, they are all home to numerous villages with strong ties to the Mouride and Tidjane Sufi Brotherhoods that dominate Senegal's Islamic practice, and the ethnic majority in each is Wolof. Of course, this is never a perfect exercise; centralized Kebemer's population is both lower and more densely inhabited, though it still falls far below the national average for historically centralized areas of 102 residents per square kilometer. Further differences were found once I arrived on the ground. Koungheul had fifty-one villages listed in the official village repertoire that I had obtained in Dakar,

---

[3] The cases were selected from the models presented in Figure 5.2 by identifying cases that were on-liers across the three dependent variables presented in Panel B.
[4] Seawright (2016). This effectively means communities that were always centralized or never centralized in the 500 years before colonization.

TABLE 6.1 *Description of case selection*

	On-the-line		Off-the-line
	Kebemer	*Koungheul*	*Koumpentoum*
Precolonial Heritage	Centralized	Acephalous	Mixed
Settlements	17th–18th c	early 1900s	1940s–1980s
Population	~14,000	~20,000	~14,000
# Villages	38	61	41
Wolof (%)	74	73	67
Peulh (%)	15	22	19
Serer (%)	<1	4	9
Maure (%)	10	<1	<1
Mandingue (%)	<1	<1	4
Pop. Density (per km²)	53.4	33.8	27.6
Economy	Agriculture, Animal Husbandry	Agriculture, Animal Husbandry	Agriculture, Animal Husbandry
Religious Composition	Maj.: Mouride Min.: Tidjane	Maj.: Mouride Min.: Tidjane, Fala	Maj.: Mouride Min.: Tidjane, Catholic

but I soon learned that ten new villages had been created by the previous mayor (though, as I will detail below, this itself proves to be valuable data for my argument).

Descriptive information on the selected communities can be found in Table 6.1, where I also offer a comparison with the third case of Koumpentoum introduced in the chapter's second half.

The research was conducted with the help of two Senegalese research assistants during an approximately two-week stay in each local government. Open-ended interviews were conducted with a large swath of local elites, during which we posed a series of questions about the history and demographics of their villages as well as what they had received from the local state and when. We discussed local political life, including the most recent local elections (held in 2014) at length, asking politicians about their entrance into politics and political campaigns while village chiefs were asked about their experience with local state politics. The only standardized part of the interviews came at the end when we collected social network data for each respondent, inventorying their social ties to other elected officials and village chiefs in their communities, categorized as acquaintances, friends, extended family members, or immediate family members (e.g. a daughter-in-law or brother).

Table 6.2 presents descriptive statistics on the entire sample of interviewees. Though the objective was to speak with as complete a list of village chiefs as possible, this was not achieved in any local government, primarily due to chiefs

TABLE 6.2 *Descriptive statistics for case study interviewees*

Case	Respondent type	N	% interviewed	% related to village founder	% related to chief	Avg # Network Ties	Average years chief/ # Mandates
Kebemer	Chiefs	34	89.5	100		3.7	15.4
	Elected Officials	8	20		88		1.3
	Misc. Others	5					
Koungheul	Chiefs	56	90	98		2.09	19
	Elected Officials	8	17.4		37.5		1.6
	Misc. Others	8					
Koumpentoum	Chiefs	40	97.5	86		1.73	17.1
	Elected Officials	10	22		10		1.24
	Misc. Others	5					

traveling or being too ill or old to be interviewed. Nonetheless, nearly 90 percent of chiefs were interviewed in each case. Repeated interviews were conducted with the mayor of each local government in addition to one if not both of the mayor's adjoints. Beyond this, we sought to speak to five to six local councilors, with priority given to local opposition party leaders. Because I was interested in local governance since 1996, I additionally interviewed former mayors and councilors who had served multiple mandates on the local council. A number of village chiefs in all three communities noted that they had previously served as councilors as well. When possible, I also met with other state agents, including the subprefect and local development agent in each *arrondissement*, griots (traditional praise singers) who recounted the community's history and the secretary posted by the central state to each local government.

These more formal interviews were paired with the informal interactions that arise when one stays in a small community, conversations with neighbors who stop by to introduce themselves, with state agents who pass through the local government, or with the horse cart and motorcycle drivers we hired to transport us to different villages. Consequently, while the stay in each local government was too short to be considered ethnographic, each case offers a snapshot of the political debates and evaluations taking place within each community at the time of research. To preserve the anonymity of respondents, I have changed the names of respondents and identified each local government by the department – a higher-level administrative unit – that it falls within. Because Senegal's administrative units are named after their capital city, I identify the capital village (or *chef-lieu*) of each local government as, for example, "Kebemer-Village."

As with the survey data presented in Chapter 4, I was cautious about priming respondents to discuss the precolonial past. Accordingly, I instructed my research assistants to not explicitly raise questions about this period until a respondent did, asking more generic questions about their village's foundation instead. Across interviews, we heard largely consistent narratives within each local government. Indeed, in many cases, respondents inadvertently cross-validated each other. For example, villages founded in new territories such as Koungheul often engaged in chained patterns of migration; arriving in a new zone, individuals would seek a "host" in an existing village before founding their own settlement nearby in the following years, once a well had been dug and fields plowed. These entwined histories of settlement were always told on both sides: in the village that first hosted newcomers and in the villages that the newcomers went on to settle.

Of course, the risk that these stories were inflated remains, but the shared nature of their telling remains important even if the facts stray into local mythologies. In this way, the stories I heard reflect a localized process of meaning-making as much, if not more, than an accurate retelling of history. We could, however, imagine that in an age of autochthony debates, individuals may claim to an outsider, such as myself, that their village is older or that it played a particularly weighty role in local history. Yet I saw no such opportunism. Indeed, recently founded villages were often headed by the founder himself

Case Selection and Methodology

or, at times, a son, both of whom would detail with pride their village's founding story. Though many of the stories recounted below are likely inflated and partially reimagined, therefore, I have little reason to think that they are invented *de novo*.

At the time of research, all three local governments were facing a common set of structural challenges. First, local councils struggled with the realities of President Sall's *Acte III* of decentralization, introduced in Chapter 2. Though this had earned them the titles of *commune* and *mayor*, many were disappointed with the reforms, which had done little to alleviate the most central concern of local elected officials: finances. Yearly fiscal transfers had only barely increased, officials noted, yet they were being asked to take on more responsibilities at the same time that local populations had come to expect more activity at the local level.

This was further complicated by President Sall's second major initiative, *Le Plan Senegal Émergent* (PSE), a medium-term plan designed to transform the country's economy. For local officials, the felt consequence of the PSE was the elimination of a number of state programs that had previously provided fiscal transfers for local governments that, though earmarked by sector, granted the local council full autonomy over their use. While yearly transfers of the FDD, the financial lifeline for local governments, remained constant, Sall introduced instead the United Nations Development Program co-sponsored *Programme d'Urgence de Développement Communitaire* (PUDC), effectively removing local control over program funding to centralize it in the prime minister's office. This is not without benefit for rural livelihoods. The PUDC is focused on large-scale investments such as roads and boreholes that are far beyond the means or competency of the local state. But local officials elected in 2014 found themselves with a significantly reduced set of fiscal assets than their predecessors. This was widely recognized; across all three cases, local councilors, village chiefs, and other stakeholders observed a sharp decline in local government activity.

At the same time, Senegal's rural mayors were working within a weak and fragmented local party structure. Echoing a common story of the 2014 local elections, the communities were animated by political jockeying within the relatively weak Presidential majority coalition, *Benno Bokk Yakkar* (BBY) or, alternatively, within Sall's own party, the *Alliance pour le République* (APR). The consequence was the splintering of lists within the party itself, meaning that some voters saw multiple lists from the same political camp on their ballots. In many cases, for example, the APR ran lists against their own coalition, BBY. This reflects, in part, a long-standing tendency toward intraparty factionalism in the country, but it speaks more immediately to the weak structure of the relatively young APR at the grassroots.[5] While the previous ruling parties, the long-ruling *Parti socialiste* (PS) and the *Parti démocratique sénégalais* (PDS),

---

[5] See Cruise O'Brien (1975).

maintained robust local party apparatuses, few rural areas had a meaningful APR presence until Sall's election in 2012, which prompted significant bandwagoning to the majority party by elected officials and village chiefs. As detailed below, this meant the outcome of the 2014 elections was not a given for any candidate in the cases under study.

Each case under study had seen a new mayor elected in 2014, and together the three factors detailed above meant they all found themselves facing unforeseen top-down constraints on the resources at their disposal and bottom-up constraints imposed by weak local party structures. Despite these similarities, however, I document below three very different outcomes for local governance.

ASSESSING THE THEORY IN KEBEMER AND KOUNGHEUL

I introduce the cases of Kebemer and Koungheul by focusing on the three component parts of my theory: the (a) identity and (b) network mechanisms that sustain (c) cross-village social institutions when both are present. The section "Representation and Redistribution across Social Networks" goes on to compare why the presence of social institutions that encompass the majority of villages enables local officials in Kebemer to better overcome the social dilemmas they face in the local council.

The Identity Mechanism

Kebemer is the home of the mayor at whose party this chapter opened. Despite being erected as a local government in 1976, few local elites discuss Kebemer's history as if it was a mere forty-years-old, placing local history firmly within a legacy of the Cayor Empire, a major precolonial state in the Senegambian region.[6] During the era of the Cayor, most villages in the kingdom were highly stable social units, linked together through clientelist ties, shared histories, and mythology.[7] Evidence collected during my stay suggests that these patterns have persisted and residents widely expressed great pride in the shared heritage they believed their community represented. Indeed, the mayor, Alou Gueye, welcomed me first and foremost to the "heart of the Cayor."[8]

The community's uncontested founding narrative was that the zone had been settled over 400 years earlier by five families who had departed the Djoloff Empire, under which the Cayor had long been a vassal.[9] Together, each family had founded their own village, with their descendants expanding to establish new settlements over time.[10] As a result, most villages in the

---

[6] Note that the local government did not fall in the territory annexed by the French General Faidherbe in the 1860s. Nor does the current territory of the local government included any of the kingdom's centers of power.
[7] Diouf (1990, 17). [8] Interview, February 6, 2017.
[9] The Cayor seceded in the mid-fifteen-hundreds. [10] Interview, February 8, 2017.

community traced their descent from one of the five founding lineages and 85 percent of community's villages were settled before the onset of colonial rule. Of the handful created after 1880, only three were established by inmigrants with no ties to the zone. Because of this shared descent, the local government is dominated by the Wolof ethnic group, the ethnicity of four of the five founding families, though one of the Wolof families was casted. The remaining founding lineage was ethnically Maure. These families had been joined during the precolonial era by Peulh pastoralists, whose settlement in the zone created friendships and reciprocal ties between "new" and "old" villages, reflecting a broader pattern in the kingdom which was home to Mandingue, Maure, Peulh, and Serer minorities.[11] Now, one Wolof chief said of his Peulh neighbors "we are the same family."[12]

The identity of a shared descent from the Cayor generated a commonsense framework that individuals drew on when describing their community. Most residents shared a deep respect for their history and were extremely hesitant to betray this common identification.[13] In particular, a prominent role was played by the shared claim to the final resistance thrown up by the Cayor as the French advanced into Senegal's interior; "this is a historic zone," one village chief explained, "we always resisted the whites with Lat Dior [the last king of Cayor]. We are not cowards."[14] As the local development agent explained that "this history is still very powerful here ... everyone's ancestors were involved." As articulated by the former mayor in no unclear terms: "these century old relations gave [Kebemer] a historical consciousness and identity." The history may have been bloody, he continued, but the impact today is only positive.[15] The current mayor, one chief noted, won in the 2014 local elections explicitly because he had successfully "played the card of unity," highlighting his descent from a prominent, aristocratic family rather than seeding partisan competition.[16]

The second case, Koungheul, is located to Kebemer's southeast in Kaffrine Region which falls in the eastern stretches of Senegal's peanut basin, the epicenter of the country's cash crop production. Prior to French colonization, Koungheul was acephalous, home to a sparse population living independently outside the control of a centralized polity. In an 1896 report, an early colonial administrator described the region by what it was not rather than what it was: "For the commodity of language, I designate under the generic name of 'Coungheul' the group of heterogeneous cantons ... bordered to the west by the Saloum, to the north by Djoloff ..."[17] Densely forested and primarily inhabited by nomadic Peulh pastoralists in the precolonial era, no existing

---

[11] Diouf (1990, 20–21). Traditionally, minorities were administered under a distinct political hierarchy. Peulhs, for example, could choose an *ardo* as their chief, but a Wolof *jarga* served as an intermediary and could control a given *ardo* if they wanted (Diouf 1990, 68).
[12] Interview, February 9, 2017.   [13] Interview, village chief, February 12, 2017.
[14] Interview, February 10, 2017.   [15] Interview, February 12, 2017.
[16] Interview, February 11, 2017.   [17] Orbessier (1896).

village in the local government was founded prior to 1900. The first wave of modern implantation occurred in the early years of French colonization and many chiefs recounted how their grandparents had spent years clearing the land, digging wells, and, in many cases, fighting off wild animals that inhabited the forest. These settlers searched for new land for their families and herds, seeking to escape overcrowded villages and the social upheaval generated by the early stages of colonial occupation.[18] In other cases, marabouts (Islamic religious guides) moved to the area to found *Dahiras*, or Koranic schools, away from French interference. More recent waves of implantation came as Peulh herders settled in the area, in particular following the droughts of the 1970s and 1980s.

Unlike in the Cayor, stories of settlement in Koungheul are largely specific to each village, though in some cases clusters of villages shared a unifying settlement history. For example, one maraboutic village had been the initial point of arrival in the zone for the families that went on to found a number of surrounding villages. In this way, these villages possessed a group identity – their shared allegiance to the marabout – but it encompassed only a small percentage of villages in the local government. Across the local government as a whole, no narrative about what it meant to be Koungheulese was heard. This is revealed in the comments of a retired school director who explained that the local government capital, Koungheul-Village, had long reclaimed that the mayor be from their village, since they had only held city hall once. Being administered by mayors from other villages is "like a technical administration always coming here to rule us," he sighed.[19] Social identities are present in Koungheul, therefore, but they are splintered across villages within the local state.

The cases of Kebemer and Koungheul echo many of those presented in Chapter 4. The availability of a shared history of descent from a precolonial kingdom united Kebemer's villages into a cohesive local identity that revolved around the glory of the Cayor. Because no comparable touchstone was available in Koungheul, no overarching political identity emerged, with individuals attached to their villages, religious leaders, or their ethnic groups. Koungheul, in other words, is a case of multiple, sub-local government identities.

The Network Mechanism

Local social network ties also differed across the two cases. Again and again, elected officials and traditional authorities in centralized Kebemer claimed that these very family relations and shared histories of cohabitation had generated a "mentality of solidarity," thus that whenever political disputes arise, everyone moves quickly to protect local social relations.[20] In contrast, interviewees in Koungheul reported pockets of social connections between villages whose

---

[18] As discussed by Klein (1968b, 211).   [19] Interview, February 16, 2017.
[20] Interview, local government councilor, March 9, 2017.

grandparents had migrated together to settle or, as in the case of Peulh pastoralists who had settled in the area, connections built through intermarriage over the past half-century.

Preliminary evidence for the network mechanism was found in the survey data presented in Chapter 4, but the case studies offer a means to test this more robustly. I collected the reported social ties of each village chief and elected official interviewed. Though individuals' social networks extend far beyond the borders of the local government, I bound the network to villages and councilors within the local government. This meant that I asked each village chief if they personally knew the chief of each village in the local government and, if so, how they would describe their social relationship. I additionally asked each village chief if there was a councilor from their village or if there had been since 1996 as well as their relationship to these individuals. Later, I more generally asked if they were related to any other political actors in the local government to catch any missed connections. Because I only interviewed approximately 20 percent of elected officials in each local government, I primarily rely on reporting by chiefs about their connections with the councilors in their village.[21] Though respondents at times disagreed over whether or not they were friends, no one identified someone as family without their pair reciprocating that identification.[22]

Figure 6.1 displays the extended family ties between village chiefs in each local government as a baseline for intervillage connectivity. Each node represents a village chief in the network, with ties between nodes indicating a reported relationship between them. Figure 6.1 displays these ties categorically by the nature of reported relationships, either extended (e.g. second cousins) or immediate family (e.g. sibling, uncle, or in-law).[23] Figure 6.2 displays friendship ties. Nodes are disaggregated by ethnicity in both Figures 6.1 and 6.2. Lastly, Figure 6.3 compares reported relationships between village chiefs and councilors (disaggregated by gender) who were serving at the time of research (meaning those elected in 2014), with nodes color-coded by village of origin.

The networks look starkly different. In Kebemer, the social network is largely well-connected and centralized, with all but one village reporting multiple family ties to other village chiefs. While there is some indication of ethnic segmentation, there is evidence of intermarriage across villages. In contrast, we see clustering effects in Koungheul where a densely connected subnetwork of small, Peulh villages have heavily intermarried (though three villages of Peulh in-migrants from Guinea report no family ties at all). Wolof and Serer elites remain loosely connected. Friendship ties, seen in Figure 6.2, show slightly

---

[21] Interviews with elected officials allowed me to cross-validate, revealing perfect reliability.
[22] In cases of disagreement, I revert to the most distant type of social connection. For example, if one chief identifies another as a friend while the pair identifies the chief as an acquaintance, I code this as an acquaintance.
[23] The visualized spread of villages does not reflect geographic placement of villages.

166 Congruence and Incongruence in Action

(a) Kebemer

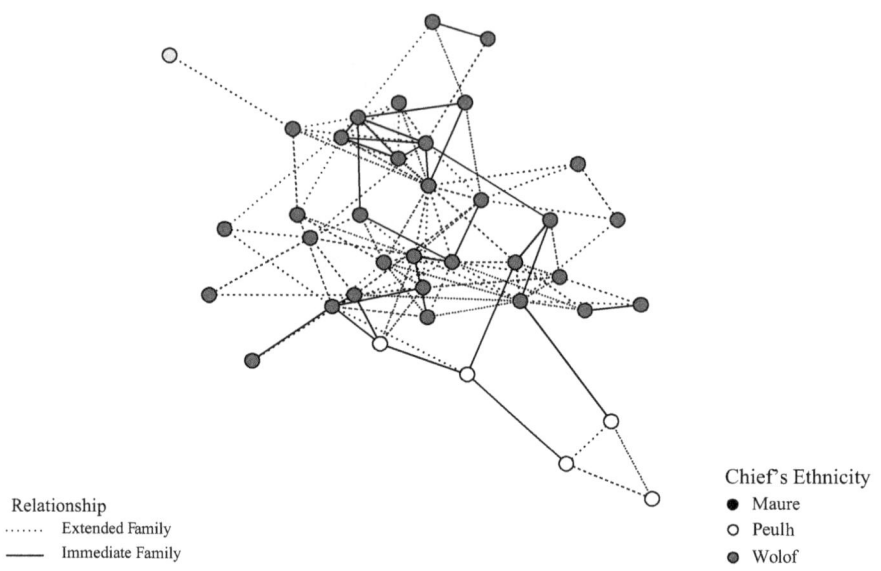

Relationship
.... Extended Family
——— Immediate Family

Chief's Ethnicity
● Maure
○ Peulh
● Wolof

(b) Koungheul

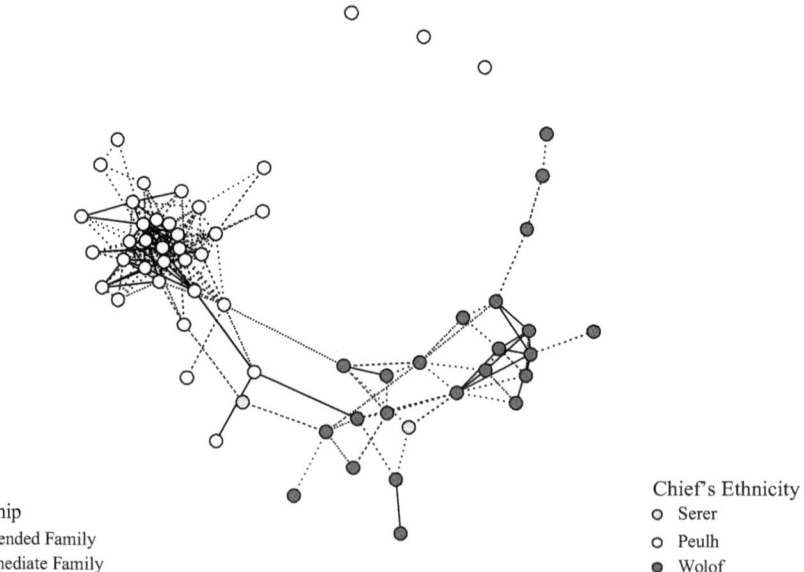

Relationship
.... Extended Family
——— Immediate Family

Chief's Ethnicity
○ Serer
○ Peulh
● Wolof

FIGURE 6.1 Family network relations between village chiefs: (a) Kebemer and (b) Koungheul

(a) Kebemer

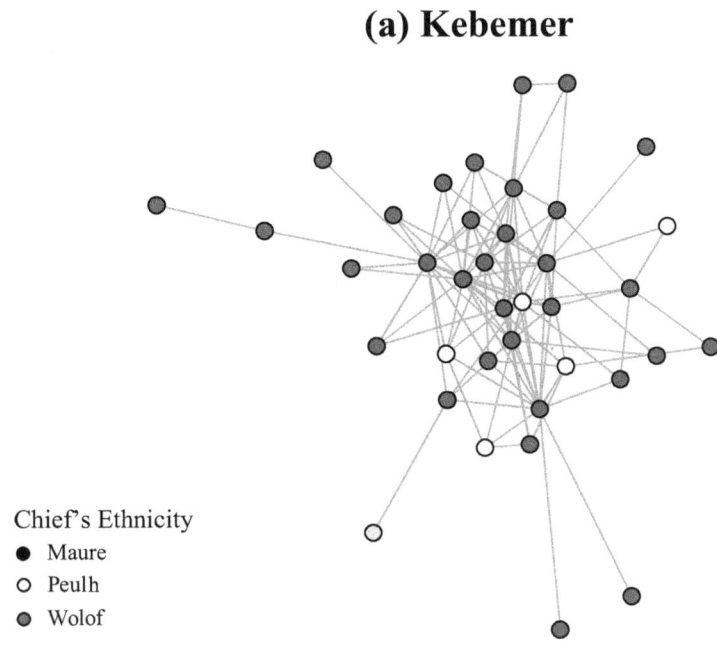

Chief's Ethnicity
- Maure
- Peulh
- Wolof

(b) Koungheul

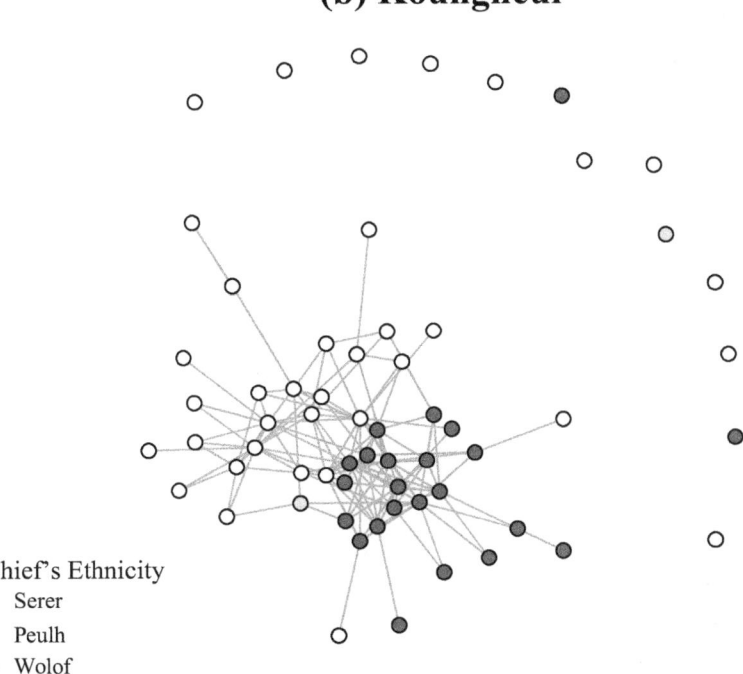

Chief's Ethnicity
- Serer
- Peulh
- Wolof

FIGURE 6.2 Friendship network relations between village chiefs: (a) Kebemer and (b) Koungheul

168   *Congruence and Incongruence in Action*

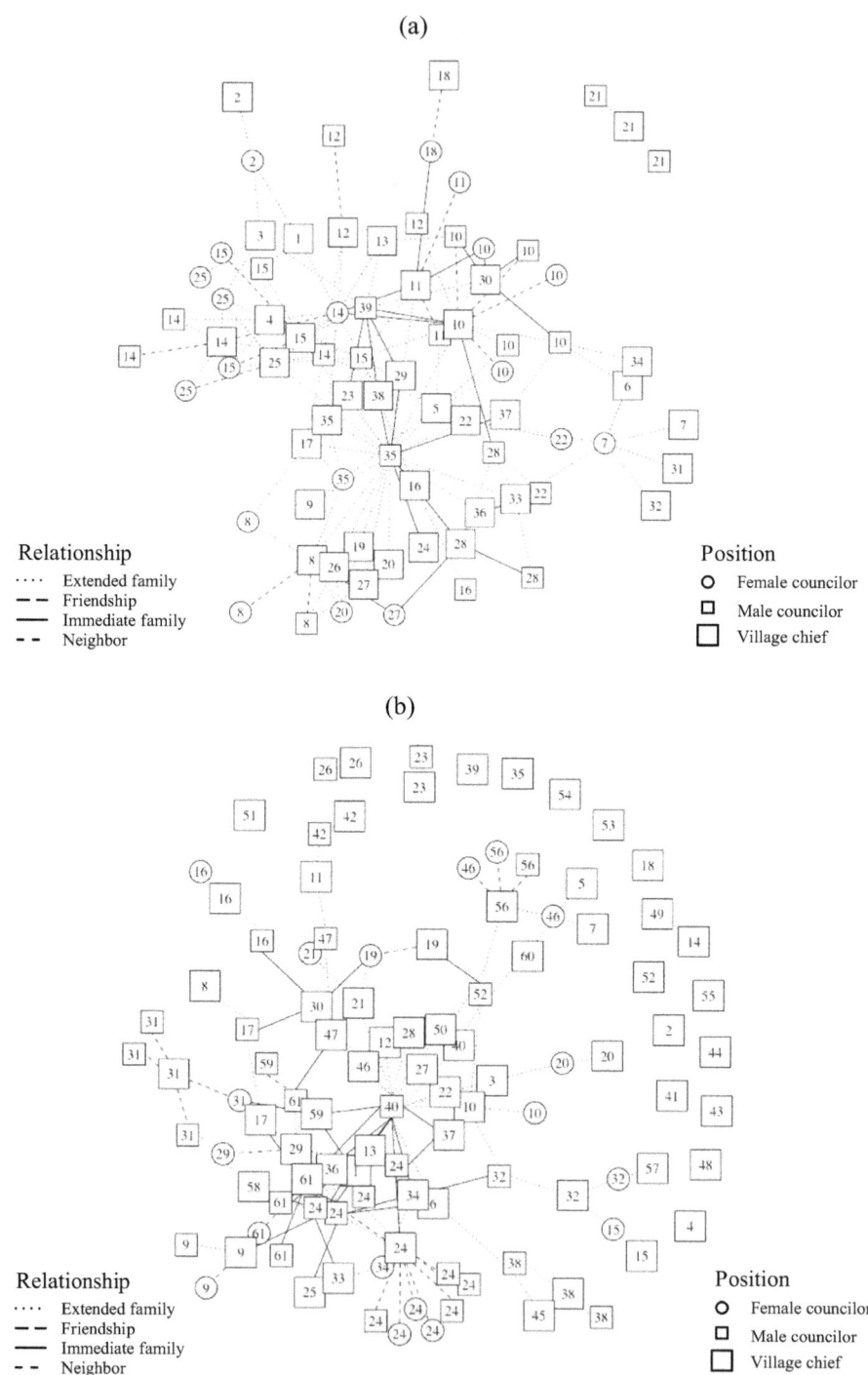

FIGURE 6.3 Network relations between village chiefs and local elected officials: (a) Kebemer and (b) Koungheul

more centrality in Koungheul. Nonetheless, a large number of village chiefs report no friends in other villages at all, and across both family and friendship networks, acephalous Koungheul displays a much larger number of isolated or near-isolated nodes. This has no parallel in Kebemer, where all elites report at least one family and friendship ties, and most report multiple ties of each type.

These dynamics are particularly acute when we examine the relationships between village chiefs and elected councilors; here the centrality present in Kebemer across local elites is clear. As displayed in Figure 6.3, one clear network appears in Kebemer. Koungheul likewise has a central cluster, but we see the presence of far more weak connections at the edges. Nearly one-third of villages are not connected to another village at all, though a few report connections to their village's own councilors. Together, these network plots reflect what comes out in the interviews. Social networks in Kebemer are more coherent and interconnected than those in Koungheul, where network centrality clusters within ethnic groups while a number of villages report weak or nonexistent social ties.

How the Mechanisms Support Cross-Village Social Institutions in Kebemer but Not Koungheul?

Respondents in Kebemer repeatedly invoked shared social expectations for public life. As norms of appropriate behavior in the public sphere demarcated by group boundaries, social institutions rely on dense social networks and strong identities to motivate individuals to adhere to their logic. Actors abide by any given social institution both because they perceive costs to not doing so and because they think to do so is proper or good. Parallel to those identified by survey respondents in Chapter 4, social institutions in Kebemer were most frequently invoked along two axes. The first is around conflict resolution and prevention, most often discussed with reference to the concept of *"democratie de palabre,"* or democracy by ongoing discussion. The tradition of community leaders sitting together to discuss an issue until they find a mutually agreeable solution echoes the practices described by Schaffer (1998, 80). Writing on Senegal's Wolof heartland, Schaffer argues that Senegalese peasants and rural elite think of democracy not just as electoral practice, but as reflecting "consensus, solidarity and evenhandedness." This was reported widely in Kebemer. As phrased by one chief in Kebemer, "the tradition of discussion has always been the secret behind our social force."[24]

The broader manifestations of this norm had direct bearing on local political practice. The declaration of the former mayor of Koungheul that politics is "a confrontation like chess" could not be in sharper contrast to the position of Mar Ndaw, Kebemer's former mayor, who argued that even someone who is

---

[24] Interviews, February 11 and 13, 2017.

your enemy today could be your ally in the future so it was best to not risk offending them. Explicitly citing the cost to local social relations, local elites in Kebemer all boasted that they would never call in the police or state agents to resolve disputes; "even if there is a complicated problem, we call the mayor. We will do everything to not call the police."[25]

This "mentality of solidarity" serves to prevent the escalation of conflict and, when it does arise, to protect the reputations of those involved.[26] Kebemer's former mayor, Ndaw, reported going to great lengths to resolve potential points of conflict, especially when applying the law may adversely impact family members. "I would prepare the terrain, talking to people and informing them," he recalled, working through trusted intermediaries, such as village chiefs, notables, or mutual friends, when the situation called for it. He continued, "you cannot just impose things ... Especially when you are related, you have to go with humility, know-how and then be willing to work with them" on any given issue. Such practices are not only time-consuming, he acknowledged, but they limited his political choices.[27] Social networks, in other words, were directly cited as shaping political strategies. "Politics is complex," one elderly chief in Kebemer recalled, but no matter how complicated, "you should never do things that dirty your family name and you should certainly never damage family ties for the sake of politics."[28] Here we see clearly how the theory's twin mechanisms are activated to reinforce powerful social institutions that constrain political strategies.

Such informal institutions exist everywhere and almost all village chiefs in rural Senegal describe one of their central obligations as "guarding social stability in the village."[29] But it is only in communities like Kebemer that they stretch across villages to encompass the vast majority of elites. Consequently, cross-village, extended family ties were sacrosanct in Kebemer, but they were not so in acephalous Koungheul. "In politics, there is no family," stated Koungheul's former mayor acerbically.[30] Indeed, his local government illustrated this well: the current and former mayors were cousins, but they were also engaged in a bitter, ongoing rivalry within the same political party. Some in their large, extended family scolded both men for creating tension in the family and others stayed clearly in one camp or the other, but most prioritized keeping peace with their relatives, noting that "we are family and everyone has problems sometimes."[31] Locally understood and institutionalized norms of resolving conflicts are not specific to Kebemer, therefore, but *who* they apply to – a village, an extended family, or, as in the case of Kebemer, to all descendants of the Cayor – differs.

---

[25] Interview, village chief, February 9, 2017.   [26] Interview, councilor, March 9, 2017.
[27] Interview, February 12, 2017.   [28] Interview, February 9, 2017.
[29] Interview, village chief, Kaffrine Region, February 21, 2017.
[30] Interview, February 18, 2017.   [31] Interviews, February 19–21, 2017.

The second influential social institution in historically centralized areas is the prioritization of balancing across group members. It was quite rare in Kebemer to hear complaints of favoritism; most village chiefs, for example, thought that the local government recognized each village's needs without attention to ethnicity or caste and without ignoring smaller villages. This was not explained as a function of democratic ideas, but rather to the idea that the local government's constituent villages had equal claim to its resources by virtue of their shared history.

While individuals noted equality as an aspirational goal in both communities, it was only in Kebemer that local elites spoke of their government as actually attaining it. In Koungheul, it was quite common for individuals to argue that officials should fight narrowly for the interest of their own village. The description of one chief's ideal candidate for local government in Kebemer as "a good leader for the municipal council is someone who puts everyone on equal footing and who works hard" is at odds with a common response in Koungheul, "the councilor should help the population of his village and defend them in the council."[32] If in Kebemer local elites had all embraced the value of equality among villages, elsewhere elites had either internalized the comparative inequality they lived under or had learned that their villages and clients would never get anywhere if they waited for the local council to bring it.

Social Institutions in Action: Evaluating the 2014 Local Elections

The dynamics of institutional congruence are illustrated with particular clarity in the outcomes of the 2014 local elections. Both local governments saw the defeat of the incumbent mayor by a relative newcomer to the political scene, yet while the consequences of this upset continued to generate political tensions in Koungheul, they had largely been papered over in Kebemer.

In 2014, Kebemer saw Alou Gueye, running with the new Presidential Coalition, BBY, defeat the two-term incumbent, Mar Ndaw. As introduced at the start of the chapter, Gueye was a recently retired bureaucrat who had returned to the local government as a vocal ally of the president. Ndaw had been elected twice with former President Abdoulaye Wade's PDS and ran again with the PDS in 2014. Both men were educated and came from locally prominent families. Ndaw was considered to have done much for the local government, investing broadly and prolifically, but he faced a difficult contest with Gueye, who was seen by many as a potential asset given his experiences in the bureaucracy. In line with social institutions of balancing, the sentiment prevailed that it was only fair to give someone else a chance; as one chief reasoned about the choice to vote for Gueye over the incumbent Ndaw, "Ndaw already

---

[32] Interviews, Louga Region, February 13, 2017 and Kaffrine Region, February 21, 2017.

served two mandates and the population thought they should give it to someone new."[33]

The election was incredibly close. Gueye's BBY coalition only won with the help of the nearly unanimous support of a large Peulh village, run by an influential marabout. Two details of Senegal's electoral system are key to understanding the political intrigue that followed. Senegalese political parties run a majority and a proportional list and if a party wins, all of the candidates on its majority list pass as well as the equivalent percentage of their vote share on the proportional list. In Kebemer, the sitting mayor, Ndaw, had made the usual move of placing himself at the top of the proportional list ("I take this as a sign he knew he couldn't win," his successor jabbed) and was accordingly elected into the opposition. A second peculiarity of Senegal's local elections is that local government leadership, the mayor and his two adjoints, are only elected indirectly by members of the new council following the general elections. This means that even though Ndaw's party lost the majority, he was still eligible to be elected mayor, which, in fact, he tried to accomplish by recruiting votes from three councilors elected under Gueye's APR lists. Upon learning of this betrayal within the APR, Gueye sensed that his candidacy was imperiled, leading him to go back on a campaign promise that his first adjoint would come from his coalition partners in the Socialist Party, promising it instead to a member of a nonaligned minority party as a means to buy himself the three necessary replacement votes. The move worked, but it continued to raise eyebrows three years later.

Communities like Kebemer are clearly not without political conflict. Politicians want to win, and they will pursue this at length. What is distinct, however, is the degree to which community members bound these interactions. Though heated at the moment, therefore, political memories in Kebemer are uniquely muted. When probed about the three councilors' betrayal in 2014, for example, Gueye dismissed my questions, stating that he "had forgotten all that and who voted for whom."[34] Ndaw concurred, observing that the community had "barriers" to who can become one's enemy or adversary. "We are here amongst ourselves," he explained, continuing "the lead-up to elections is the time for politics ... afterwards, everyone returns to their work since everyone knows everyone else."[35] The outcome is not collective amnesia. Individuals speak with relative openness of past disagreements, but they embed them within social ties. Admitting that he sometimes disagrees with friends and family in the local government, one former councilor and current advisor to

---

[33] Interview, village chief, February 11, 2017. A second factor raised by a handful of respondents was that Ndaw had built a small project in his own village rather than in the much larger capital village, located 2 kilometers away the year before the election. Whether the project was truly best placed in Kebemer-Village or not remains unclear, but for some Ndaw had actively violated local norms around how public goods should be allocated.
[34] Interview, February 6, 2017.   [35] Interview, February 12, 2017.

the mayor explained that this simply could not take priority. "Other relationships are stronger, more important than the council," he stressed.[36]

Koungheul also saw a political betrayal in 2014. Like Kebemer, Koungheul had elected the majority Wolof local government's first Peulh mayor, Mamadou Dia, with the PDS in 2002 and again in 2009. In 2014, Dia's cousin and a sitting local government councilor, Abdou Balde, challenged him in – and ultimately won – the local elections. Though Dia had been elected to both terms with the PDS, like many mayors he had joined the APR in 2013. This understandably upset his cousin, who had himself been preparing to run with the APR, only to find himself cast aside by departmental APR officials who believed that Dia was a more promising candidate. Angered, Balde quit the party and approached the PDS who, interested in obtaining a well-known and, not inconsequentially, wealthy candidate to their camp, quickly altered their electoral list to accommodate him. In what to many was a surprise victory, Balde beat his cousin by running with the latter's former party. And within just days of his election under the banner of the PDS, Balde rallied to his former party, the APR, to bring himself and many of the candidates elected with him into the Presidential majority.

In Koungheul, family ties did little to smooth over Dia and Balde's mutual dislike and both men reported virtually no social contact. In direct contrast to the frequently heard desire to protect social relations in Kebemer, a councilor in Koungheul stated in no unequivocal terms that "family doesn't play in politics." What differs is that in Koungheul, no cross-cutting social institutions have emerged to check the political repercussions of both old and new political divisions. "Well," concluded one of village notable, "politics is like this. A friend today can become your enemy tomorrow."[37] This lesson, in turn, had been learned by Mamadou Dia who was still visibly angry over his cousin having ousted him in 2014.

The 2014 elections created a number of lingering political tensions. The residents of Koungheul-Village were anxious to elect a member of their own village as mayor, yet despite having a strong candidate on the PDS list, many Wolof councilors from the village defected at the last minute to support Balde for mayor because their village's own candidate was a member of a lower social caste. Prominent elites in the village, the mayor explained, could not bring themselves to vote for someone whose grandparents had danced and sung for their grandparents, a reference to the casted councilor's descent from griots.[38] As the local government secretary stated early in our first meeting, "the Wolofs here do not get along and the Peulhs profit."[39] The heated political campaign in 2014 still actively colored political allegiances in Koungheul in the winter of 2017. Dia remained the local APR party coordinator, protected by his close

---

[36] Interview, February 13, 2017. [37] Interview, February 22, 2017.
[38] Interview, February 23, 2017. [39] Interview, February 23, 2017.

friendship with the party's departmental leader, much to the chagrin of Balde, who felt that the position should be his as mayor. Rumors swirled. One councilor, loyal to Dia was skeptical "he [Balde] says he rejoined the APR, but I heard he may be with another party ...."[40]

Though we may be tempted to understand Koungheul's politics as ethnic, this would be a simplification of the situation. At base, what divides the local government is those who lament the departure of Dia, who was a strong patron to those who supported him, and those who have rallied behind Balde, who struggles to deliver to his supporters. Both men actively report their first political objective as rewarding their core supporters, no matter their ethnicity or caste, reflecting an ability to politicize social network ties opportunistically. This stands in stark contrast to the prevailing rhetoric in Kebemer, which emphasized putting electoral rivalries aside and working for the good of the local government specifically to preserve social relations.

REPRESENTATION AND REDISTRIBUTION ACROSS SOCIAL NETWORKS

If social institutions vary in the degree to which they embed local officials across villages, then this should create different solutions to the redistributive dilemmas generated by decentralized governance. I examine this in two issue areas, village representation on local electoral lists and, second, local government public goods delivery over a fifteen-year period between 2002 and 2017.

Representation

The goal of improving representation is central to democratic decentralization. Beyond its value in its own right, facilitating the ability of local citizens to voice their preferences is among the most desired of decentralization's many claimed benefits. Citizens who feel represented by the state should see the state as more legitimate and hold their governments more accountable to help make governance more efficient.

This makes allegations of bias and neglect – such as one village chief in acephalous Koungheul's statement that the local council "has never taken care of us, even though we are part of the municipality too" – all the more troubling. The village had never had a councilor and, according to the chief, every village had been helped but his.[41] The latter statement was factually untrue, but the perception among villages that they were singled out and treated as lesser community members has profound consequences for state consolidation at the grassroots. When communities feel that "we are only there to elect them

[40] Interview, February 16, 2017.   [41] Interview, February 17, 2017.

Representation and Redistribution 175

and nothing else," it is not surprising that, over time, some segments of the population disengage from their local government.[42]

The easiest measurement of these dynamics is found in discussions of electoral list construction. "It's very hard to make party lists," the former mayor of Koungheul stated. "There are those who can do the work well, but do not have a mass [followers] behind them, and then there are those who do not know how to work, but who have a mass with them," and in this case, he continued, you have to take the latter.[43] The practice of seeking candidates with influence – be it in their village, with area women or youth, etc. – is common around the country, but deciding which villages obtain candidates is another question altogether.

In Koungheul, these decisions were recounted as being bitter and deceptive. It was not uncommon for village chiefs to report that party leaders had promised to put someone from the village on their party lists, leading villagers to declare their allegiance for and campaign with the party, only to find on election day that their village's candidate had never been on the list at all.[44] Such deception was not easily forgiven. The village chief of Koungheul-Village reported with pride that he had taken his horse cart across the local government to campaign against Dia in 2014, explicitly stating that his endorsement of Balde was to spite Dia, who had promised the chief a spot on the 2009 PDS electoral list, only to omit his name once the official lists were posted.[45] Though lists are often made during meetings with all local party officials, it was widely agreed upon in Koungheul that "once the leader is alone, they can change the names."[46] Smaller villages or those that felt disadvantaged spoke of this process as compounding their inability to get anything from the state. "Party leaders just pick people who will follow them," stated one disgruntled chief.[47]

Such contention is largely absent in centralized Kebemer, where respondents by and large tell a similar tale of how lists are made: party leaders go to villages looking for influential people, often by consulting with village leaders. Once a list of potential candidates is in hand, the party decides how many councilors to take from each village (largely according to village population) and then consults with the village to help narrow down the list of potential candidates. Invoking the community's dense networks, Kebemer's mayor reported that making electoral lists was not very hard at all ("we all know each

---

[42] Interview, village chief, March 2, 2017.   [43] Interview, February 18, 2017.
[44] Party lists are posted at the subprefecture in the days before the election. Because most villages are quite far away and, in any case, many rural Senegalese are illiterate, this means that it is hard for most villagers to verify who is or is not on the list until the election.
[45] The rivalry was personal, but it took on ethnic undertones. Overhearing our conversation, one friend of the chief murmured "well I told you at the time you shouldn't let a Peulh from the Djoloff rule over you," referencing Dia's ethnic origins (Interview, February 16, 2017).
[46] Interview, February 22, 2017.   [47] Interview, February 26, 2017.

other after all"), and they simply proceeded by asking each village to put forward names of influential and qualified people. While the mayor admitted to having given the chef-lieu more spots than he would have otherwise – only to face an unexpectedly tight competition there – most villages were assigned as many spots on party lists as their population merited.[48] Certainly, this does not mean that everyone is content with the number of councilors they receive, but most accepted that this followed local norms of maintaining balance across villages. Importantly, when grievances were voiced, village chiefs engaged in a form of excuse-making prevalent in historically centralized areas. Noting that his village had not had a councilor in years, even though he always asks for one, one chief quickly suggested that this was probably because his village had moved closer to a larger village home to their marabouts a few decades before. "They likely don't consider us our own village anymore, since we are so close ..." he observed, noting that the marabout's village did have a councilor who he considered to represent his village's interests.[49]

Redistribution

Perceptions of bias and favoritism are not only more prevalent in historically acephalous areas, they are also sharper, neatly articulated along locally demarcated political cleavages. In contrast to the 6 percent of chiefs who made any allegation of unequal treatment by the local government (for their own village or others) during the course of the interview in Kebemer, 57 percent alleged some form of inequality in Koungheul. Even chiefs who did criticize the local government of Kebemer reflected norms of conflict avoidance by excusing such behavior. For example, one chief whose village had not been among those to receive a solar panel for their mosque was not sure why his village had been left out. Invoking a norm of equality, he argued that if most villages were receiving something, then all villages should do so, though he caveated that the fact that his village mosque already had a solar panel might have something to do with it.[50] Still, across the board, respondents in Kebemer reported that distributional choices are "not overly political" the way they might be elsewhere.[51] More often than not, village chiefs and councilors had a clear understanding of why things were placed where they were, revealing how information circulated within their dense social network: to take a few illustrations, "[the recipient village] is a large village, so it is normal that the health hut there was rebuilt"; the council "tries to look for which village is the most needy and the situation of neighboring villages"; "we know each other, we may all have the same needs,

---

[48] Interview, February 6, 2017.
[49] Interview, February 10, 2017. Indeed, the villages were effectively functioning as one coherent settlement.
[50] Interview, February 9, 2017.   [51] Interview, local development agent, February 8, 2017.

but we also know whose needs really are urgent."⁵² In Kebemer, redistributive choices were widely seen as fair and following a sufficiently transparent logic.

There was also little debate over how things were distributed in acephalous Koungheul: the political allies of the mayor are given priority eight times out of ten, contended one chief, an equation he claimed was true of the current mayor as well as his predecessor.⁵³ Some had been favored under one administration, but consequently ignored by the next. For this reason, another chief expressed skepticism that the current council would ever repair his village's broken water pipeline since he had served as a loyal councilor with the previous mayor for two terms.⁵⁴ Even the most basic interactions with the local government, including the delivery of birth, marriage, and death certificates, were subject to political interference. Koungheul's former mayor was widely reported to have denied signing any *etat-civile* paperwork (such as birth or marriage certificates) for villages that did not support him. One councilor, a local health agent, reported that it had been nearly impossible for her to get birth certificates for newborns in her village, "Mohamadou Dia [the previous mayor] didn't like the village because, even if he had a few followers in the village, most of the village was not with him. He wanted all of the villages ... so he blocked our paperwork as punishment."⁵⁵

Technically, delivering paperwork is not a devolved competence, but it is the most burdensome task that the local state is charged with, requiring extensive hours of copying and recopying paper records of all declared births, deaths, and marriages. The incoming mayor, who had served as a councilor in the previous term, said he had processed thousands of *état-civile* requests since taking office.⁵⁶ All children who wish to enter primary school must present a birth certificate, and denying birth certificates for children for more than a year after birth requires a more elaborate – and expensive – process later on. The most frequent interaction that most rural Senegalese have with the local state involves *état-civile* paperwork and for many, it is their only interaction. Despite this, one of Koungheul's chiefs surmised that the politicization of this most bureaucratic of tasks was not surprising; "Mohamadou Dia was always in campaign mode, when he knew that your village wasn't with him, he did nothing for you."⁵⁷

Politicians are acutely aware that they need to deliver "development" to their constituents if they wish to win reelections. Despite the restricted financial resources he had to work with, for example, the mayor of centralized Kebemer proudly recounted the many things he had accomplished in his term, including an ongoing project to digitize the *état-civile,* rebuilding a health hut, the

---

⁵² Interviews, village chief, February 7, 2017; opposition councilor, February 13, 2017; and village chief, February 10, 2017.
⁵³ Interview, February 16, 2017.   ⁵⁴ Interview, February 17, 2017.
⁵⁵ Interview, February 19, 2017.   ⁵⁶ Interview, February 23, 2017.
⁵⁷ Interview, February 20, 2017.

construction of a new vaccination center for livestock, remodeling an old community building where he planned to put a library as well as the aforementioned solar panels, and the purchase of six millet mills introduced at the start of the book. By and large, Alou Gueye followed the strategy of balancing outlined by his predecessor: the latter explained that he had explicitly targeted villages that had not voted for him when he first took office, recognizing that "I would lose later if I didn't work with everyone" and that one was "first and foremost a development agent as the PCR [mayor] and a leader should not leave people out or put politics before development." As a result, Ndaw had spent a little more than $9,000 bringing water to a large village he had lost during his first campaign in 2002. "They are still very happy with me there," he laughed.[58]

This strategy was not universally shared. In contrast to Kebemer, where the mayor had yet to deliver anything to his own village, politicians in Koungheul frequently made such investments. For his part, Koungheul's mayor stated that the most pressing need in his local government was to build a new health post in the village immediately neighboring his own, even though they were only 6 kilometers from the post in Koungheul-Village, far closer than the local government average. His first act, he reported, was to bring water to two villages where more than 95 percent of the polling station had voted against him.[59] But this telling was incomplete. The mayor had in reality brought a pipeline to his own village and, as clarified by one of the chiefs whose village also received a connection from the pipeline, "even he [the mayor] wouldn't dare not give it to the villages along the way."[60] In a now-familiar story, Koungheul's former mayor, Mohamadou Dia, said his proudest accomplishments after ten years of service were bringing water to his village and those surrounding it, as well as building a health post a few hundred meters from his compound and, in a particularly costly endeavor, grating a new road between the chef-lieu and the village immediately adjacent to his.[61]

I map the projects delivered to each village by the local government over the past fifteen years in Figures 6.4 and 6.5. The same data are calculated per capita in the second panel to account for village size. Together, these network plots validate the themes in the qualitative data – there is more evidence of clustering in Koungheul as opposed to Kebemer where projects are redistributed more evenly across the network. Numerically, slightly over half of Koungheul's villages report receiving an investment since the passage of Acte II in 1996, in contrast with nearly 90 percent in Kebemer.

Figure 6.5c also shows a unique form of "redistribution" in Koungheul, where the former mayor, Dia, had created nine new villages for his extended

---

[58] Interview, February 12, 2017.   [59] Interview, February 15, 2017.
[60] Interview, February 16, 2017.
[61] Interview, February 18, 2017. Grating a road is a highly unusual investment for a local government.

(a) New Public Goods

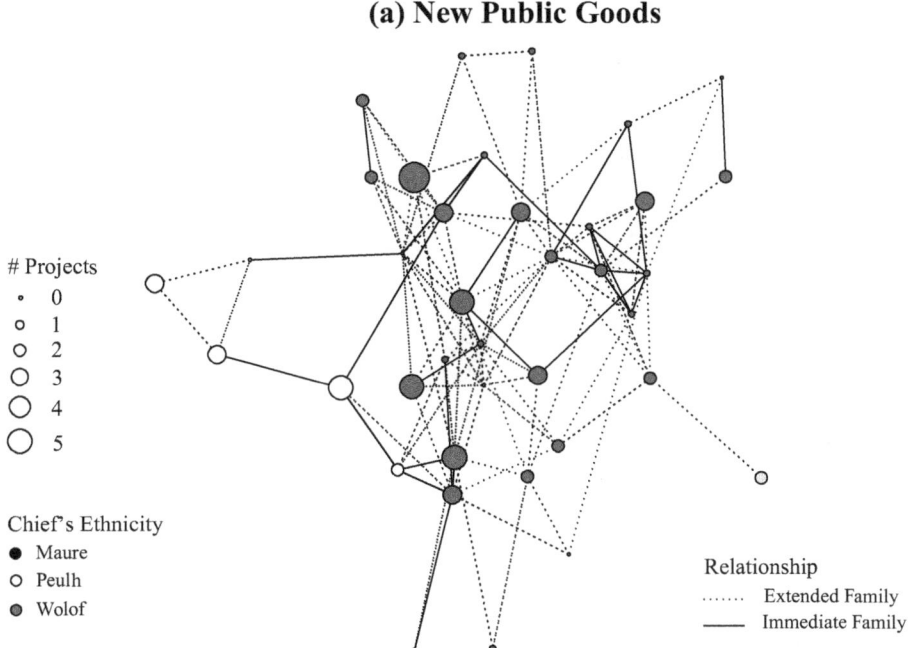

(b) % New Public Goods as % of Pop Share

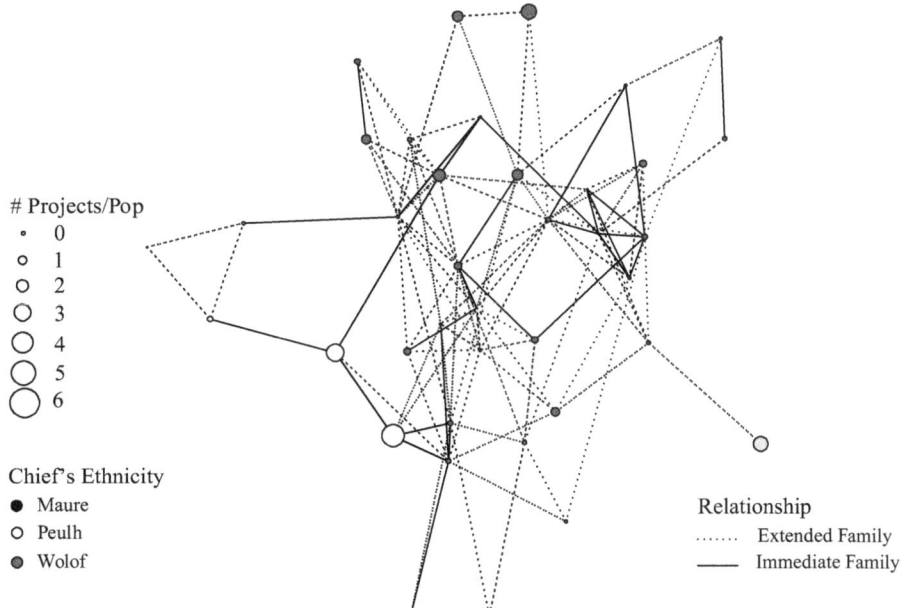

FIGURE 6.4 Kebemer public goods delivery: (a) new public goods and (b) percentage of new public goods as percentage of pop share

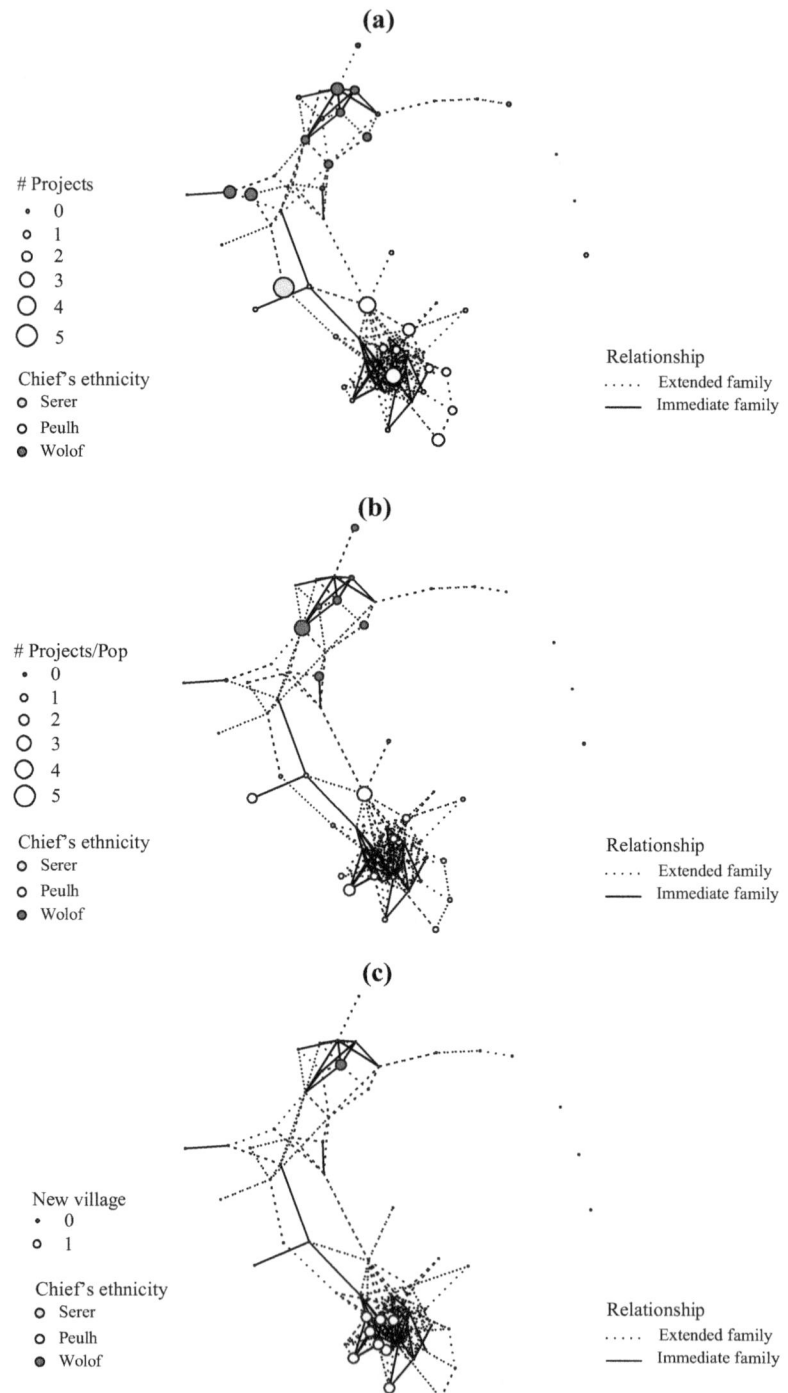

FIGURE 6.5 Koungheul public goods delivery: (a) new public goods, (b) percentage of new public goods as percentage of pop share, and (c) new village creation

family members over the course of the term. Obtaining the status of an official village is highly desirable since being an official village both entitles one to certain central government deliveries, such as seed and fertilizer before the growing season, as well as better positioning a community to make claims on the local state.[62] This is not uncontroversial. Allowing part of a village to effectively "secede" or recognizing a preexisting hamlet as an official entity in its own right often violates local social standards over who is the rightful claimant to both symbolic goods, such as standing in the community, as well as material ones, notably land. In a political strategy that created loyal allies to the present, Dia's solution to family feuds was simply to create new villages, but it was also a means by which he could punish his political opponents by reducing the population under a rival chief's authority. Many mocked these new villages – "it's a village of three houses," one chief joked when we told him we were headed there next, before sighing "politicians, they create enormous difficulties for us."[63] Though Balde, the current mayor, had publicly decried Dia's strategy, he himself had created one new village in a move that many saw as a comparable reward to his supporters.

Evaluating a complete inventory of projects delivered in Kebemer and Koungheul since the onset of decentralization corroborates the findings presented in Chapter 5. The politics of institutional congruence generates incentives for politicians to deliver broadly across space and, in line with these expectations, we see Kebemer's elected officials distributing projects across the community irrespective of ethnic or political affiliation. In sharp contrast, redistribution is more targeted in Koungheul, with some villages favored at the expense of others according to explicitly political criteria.

STATES WITHOUT LEGACIES: THE EXAMPLE OF KOUMPENTOUM

The paired case studies of centralized Kebemer and acephalous Koungheul demonstrate how the legacy of precolonial statehood in the former generated social institutions around balance and social harmony that stretch across villages, carrying them into contemporary politics following decentralization. To further illustrate that it is these mechanisms and not some other, unobserved feature of regions that were able to support precolonial polities that generated these differences in contemporary political performance, I include an "off-the-line" case, one that is not well-predicted by the model, but which is ostensibly similar to Kebemer and Koungheul on most dimensions (see Table 6.1) apart from its precolonial history.

The local government of Koumpentoum falls in the territory of the Mandingue-dominated precolonial state of Niani, which rose by consolidating

---

[62] See discussion in Chapter 2 on village creation.   [63] Interview, February 22, 2017.

power as an intermediary in the Atlantic slave trade, controlling slave routes from the Upper Senegal Basin and Guinean highlands to the coast. Unlike other states that more adeptly pivoted their economic orientation following the abolition of the Atlantic trade in 1807, the Niani saw a sharp decline in fortunes.[64] As the state lost dominance of its territory, the region of present-day Koumpentoum saw near complete out-migration of residents of the Niani. New settlers arriving in the early twentieth century claim abandoned wells as they established new villages in the Niani's ruins. In contrast to the long histories of centralized Kebemer, the majority of Koumpentoum's villages were founded following independence. As a consequence, neither the identity nor network mechanism from the Niani has reproduced social institutions for the local government's residents.[65]

Like Kebemer and Koungheul, the 2014 elections saw the victory of the APR and the defeat of two terms of PDS rule, though in this case the incumbent mayor had stepped down. The winner, Daouda Diallo, was a state agent who, though not originally from the region, had long worked in the arrondissement. Diallo made much of the fact that he was educated – which neither his predecessor nor his immediate competition was – a strategy that was quite persuasive to the population who thought that a literate mayor would improve their livelihoods. But "now people feel fooled."[66] Diallo had repeatedly and quite openly admitted to "eating" the local government's meager tax revenue and was accused across the board of a "nebulous" management of the commune's resources. Halfway through the council's term, the local government was at an effective standstill. Factionalism in the ruling APR was rampant, leading one opposition councilor to observe that "there is almost no party."[67] Particular evidence of the mayor's political weakness was seen in the fact that he had lost his own village, the local government capital, in the country's 2016 constitutional referendum, widely interpreted as a barometer of support for his party.

Koumpentoum as a Case of Institutional Incongruence

Why is such political dysfunction present in Koumpentoum despite falling in the territory of a precolonial state? I argue that Koumpentoum is a case of institutional incongruence because it lacks both mechanisms necessary to carry cross-village social institutions from the past into the present. Because the zone saw significant out-migration in the nineteenth century as residents on the Niani left the territory, the village-based social hierarchies that I identify as

---

[64] Quinn (1972).
[65] This is a difference between some of the cases mentioned in Chapter 4 where such out-migration had not taken place. As discussed there, in some areas, such as the territory of Boundou or Ouli to the east, descendants of these states remain, often generating sharp clashes with in-migrants precisely because they make *non-majoritarian* claims to community "ownership."
[66] Interview, village chief, February 27, 2017.   [67] Interview, March 2, 2017.

States without Legacies   183

the mechanism of persistence for social institutions were abruptly displaced. Although in-migrants established new status hierarchies in their villages, these do not trace their legitimacy or claim to territory to the era of the Niani, meaning that there is neither a shared sense of identification nor sufficiently dense social network ties among elites to embed the majority in cross-village social institutions capable of constraining elite behavior.

This is illustrated clearly in the pervasive corruption allegations made against the mayor. When asked about missing funds during the annual budget meeting, the mayor attempted to defend himself by claiming "I will not tell anyone the details of why the process is delayed, I am not going to run away, we live here together!"[68] In Kebemer, such narratives of cohabitation are potent, pulling local political crises back from the brink to preserve family ties and reputations. But in Koumpentoum, councilors merely laughed and doubled down on their critiques. The perception among local elites was that they could not effectively sanction the mayor because he had weak social ties to the zone. "Really, it's the commune's fault for electing someone who is not from here," began one chief, "why would he care if the commune advances or not? He has no family here ... so he can do whatever he wants because his family does not suffer, and they do not know."[69]

The splintered nature of social ties had ramifications beyond Diallo alone. The community was defined by its distinct waves of settlement which generated village-based identities, meaning that Koumpentoum lacked all but the weakest of cross-village identities. The head nurse of Koumpentoum's health post surmised this neatly, "people are not proud to be from Koumpentoum ... people have to be proud to live here for things to get better. But, up until now, no leader has done this, has tried to make 'Koumpentoum' a meaningful entity."[70] Disengagement became the standard response. "The mayor doesn't work, there is nothing to say to or about him," dismissed one councilor, an attitude reflected in the fact that the local council was reported to be regularly below the required quorum as councilors lost interest.[71]

Critically, the lack of cross-village social institutions meant that no unified effort to counter Diallo's rapacious behavior emerged. In contrast, the ensuing political debate was over who could best succeed him, a question that reignited the local government's long-standing rivalry between its three largest villages. Babacar Diouf, a dynamic, educated young councilor from the largest village had surprisingly won five seats for his small party in the 2014 elections and was one oft-mentioned contender. As the son of his village's first candidate for mayor in 1984, residents of the Koumpentoum-Village did not mince words in expressing their distaste for Diouf, even though he had gained substantial popularity among the small villages in the local government's neglected

---

[68] Interview, February 15, 2017.   [69] Interview, February 28, 2017.
[70] Interview, March 2, 2017.   [71] Interview, February 27, 2017.

southeast. "[Koumpentoum-Village] thinks I am looking for revenge," he noted, "they think I am out to trick them as payback" for my father's loss in 1984.[72]

Figure 6.6 replicates the family and friendship networks between village chiefs in the local government and between chiefs and councilors. As is immediately obvious, family ties are much weaker between elites; social networks here are more tree-like, relying on single connections between elites rather than the multiple and reinforcing connection seen in centralized Kebemer and within subsets of Koungheul's population. While there is more centrality in friendship ties, nearly half of chiefs report two or fewer friendships with other chiefs in the local government.

Representation and Redistribution in Koumpentoum

As predicted by my theory, Koumpentoum as a case of institutional incongruence displays representational and redistributive patterns more akin to acephalous Koungheul than centralized Kebemer. Allegations of unequal treatment were made by three-quarters of the local government's village chiefs and coalesced most clearly around local government work. The majority of villages reported confusion, concern, or outright ignorance on why they received nothing while others, in their view, were favored by the local government. The most common comment was a variant of "the mayor distributes things by affinity and appreciation, there is nothing clear in how he runs things."[73] On this issue, the numerous villages along the local government's southeast border were indisputably neglected; "us, the small villages, we are not considered by the commune. We fulfill our obligations to the council [e.g. pay taxes], but they have never done anything for us even though we have over 250 residents," argued one chief.[74] Here the effects of not having a councilor were perceived as compounding the ability of the council to ignore certain villages. "Villages like [name], [name], [name] which have a lot of councilors are the ones with influence here ... they have people to defend them in the council."[75]

As was introduced for Kebemer and Koungheul in the introduction to this book, Koumpentoum also purchased and delivered three millet mills in

---

[72] Interview, March 2, 2017. This was confirmed. "The residents of [Koumpentoum-Village] did not want someone from [Diouf's village] to run the commune," stated a long-standing councilor from Koumpentoum-Village; "[his father] tried to be mayor before, and that didn't work." (Interview, March 2, 2017).
[73] Interview, village chief, February 26, 2017.
[74] Interview, March 1, 2017. Others argued that politicians were easily able to separate smaller villages by buying votes to split the power of any opposition coalitions. It's hard to fight this, one chief argued, because even if you try to discuss with people, "ideas do not fill bellies," and people are very poor (Interview, February 27, 2017).
[75] Interview, February 27, 2017.

States without Legacies

(a) Family Network Relations between Village Chiefs

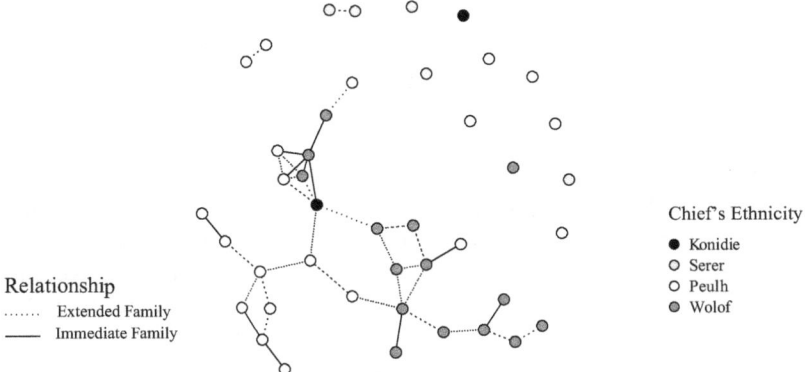

(b) Friendship Network Relations between Village Chiefs

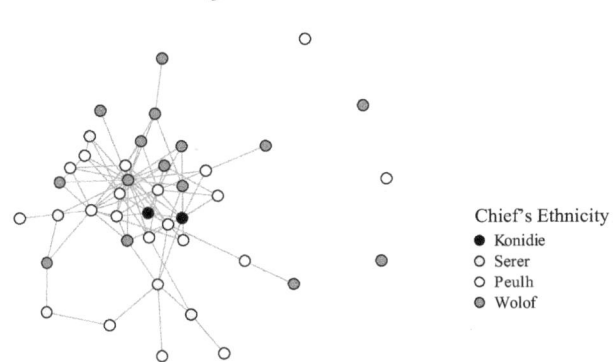

(c) Network Relations between Village Chiefs and Local Elected Officials

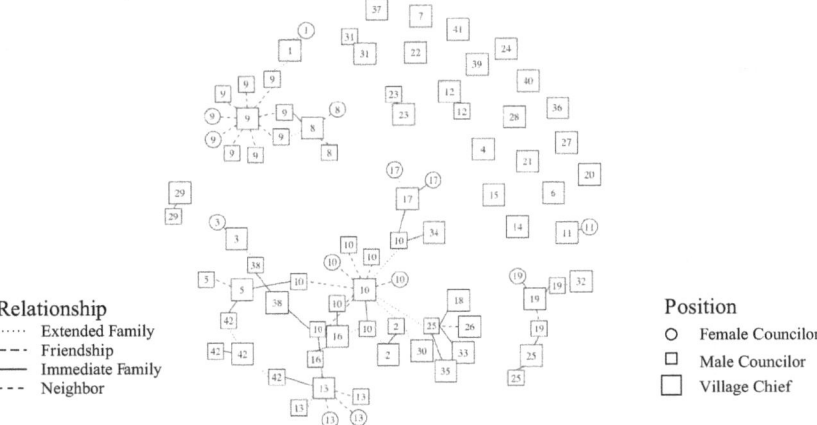

FIGURE 6.6 Elite networks in Koumpentoum: (a) family network relations between village chiefs, (b) friendship network relations between village chiefs, and (c) network relations between village chiefs and local elected officials

2016.⁷⁶ The first mill went to a small village of approximately eighty residents, the second was delivered to a village that had a mill run by a private operator, and the third went to the mayor's own village, already home to three functioning mills. Recalling the council meeting where the choice of villages had been announced and forced through to a vote, a village chief laughed with dismay, "there was a lot of conflict that day ... that meeting did not follow *any* standards."⁷⁷ For his part, the mayor justified the choice as one of ethnic balancing: an ethnically Wolof, Peulh, and Serer village had each received a mill. Even if we accept this as a legitimate criterion, the mayor himself explained that he had carefully chosen from among all possible Wolof, Peulh, and Serer villages those that had most actively supported him in 2014.⁷⁸ As one councilor aligned with Diallo laid bare, the party's approach was to take need into account, "but if the village is not with the mayor, we will not do anything."⁷⁹

As in Koungheul, this favoritism impacted even the most basic of local government duties. One opposition councilor in Koumpentoum noted he had more than fifty requests for new identity cards in his briefcase, the result of Senegal's adoption of biometric identity cards for the approaching legislative elections a few months later, but the mayor had been delaying signing them for weeks, requiring the councilor to travel back and forth to the chef-lieu. "They say he is sick," the councilor confided, "but I know he is signing paper for others."⁸⁰ Critically, there is little evidence that such patterns were specific to Diallo's administration. As Diallo's predecessor stated, given three projects, a politician should give two to those who are with you and one to those who are not.⁸¹

Figure 6.7 illustrates the delivery of new public goods since 2002 in absolute and per capita numbers, respectively. While the largest village had seen four projects, far above the average of 0.8, looking at these numbers per capita reveals the favoritism of the two mayors in power during this period to their mutual home village (and capital) as well as a small number of politically loyal villages.

The case of Koumpentoum offers two critical insights for my argument. First, because the territory was capable of sustaining a precolonial state for nearly 200 years, it indicates that there is not some unobserved variable that both fostered state formation in the past and enables broad redistribution in the present. In contrast, it illustrates the necessity of a mechanism of persistence to carry social institutions from precolonial states into the decision calculi of politicians following decentralization. Because the population of the Niani

---

⁷⁶ The price at which they were reported to have been bought – approximately $6,000 a piece – was rightfully declared "outrageous" at the following year's budget meeting. The inability of the local administration to produce receipts led many to conclude that this was yet another instance of gross embezzlement by the mayor and his entourage.

⁷⁷ Interview, February 27, 2017. ⁷⁸ Interview, March 1, 2017.

⁷⁹ Interview, March 2, 2017.

⁸⁰ Interview, February 27, 2017. This allegation was true, the mayor was seen signing similar paperwork for others during this time. Many viewed this tactic as a form of voter suppression.

⁸¹ Interview, February 28, 2017.

States without Legacies 187

(a) New Public Goods

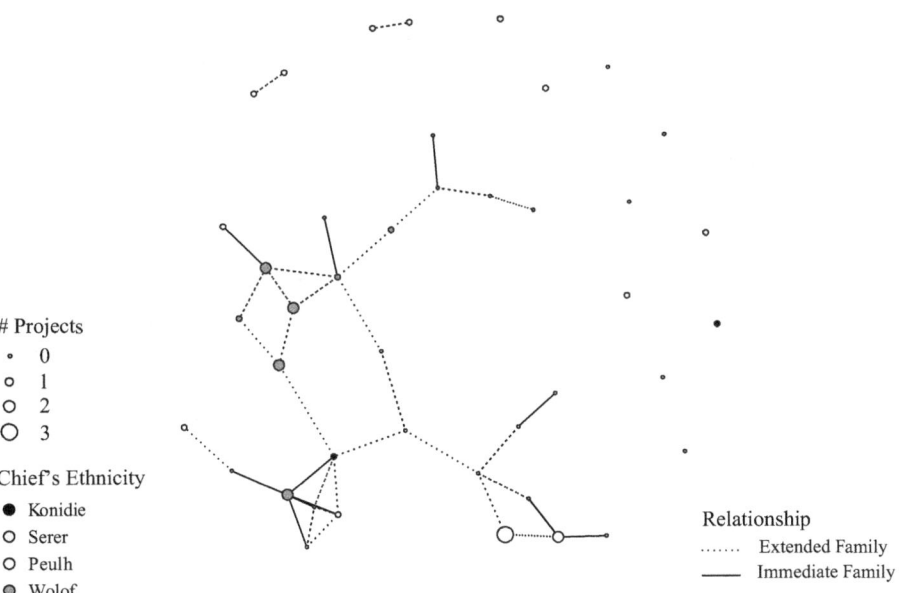

(b) % New Public Goods as % of Pop Share

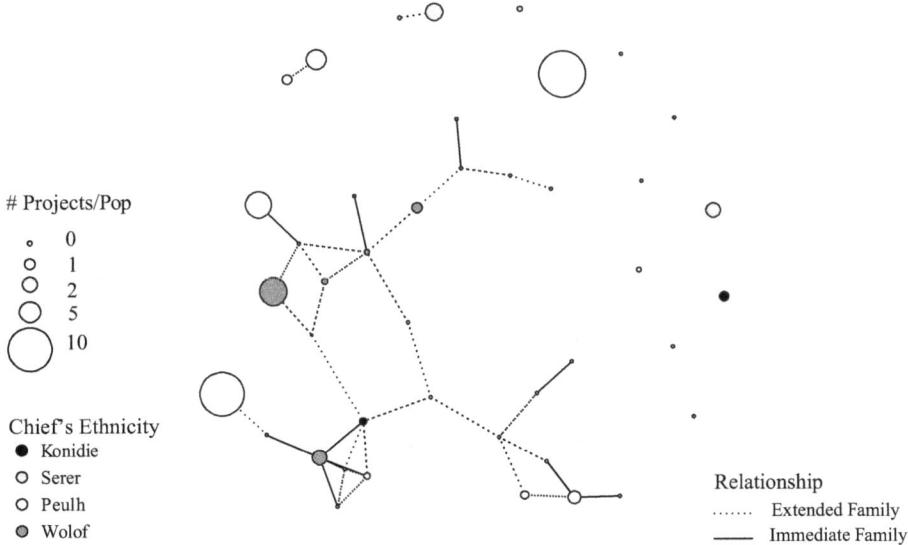

FIGURE 6.7 Koumpentoum public goods delivery: (a) new public goods and (b) percentage of new public goods as percentage of pop share

out-migrated, the local government's contemporary residents lack robust cross-village social networks to circulate reputations and ensure social sanction for poorly performing behavior. They also hold disparate and competing social identities. The social institutions that prevent political opportunism and conflict in centralized Kebemer thus fail to emerge between villages and local elites because they never existed for the population in question in the first place.

Second, though many village chiefs correctly identified the territory as having been ruled under the Niani prior to their arrival, there was not a single attempt – veiled or otherwise – to claim this history. Rural elites appear to be either uninterested or unable to latch onto a mythology of precolonial glory when they have no credible claim to doing so. In stark contrast, elites in Koumpentoum proudly recount how and why their grandparents settled the zone, revealing divided and atomized village identities, cumulating in disjointed and competing historical narratives. Put otherwise, absent the mechanism of persistence, we do not see opportunistic claim-making to an alternative history.

ASSESSING ALTERNATIVE EXPLANATIONS

A priori, there is no reason to assume that politicians in centralized Kebemer are inherently more benevolent than in acephalous Koungheul or in the off-the-line case of Koumpentoum. Rather, my argument is that politicians in Kebemer inhabit distinct social worlds that reward prosocial behavior while also raising the costs of predatory behavior. Could Kebemer's broadly redistributive behavior be driven by something else?

Perhaps, for example, the fact that the local government has been dominated by Wolof elected officials has unrecognized properties. Gennaioli and Rainer (2007), for example, argue that centralized ethnic groups facilitate greater accountability between chiefs and local populations, relations that have persisted over time. Anthropological evidence abounds that ethnic categories and identities were radically transformed by the colonial encounter, and most precolonial states, in particular those in West Africa, were multiethnic.[82] But if there are ethnic legacies – say in this case among the Wolof – that facilitate collective action, we may very well expect that *any* local government run by a Wolof majority would perform better.

This begs the question of why Wolofs – the majority ethnic group in all three cases – were able to politically unite in centralized Kebemer, while in acephalous Koungheul they are described as "lacking a common heart" in contrast to their Peulh neighbors.[83] The back-to-back mandates of Peulh mayors in

---

[82] See Chanock (1991); Fortes and Evans-Pritchard (1940); and Colson (1969).
[83] For example, interview, adjoint mayor, February 19, 2017. A similar narrative was heard in Koumpentoum. As one village chief argued, "if you slap a Maure, the Maures get up. If you slap a Peulh, the Peulhs get up. If you slap a Wolof, the Wolofs cross their arms" (Interview, February 28, 2017).

Assessing Alternative Explanations

Koungheul were explained (with no lack of judgment) by Wolofs as the result of the willingness of Peulhs to "get out their money" to buy votes.[84] But during Kebemer's 2014 local elections, both the Wolof incumbent and his Wolof challengers were widely reported to (and indeed admitted to) giving "small gifts" to influential local actors.

Ethnic stereotypes abound in all three cases, but ethnicity is only occasionally how local actors understand the boundaries of their social solidarity. While Wolofs in Koungheul or Koumpentoum were said to "easily divide" along lines of caste or settlement waves, inter- and intra-ethnic relations in Kebemer were described as broadly harmonious.[85] Listening to local elites reveals more variable understandings of what group boundaries are salient. The Wolofs in centralized Kebemer report feeling tied together through dense family relations and their shared identification with the precolonial past, but critically this category and network encompass most local minorities. I find no evidence that Wolofs have different cultural characteristics than Peulhs or Serers, or that Wolofs are somehow culturally different in Kebemer than elsewhere. Rather, political leaders in Kebemer are constrained in their ability to play with local social relations to win office and, crucially, these constraints cross ethnic and caste lines.

A second alternative explanation is that the varying nature of representation and redistribution reflect patterns of electoral targeting – say of core or swing voters – and nothing more. Certainly, electoral dynamics in historically acephalous Koungheul reflected a clear bias toward a core constituency for each candidate, with larger Wolof villages serving as swing votes. As one nonaligned village chief explained, it was to be expected that the mayor favors certain villages "because some villages supported him and its only normal he would favor them as repayment."[86] Little agreement on this strategy emerged, however. Koungheul's former mayor observed that he preferred to more aggressively pursue votes in swing villages, since "your base is already won,"[87] but a minority party councilor explained that a politician ought to constantly deliver to their base.[88]

In contrast, core voters were harder to assess in the off-the-line case of Koumpentoum, where politicians' self-described electoral strategies can be more accurately summarized as reflecting a logic of minimum winning coalition formation. Here, the mayor had established an uneasy alliance to win the 2014 local elections by carefully including candidates from the long-neglected

---

[84] Interview, village chief, February 15, 2017.
[85] As evidence of the former: one Wolof chief in Koungheul argued that it was the Wolofs' own fault for letting themselves be so easily divided (Interview, February 22, 2017). As evidence of the latter, one village chief mused about the Peulh minority that had long lived in his village: "If there is a joy, we share it. If there is a tragedy, we live it together" (Interview, village chief, February 9, 2017).
[86] Interview, February 21, 2017.   [87] Interview, February 18, 2017.
[88] Interview, February 19, 2017. To the extent that "core" voters existed, it was personalized rather than partisan. "My father told Mohamadou Dia [the former mayor] that the village belonged to him," stated one village chief, and the village remained loyal even after Dia's defeat in 2014 (Interview, February 16, 2017).

southeast of the local government and by promising key spots to members of each of the local government's major ethnic groups to ensure that they would get the necessary votes to win.[89] In the end, he had won with just fewer than 50 percent of the votes, with minority parties splitting the remainder. Since then, villages that had not been in the mayor's coalition had received nothing from the local state.

Neither dynamic explains the case of Kebemer, where politicians describe their political coalitions broadly and report a relative inability to alienate community members regardless of ethnicity, partisanship, or caste. In contrast, Kebemer's current mayor's electoral strategy is easily summed up as a classic turnout strategy. The mayor reported visiting each village to help residents get on the electoral rolls, quickly adding here that it was every citizen's right to vote and that possessing an identity card was important for rural citizens beyond just elections.[90] This was largely confirmed by village chiefs. This was eminently political, but it was a distinctly less divisive strategy in comparison to his colleagues in Koungheul and Koumpentoum. As one notable described the mayor, "his party is the locality."[91]

A final potential explanation emerges from the case studies themselves. Elections, many rural Senegalese tell me, are won for many reasons, not all of them "visible."[92] A village chief in acephalous Koungheul, for example, said that it is really no surprise that the community's Peulhs were more active in local politics than Wolofs like himself: "the mystical aspect is important. The Peulhs are very strong [mystically]. The Wolofs are really too religious here to engage in this, but the Peulhs, they will not hesitate to sacrifice an animal."[93] The role of the invisible in local political life was unusually acute in Koumpentoum, where the mayor had recently taken ill. Rumors swirled and everyone in the local government had a theory about who had "done this" to the mayor. One villager informed me that the mayor's pain worsened every time a donkey cried, a not infrequent occurrence. Others claimed that they had found *gris gris*, or a mystical charm, in the batteries of the local government office's solar panels. Elsewhere, I heard that the mayor's office chair had been stolen after he was elected only to be returned shortly before he fell ill. This, one horse cart driver informed me, was certainly how the affliction was cast. Regardless of the specific nature and origin of the cause, there was no disagreement that the mayor was not simply ill, but that he had been made ill as a result of his poor behavior.

If Koungheul and Koumpentoum are simply more spiritually active, can this explain why Kebemer is more peaceful? How are we to wrestle with the idea that local political outcomes are a function of mysticism and not, as I have argued, the historical legacies of precolonial statehood? Political science rarely addresses such alternative explanations, yet this is often the most frequent explanation offered

[89] Interview, February 26, 2017.
[90] Interview, February 5, 2017.
[91] Interview, February 8, 2017.
[92] To adopt Ellis and ter Haar's (1998) language.
[93] Interview, February 18, 2017.

by respondents on the ground. Regardless of whether or not we share these beliefs, they are undeniably consequential for politicians' behavior. By invoking invisible forces, politics in Koungheul and Koumpentoum was understood less in terms of partisan divisions than by who did or did not have the social or mystical authority to run for office. One well-educated councilor noted that he always changed into traditional clothes before returning to the local government, clarifying that he had to "be very careful here" lest he too falls victim to mystical powers.[94] Such mysticism led youth and some minority groups to opt out of running altogether. A youth activist in Koungheul expressed skepticism that the frequently better educated younger citizens in the zone would get more involved in politics; "their parents won't let them," he argued, since "it's a little dangerous" given the perceived mystical abilities of someone like the mayor.[95]

In direct contrast, a young councilor from centralized Kebemer who was finishing up his studies in Dakar, laughed when I asked him if youth in his area shared these concerns. "Like in all of Senegal, those ideas are there. But youth believe it less and there is less reason to worry if you are not the mayor," he responded.[96] In line with this more skeptical stance, the idea that invisible factors influenced local politics in Kebemer went entirely unmentioned by respondents. It is plausible, of course, that this simply reflects a local tendency to not advertise local political issues, but it is just as likely that the same social institutions that constrain political behavior likewise exercise control over what is and is not an appropriate invisible sanction as well.

CONCLUSION

Taken together, the three case studies presented in this chapter allow me to pinpoint the mechanisms behind my argument and to bolster my claim that the nature of political life under decentralization is historically contingent. Certainly, the cases suggest that politicians may pursue minimum winning coalitions or target core or swing voters strategically, but that we cannot explain local politics with these dynamics alone. In all three cases, elites have ambitions for their communities and their children's future; the mayor in acephalous Koungheul had as many development initiatives planned as his counterpart in centralized Kebemer. What differs, I have argued, is not the personalities of who is elected nor their political ambitions, but the broader communities that they are embedded within. When local elites are connected across villages through shared webs of social institutions, the presence of shared group identification and dense social ties extend who they think they are obligated to beyond their own family or village. This is the enduring legacy of the precolonial past.

---

[94] Interview, March 2, 2017.   [95] Interview, February 20, 2017.
[96] Interview, March 9, 2017.

7

Decompressing Legacies of Public Goods Delivery, 1880–2012

In this chapter, I turn to an original dataset of historical public service investments to test a final implication of my theory. While the previous two chapters demonstrated that congruent local governments engage in spatially distinct redistributive politics, my argument holds uneven temporal predictions: the influence of the precolonial past on redistributive politics should be contingent on its congruence with formal institutions. As I show in the following pages, the precolonial past only influences social service delivery following the 1996 decentralization reforms that transferred authority over public goods placement to local governments.

Built from archival documents, my historical dataset also enables me to assess a set of possible alternative explanations first raised in Chapter 2. The colonial era brought numerous changes to rural Senegal that have been shown elsewhere to radically alter development trajectories. Could the findings I document be driven by divergent experiences with the colonial state and not exposure to precolonial centralization? I test a range of arguments about colonial influences on long-run development trajectories but find little evidence that colonial legacies mediate those of the precolonial past. Thus, while French colonization did intimately influence the contours of Senegal's social service infrastructure, the political and economic interests of the colonial state only appear to have shaped proximity to basic services in the colonial and immediate postcolonial period. Colonial effects have almost entirely faded by the early 2000s.

In this way, this chapter "decompresses" history to engage in two broader debates animating the recent turn to history among students of political economy of development. By explicitly examining the impact of precolonial and colonial legacies *over time*, I offer a corrective to the tendency to gloss over the question of temporal process that defines much of our recent interest in historical legacies. As the empirical evidence marshaled in the following pages shows,

I find no support for arguments that areas that were home to precolonial states are doing better today because they have *always* done better. In sharp contrast, my data reveal that legacies can persist at the grassroots only to reemerge to influence the outcome of interest under specific institutional arrangements.

From here, I draw out a second, related tension in much of the recent scholarship on historical legacies. This work has largely assumed that historical legacies are long-run equilibria, generating the expectation that they should persist absent some exogenous shock. Yet as I document, empirical trends in the legacy of colonial service delivery seem better suited to evolutionary logics that are more consistent with the changing political dilemmas of the colonial and postcolonial African state.[1] Without taking temporal logics seriously, I caution that we risk making inaccurate predications about how and why the past influences the present.

The chapter is structured in three parts. I begin by introducing the historical data, before establishing that the effect of falling within the territory of a precolonial polity only becomes consequential for public goods delivery following the 1996 decentralization reforms. I secondly examine whether this obscures or ignores an important role for colonial legacies, only to find that these effects have largely faded by the 1990s. A third and final section develops the implications that these findings hold for research on historical persistence in the study of political economy of development.

WHEN DOES THE PRECOLONIAL PAST MATTER?

In identifying a robust legacy for West Africa's precolonial kingdoms, this book contributes to the increasing recognition that African centralized precolonial organizations have long-lasting impacts on development outcomes.[2] Prominent arguments in this literature suggest that areas that were home to precolonial states have better living standards today because they were home to distinct cultural norms, more accountable chiefs or because they were better able to adopt new technologies to name a few examples.[3] Like most work on historical legacies, the overarching assumption among these arguments is that something about the precolonial past matters, that it has consistently done so, and that its impact is cumulative.

My own argument departs from this linear causal story: precolonial states left behind robust cross-village social institutions that today generate distinct forms of distributional politics. Social institutions have not always mattered for development, however, because their ability to shape public goods delivery is contingent on the formal institutional configuration that they operate within. Key for my argument is that the 1996 decentralization reforms were an

---

[1] Huillery (2009) and Frankema (2012).   [2] For example, Gennaioli and Rainer (2007).
[3] Respectively, Michalopoulos and Papaioannou (2013); Gennaioli and Rainer (2007); and Bandyopadhyay and Green (2016).

exogenous shock that facilitated the (re)emergence of social institutions as a key driver of subnational distributional politics. Accordingly, I examine whether we see evidence of interactive effects between precolonial legacies and formal institutional structure, only to find that precolonial legacies do not become a significant factor until the 1996 decentralization reforms.

Historical Data

To trace the impact of precolonial political centralization on development outcomes, I use archival data to extend my village-level dataset back to 1882, coding the construction of new primary schools and basic health facilities in rural Senegal at roughly ten-year intervals to the present.[4] To do so, I rely on annual colonial reports by sector, notably the *Rapports Statistique Annuel de Santé* and *d'Enseignement*, accessed at the French *Archives nationales d'outre-mer* (ANOM) or the *Archives nationales du Sénégal* (ANS) in Dakar.[5] For the first decades of colonization, the data are completed with the *Annuaire du Senegal et Dependences*.[6] This allows me to generate a dummy variable of whether or not a village has access to a primary school or a health facility, which may include a health center or *dispensarie* ("poste" post-1975), in a given year using the same definition of access introduced in Chapter 5. Health huts (*cases de sante*), more basic health facilities administered under health posts, were not pioneered until the early 1980s and are regrettably not included in the dataset due to a lack of information about their locations prior to 2000. Unsurprisingly given the state crisis of the era, village-level data are not available between the mid-1970s and 2000, leading me to complement the village-level data with alternative measures that, though aggregated at a higher level, help fill this temporal gap. These are introduced below.

Because many villages were settled following the onset of colonial rule, I restrict my analysis for the early years of colonialism (1902–1912) to villages (n = 3,301) that are listed in the first censuses conducted by the French between 1890 and 1904.[7] Early census data could not be located for some parts of the country during this time period and missing zones span the country's precolonial political geography. Notably, acephalous zones of Kedougou Region and the Ferlo Desert are missing, as well as present-day Kolda Region, which had a

---

[4] Intervals are not precisely set to ten years because they are subject to data availability – the reports from which I code the locations of basic social services are not available for all years.
[5] Service de Sante (Misc. Years) and Service de l'Enseignement Primaire (Misc. Years).
[6] AOF (Misc. Years).
[7] The primary source for early colonial census is Becker (1983), which compiles a number of archival documents with early census data. This is combined with a series of report commissioned by the French in 1904 (dates of completion vary between 1904 and 1906) of all *cercles* under their administration (though some are not available in archives) that frequently list villages and their chiefs (Afrique Occidental Française 1901; AOF 1903a, 1903b; AOF 1904a, 1904b, 1904c, 1904d, 1904e, 1904f).

When Does the Precolonial Past Matter?

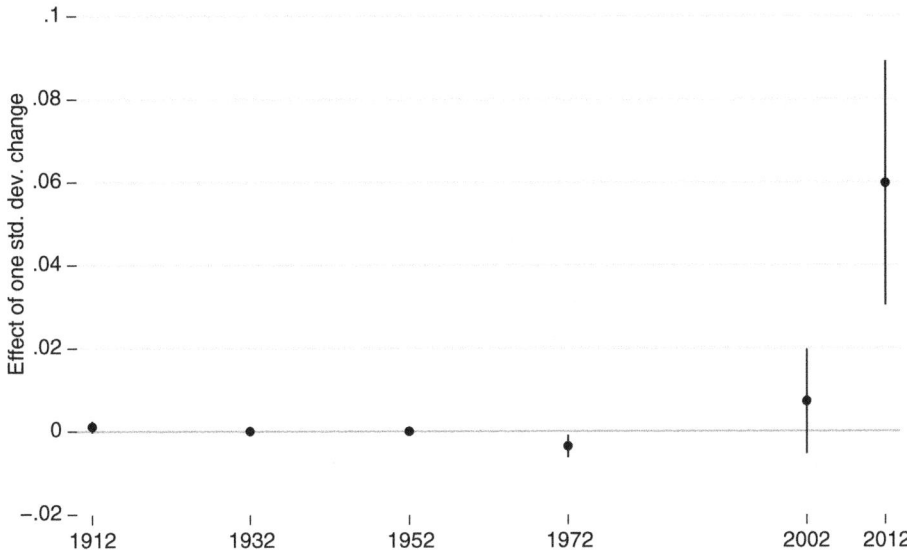

FIGURE 7.1 Effect of institutional congruence on new social service access over time

mixed political history, and Tivaouane Department, which was home to the heart of the precolonial Cayor Kingdom. I use data from the 1956 *Repertoire de villages* to expand the scope of villages in existence for the 1922–1972 period (n = 10,877).[8] Restricting the data in this manner helps mitigate the risk of estimating the nondelivery of public goods to villages that were not in existence and hence not eligible for selection, though of course using reduced samples is an imperfect solution because I am unable to precisely estimate when villages entered the sample.[9] Due to a lack of digitalization for the archival records, all data were hand-matched.[10]

Estimating the Legacy of Precolonial Statehood

I begin by assessing the ability of precolonial centralization to explain a village's likelihood of receiving school or clinic access over time. Figure 7.1 shows the effect of one standard deviation shift in institutional congruence on whether a village gains new social service access (a primary school and/or health clinic) at

---

[8] Ministere de l'Interieur (1956).
[9] The French may have been more likely to miss villages in historically acephalous areas given the relative upheaval seen in these areas (see Chapter 2). This would lead me to underestimate the effect of precolonial centralization on service delivery during the early colonial period, however, rather than to find an effect where it does not exist.
[10] Both sets of colonial censuses include villages that have no match in the current repertoire of villages. This is likely due to villages that were abandoned.

approximately twenty-year intervals from 1902 through 2012 from a series of naive models. As is abundantly clear, the effect of precolonial centralization on social service access in any given village is only statistically significant post-2002. There is no significant effect in earlier eras. As late as 1972 the effect is actually negative, suggesting that historically uncentralized areas received more investments from the late colonial and early postcolonial states.

Though suggestive, missing periods of observation in the village-level data limit my ability to pinpoint the mid-1990s as a pivotal moment. More complete time series can be found at the department level, a higher level of aggregation for which ministerial data are available for the period missing in Figure 7.1. Colonial-era data are aggregated upward to these boundaries. Figure 7.2a shows the average number of schools by department, with diamonds indicating the years for which data are available. The figure illustrates a marked flip between the average number of schools in departments that were dominated by a precolonial state and those that were not following the 1996 administrative reforms. While historically acephalous areas had more schools on average from the 1940s through the early years of independence, this effect switches dramatically following the devolution of authority over primary school construction to local governments.[11] Between 1998 and 2002 for example, departments that were dominated by precolonial states areas outbuilt acephalous ones by 2.7 schools to 1. Between 2002 and 2012, this ratio was 1.8 to 1.

Figure 7.2b replicates Figure 7.2a for the average number of health posts by department. Here areas that were home to centralized states in the precolonial era have slightly more health posts on average beginning in the 1940s (though the difference is small at less than one post per department until 1976). While there is no switch as was seen with primary schools, the growth rate in average health post construction following 1998 is accelerating at a faster pace in departments whose territory housed a precolonial state than those that did not by roughly two to one.

To reinforce my argument that these changes in building patterns are unique to locally delivered public goods, Figure 7.2c shows comparable data for borehole construction. Major waterworks like boreholes are equally if not more in demand by rural populations, yet this is not a devolved competence and such projects are far beyond the capacity of even the most well-financed local governments. Borehole construction has always been in the control of the central government and, as Figure 7.2c illustrates, it has been biased toward centralized areas from the postcolonial period on; most of this difference is driven by investments in Senegal's peanut basin. Still the data suggest that if anything there has been a reduction in this bias in the 2000s as historically acephalous zones have received more boreholes relative to historically

---

[11] Importantly, there is no systematically different change in population during this time period that might be driving this.

When Does the Precolonial Past Matter?

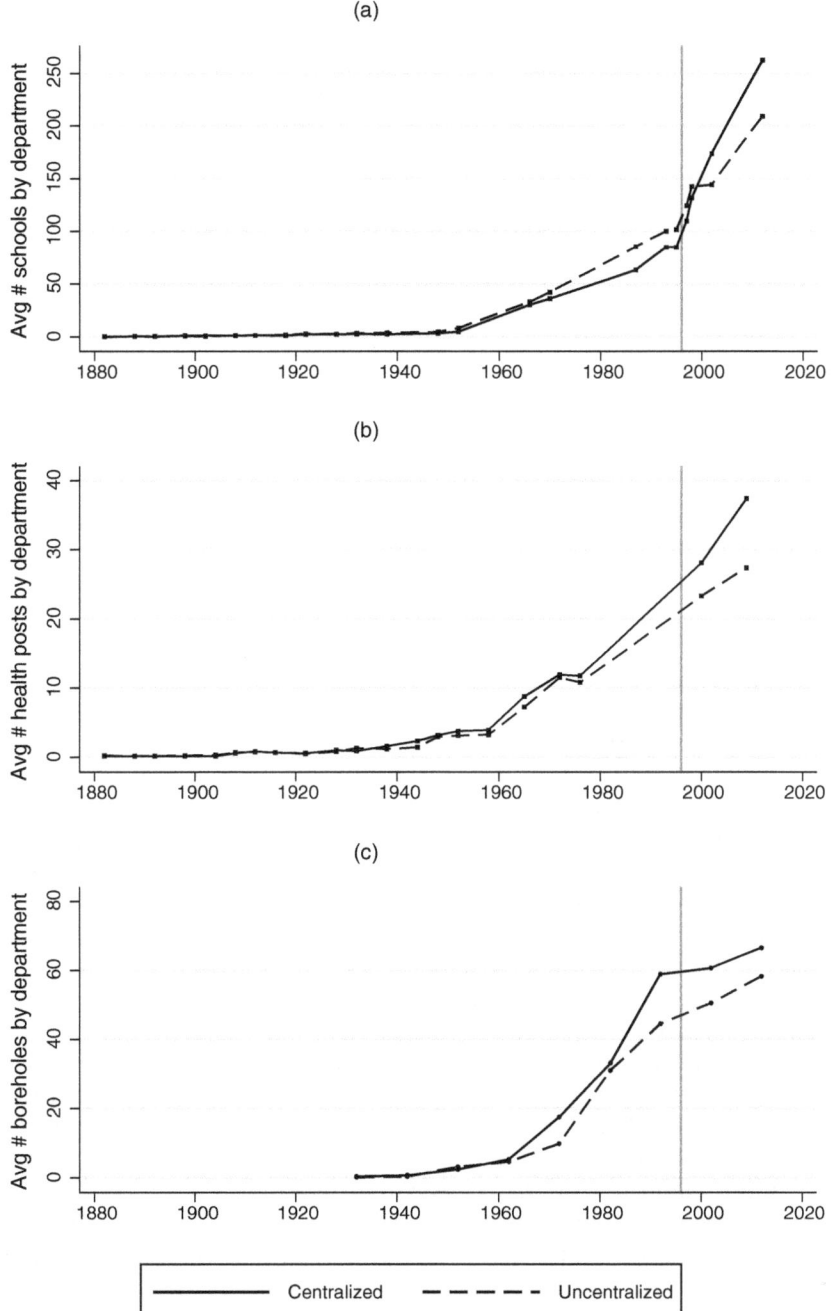

FIGURE 7.2 Basic services over time: (a) primary education, (b) basic health facilities, and (c) boreholes

198   *Decompressing Legacies of Public Goods Delivery*

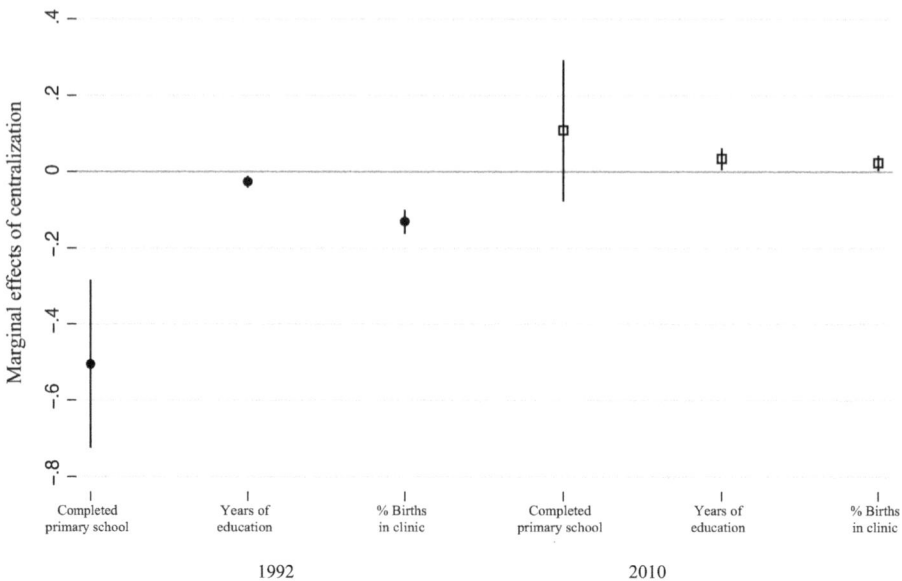

FIGURE 7.3 Marginal effect of centralization on education and health attainment

centralized areas than in the post-decentralization era. Central-state-provided goods seem to behave more consistently over time than locally provided goods, which see a visible change in patterns of their delivery following decentralization.

As a final means to address data limitations, Figure 7.3 shows the marginal effect of centralization on educational outcomes as reported by rural respondents in the 1992 and 2010 Demographic and Health Surveys (DHS) for Senegal. The DHS surveys are nationally stratified surveys, such that households have equal probability of being sampled within each census enumeration zones of a given country. The surveys collect a complete inventory of household members as well as their individual demographic attributes. Given the DHS's wide sampling of respondents across the country both before and after decentralization, I am able to estimate differences in "stocks" of education in rural residents as a means to establish the availability of public goods across space and time.[12] The sample is truncated to those who would have been primary school aged in 1996 and onward; hence the 2010 data are limited to those between the ages of fourteen and twenty-one. To ensure comparability, the 1992 data are limited similarly. I estimate health outcomes by looking at the percent of births per woman over the previous five years that took place in a public clinic. The data tell a now-familiar story: young rural Senegalese were less likely to be educated if they lived in areas that were home to centralized

[12] Kramon and Posner (2013).

states in 1992, but this gap has closed by 2010, reflecting the gains in primary school investments made over this period. Similarly, women living in areas that were home to a precolonial state were significantly less likely to have delivered their youngest babies in a clinic in the early 1990s, but the effect flips direction by 2010 when they are more likely to deliver in a clinic. Importantly, there is no reason to expect that this would be driven by cultural shifts. It is hard to imagine why attitudes about Western education or, in particular, health care, would only accrue in historically centralized areas and to a significant enough degree to generate shifts of this scale.

What Precolonial Centralization's Intermittent Effects Say about Historical Legacies?

Figures 7.1–7.3 cumulatively reject the argument that precolonial centralization has been a constant force for improving access to public goods. I find no support for the idea that precolonial polities disproportionately attracted colonial investments, thus that I would conflate a colonial for a precolonial legacy. This does not appear to be specific to Senegal. Ricart-Huguet (2021) likewise finds little impact of precolonial statehood in driving district-level colonial investments across sixteen West and East African colonies, suggesting that precolonial statehood did not robustly influence colonial investment strategies.

The sudden significance of precolonial centralization seen in Figures 7.1–7.3 is not easily explained by anything other than Senegal's decentralization reforms. Still, I note here three other significant changes took place in this general time frame that may strike some as plausible alternatives. As I discuss, however, none are likely drivers of the shifts observed in the data.

First, we might think that structural adjustment reforms, adopted widely across the continent in the 1980s, may have had uneven subnational effects.[13] Certainly, structural adjustment programs encouraged governments to scale back spending. To illustrate, Senegal's health spending – which averaged 8–9 percent of the national budget in the early years of independence – had dropped to 5.4 percent by 1985, evidence of the drastic cuts that took place during the early years of structural adjustment.[14] Ultimately, however, the neoliberal reforms of the era did little to fundamentally alter the structure of service expansion, having its most focused impact on central government bureaucracies on the one hand and, on the other, end-line users through the introduction of cost recovery programs in the late 1980s.[15] There is no evidence that structural adjustment altered the clearest distributional pattern of the postcolonial state: a durable bias toward urban service investments.[16]

---

[13] Senegal received its first structural adjustment program in 1979.   [14] Menes (1976, 86).
[15] Foley (2010, 59).
[16] Education spending was also long-biased toward secondary and tertiary education, primarily located in urban centers. More than 60 percent of the health budget went to the three largest

A second notable change was the significant uptick in development funding, specifically focused on basic services. By the mid-1990s, only 58 percent of the eligible student population attended primary school and only 27 percent of adults were literate, far below the continent's average which hovered around 50 percent.[17] The international community sought to address such disparities with renewed vigor from the 1990s onward. This means that Figures 7.1–7.3 may reflect the ability of the state to politically target certain populations with new donor funding rather than these effects being driven by local social dynamics.[18] If this were the case, however, it is unclear why the regime would engage in inconsistent patterns across goods, favoring historically centralized areas with primary schools and clinics while favoring historically acephalous zones with high-demand goods like boreholes.

The election of Abdoulaye Wade in 2000 – the country's first electoral transfer of power that saw the defeat of the PS – is a third and related important change during this time period. How do I know that it was the 1996 decentralization reforms introduced under President Abdou Diouf and not his loss to Wade four years later that drives these distributional changes? Though I cannot establish this with absolute certainty, Wade's regime is not considered to have radically altered Diouf's general political orientation. Indeed, on many metrics their regimes were very similar: both ruled through rural clientelist networks, reinforced the role of the presidency, and co-opted challengers.[19] This is not to deny their differences. Though both regimes relied on tight alliances with Sufi leaders as vote brokers, Wade's regime was notable for its shift toward Touba, the seat of the Mouride Brotherhood, at the expense of the Tidjanes, based in Tivaouane.[20] Still, both men represented what Kelly (2020) has called "insider-induced turnovers." Wade served in Diouf's government in the early 1990s and had long been involved in Senegalese politics, meaning that while his election was monumental, the 2000 alternation of power largely did little to challenge the constellation of national elites as Wade continued Diouf's strategy of encouraging the formation of patronage-seeking parties that the regime could co-opt. Analysis of the two men's regimes offers little reason to think that Wade systematically shifted service delivery toward regions of the country that had been home to precolonial states.

Rather, I argue that the devolution of authority over the construction of primary school and basic health facilities to local governments that came with Acte II of Senegal's decentralization project offers the most leverage on the changing patterns we see in the data. These reforms were arguably the most significant change to the structure of primary education and health delivery in postcolonial Senegal. Foley (2010, 58) corroborates this, writing that the local

urban areas of the country in 1974, for example, despite housing only a quarter of the country's population (Keita 2007, 133).

[17] World Bank (1995). [18] As recently demonstrated by Briggs (2014).
[19] Diop (2006b, 104). [20] Mbow (2008, 161) and Galvan (2001, 53–55).

officials she interviewed in the late 1990s saw Acte II as much more significant than the previous decade's neoliberal adjustment given the significant administrative restructuring of responsibility that it brought to local actors. Beyond creating new political space locally, Acte II also nuanced the authority of long-standing patronage structures, most notably the role of the Muslim Brotherhoods as key brokers between the state and rural communities.[21] This is widely remarked upon in my own interviews as well. One former mayor described how no one in his community was very interested in the first elections in his local government, held in 1976, because the local government was seen as largely irrelevant. It was only after 1996 that the availability of real resources garnered the attention of local elites who were attracted to the new authority granted to the local state.[22]

This is an important corrective to recent work on precolonial legacies, which tends to assume an equilibrium dynamic. Much of this literature invokes "catch-all" mechanisms that are unable to explain variation in the antecedent cause's effects over time. For example, Hjort (2010, 689) argues that centralization among the Tswana perpetuated norms of individual property rights, inter-ethnic unity, and democratic traditions as an explanation for Botswana's postcolonial economic growth. In assuming that these mechanisms are constant over time, however, Hjort and others who find similar legacies cannot explain why we might expect a positive effect at some points in time but not others. If Senegal's precolonial states similarly left behind, say, a legacy of inter-ethnic unity, why wouldn't this have impacted state redistribution from at least independence onward? This question is important because one clear measure of an argument's strength is the plausibility of its mechanisms as a link between the outcome and the antecedent condition.[23] This necessitates taking historical processes seriously and developing mechanisms that are consistent with temporal processes. Doing so reinforces my theory of institutional congruence: the legacy of the precolonial past is dependent on formal institutional arrangements. It is only when formal and informal institutional boundaries are congruent that we see an effect on precolonial statehood.

ASSESSING ALTERNATIVE HISTORICAL LEGACIES: WHAT ROLE FOR THE COLONIAL STATE?

Above, I document little evidence that the colonial state targeted investments to the territory of Senegal's precolonial kingdoms. In view of the stunning reinvigoration of academic interest in the impact of colonization on development

---

[21] See Beck (2001). [22] Interview, Louga Region, February 12, 2017.
[23] See here Wittenberg (2015). The question of mechanisms is not unacknowledged in this literature. Michalopoulos and Papaioannou (2013, 19) note that work should look in more depth at how "ethnic-specific attributes" shape economic performance. Others, like Bandyopadhyay and Green (2016) look at different dependent variables to identify more or less plausible mechanisms.

outcomes, however, colonial legacies may not be so easily dismissed.[24] Increasingly, this has led scholars to turn their attention to subnational variation in colonial rule, enabling us to nuance our understanding of how colonialism matters by revealing how colonization was a spatially and temporally uneven exercise in state-building.[25] As a result, causal primacy has been ascribed to the colonial state in lieu of precolonial or postcolonial legacies. Although some scholars have begun efforts to adjudicate between seemingly contradictory conclusions, the key tenet of this literature continues to be that exposure to some aspect of colonization (for instance, specific institutions or forms of human capital transfer) generated path-dependent effects that persist to the present.[26] In this view, contemporary conditions in the Global South are a function of a series of colonialism-induced equilibria.

For many, this will make my claim that it is *pre*colonial legacies that are influential in the present puzzling. Could the effects I ascribe to precolonial political geography be masking what are ultimately colonial-era changes? To account for the possibility that my data may obscure legacies induced by the distributional logics of the colonial state, I test three common claims about the impact of the colonial encounter below. First, I examine whether contemporary development is a function of location fundamentals. This logic would predict that patterns of social service access were determined by proximity to the colonial state. A second and related argument is that service delivery is spatially "sticky," with early exposure to social services predicting long-term access. Finally, I address a more diffuse set of arguments that the colonial state delivered services to fulfill its own specific political agenda with lasting impacts.

Did Early Colonial Exposure Drive Outcomes?

Early colonial investments were thin and clustered near points of French strategic investments. Prior to French expansion inland, the first schools and health facilities were founded in the ports and *escales* dominated by French traders, principally based in and around the early urban centers of Saint-Louis and Dakar. Education slowly expanded outward on three axes: in an expanding network of trading centers as French commercial interests spread along the Senegal River and, later, along the Saint-Louis–Dakar railroad constructed in the late 1880s; via missionary stations along the coast; and in the early administrative posts of the young colonial states as French officers made tentative efforts to provide primary health and education services. Health facilities were much slower to expand beyond major population centers and much of the country, even areas that had seen relative advances in education, remained

---

[24] Perhaps best well-known in a series of papers by Acemoglu et al. (2002) and Acemoglu et al. (2001).
[25] For example, Pierskalla et al. (2017) or Berger (2009).
[26] For example, Bruhn and Gallego (2012); Foa (2017); and Letsa and Wilfahrt (2020).

drastically underserved. Neither rural Diourbel nor Fleuve (present-day Saint-Louis and Matam) Regions had a doctor prior to 1910, for example.

In part, this reflected prevailing beliefs in Europe at the time that economic and social activities were the responsibility of the private realm with the state focused on providing internal and external protection. While over time it became clear that the colonies would never attract private investment without some state-led development of infrastructure, such as railroads and basic social services, the constraints of colonial budgeting, which required colonies to be economically self-sufficient hampered significant development efforts.[27] Early revenue raised in French West Africa was largely destined to finance the colony's own administration.[28]

The consequence was that while the colony's small European populations did have access to basic social services, most colonial subjects effectively received nothing in terms of investment from the colonial state in the first decades of colonization. What impact was felt in outlying areas was the expansion of transportation and communication networks, the introduction of a uniform currency, and the alienation of peasants from traditional land-holding practices.[29] Though many colonial administrators bemoaned the lack of development effort on the part of the state, with high-profile actors like Gouverneur Général Ponty calling for greater investment in the domains of health and education in 1908, efforts remained weak. From the 190 primary schools in operation in French West Africa in 1909, there was no meaningful increase by the end of First World War a decade later.[30]

What public goods were built were often done so on the whim of individual administrators, who had absolute authority in their *cercles* far from the oversight of their superiors.[31] In contrast to the dominant view of the French colonial administration as a centralized, homogenous entity, in reality, the early years of colonization are best characterized as a "decentralized administrative structure [that] virtually gave a free hand to the man who wanted to build a bridge, establish a schoolhouse, or help increase local peanut production...."[32] The French lacked a coherent vision for their massive territorial acquisitions, which granted substantial authority to the understaffed territorial administration, though this also meant that any given official's individual efforts were largely circumscribed to the most accessible areas around his post and easily abandoned upon his departure.

The only coherent education policy in the early years of colonial administration in French West Africa was a desire to create and reproduce a stratum of

---

[27] Take, for example, an early effort to expand schooling outward from Saint-Louis into the newly annexed territory of the Walo under General Faidherbe in the 1850s. Despite the belief that such education was necessary to train a colonial workforce, the schools were all closed within fifteen years as the Franco-Prussian war tightened colonial budgets (Duke Bryant 2015, 15–16).
[28] Fage (1969, 201–202). [29] Crowder (1968, 275). [30] Crowder (1968, 284).
[31] Cohen (1971) and Colombi (1991). [32] Cohen (1971, 61, 79).

Africans able to perform vital functions for the colonial economy: government clerks, technicians, veterinarians, teachers, and doctors.[33] Following the 1912 request of the government of French West Africa government that each colony create its own Education Department (Senegal's was created in 1913), schools were organized in a pyramidal fashion: village schools at the base, regional schools serving as a middle layer, and a few elite schools, based in Dakar and Saint-Louis, that trained future elites at the top.[34] What schools were built in rural districts often suffered from weak attendance.[35] Early health intervention was simultaneously geared toward meeting colonial needs and structured along racial and class lines.[36] Although the French made significant advances in expanding access to health care relative to other colonial powers on the continent, in large part because they invested in training African doctors, clinics remained concentrated in administrative centers much like schools; the average distance to a clinic in the 1920s, for example, was just shy of 50 kilometers.[37]

The clustered nature of early colonial investments raises the possibility that social service access was merely driven by the happenstance of proximity: being located near a European population center, a trading post, or an administrative center with an ambitious colonial officer were all likely to increase access to services. Alternatively, if exposure to precolonial coastal trade influenced district-level colonial investments or if subsequent investments diffused outward from early missionary posts, for example, we might find certain path dependencies in service access.[38] Given that the early colonial state made few investments, am I actually capturing persistent "spatial equilibrium" that is truly a function of early proximity to colonial infrastructure?[39]

To answer this question, I turn again to my dataset of historical public goods delivery. I estimate the effect of proximity to the colonial state in four ways. First, I look at whether distances to European population centers can explain social service access over time. I measure this with (a) a village's logged distance

---

[33] The government emphasized recruiting students from among local elites, sons of notables and chiefs as well as the children of ex-soldiers, colonial functionaries, and merchants. As Gouverneur General Rome wrote in 1924: "because our current means do not allow us to yet reach the masses and restrict our efforts to a minority, choose judiciously among this minority ... Chose our students first from among the sons of village chiefs and notables, the indigenous society is very hierarchical. Social classes are clearly determined by hereditary factors and customs. It is on this that our authority relies in the administration of the country" (Moumani 1967, 56).

[34] Though the first Western schools in the colony were built by missionaries or local Catholic churches, the colonial government began regulating primary education in 1903, replacing religious teachers with laymen in state schools and cutting off all support to missions. Unlike in British colonies, which relied on school fees as a means to supplement the costs of government-run schools, schooling was free in French West Africa and many students, especially at elite or regional schools, received free lodging as well (Mumford 1970 (1935), 63).

[35] Duke Bryant (2015, chapter 1). [36] Keita (2007). [37] Crowder (1968, 327).

[38] Ricart-Huguet (2016) and Gallego and Woodberry (2010).

[39] To adopt the language of Burgess et al. (2015).

to the nearest French outpost – fort, mission, trading post, or rail station – before the full onset of colonial rule (pre-1890) and (b) a locality's European population in 1912.[40] I secondly measure exposure to the colonial administration with the logged distance to the nearest French administrative center in 1902 and again in 1922, when the colonial state was more entrenched. Third, I take into account transport infrastructure by looking at the logged distance to the nearest point on the French railway in 1910, when it was largely completed, and to a major road as of 1940, when road travel had come to surpass rail in much of the countryside. Lastly, I examine exposure to missionaries with the logged distance to the nearest mission in 1900 and 1918, after which the map of missionary activity was largely fixed in rural areas.

Results from a series of OLS estimates are displayed in Figure 7.4. These models control for the same geographic variables introduced in Chapter 5 because geographic factors may have both encouraged French settlement or investment decisions while also influencing subsequent development processes. Models are run with fixed effects at the *cercle*, an early administrative unit that is pegged here to its 1915 boundaries, the first year for which complete French colonial maps are available. While choosing a geographical boundary that was created following colonization is far from ideal, these boundaries are arguably less politically informed than subsequent administrative divisions because early efforts to delineate the colony quickly amalgamated large swaths of land as the French moved inland. All models include robust, clustered standard errors at this level as well.

Two things are immediately obvious. First, proximity to the colonial administration and Europeans – via missions or those living near French administrative centers – is almost always significant in the early colonial period. Likewise, areas that had earlier access to road and rail networks see similar boosts in their exposure to services during the colonial era. This suggests that early points of accessibility into the rural countryside did catalyze the delivery of social services. The second conclusion that we can draw is that while these effects are remarkably sticky through the end of the twentieth century, they disappear entirely by the start of the second decade of decentralized governance if not earlier. Location fundamentals induced by the colonial state do not appear to be driving the distributional patterns documented in earlier chapters of this book.

Are Colonial Development Policies Durable?

A variant of the argument explored above is found in Huillery's (2009) paper that argues that infrastructural investments, such as clinics and schools, are sticky: colonial investments tend to produce persistent patterns of access over time. If, as Huillery (2009) argues, colonial-era investments drive subsequent ones, then contemporary patterns of access may simply reflect

[40] The latter is coded from AOF (1912).

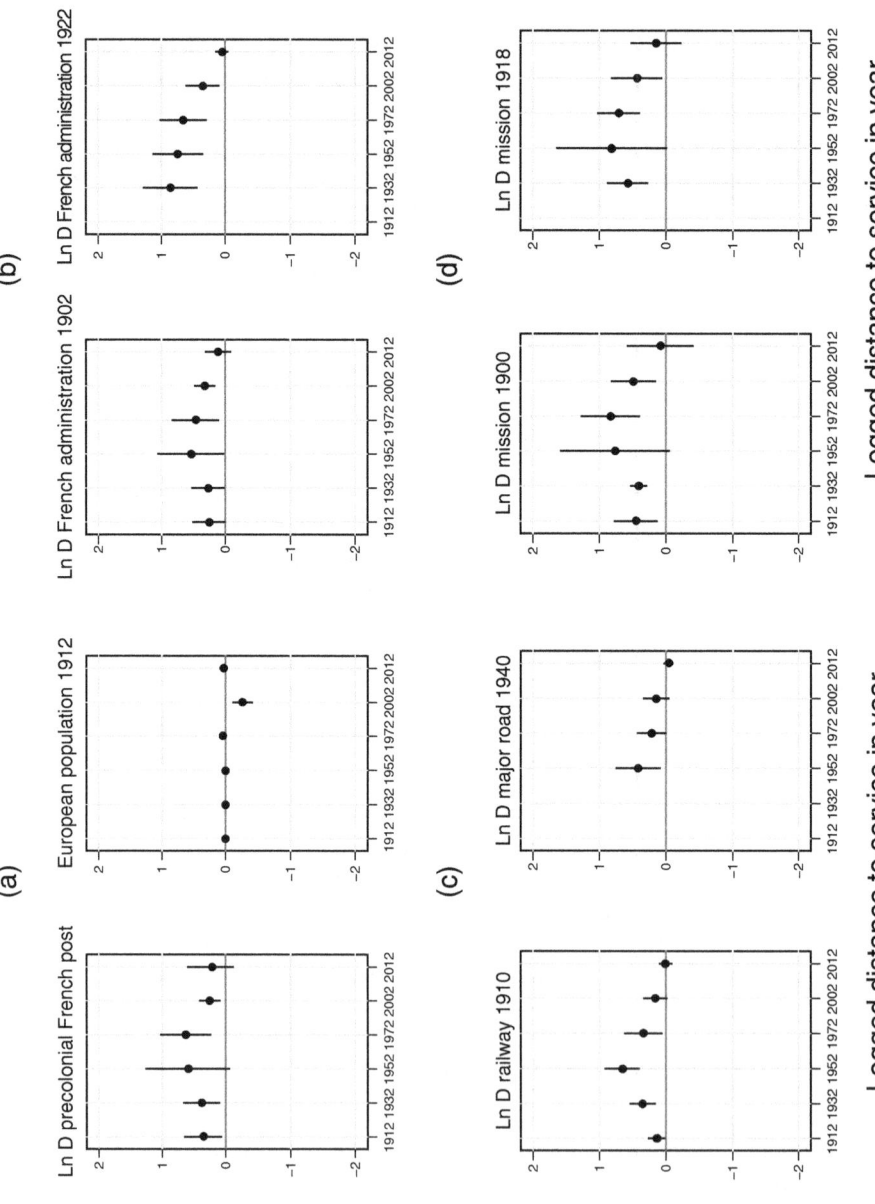

FIGURE 7.4 Effect of colonial exposure on service access over time: (a) proximity to Europeans, (b) proximity to

Assessing Alternative Historical Legacies

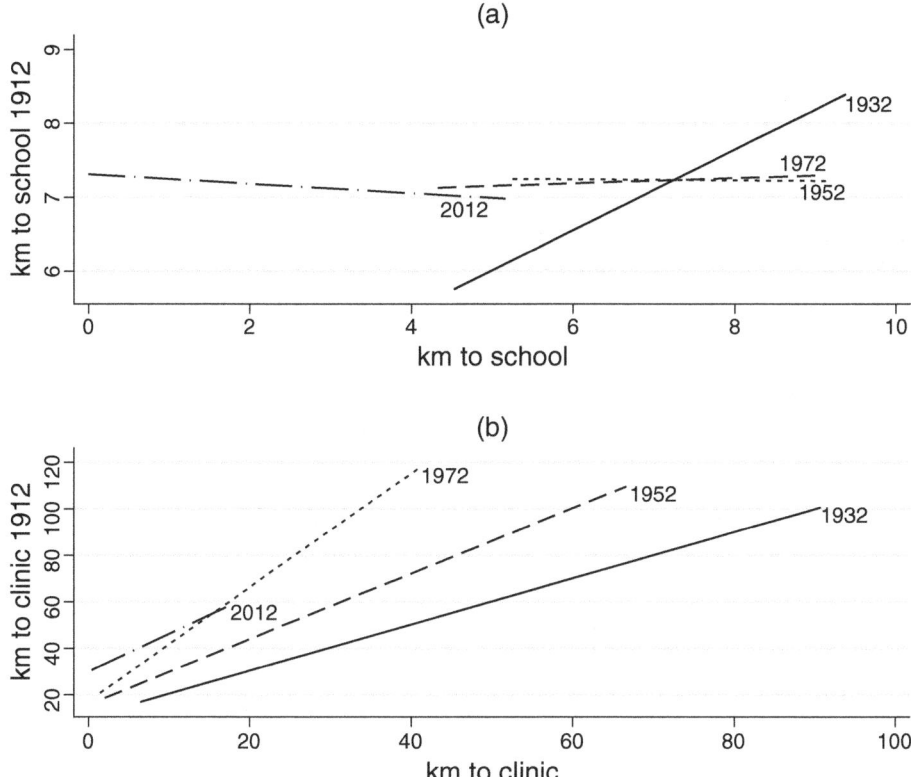

FIGURE 7.5 Linear fit between early colonial and subsequent service access: (a) education and (b) health

economies of scales in areas that received higher levels of investment during French colonial rule.[41] To evaluate whether this is the case, I examine whether access to services during the colonial era can predict subsequent access.

Figure 7.5 shows the line of fit between a village's distances to the nearest school (Figure 7.5a) and health center (Figure 7.5b) in 1912 and at four other points in time: 1932, 1952, 1972, and 2012. Panel A suggests a positive correlation between distances to education facilities in 1912 and 1932, but this relationship flattens by the late colonial era and remains so to the present. Panel B shows that healthcare access correlates more strongly over time, though this relationship has also weakened considerably by the early 2000s.

The flattening in Panel A reflects in part the uptick in colonial investments following the Second World War. At the 1944 Brazzaville Conference, convoked by French President Charles de Gaulle to outline a plan for the African

---

[41] Huillery's outcome data come from 1995, which would predate decentralization for most of the countries in her sample.

colonies following France's liberation from Germany, a massive expansion of education and health services was proposed, motivated by the belief that the colonial state was "building Frenchmen."[42] During the same year, the Governor General of the AOF commissioned a fifty-year plan to ensure mass education of African subjects that resulted in primary education reform in August of 1945, whereby colonial schools adopted the standards of metropolitan France.

The ten-year plan for the Modernization of Overseas Territories of 1946 aimed to double school enrollment in five years and triple it by 1956 to meet an overall goal of 50 percent enrollment throughout West Africa. In 1948, primary school enrollment was opened to all.[43] Although the region fell well short of these numbers, more than 1,000 schools were built in French West Africa between 1949 and 1950 through the *Fonds d'Investissement pour le Developpement Economique et Social des Territoires d'outre mer* (FIDES).[44] FIDES brought not only money, but technicians, substantially restricting the latitude previously afforded administrators as service delivery was increasingly bureaucratized.[45] Perhaps most notably, the FIDES era saw significant expansion into areas that had previously seen little investment as the colonial state, now more secure in its hegemony, began extending a more comprehensive reach across the countryside. These gains were meaningful but insufficient.[46] While the budget for primary education tripled from 1,595,000 CFA to 5,311,000 between 1950 and 1955, the impact on student enrollment remained low: with 4 out of 1,000 students educated in 1947, this number only increased to 10 in 1,000 by 1957.[47]

The significant expansion of services during the FIDES era calls into question the assumption that it was the colonial states' earliest investments that drive long-term access. I test to see how early versus late colonial investments are compared in Figure 7.6, which provides a more rigorous analysis of over time trends. I model the impact of the logged distance to the nearest clinic or primary school in 1902, 1912, 1932, and 1952 on the equivalent measure in the following decades. Although there is initially a strong relationship for each in the shorter term, the effect of pre-First World War investments fades by the early postcolonial period. A similar pattern is seen in the distances to services at later points in time, whose effects fade by the era of decentralization. Looking at village-specific access, my data suggest less long-term persistence at the village level than Huillery's (2009) measurement of colonial legacies at the level of the colonial *cercle*.

Overall, the evidence is mixed for Huillery's argument. Any early "stickiness" of colonial investments appears to have largely faded by the postcolonial

---

[42] Kusiak (2005, 104).   [43] De Bénoist (1982, 142–143).   [44] Gardiniere (1985, 339).
[45] Cohen (1971, 173) and Colombi (1991, 129).
[46] As Colombi (1991, 1919) writes, however the FIDES money "arrived fifty years too late" to be of use in helping the country prepare for independence.
[47] Moumani (1967, 56).

Assessing Alternative Historical Legacies

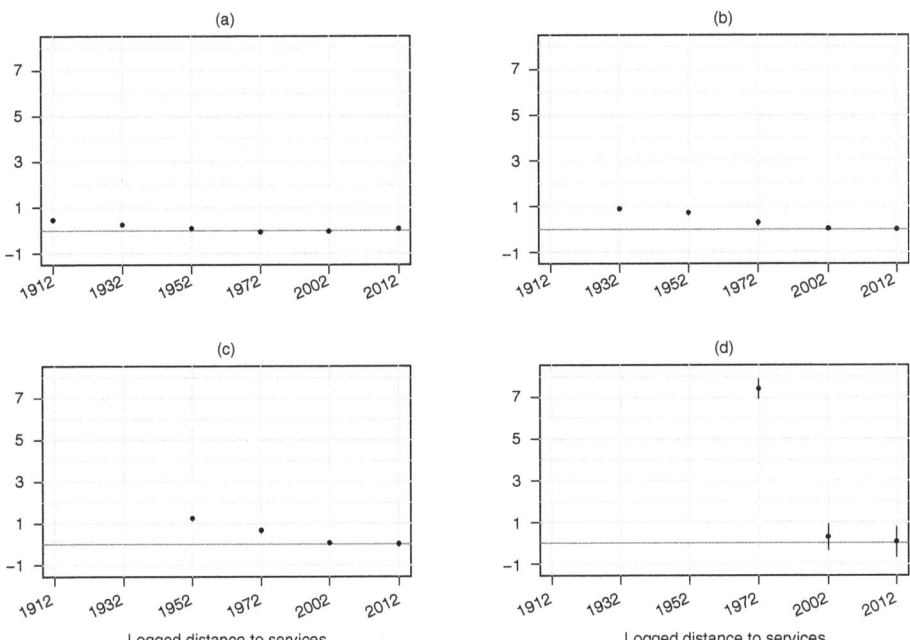

FIGURE 7.6 Effect of early investments on later investments. Distance from services in (a) 1902, (b) 1912, (c) 1932, and (d) 1952

era, which may mean that these starting points matter, but that over a longer run more proximate factors hold more influence.

Colonial and Postcolonial Political Favoritism

In 1960, 2 in 1,000 rural Senegalese had their *certificate d'etudes primaire* (CEP), but this number was much higher at 6–8 per 1,000 in the lower Casamance (present-day Ziguinchor Region).[48] That the region of Cap-Vert (home to Dakar) and the lower Casamance were better educated was largely the legacy of the early and intense efforts of Catholic missions, which encouraged families to send their children to school.[49] Patterns in healthcare access were altogether different. The Casamance, along with Louga and Senegal Oriental, was significantly underserved in health through the early 1980s.[50]

These inequities – already evident by mid-century – return us to the question of what characteristics of the colonial state should bias against the persistence

---

[48] Colonial administrators often ascribed these differences to cultural differences among ethnic groups; the Diola, Sarakole, and Serer were seen as being more open to French education as opposed to the Peulh or the entirety of Kedougou Region (Colin 1980, 499).
[49] Colin (1980, 503).   [50] Keita (2007, 137).

of precolonial legacies. Subnational variation in access may have little at all to do with proximity or spatial diffusion, but instead be driven by the political ambitions of the French colonial state, which sought first and foremost compliance and tax revenue. To this end, French strategy toward the countryside largely revolved around the peanut economy, with the Sufi Islamic Brotherhoods acting as valuable intermediaries. Despite adopting a language of "modernizing" the link between France and her colonies in the 1950s and the introduction of local elected assemblies, the French kept its political negotiations focused around an urban political elite while granting autonomy to rural brokers, often Sufi leaders, in the countryside.[51] The postcolonial state demonstrated unusual continuity in these priorities, by and large relying on the same stratum of rural elites that had worked closely with the French.[52]

This produced distinct tensions for the postcolonial state. "Political integration," which sought to reduce inequalities in access to social services and to bring areas that had been largely isolated during the colonial era more fully into the country's economy, figured prominently in the first four-year plan of President Senghor and his Prime Minister, Mamadou Dia.[53] The early postcolonial state's efforts to transform the lives of the peasantry resulted in more than 50 percent of the state's annual spending going to the "social budget" in the first years of independence.[54] At independence in 1960, Senegal counted 106,911 primary school students, a number that rose by more than 20,000 to 127,000 in 1962.[55] By and large, primary school construction and the construction of rural dispensaries were among the most popular services provided by the newly independent state.[56] This trend eventually abated in the late 1960s, however, as Senghor's government realized that it could not support the costs associated with such rapid expansion, notably salaries and facility maintenance.[57] The government also emphasized preventative rural health, but even these early goals were never met as French medical training and practices continued to dominate. By 1974 the country had only 281 doctors.[58] Primary school construction slowed considerably as did the growth in enrollment rates, which went from a 11.2 percent annual increase in 1964 to a mere 2.7 percent in 1971.[59] Although reaching complete primary school enrollment remained a goal in subsequent government plans, the expected date of this achievement was pushed back to 2000, with short-term objectives hovering around

---

[51] Cooper (1994, 171–172). This should not lead us to assume, however, that these investments were done with an eye toward independence; Cooper (1994, 178) argues that these efforts were reactive, "a tenacious holding operation."

[52] Boone (2003b). Unlike neighboring Mali and Guinea, for example, Senegal retained its canton chiefs, rebaptizing them as *chefs d'arrondissement* following independence (though the position was eventually eliminated).

[53] Gellar et al. (1980, 52). [54] Colin (1980, 597). [55] Moumani (1967).

[56] Gellar et al. (1980, 70). [57] Boone (1992, 92) and Gellar et al. (1980, 86).

[58] Menes (1976, 96). [59] Colin (1980, 605) and Le Brun (1979, 185).

40 percent. Senegal has yet to meet the goal of complete primary school attendance; in 2019, it hovered around 75 percent.

Did the expansion of services by the colonial and/or postcolonial regime map onto these political objectives? If the colonial and postcolonial states systematically allied themselves in rural areas with the Wolof, peanut-producing heartland, we might expect investments to cluster in these areas. This would be the key prediction of Roessler et al. (2018) who find that colonial development centered around cash crops zones, generating persistent spatial inequalities in African states to the present. Alternatively, we might expect goods to accumulate in the Mouride heartland. Figure 7.7 presents a series of OLS regressions estimating the impact of numerous potential sources of political favoritism on a village's access to social services over time. I begin by looking for evidence of ethnic favoritism to Wolof and Serer (Figure 7.7a) dominant local governments. These ethnic groups were closest to Dakar and traditionally inhabited much of the peanut basin. Second, Figure 7.7b presents the results of models examining whether areas that produced large amounts of peanuts, Senegal's main export crop, in either 1900 or, later, 1950, were favored. This allows me to account for both the original peanut-producing zones and the later expansion of production southeastward as the soils of Cayor and the Djoloff were exhausted. Finally, Figure 7.7c looks at the role of the Mouride Brotherhood, first, measured by the number of Mourides living in each *canton* in 1917 as reported by Marty (1917) and, second, whether the village falls within the large swaths of land opened to Mouride pioneers as estimated by Pélissier (1966, 316). Geographic controls and model specification are equivalent to those described above.

This is largely a story of null effects and, when these measures are statistically significant, it is often in the opposite direction than what is suggested in the literature. There is no evidence of ethnic favoritism, with the exception of 1932 when Wolof zones do appear to briefly see more improvements in service access. The peanut basin never significantly predicts new service delivery and, to the contrary, early peanut-producing zones have poorer access to social services until the 2000s. Nor is there a significant difference for a village's falling in the heart of the peanut economy as measured by its expanse in the 1950s. French colonial investments in clinics and schools, this suggests, were not targeted to key economic zones. Of course, favoritism likely took other forms, such as the distribution of agricultural inputs or the digging of wells in addition to the ways in which these economies shaped rail and road networks, but for the social services under study here, there is no evidence that the political ambitions of the colonial or early postcolonial state are driving the patterns I document.

Finally, villages that fall in the approximated boundary of Mouride pioneer settlements only see a benefit in the early 1970s. There is, however, a positive and significant effect for villages falling in cantons with high numbers of Mourides in 1932 and 1952 and, interestingly, again in 2002. This certainly reflects the powerful role played by the Mouride Brotherhoods in the late colonial and postindependence era. This effect disappears by 2012.

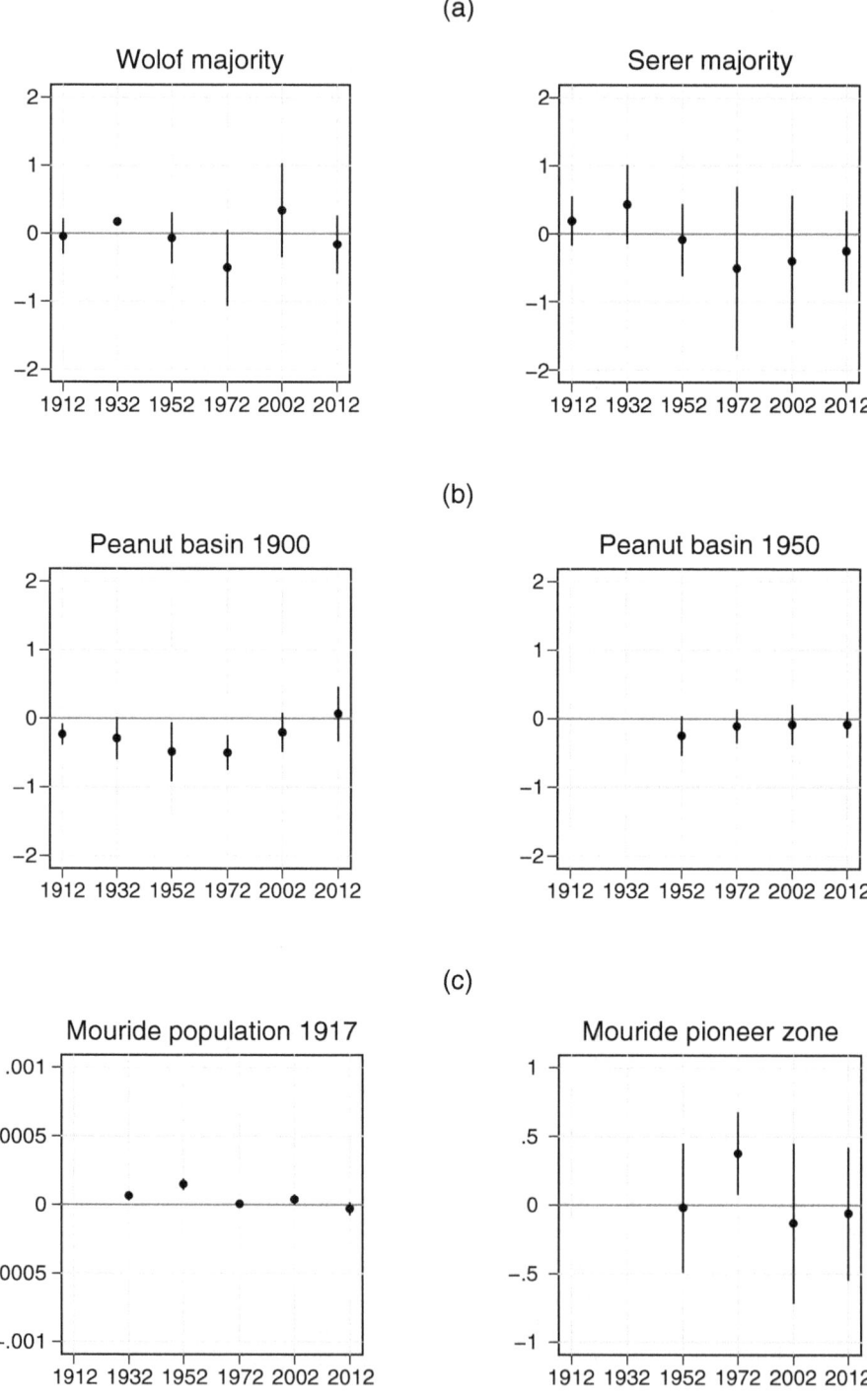

FIGURE 7.7 Colonial favoritism on service access over time: (a) ethnic favoritism, (b) peanut economy, and (c) Mouride Brotherhood

Whither the Colonial State?

The data presented above further substantiates my claim that despite their magnitude, the changes induced by French colonization cannot explain the contemporary politics of public goods delivery in decentralized Senegal. This runs counter to a long-standing assumption among scholars of political economy that we can locate fundamental causes of contemporary development disparities in the colonial period. Although proximity to the colonial state heavily influenced access to social services through the 1970s, my data suggest that the effects of colonialism on local service access have faded by the early 2000s. The contemporary politics of redistribution in rural Senegal do not appear to be driven by exposure to the colonial state, to path dependencies in its social service delivery, or by the political or economic logics of colonial rule.

Certainly, colonialism had myriad influences that I do not begin to capture here. I do not question that colonialism had broader, reverberating impacts in rural West Africa nor that there are other pathways through which colonialism impacts the present.[60] Senegalese politics is still heavily oriented toward appeasing urban citizens and working via maraboutic networks in rural zones, for example. Still, my findings echo an argument that it is no longer empirically or theoretically useful to speak of a postcolonial state after the changes brought about by the post-Cold War world of structural adjustment and democratization (no matter how thin).[61] If this is true, then it is not surprising that my data document a fading role for colonial legacies in service provision. Figure 7.6 suggests that some colonial influences have washed out by as early as the 1970s. Maseland (2018) similarly finds that within two decades of Nigeria's independence, the impact of colonialism on per capita income and institutional quality had largely faded. This may not be limited to sub-Saharan Africa. Though identifying disparities in contemporary development outcomes between areas of India that were ruled directly and those ruled indirectly, Iyer (2010) observes that this gap is narrowing over time as a function of the postcolonial state's own policies. Collectively, this suggests that colonialism may be influential but not deterministic, highlighting the risk of engaging in what Cooper (2005, 17) has called "leapfrogging legacies" that fail to unpack historical processes and, in the process, undermining the agency of local actors and the ambitions of postcolonial leaders and bureaucrats alike.

DISCUSSION: WHY DON'T ALL LEGACIES PERSIST?

This chapter has shown evidence of two legacy effects: one that reappears after over 100 years and one that fades over time. In unpacking both precolonial and

---

[60] Notably, communities with early exposure to education undoubtedly saw greater opportunities for careers in the colonial and postcolonial bureaucracy in ways that were consequential for private wealth and mobility. The inequalities generated by this pathway are most likely to accrue in urban areas and in private wealth acquisition, however.
[61] As argued by Young (2004) and Piot (2010).

colonial legacies during the course of the twentieth century, I have attempted to respond to one of the most prominent criticisms of recent work on the long-run historical causes of contemporary political and economic development: scholars make "heroic assumptions" about historical processes that strain credibility by omitting decades of history.[62] This "compression of history" relies on two assumptions about unit homogeneity, the idea that causal processes unfold the same in all cases.[63] First, this work supposes that historical institutions have universal effects and, second, that this places certain countries or communities in different equilibria that become path-dependent. The dominant approach in the "historical renaissance" therefore is that history matters because it can explain why some societies become "stuck" on more or less developmental paths.[64]

This is a powerful view of history, assigning great weight to say the intergenerational persistence of attitudes (as argued by Nunn and Wantchekon 2011, for example) or to the lock-in effects of institutions. Acemoglu et al. (2001), to take a prominent example, argue that institutions brought by settlers have sunk costs, generating path dependencies as the cost of switching to other institutional forms rises for subsequent generations. Huillery (2009), introduced above, makes a structurally similar argument: French colonial investments placed some districts on a "virtuous circle," as the at times happenstance placement of a school in one district over another created long-run path dependencies in investments. This perspective thus predicts persistence, meaning that change should only arise following strong shocks, such as those that correct an unproductive equilibrium or, to embrace a different language, that produce critical junctures for institutional change. Putting aside, if we can, the question of more or less plausible historical processes, one of the most remarkable features of this scholarship is that there is limited room, if any, to consider whether and when legacies simply fade away.

Yet, this is exactly what I observe. My data on social service access find no evidence that the French strategically targeted certain areas of the country over others in their early colonial efforts, but rather settled according to convenience. Once faced with the need to actually govern vast swaths of territory, early investments were largely driven by the various attitudes of local administrators, choosing to invest in areas over which they had the most oversight, effectively meaning their own settlements and those in close proximity. When the French government was finally willing to invest in its colonies, social services expanded outward in an attempt to equalize access across the country, a project largely continued in the postcolonial period. To the extent that the colonial state had political and economic objectives, I find no evidence that this was systematically

---

[62] Hopkins (2009, 165). [63] See Austin (2008) on the compression of history.
[64] Nunn (2009, 75–77).

correlated with precolonial centralization or even investments made during earlier phases of the colonial state construction.[65]

This suggests that not all historical legacies persist equally and, in turn, that we have insufficient leverage over why and when they are more likely to do so. One clear implication of my findings is that colonial effects may be better modeled as a slow evolutionary process than as equilibria that necessitate an exogenous shock to create change. This should not be a radical position. To the extent that scholars have established how empires (e.g. Barkey 2008) or the colonial state itself (e.g. Young 1994) evolve, consolidating and eroding their authority over time, it is eminently rational to expect the same from the legacies they leave behind. This makes equilibrium approaches ill-suited to explain the patterns I document in this chapter. Rather than isolating one discontinuous moment of change, development initiatives in Senegal's countryside have adapted and responded to new political imperatives: peasant malaise led to the creation of rural communities early on, but it was structural adjustment and the political upheaval of the early 1990s that generated the move toward *Acte II*, for example. Past investments may be sticky, but they do not appear to be "stuck."

Yet aren't my findings suggestive that rural Senegal is simply returning to a longer-run equilibrium? In many ways, this is the case. As laid out in Chapter 2 and substantiated with data presented in Chapters 4 and 6, precolonial legacies are tied to the persistence of local elite social status, which validates and reifies narratives of descent from a centralized precolonial past. I theorize that politically latent social institutions are redeployed for new purposes as political actors adapt to changing institutional circumstances, such as the advent of decentralization.[66] The social institutions that I identify as critical may be an equilibrium, therefore, but this only matters for the outcomes of interest under specific formal institutional configurations.

In this vein, I suggest that contemporary differences can be traced to the distant past but that this may not become causal until an exogenous institutional shock fosters institutional congruence. Paying attention to such political interactions is critical. For example, Acemoglu, Reed et al. (2014) observe a strong legacy of indirect rule in Sierra Leone, but note that such persistence was not uniform. In states such as Ghana or Uganda, the presence of a large, centralized precolonial state generated chiefs with sufficient authority to challenge postindependence elites. In the face of these challengers, elites consolidated power to rule more directly as a means of co-opting potential rivals, a political strategy endogenous to local interactions between formal and informal

---

[65] Of course, in cases where early French settlements facilitated rapid economic growth thus that a village obtained "urban" status, there is a strong correlation between French investments and postcolonial favoritism. This is not within the scope of this project, however, which only focuses on rural areas.

[66] See discussion in Thelen and Steinmo (1992, 13).

institutions. If we recognize the redistributive effects of institutions, then any shift in the power coalitions controlling state institutions should reshape who benefits from social service investments.[67] Crucially, this can happen even absent major institutional shocks.

As Cooper (2005, 25) has argued, "there is a danger that ahistorical history encourages an apolitical politics." By unpacking history, I have attempted to restore some agency to both the postcolonial state, whose policies appear to have at least sometimes muted the disparities of the colonial era, as well as the agency of local communities to embed institutional reforms in their own local political narratives. If the appeal of legacy arguments lies in our recognition that "real social processes have distinctly temporal dimensions," my framework offers a means to reinsert social mechanisms more clearly into our understandings of why things do (and do not) persist over time.[68]

One potential reading is that institutions imposed from above, such as the extractive logics of the colonial state, may be more prone to peter out rather than to persist, while the more organic legacies of the precolonial past retain an ability to adapt to changing political, social, and economic realities as they are repurposed by local communities at the grassroots. This is because such "cognitive" legacies are most likely to be resilient within closed groups and when they invoke strong prescriptive norms.[69] Still, the social institutions at play in rural Senegal may both persist for generations and remain particularly vulnerable to shocks. Still, that they have survived the colonial encounter as well as the transition to independence suggests a remarkable durability. At base, however, the ability of social institutions to shape development outcomes is contingent on their overlap with formal institutions. This means that if decentralization was to be abolished or, more limitedly, if authority over public goods was to be transferred back to the state, then the effect I observe should disappear.

CONCLUSION

Together, the findings of this chapter reveal that historical legacies may face different prospects for persistence. While understanding the contours of the temporal variation of our outcomes under study is a valuable empirical pursuit in its own right, it simultaneously allows me to question the assumption behind the majority of mechanisms that have been put forth in work in the "historical renaissance": that the geography of subnational inequalities has not dramatically changed and that these disparities have amplified over time.

In contrast, I reveal changing landscapes of political logics and political favoritism. This reinforces my theory of institutional congruence because the legacy of the precolonial past is dependent on formal institutional arrangements.

---

[67] Following Mahoney (2010).   [68] Pierson (2004, 13).   [69] Simpser et al. (2018, 426).

Conclusion

It is only when formal and informal institutional boundaries are congruent that we see an effect on precolonial statehood. This results in a striking ability of precolonial geography to shape outcomes in the present, but this is not the result of a uniform or uninterrupted process. In this way, my argument can be read as a response to the recent tendency to pretermit decades, if not centuries, of history within the historical renaissance sweeping development economics and political science. In rural West Africa, historical antecedents matter, but without understanding when and for how long leaves us vulnerable to assuming improbable causes. This pushes forward debates on institutional persistence by specifying clear mechanisms of persistence, as called for by Nunn (2009), while remaining sensitive to how plausible those mechanisms are at different points in time.

The second argument advanced in this chapter is that not all legacies persist with equal robustness to the present. Studying what fades away can be as intellectually useful as studying what persists. In the face of mounting evidence that important subnational trajectories exist in developing countries and that they can be explained by the distant past, it is imperative that we take seriously how these processes actually work themselves out over time. Scholars have been quick to highlight the need to disaggregate by type of public good or across countries.[70] By demonstrating the value of unpacking temporal process, this chapter suggests that we must also take seriously who makes these decisions and when.

---

[70] For example, Kramon and Posner (2013) and Franck and Rainer (2012).

8

Institutional Congruence beyond Senegal

Communities around the world possess norms that stipulate appropriate social comportment and acceptable ways to exercising political authority. Political scientists are increasingly interested in these dynamics, suggesting that governance may be improved by "harmonization" of traditional and legal forms of governance.[1] I join this broader research agenda by documenting how social institutions around conflict avoidance and principles of balance shape local governance in historically centralized areas of rural Senegal when they overlap with formal institutional boundaries. Because decentralization reforms have been put in place across West Africa, this raises the question of whether we see similar patterns elsewhere. Is there a robust effect of precolonial centralization on local development outcomes across the region? This chapter offers a tentative answer to this question by pairing an expanded coding of precolonial states across West Africa with data from the Demographic and Health Surveys (DHS) and public opinion data from the Afrobarometer survey. This allows me to estimate whether the location of precolonial states correlates with attitudes toward local governance and development outcomes across decentralized West Africa. Afrobarometer respondents in areas that were home to precolonial states report distinctly more positive attitudes about their local governments and democratic practice than their counterparts in historically acephalous zones. The DHS data shows that these same areas also see improvements in local development outcomes in line with both my expectations and the patterns I have documented in Senegal.

The second half of this chapter explores the argument's theoretical generalizability by returning to the central question animating this book: why are some

---

[1] As recently phrased by Holzinger et al. (2016).

communities imbued with prosocial attitudes that help them improve their collective good while others are not? My evidence from Senegal suggests one answer can be found by studying how social institutions inherited from the precolonial past facilitate cooperation under decentralization when they overlap with the contours of the local state. But can the argument shed light on empirical phenomena that stray from the specifics of precolonial legacies or decentralization as an institutional reform? To answer this, I highlight how the two mechanisms animating my theory – shared social identification and dense network ties among elites – offer a flexible and generalizable framework for understanding variation in how distributive dilemmas are resolved. I draw on a wide range of research to illustrate the broad applicability of the mechanisms, identifying comparable dynamics at different levels of government and across varying cultural and institutional contexts. I conclude by outlining a series of scope conditions for the argument.

LEGACIES OF PRECOLONIAL STATEHOOD ACROSS WEST AFRICA

My focus on precolonial legacies contributes to a growing recognition that areas of Africa that were home to centralized precolonial organizations have better levels of contemporary development today by refining our understanding of why the precolonial past continues to shape the present. To do so, I have limited the historical treatment under study to look at Senegal's microstate system in the centuries before French colonization. But is the argument specific to the legacies of precolonial states in Senegal alone? Though scholarship has shown that exposure to precolonial statehood generated continent-wide effects, I focus on the West African state system[2], which stretched east to the edges of the Sokoto Caliphate in Nigeria, and south to the coastal states that were most directly touched by the Atlantic trade.[3] The majority of West African countries were home to a multitude of smaller precolonial polities. As a result, like Senegal, these cases offer unique subnational leverage on the independent variable. At the same time, though more variations on state form are found once we look beyond Senegal, key commonalities defined West Africa's precolonial polities as lineage structures remained the basic sociopolitical institutions, for example, and leaders faced a common dilemma of how to rule dispersed populations.[4]

---

[2] West Africa is defined here as Benin, Burkina Faso, Cote d'Ivoire, The Gambia, Ghana, Guinea, Guinea-Bissau, Liberia, Mali, Niger, Nigeria, Sierra Leone, and Togo.
[3] For example, Gennaioli and Rainer (2007).   [4] Colson (1969, 37, 53).

Decentralization in West Africa

The last three decades have seen a wave of decentralization reforms sweep the African continent, often concurrent with broader processes of political liberalization. Some West African countries, like Ghana or Nigeria, have joined Senegal in expanding earlier decentralization efforts, while others, such as Sierra Leone or Burkina Faso, decentralized more recently in the 2000s. Table 8.1 offers a brief comparison of decentralization reforms in the West African states for which I have data, specifically among those surveyed in Round 6 of the Afrobarometer. These reforms varied in timing and form. Francophone countries have largely followed a similar model that hews closely to France's own administrative structure: decentralization created urban and rural communes nested with either elected regions (e.g. Mali) or within deconcentrated departments (e.g. Cote d'Ivoire, Senegal).[5] In contrast, Anglophone countries display more variation, from fully democratically elected local governments in Sierra Leone to Nigeria's Local Government Authorities (LGAs), where elections are held at the discretion of the state governor. As a result, only a quarter of Nigeria's LGAs are run by an elected council with the rest administered by a caretaker committee.[6]

Table 8.1 also reveals wide diversity in the depth of reform, as many governments have announced decentralization schemes but stopped short of full implementation. Burkina Faso established decentralized administrative principles in its 1991 constitution, but did not hold founding elections until 2006.[7] Likewise, while decentralization was first discussed in Benin's National Conference in 1989, the law took ten years to complete and local elections were only held in 2002.[8] Still elsewhere, decentralization reforms are only now being enacted (and weakly so at that) after years of discussion. Togo has long debated and passed decentralization laws, for example, but has yet to meaningfully transfer authority to the local level and only held its first local elections in June 2019.[9] Similarly, Guinea's local government code, decreed in 2006, has yet to be published. Liberia included decentralization reforms in its postwar reconstruction plan but has proceeded slowly since the return to civilian rule. For example, the County Development Fund was introduced in 2006, transferring funds to the lowest administrative unit of the county, but a draft Local Government Act was only circulated in 2013. Due to the 2014–2015 Ebola Crisis, the process was delayed, with the final decentralization laws signed in September of 2018.

In most cases, urban communes have benefited more meaningfully from these reforms than their rural counterparts. Perhaps unsurprisingly, the latter have also seen substantial interference with their borders. In Cote d'Ivoire,

---

[5] Brosio (2000). Cote d'Ivoire initially adopted a model of deconcentration (see Blundo 1998a).
[6] As of 2017 (Ojebode et al. 2017). [7] Mathieu and Yilmaz (2010, 331).
[8] Mongbo (2008, 50). [9] World Bank (June 2019).

TABLE 8.1 *Decentralization in West African countries surveyed in Afrobarometer Round 6*

Country	Decentralized?	Year	Lowest elected unit	# Lowest rural units	Local election years	Social services effectively transferred
Benin	Yes	1998	Communes	77	2002, 2008, 2015	Primary Education, Basic Health, Marketplace Management, Transport
Burkina Faso	Yes	2006/2009	Communes	351	2006, 2012	Primary Education, Basic Health, Water and Sanitation
Cote d'Ivoire[a]	Yes	1985/2011	Communes	201	2013, 2018	Primary Education, Basic Health Care, Local Roads, Urban Services
Ghana[b]	Yes	1993	Metropolitan/Municipal/District Assemblies	254	1994, 1998, 2002, 2006, 2010, 2015	Primary Education, Basic Health, Water and Sanitation, Local Road Maintenance
Guinea	Yes	1986, 2006	Rural Development Communities	303	2005, 2017	Primary Education, Basic Health, Local Roads, Urban Services
Liberia[c]	Proposed	2018	Counties	15		
Mali	Yes	1996	Communes	701	2004, 2009, 2016	Primary Education, Basic Health, Urban Services
Niger	Yes	1991, 2002	Communes	265	2004, 2011	Primary Education, Basic Health, Sanitation
Nigeria	Yes – Federal System	1976	Local Government Authorities	774	Various[d]	Primary and Vocational Education, Health Services, Social Welfare, Sewage

(continued)

TABLE 8.1 (continued)

Country	Decentralized?	Year	Lowest elected unit	# Lowest rural units	Local election years	Social services effectively transferred
Senegal	Yes	1996	Urban and Rural Communes	385	1996, 2000, 2002, 2009, 2014	Primary Education, Basic Health, Urban Services
Sierra Leone	Yes	2004	Local Councils	19	2004, 2008, 2012, 2018	Primary and Jr. Secondary Education, Basic Health, Sanitation, Feeder Road Maintenance
Togo[e]	Yes	2019	Communes	117	2019	Not yet transferred

[a] Cote d'Ivoire began its decentralization reforms in the 1980s, devolving authority over the construction of primary education facilities, local market and bus station maintenance, etc. in 1985, but economic crises in the early 1990s led the state to retrench from local communes (Crook 1998, 143).
[b] Ghana's District Assemblies are headed by the District Chief Executive, who is appointed by the President. The District Assembly is 70 percent elected by adult suffrage in nonpartisan elections, with the remaining 30 percent appointed.
[c] Liberian President Ellen Johnson-Sirleaf launched a National Policy on Decentralization in 2012, but the legal framework for decentralization, the Local Government Act, was not signed until September 2018.
[d] LGA elections are held at the discretion of the state governor, with the majority of LGAs run under a "caretaker committee" appointed by the Governor.
[e] Togo originally enacted decentralization laws in 1998, but these remained unimplemented. Urban and Rural communes held elections in 1987, but all subnational units have been administered by the central-state-appointed officials in the interim (Breuer 2017).

former President Gbagbo attempted to increase the number of communes nearly fivefold, though the process was aborted in 2012; today the country has 197 municipalities.[10] Similarly, Ghana decentralized with 110 District Assemblies in 1993, but the number of districts more than doubled to 254 by 2019.[11] An inverse version of these dynamics is found in Mali, where the decision to involve local populations in commune creation following the establishment of a decentralized territorial administration in its 1992 constitution led to a proliferating set of demands for increasingly small administrative units as the government sought to find compromises between bottom-up preferences and top-down needs for administrative efficiency. In the end, the country created 701 communes, nearly double the original goal.[12] At the other extreme, however, Niger simply decentralized by granting more power to preexisting cantons, themselves inherited from the colonial era.[13]

Local governments across the region have been charged with a broadly similar set of responsibilities, though in all cases, state transfers are insufficient and local tax collection weak. Unlike in Senegal, responsibility over basic service provision was promised from the start for most countries in the region, even if they were only bestowed gradually. Mali's local governments obtained minimal authority over primary education, basic health, sporting and cultural events, and a handful of other policy areas in 1996, but these were not transferred until 2002.[14] Similarly, local governments in Burkina Faso are officially tasked with eleven policy areas but at the end of the initial three-year timeline set forth by the state, only four of these had been devolved.[15] In many cases, authority is decentralized but remains effectively concurrent; state and local governments alike are active in basic health and primary education in countries like Nigeria. Note, moreover, that in some cases this authority is circumscribed: Burkina Faso and Guinea remain under the *tutelle* of the central state, meaning that all decisions must be approved by higher-level officials.

We can draw two tentative conclusions about decentralization in West Africa. First, decentralization remains an incomplete reform, at times blending responsibility in unclear ways. Nevertheless, even though local governments have yet to be granted the full authority promised to them by the center, in all cases they have begun exercising local authority in some domains. Second, most countries have held at least two rounds of local elections. Even if these reforms may be "incomplete" in the eyes of proponents, the combination of these two factors has been sufficient to create new arenas of political competition that are tied to questions of local solidarities, historical settlement patterns, and local distributional politics as I document in the section "Evidence of Institutional Congruence Following Decentralization."

---

[10] Bouquet and Kassi-Djodjo (2014). [11] See Ayee (2012). [12] Idelman (2009).
[13] Hagberg (2010, 9). [14] Wing and Kassibo (2014, 120).
[15] Mathieu and Yilmaz (2010, 340).

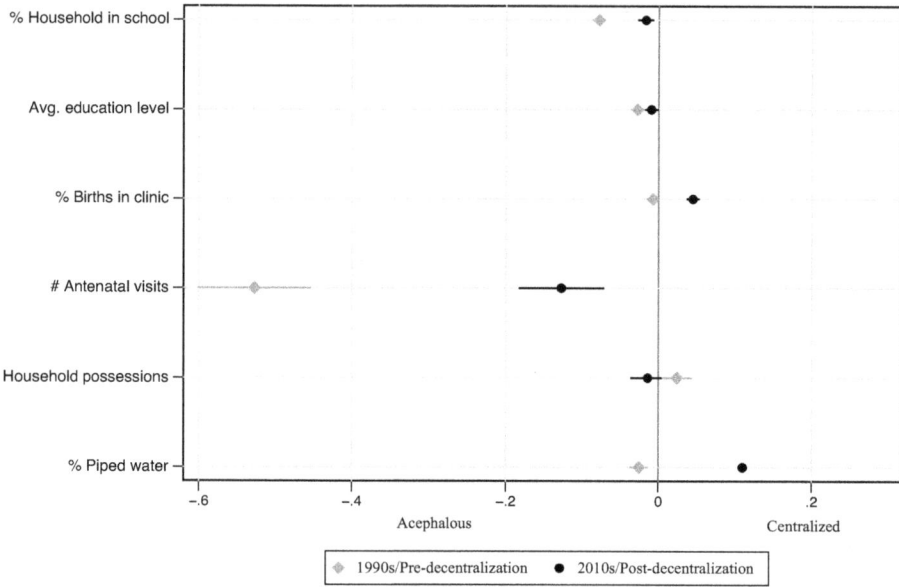

FIGURE 8.1 Difference of means – DHS data

Evidence from the DHS

If broad trends in decentralization are similar, as shown in Figure 8.1, then the fact that West Africa was home to a series of interconnected microstate systems means that the properties for institutional congruence should be available throughout the region. I begin by examining whether or not there are systematic differences in local gains in public goods access between areas that were home to precolonial states and those that were not. Put otherwise, is there evidence that precolonial statehood impacts the contemporary politics of redistribution similarly across West Africa?

To do so, I test changes in social service access with data from the DHS. The DHS surveys are collected around the world, surveying a nationally representative sample about household demographics, health, and nutrition. I compare reported access to locally delivered social services in the early 1990s – before democratic decentralization was enacted – with data collected post-decentralization, between 2010 and 2012. Because some countries in the sample have only made tentative steps toward decentralization by the early 2010s, notably Togo and Liberia, I drop them from the analysis.[16] As has been noted by others, DHS data may best be thought of as estimating the flow of goods through individuals, rather than the actual physical location of services

---

[16] The Gambia and Guinea-Bissau are also not included because they have not decentralized.

Legacies of Precolonial Statehood across West Africa 225

themselves.[17] I limit the sample to rural respondents, where the assumption that individuals are most likely to obtain access to such flows, like education, at facilities that are in close proximity, is most plausible.

In order to estimate the impact of precolonial statehood on reported access to basic social services in the DHS, I have to match sampled households to the location of precolonial states. I follow a similar procedure as that described in Chapter 5 to expand my coding of precolonial statehood for the precolonial polities listed in Table 8.2, all of which meet my criteria for statehood. DHS respondents are coded as falling within the territory of a precolonial state if their geolocation is within a 20-kilometer buffer of the capital of these states.

To avoid imposing assumptions on the form of the data as well as "bad" or post-treatment controls, I present the results of a series of simple difference of means tests in Figure 8.1.[18] Since most local governments in West Africa are charged with building and maintaining primary education and basic health facilities, I examine measures for both. For education, I look at what percent of children under the age of ten in each surveyed household was enrolled in school at the time of the interview. I also examine the average levels of education of household members. Similar to the strategy adopted in Chapter 7, I limit the sample to household members under ten years of age to ensure that I am only measuring those who could plausibly have benefited from new infrastructure built following decentralization reforms. Data from the early 1990s are truncated similarly for comparison. To measure improvements in healthcare access, I calculate the percent of all children born to surveyed women in the past five years that were delivered in a public health clinic as well as each woman's reported number of antenatal visits for her most recent birth. As with education, these data are limited to births that would have occurred post-decentralization.[19]

Figure 8.1 presents the results of difference of means tests for these variables. For all four outcomes, the data suggest that there have been disproportionate improvements in areas that were home to precolonial states.[20] Prior to decentralization, households in historically centralized areas had a lower percent of

---

[17] For example, Kudamatsu (2007) and Kramon and Posner (2013).
[18] Angrist and Pischke (2010).
[19] Of course, the data presented in Figure 8.1 rest on the assumption that women prefer to give birth in a clinic and to have antenatal visits and that they will do so if possible. In other words, I assume that there has not been a norm shift in historically centralized areas thus that women are increasingly seeking maternal health care or that families are now more amenable to primary education.
[20] The results do not appear to be driven by population density, measured at the regional level. Splitting out areas with low population density (measured as those in the bottom 25 percentile of regional population density) or high population (eliminating the top 25 percent densest areas) produces consistent results with one exception. The number of antenatal visits loses significance once high-density areas are dropped. In the DHS data, this would include respondents in any region with more than 189 residents per square kilometer.

TABLE 8.2 West Africa's precolonial states in the nineteenth century

Benin	Dahomey	**Ghana**	Akuapem	**Niger**	Adar	**Senegal**	Baol
	Borgu		Akwamu		Agadez		Boundou
	Yoruba States		Akyem		Arewa		Cayor
	Nikki		Ashanti		Damagaram		Djoloff
	Porto Novo		Dagomba		Dosso		Gajaaga
Burkina Faso	Mossi States		Gonja		Gobir		Fouladou
	Liptako	**Guinea**	Fouta Djallon		Tessaoua		Fouta Toro
	Yagha		Samory	**Nigeria**	Benin		Kaabu
Cote d'Ivoire	Abron-Gyaman	**Mali**	Kaarta		Calabar		Saloum
	Bouna		Kenedoguou		Kanem-Bornu		Sine
	Morounou		Khasso		Sokoto Emirates	**Togo**	Kotokoli
	Sanwi		Macina		Yoruba States		Chokossi
			Segou	**Sierra Leone**	Sherbro		
			Segou-Toucouluer				

household members enrolled in school than historically acephalous areas, but this relationship flips completely by the early 2010s. Likewise, these areas have nearly closed the gap in the average education level of household members fewer than ten. Nearly identical trends are found in maternal health: women in historically acephalous zones were more likely to deliver in a clinic in the 1990s, but the bias has flipped by the early 2010s. And while women in historically acephalous zones do have more antenatal visits, this gap has narrowed considerably since decentralization.[21] These results mirror the trends reported in the DHS data for Senegal in Chapter 7.

Finally, I examine whether or not this could be driven by a wealth effect; areas home to precolonial states have been argued to have accumulated higher levels of private wealth, as has been argued by Bandyopadhyay and Green (2016), which would suggest that the effect of precolonial statehood does not run via the local state, but more simply because families in these areas accumulated more wealth early on. There is no statistically significant difference in the DHS's household possessions index in either time period. We do see an improvement in access to piped water, however. Households surveyed in areas that were home to precolonial states were statistically less likely to have clean water prior to decentralization, but more likely to have access afterward. Because water is not decentralized everywhere in the region, note that the results for these estimates come from a reduced sample of countries that have devolved water and/or sanitation. The DHS results parallel neatly those presented in earlier chapters for Senegal: private wealth does not seem to positively correlate with precolonial statehood, but access to public goods that are delivered by local governments in the majority of decentralized West African countries does appear to be higher – and improving at different rates – in areas that were home to precolonial states.

Figure 8.1 provides support for my claim that the empirical pattern I document in Senegal has broader empirical traction in the region. But these figures risk conflating the diversity of experiences that West African states have had with decentralization reforms discussed above. A key property of my theory is that institutional congruence embeds decision-making within local social relations, meaning that local governments that see substantial top-down interference may not see congruence despite ostensible decentralization. For example, the fact that many – though not all – of Nigeria's LGAs are run by caretaker committee may suggest that other redistributive logics prevail because decision-making is removed from the social institutions that I claim alter local elite behavior.

To address this possibility, I replicate the results presented in Figure 8.2 but distinguish between local governments that enjoy full legal autonomy and those

---

[21] These effects are weaker in households where the average-level of adult education is a secondary level or higher. Results do not change for female-headed households.

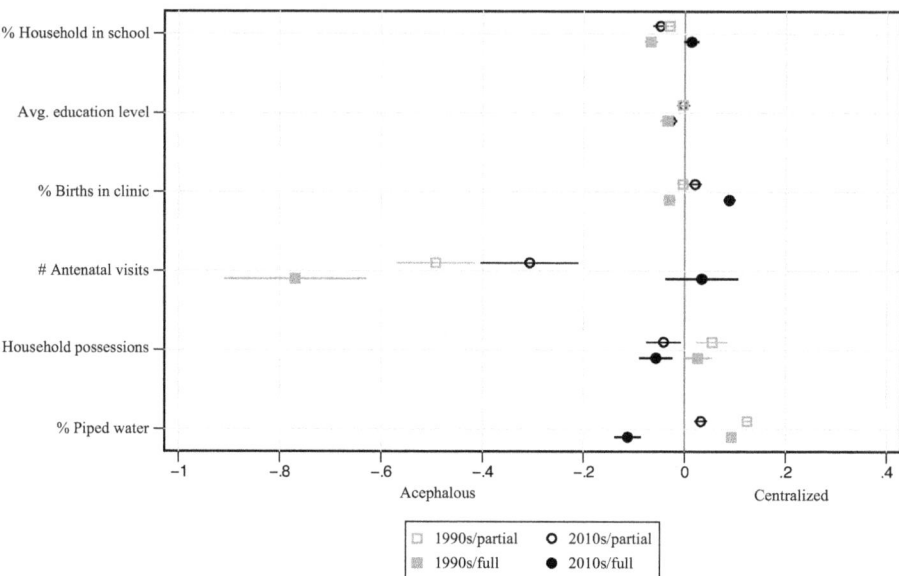

FIGURE 8.2 Difference of means – DHS data, accounting for variation in level of decentralization

that see substantial top-down interference. The latter includes Burkina Faso and Guinea, which remain under the *tutelle* of the central state, as well as Ghana, where the District Chief Executive (akin to a mayor) is appointed by the President. I code Nigeria's LGAs as being subject to top-down influence when less than 50 percent of a state's LGAs were ruled by elected local councils for the majority of time between 2008 and 2013, the date of the last DHS round in my sample, as coded by Kyburz (2018).

Figure 8.2 displays the average change in the same metrics between historically centralized and acephalous sample clusters, breaking down the difference between decentralized units that have substantial (or "full") local authority over local redistribution and those with "partial" authority that sees central state interference. In general, historically centralized areas appear to perform better than historically acephalous zones regardless of the degree of local autonomy. Nonetheless, recent development gains are greater for respondents who have seen more significant decentralization of authority to the local level than those that have seen decentralization with considerable central state oversight. This indicates a strong role for local governance as a driver of local development when there is significant spatial overlap with longer-run histories of cooperation.

Evidence from Attitudinal Data

Next, I turn to geocoded public opinion data from the Afrobarometer public opinion surveys to examine whether rural citizens evaluate their local

Legacies of Precolonial Statehood across West Africa 229

governments differently in areas that were home to precolonial states. Using data from Round 6, which covers all eight countries of French West Africa, absent Mauritania, and key Anglophone states in the region, including Ghana, Liberia, Nigeria, and Sierra Leone, I match respondents' villages to the expanded coding of precolonial states introduced in the previous section.

Employing Afrobarometer data allows me to assess the general plausibility that something about governance in areas that were home to precolonial states differs from historically stateless zones. Although the data are necessarily imprecise as to the mechanisms I derive from the Senegalese case, Round 6 offers a number of questions that offer indirect assessments of the theory's broad contours. These fall into two broad categories. First, the Afrobarometer asks respondents a suite of questions about how they evaluate their local government's work and, second, the survey asks a number of questions that I use to estimate respondents' general sense of political satisfaction.

The first five estimates presented in Panel A of Figure 8.3 suggest that by and large respondents who fall in areas that were home to precolonial states are more positive about their local government. Specifically, respondents in historically centralized areas are more likely to think that their local councilor listens to them, to trust their local elected officials, to positively evaluate their council's work, and to report that it is easy to obtain an identity card, a service frequently (though not exclusively) performed by local governments. There is no difference, however, in the reported likelihood of having contacted one's local elected official in the past year.

In an effort to distinguish between what is driven by a local versus a national effect, I also look for differences in how respondents evaluate the President's performance. As reported in Panel A, there is no difference in evaluations of the President between historically centralized and historically stateless zones, suggesting – though of course not establishing definitively – that respondents are not conflating their satisfaction with local and central state officials. General political satisfaction is proxied with the last two estimates in Panel A. Respondents in areas that were home to precolonial states report being more satisfied with democracy and are less likely to believe that political parties create conflict. Results are consistent when subset by gender and education, and whether or not one is an ethnic minority within their survey cluster. The findings fall broadly in line with the expectations derived from my qualitative data from rural Senegal.

Because Afrobarometer enumerators ask questions about household wealth while also making their own observations about the quality of a respondent's dwelling, I am again able to test for differences in local development. Specifically, I look at whether there is a difference in access to locally supplied public goods or those provided by the central state and, finally, I test the robustness of the wealth findings from the DHS data reported in Figure 8.1. I measure locally supplied public goods by looking at reported access to water and sanitation (latrines). Because water and sanitation are only devolved

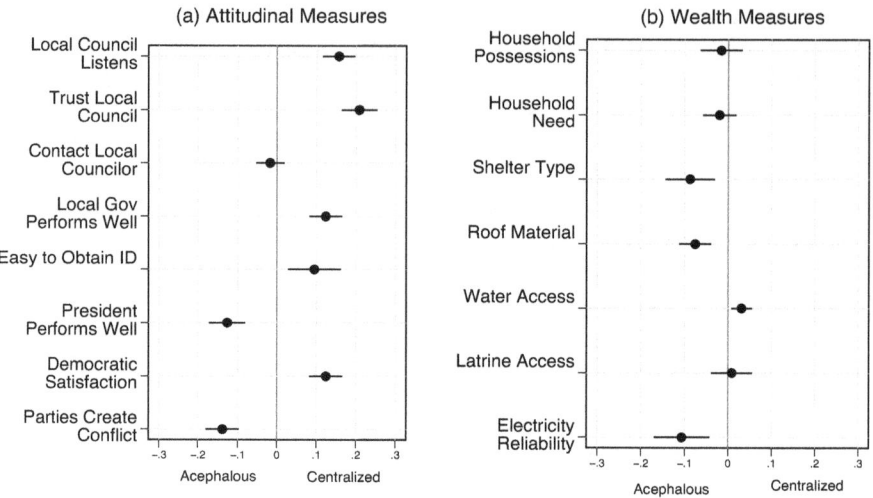

FIGURE 8.3 Difference in means – Afrobarometer data: (a) attitudinal measures and (b) wealth measures

competences in some countries in my sample, I only estimate this for countries that have officially transferred responsibility over water and/or sanitation to the local state (as reported in Table 8.1). I measure central-state-provided goods by whether or not a respondent has reliable access to electricity (if at all). Lastly, I estimate the effect of precolonial centralization on household wealth through a standard wealth index of household possessions, an index of household need, the type of residence a respondent lives in (ranging from temporary structure to a permanent house), and the material of their residence's roof (ranging from thatch or grass to a permanent roof).[22]

These results, seen in Panel B, give no evidence of a private wealth effect, in line with the DHS data. If anything, households in areas that were home to precolonial states seem to fare worse. While there is no difference in household possessions or conversely household needs, West African respondents in historically centralized zones have poorer roof materials and live in less permanent or more traditional residential structures. Historically centralized areas do not seem to benefit more from goods delivered by the central state. In fact, these areas are *less* likely to have reliable electricity access than historically stateless areas, mirroring the results of the placebo tests presented in Chapter 5. Still, Panel B does indicate that West African respondents residing in areas that were home to a precolonial state have better access to clean water in countries where

---

[22] Specifically, wealth is measured as whether a household owns a mobile phone, a car, a television, or a radio. Need is measured by whether the household reports lacking adequate food, water, medicine, household cooking fuel, or cash in the last twelve months.

local governments are charged with their delivery, though there is no effect of broader sanitation efforts, as seen in the null effect for latrine access.

Of course, these findings are only suggestive. The positive bias toward the local state in historically centralized areas could simply reflect more deference to elites rather than actual performance. Nonetheless, Figure 8.3 supports my core contention that there is something systematically different about areas home to precolonial states in the region and that the positive effects of precolonial statehood appear to be limited to locally provided public goods.[23]

Evidence of Institutional Congruence Following Decentralization

Statistical analysis of data from the DHS and Afrobarometer suggests that broadly similar outcomes are emerging in decentralized West Africa, as individuals in historically centralized areas reporting greater satisfaction with the local state and seeing better on average improvements in local development outcomes. This finds traction in case studies of community-specific experiences with decentralization in the countries under study. Reviewing these case studies provides support for three broad elements of my theory: decentralization reforms have elided with local social status hierarchies, this has generated new political arenas for local cooperation (or conflict) akin to a two-level game, and, finally, that local governance has been imbued with social institutions that shape how elites approach the local state.

I begin with the most studied of these questions. The advent of decentralization across West Africa produced a "resurgence of tradition," as the establishment of new arenas of power produced novel avenues to local authority and local resources.[24] The creation of local governments – even when fiscal and distributional capacities have been slow to arrive – has paradoxically both reconfigured and reinforced local legitimacies. This is particularly true for traditional authorities who have (re)emerged as powerful figures in local politics in an institutional "layering" of power.[25] Many chiefs, for example, have seen decentralization as an opportunity to reassert their authority.[26]

---

[23] As with the DHS data, the results do not appear to be driven by population density. Splitting out areas with low population density (measured as those in the bottom 25 percentile of regional population density) or high population (eliminating the top 25 percent densest areas) produces consistent results with a few exceptions. Without low-density areas, there is no significant difference in eases of obtaining an identity card or in household possessions. Without high-density areas, historically centralized areas appear to be less likely to contact their local councilor, to have higher household needs, and to have worse latrine access.

[24] Erk (2014).   [25] To paraphrase Bierschenk and Olivier de Sardan (2003).

[26] Englebert and Sangaré (2014). This is particularly interesting given the varied fate of precolonial chieftaincies in the subregion. Niger's first President, Diori Hamani, formed a close alliance with canton chiefs, meaning that the chieftaincy has largely persisted by adapting to new regimes over time, but in sharp contrast, the chieftaincy was abolished in Guinea, as well as in Burkina Faso

In the short term, this raised alarm among proponents of decentralization, who viewed the implication of traditional authorities as evidence of elite capture. Over time, however, this has become less clear. While local notables typically won in the first round of elections, for example, subsequent local elections have seen more competition as local populations came to appreciate the role that the local state would play in their lives. Yet even as candidates who are seen as dynamic and resourceful have made gains, this has not eliminated the role of local social status and being a non-notable or in-migrant remains a potent means to discredit another's candidacy.[27] As a consequence, longer-term understandings of local moral communities and not ideological or even partisan dynamics animate local governance in the region as local political dynamics and even vote choice are informed by local social alliances and conflicts. In this way, "discourses of locality, of autochthony, of state authority, of religious belonging, of frontier ..." bring local elites and their social networks into the realm of decentralized governance.[28]

Even as interest in the local state has grown and diversified, therefore, customary holders of local social status remain prominent in the local state. Echoing my findings from Senegal, case study evidence documents a tendency of local politicians to claim their right to local social status – including seats in the local council – as a function of their descent from village founders, reflecting the deeply held view that preexisting sociopolitical hierarchies have a particular claim to these new political fora following a logic that "a good leader should be a home grown person."[29] Within Niger's local governments, politics remains closely tied to local solidarities; "The canton chief is first and foremost the representative of a lineage ... The president of the cereal bank management committee is first and foremost a man of the neighborhood ..." Olivier de Sardan (2009, 45) writes. Candidates draw on broad social networks for political support as they enter the arena of the local state, with lineage structures and historical ties between families serving as important a role as partisanship.[30] This involved not only family ties, but also friendship and allied villages, suggesting similar dynamics to those I observe in Senegal: shared histories of settlement and cohabitation shape the networks that local elites rely on in local governance.

By generating a new focal point of authority, decentralization has raised thorny questions about who should govern at the local level both within and across villages as local administrative units across the region pool numerous

---

under Sankara. Despite the fact that state reinforcement of traditional authorities has varied across space and time, therefore, decentralization seems to have nonetheless offered a venue for old and new forms of social status alike to lay claim to these new political spaces.

[27] Hagberg (2019, 14).
[28] Le Meur (2006, 891) writing on Benin; see also Bierschenk and Olivier de Sardan (2003).
[29] Iwata (2011, 105) and Hetland (2008, 31). [30] Koné and Hagberg (2019).

Legacies of Precolonial Statehood across West Africa 233

villages together into new jurisdictions.[31] To this end, local histories of settlement have created either disparate or compatible claims to the right to govern following decentralization, reflecting how "discourses of the local" remain a core dynamic within West African political culture.[32] Existing work has most often studied this in the framework of autochthony claims. Béridogo (1998) and Hahonou (2002) observe how autochthony and party politics interact to generate divisive local politics in historically acephalous areas of Mali and Niger in a way that echoes the dynamics I illustrate in Chapter 4.

Evidence from Mali's experiences with decentralization, perhaps the most studied case in the region, shows how these discourses interact with cross-village dilemmas raised the creation of rural communes.[33] Mali's process of commune creation was slowed down considerably as villages refused membership in prospective local governments because the commune's capital was proposed in the villages of non-autochthons, because they would be numerically dominated by non-co-ethnics or those who were casted or because the boundaries grouped villages with contentious historical relations, to name but a few of the most commonly cited examples.[34] In southern Mali "the new territorial collectivities concentrate a diversity of village and inter-village interests," rendering the commune an "'arena' of inter-village dynamics, ... subject to local social rules that can be identified and which must be taken into account."[35]

Here a second key component of my theory finds a parallel: decentralization generates a dynamic akin to a two-level game. Across West Africa, decentralization simultaneously offered new venues for village-based elites to expand their authority while also challenging the ability of any village hierarchy to capture the local state, shifting the focus of local political contestation to control of the commune itself.[36] Importantly, also embedded within the Malian case is a story of inherited cross-village solidarities that can generate institutional congruence. During the country's consultative process of commune creation, "social solidarity between villages soon became the driving force behind the new communes."[37] Local Bamana elite in Mali's Tinkolé commune, which falls in the territory of the precolonial state of Segou, stressed the past as an organizing principle of local social organization, for example, with "its non-respect constituting a deviation quite detrimental to all life of society."[38]

Though not himself focused on the legacies of precolonial kingdoms, we find the clearest evidence of the role of precolonial identities in Fay's (2000, 126–127) study of Mali's Tenenkou Circle, which lies in the former territory

---

[31] Touré (2012). [32] Hagberg (2010, 3).
[33] Indeed, some Malian elites promoted decentralization by invoking the purportedly decentralized nature of the precolonial Malian Empire (Mongbo 1998).
[34] Koné 1997b and Kassibo (2006, 80–81). [35] Coll (1997, 17).
[36] As observed by Englebert and Sangaré (2014, 62) in Burkina Faso.
[37] Wing and Kassibo (2014, 117–118). [38] Koné (1997a, 6).

of the precolonial kingdom of Macina. Fay documents how local communities recreated precolonial-era *janyeeli*, or provinces, when choosing the boundaries of their new communes, citing one local elite: "we are the same ... we have the same navel ... the same breasts ... we marry each other ..." At once, the quote invokes the two animating mechanisms behind my theory: a highly localized identity, or category, rooted in the past combined with dense social ties, or network, creates a sense of community solidarity and purpose. This language mirrors that heard in rural Senegal. The local development plan for Senegalese local government of Orkadiere, for example, describes the local government's many villages as sharing "an umbilical cord" with the chef-lieu, making the local government capital "a place of meetings, convergence, and services whose legitimacy is tied to history."[39]

Across the West African Sahel therefore, decentralization has generated a "traditional resurgence" as elites, who lay their claim to social status in the past, have come to embrace new roles following democratic decentralization. These dynamics take place across villages as much as within them, with the presence or absence of cross-village social networks shaping local solidarities. This raises the potential for conflict induced by the two-level game dynamics inherent in decentralization, but social institutions – when present across villages – tie elites together into shared expectations about social comportment in the public sphere. Though the form and content of social institutions likely vary from that seen in Senegal, other authors note the presence of powerful social norms tied to local identities and social networks. Olivier de Sardan (2009), for example, emphasizes norms of consensus and conflict avoidance as dominant social institutions in rural Niger, and scholarship from across the Sahel belt highlights how locally understood norms of behavior shape local governance under decentralization.[40] In Mali's Kiban Commune, which fell in the territory of the precolonial state of Segou and the subsequent Umarian state afterward, Koné and Hagberg (2019, 56) document how conflict in the commune was "silent," as the four dominant lineages in the commune moved to protect local social relations in the face of threats. In Burkina Faso's Dori Region, home to hierarchical chieftaincies in the precolonial era, understandings of poverty and mutual aid are "based in a strong moral notion of a glorious past of communal solidarity."[41] Because the citizens of Dori expect politicians to follow community values of solidarity, religious adherence, and respect for the collective good, politicians favor traditional values over pure political calculations in local governance.[42]

Though these case studies – almost all conducted by anthropologists in specific villages or local governments – lose a subnational comparative frame, we see key elements of my theory throughout. Local governments interact with

---

[39] Rural Community of Orkadiere (2006, 28).   [40] See also Coll (1997).
[41] Hagberg (2001, 53–55).   [42] Barry and Hagberg (2019, 29–30).

place and lineage-based social hierarchies and they pool villages that must negotiate over new resources delivered by a new jurisdictional body. These negotiations can be contentious, but they can also be cooperative. When case study evidence suggests the latter, scholars tend to report the key moving parts of my theory: these communities tend to have local elites with network ties across villages or lineages that support shared understandings of community solidarity and consensus.

ASSESSING THE MECHANISMS BEYOND AFRICA

The central argument of this book is that Senegal's precolonial states have left enduring legacies at the grassroots that are repurposed and redeployed by local communities under democratic decentralization. In the previous section, I demonstrated that there appears to be broad empirical traction for these dynamics across decentralized West Africa. But the question remains whether the argument offers insight for Comparative Politics more broadly. In this section, I discuss how the two jointly reinforcing mechanisms animating my theory – shared social identities and dense social networks – offer analytic leverage around the world. In this way, I show how the book's core theoretical claim, that distributional politics are shaped by the spatial overlap between the formal bounds of decision-making and localized social dynamics, can extend to a broader set of contexts, even if we relax the nature of the antecedent cause.

I support this proposition by focusing on three recent literatures that have accumulated evidence of processes that parallel those described in the preceding chapters. Collectively, they echo the assertion of Wibbels (2019, 15–16) that scholars keep an eye to "local social orders," or the social, economic, and political networks that animate any given community.

Evidence from Native American Reservations

Pioneered most clearly in a series of papers by Cornell and Kalt (1995, 2000), the first example comes from Native American reservations in the United States, where the authors find better economic development today when resident tribes have a history of shared governance. Cornell and Kalt refer to this as the existence of an "extra-constitutional agreement." Where reservations see a "match" between the constitutional rules of resident tribes and their pre-reservation systems of government, tribal governments perform better because this "match" generates agreement on how power should be legitimately exercised.[43] Cornell and Kalt articulate mechanisms not far from my own: institutions that are perceived as legitimate trigger "the private rewards and penalties of the 'social sentiments,' with the social networks that individuals are

---

[43] Cornell and Kalt (1995, 404–405).

embedded within inhibiting free-riding and defection vis-a-vis those institutions."[44] Cultural norms, they conclude, serve as "glue" between formal and informal institutions.[45]

Dippel (2014) makes a similar argument. He finds that even where residents are otherwise homogenous, reservations that pool different bands see worse economic outcomes today compared to those with a history of cohabitation. Two things in Dippel's argument make for an important parallel. First, the effect is strongest for outcomes pertaining to local governance; forced coexistence, he documents, increases internal conflict and corruption. Second, Dippel documents that this difference was minimal until the late 1980s when tribal governments gained more authority. Much like Senegal's decentralization reforms, the effect of cross-band cohabitation (or not) appears most strongly once decision-making arrives at the local level. Thus, Dippel concludes "historically determined differences in social organization can persist relatively unnoticed for long periods, before they have large and relatively sudden effects on economic outcomes when they interact with big shocks."[46]

This book effectively inverts Dippel's explanation. Where he suggests that social cleavages persist over the long run, "even when they are not tied to easily observable characteristics like ethnicity," I argue that historical sources of social cohesion can persist with equal force.[47] Evidence from Native American reservations therefore indicates that the creation of new administrative boundaries from on high paired with a later devolution of authority can generate striking divergences, even though, like Senegal, these communities were subject to brutal colonization by an external force. In both, the effect is driven by specifically local political dynamics that result from the spatial overlap between social institutions and the bounds of decision-making.

Evidence from China's Local Governments

The evidence presented in this book further resembles that presented by Tsai (2007) on local government officials in China. Tsai argues that local government officials invest more in public services when they are held accountable through informal solidary institutions that both embed officials within the village community and encompass the village as a whole. The presence of such informal institutions, namely lineage associations and temples, generates varying degrees of spatial overlap between solidary institutions and the village as an administrative unit. When this overlap is high, solidary institutions are able to hold officials accountable, even under authoritarianism, by virtue of their dense social networks and promotion of cooperative behavior. In Tsai's (2007, 253) own words, "when group boundaries overlap with the

---

[44] Cornell and Kalt (2000, 451).   [45] Cornell and Kalt (2000, 453).   [46] Dippel (2014, 2135).
[47] Dippel (2014, 2131).

administrative boundaries of local government and the group embeds local officials in its activities and institutions ... officials are more likely to carry out their duties and perform well."

Tsai's argument has been followed by a number of similar studies of village governance in rural China.[48] Most prominently, Xu and Yao (2015) find that villages home to larger clans, which often have deep historical roots in a village, have on average higher public goods expenditure. This suggests that clans themselves generate feelings of obligation to the lineage and Xu and Yao explicitly identify identity and network mechanisms. The fact that individuals so strongly identify with their clans facilitates the enforcement of local norms. By downplaying the relative role of elected officials, Xu and Yao suggest that villages that overlap with what amounts to local social institutions – proxied in their study by clan size – perform better. Tsai herself observes that the general logic has older precedents: Skinner (1965) wrote more than fifty years ago that communes created during the Mao era were hampered because they explicitly did not correspond to preexisting social networks, or, in other words, because they were intentionally *incongruent*.

A central insight from work on China is that social dynamics influence local development outcomes even under autocracy. Two implications follow for my purposes: first, it suggests that the dynamics I outline can emerge in nondemocratic settings. Second, it reveals that institutional congruence can apply downward to the village level when this is the relevant administrative unit. While my argument stipulates a role for cross-village networks, central for Tsai and others is the encompassing property of local informal institutions relative to the scale of the community in question. This likewise serves to circulate information about reputations, enabling social sanctioning and leading actors to internalize the value of group behavioral expectations.

Evidence from India

Lastly, more diffuse evidence from India indicates that variation in welfare investments is similarly shaped by different degrees of subnational territorial attachment. Singh (2015a, 2015b) compares the performance of Indian states and documents how states that have strong subnational identities outperform those that lack such shared identities. Much like local attachment to identities rooted in the precolonial past in rural Senegal, when Indian elites and citizens share a sense of subnational identity, they perceive themselves as having shared obligations to promote the "common good." Critically, this can cross other markers of diversity.[49] Ultimately, Singh (2015a, 5) draws a similar conclusion: states are more likely to invest in citizen welfare when there is "a match

---

[48] See He et al. (2017); Martinez-Bravo et al. (2017); and Zhu and Cai (2016).
[49] Singh (2015b, 510).

between the political-administrative unit that has jurisdiction over social policy and the locus of collective identification."

At a lower administrative level, Anath Pur (2007, 416) finds that informal local governance institutions within villages that maintain social norms and preserve local custom can play a positive, synergistic role within India's local governments or *gram panchayat*, precisely because these informal local associations "nest neatly," almost never crossing *gram panchayat* boundaries. This "vertical dovetailing" between formal and informal institutions, she concludes, is what makes their relationship productive for local citizens. As with the China case, this shapes how informal local government institutions have persisted within villages as Indian villages have long histories and have largely remained unchanged as territorial units.[50]

Unlike my own argument or that of Anath Pur, Singh's argument differs in the origins of such collective identification. I document deeply rooted, historical identities in Senegal, but Singh chronicles how politicians in some Indian states actively nurtured the development of subnational identities for political ends, eventually finding themselves constrained by these very subnationalisms, obligating them to meet citizens' demands for further welfare investments. This suggests – in stark contrast to my own empirical evidence or that emerging from rural China or Native American Reservations – that powerful collective identities can be forged for new subnational units even in a shorter timeframe.

Summarizing the Insights from Comparative Politics

Together, these studies indicate that a degree of "elective affinity" – or congruence between informal and formal institutions – can determine the success of institutional reforms.[51] What does this diverse set of findings mean for the two mechanisms identified in my own research? In general, scholars emphasize the role of shared identities more than the role of networks. To this end, there is abundant evidence that individuals invoke historical forms of group membership when pursuing political goals, even when these place-specific forms of group membership do not necessarily parallel objective measures of diversity. The most obvious parallel in the African context is Laitin's (1986) study of the role of ancestral cities among the Yoruba. Laitin emphasizes that ancestral cities remain the hegemonic identity for the Yoruba despite the presence of other politicized identities, notably religion. The continued identification with hometowns among the Yoruba is in no small part maintained by the fact that hometowns are, Trager (2001, 239) writes, "a place where one is known and where one's reputation is important." While for Singh the role of subnational identities is critical to her theory, for others, such as Tsai or Dippel, the role of

---

[50] Anath Pur (2007, 414–415). [51] To paraphrase Olejnik (2005, 3).

identities is implied, for example, lineage associations matter because, as clarified in Xu and Yao (2015), family lineages are a central identity for rural Chinese.

Networks are often less explicitly emphasized. This reflects the relative lack of attention among political scientists to what Tilly (2006) has called "relational mechanisms." For Tilly, the relations that individuals maintain with one another are not divorceable from the value of their social and political identities; identities thus reside within relations. Political scientists are not unaware of this – indeed key arguments often rest on assumptions about relations, say within ethnic groups – but we have only recently begun examining this empirically.[52] Yet, my findings indicate that these are inseparable; identities give meaning to networks while, in reverse, networks incentivize abiding by the behavior and norms that constitute the identity in the first place. Indeed, this book's argument is predicated on their interaction.

SCOPE CONDITIONS OF THE ARGUMENT

When are social institutions inherited from the past, such as those persisting from the precolonial era in West Africa, capable of generating institutional congruence? I articulate three scope conditions to my argument below.

Though I have focused on the legacies of precolonial statehood, there is abundant evidence that historical, place-specific identities are being resurrected across the African continent, ranging from autochthony claims to other forms of historical claim-making, such as the mobilization around colonial-era districts in debates about administrative redistricting in Nigeria.[53] This may indicate that the social requisites for congruence are plentiful. But not all social identities or social networks are capable of generating congruence even if they are otherwise "old." The first scope stipulates that there must be a clear mechanism of persistence to carry the social institutions imbued by the past into the present. The existence of a potential antecedent alone is insufficient to engender congruence.

This was illustrated in the case study of Koumpentoum, presented in Chapter 6: a positive value on the antecedent condition (here, exposure to the precolonial state of Niani) did not generate congruence because there was no mechanism of persistence to reproduce social institutions over time. In this case, residents of the Niani out-migrated in the mid-nineteenth century, meaning that the local government's current residents were not exposed to what cross-village social institutions existed during that era. This can help explain why despite an endless array of potential historical legacies, only some exert themselves powerfully in the present. Institutions are political because they are inherently

---

[52] Larson and Lewis (2017).
[53] See Geschiere (2009) on autochthony, Suberu (1991) on Nigeria.

hierarchical, ordering allocative preferences even if they simultaneously enable cooperation. The consequence is that for institutions to persist, they must be valorized and actively reproduced over time.

In rural Senegal, I locate the mechanism of reproduction in village-based social hierarchies. These hierarchies simultaneously validate the social status of individual elites, bolstering their claims to local voice as well as material goods, at the same time they necessitate that elites acknowledge the equivalent claims made by others in their communities. A lineage claiming the village chieftaincy by tracing their genealogy to the era of a precolonial state, for example, has an incentive to affirm shared identities of descent from that kingdom as a legitimate claim to community membership. In this way, shared narratives of descent from a precolonial polity are collectively reproduced by elites over time. We similarly see a clear logic of persistence in other work as well. Tsai's (2007) solidary groups, for example, have persisted in rural China because they have long offered a means to the moral standing citizens desire, meaning that they were not intentionally deployed to embed local officials. Returning to Senegal, social institutions rooted in the precolonial past continue to matter because they continue to structure access to meaningful resources, such as reciprocal obligations between families and neighbors, access to land or marriage markets, by virtue of their ties to village social hierarchies.

This further means that anything that troubles the social reproduction of local social hierarchies should overturn the effects I document. Though to date elites have proven quite capable of maintaining traditional forms of social status in the face of expanding and changing political opportunities, other longer-term dynamics could undermine these networks and, by extensions, the impact of the social institutions that elite networks carry with them on local political life. This is perhaps evidenced most clearly in my own empirical material in the presence of prominent religious authorities within local communities, who can pivot elites away from social institutions rooted in village-based social hierarchies or redefine the nature of these social hierarchies entirely around new social institutions. Alternatively, we can imagine that resettlement schemes, such as those seen in Tanzania or Ethiopia, would similarly disrupt cross-village networks and local status hierarchies by nullifying the value of "first-comer" status to a zone.

The interplay between formal governance institutions and informal social ones that animate my theory emerges from a second scope condition. If formal institutional rules reorient elites' focus outward and upward, rather than inward toward their local social networks, we should expect the effects of congruence to attenuate. My discussion in the section "Assessing the Mechanisms beyond Africa" suggested that the twin mechanisms underpinning my theory may emerge across a wide range of institutional forms with positive effects for development outcomes. This may be when congruence is initiated unintentionally from the top-down, as was seen in Senegal, or when

Scope Conditions of the Argument

the geography of cross-village social institutions altered the contours of the decentralized state itself, as in Mali, effectively rendering local government performance endogenous to the existence of robust social institutions on the eve of reform.[54] But while the argument is not necessarily tied to regime type or the nature of institutional reform, it does demand that elites view their most consequential network ties as being at the same level over which they exert authority. Put otherwise, there must be a relational component between decision-makers that subjects them to local social institutions. If they are buffered by these by top-down interference of some kind, we should be skeptical of the ability of social institutions to shape actor behavior.

This is exemplified by thinking through two alternative network structures induced by different formal institutions. Because social networks serve as a means for motivating and sanctioning behavior toward group goals, when elite networks orient actors toward the central state via the threat of sanction from above, we should expect local social dynamics and institutions to be less influential on elite behavior. For example, as described in Woldense 2018. As was shown in Figure 8.3, when local governance remains subject to central government interference, the effects of congruence are moderated. Alternatively, we can imagine cases where institutional design limits the ability of elites to sanction each other from below. A recent example of this argument is found in the Sierra Leonean case, where decentralization reforms have been captured by Paramount Chiefs exactly when they are most closely tied to elected officials. Inverse to my own findings, local public service delivery in Sierra Leone appears to improve when there is *more* conflict between chiefs and elected councilors. Conversely, service quality declines when there is more collusion.[55] Yet, as documented by Acemoglu, Reed et al. (2014), Sierra Leone's Paramount Chieftaincies were created by the British, disembedding them from local social norms and altering social networks between elites. Because these institutions were invented, in other words, they are not subject to older norms of elite cooperation that lay at the base of precolonial political order.

Individuals may possess shared identities and shared social networks, therefore, but when aspects of the formal institutional environment alter the standing of some local social network members, decision-makers can become insulated from local behavioral expectations. When elites have substantial social autonomy in this way, they have more freedom to engage in opportunistic behavior. As a result, formal institutional design must enable the network

---

[54] See Djire (2004) and Hetland (2008).
[55] Clayton et al. (2015). Replicating the findings presented in Figures 8.1 and 8.2 for Sierra Leone alone finds generally consistent results for the Afrobarometer data. Results are admittedly patchier for the DHS data. Historically centralized areas see significant gains in the percent of household members in school or in the number of antenatal visits, while acephalous areas see bigger gains in the percent of births in clinics. Other results show insignificant differences.

mechanism to carry social institutions into the calculi of local elites when they meet in the local state.

Norms "do not float freely in space," Collins (2004, 31–32) writes, "but are crystallized in institutions. The denser the environment they pervade, the thicker they tend to be." Like Collins, I advance an argument about the potency of social norms in circumscribed communities. Here looms the specter of a third potential scope condition: is the argument limited in scale?

The most obvious answer comes from Englebert (2002b) who articulates a similar logic, though distinct causal process, to explain cross-national variation in postcolonial state performance. Englebert argues that postcolonial leaders faced different incentives at independence as a function of the degree of violence that their postcolonial boundaries did to precolonial authority structures. Where postcolonial and precolonial boundaries have low congruence, bureaucrats are insufficiently loyal to the state and more likely to engage in neopatrimonial relations. The relative overlap between the postcolonial Botswanan state and traditional Tswana authority has similarly been advanced by Robinson and Parsons (2006) as a means to explain the relative success of postcolonial Botswana. In a different tradition, a large body of work has found that strong national-level identities are the basis upon which the modern European and East Asian Welfare states are built.[56] Alesina et al. (2011) globalize this view, finding that political and economic outcomes are worse in cases where states are "artificial," those whose borders do not match those preferred by its citizen, around the world.

In the intermediate spaces between the local contexts where I draw my own empirical content and the central state itself, however, lies a tricky middle ground. Few precolonial states had the geographic fortunes of the Tswana, who were numerically dominant in the postcolonial Botswanan state and the question of how identities scale subnationally within the polity appears critical elsewhere. Indeed, we might very well expect that countries like Senegal, home to microstate systems, should see precolonial identities play out differently in the postcolonial state than in cases like Uganda or Ghana, where the precolonial states of Buganda and the Ashante Confederacy presented more formidable political obstacles to postcolonial leaders. As argued by Acemoglu, Chaves et al. (2014), it was the credible threat to postcolonial elite posed by these kingdoms that led postcolonial leaders to focus on capturing domestic political compliance. This led to more reliance on the military in the short term, but both countries have more state capacity today than many of their neighbors where an immediate postcolonial threat from a rival sense of legitimacy was less pressing. When social institutions – and the political groups

---

[56] Wilensky (1975). As Hur (2018) writes on South Korea, when these are tightly linked "the welfare of one's national community and that of the state are seen as intimately related, so that the needs or demands of that state invoke an ethical obligation to comply – a sense of citizen duty."

they encompass – are neither nationally congruent nor small enough to be unthreatening to the central government actors, therefore, we may see more interventionist approaches on the part of the state in ways that alter the potential for congruence.

The argument is therefore most likely apt on a local level. Though we can see above how the identity mechanism may scale upward, say as the emergence of a national identity shifts one's sense of obligations from the local to the national level, the network mechanism should scale more difficultly. After all, it is at a localized level that both networks and identities are most ripe for collective action.[57] This does not mean that the argument is inherently limited in scale, however.[58] At higher levels of aggregation, such as Singh's study of Indian states, territorially larger than the units under study here, networks are still expected to matter, but the nature of elite ties is likely more variable and more vulnerable to pressures from outside the network.

CONCLUSION

In this final empirical chapter, I have demonstrated that the argument I develop in rural Senegal offers analytic leverage on attitudinal and development outcomes across West Africa. I find that Afrobarometer respondents residing in areas that were home to precolonial states hold more positive attitudes toward democracy and the local state than their counterparts in historically acephalous zones and, in turn, that respondents to the Afrobarometer and DHS surveys in historically centralized areas have seen disproportionate gains in locally provided public goods under decentralization. While I take this as evidence for the argument's broad generalizability, I note that these empirical regularities may be bounded and merit further analysis.

This chapter has secondly suggested that the two mechanisms that underpin my theory of institutional congruence shed light on a more universal pattern of how subnational distributive dilemmas are resolved. The contours of institutional congruence as a theoretical framework find parallels across the world and at different levels of government. This is consequential because by opening up what the content of social institutions may be, I offer a framework for unifying an otherwise dispersed literature on the effects of social identities and social institutions on access to basic welfare. While many scholars have – and indeed are increasingly – recognizing the interaction between social norms and formal institutions, I put forward a means for us to theorize when these interactions are more or less likely to induce the positive outcomes that we know they are capable of generating, but which we so often see them fail to do.

---

[57] Gould (1995, 205).
[58] As has been argued about Tsai's (2007, 263) solitary groups. See also Hur (2018).

Conclusion

The past few decades have seen rapid improvement in development outcomes around the world. Senegal halved the population living under $1.25 a day, achieved gender parity in primary education, and made great strides toward reducing child mortality. These gains – the result of high-profile objectives like the Millennium Development Goals (MDGs) and a broader push to expand basic service infrastructure – are often studied comparatively across countries. Mali and The Gambia were on track to meet the MDGs in 2015, for example, while Senegal lagged behind with neighboring Guinea and Guinea-Bissau. Yet as the preceding chapters have documented, it is just as critical to look within countries to assess how international agendas fare in practice. Following the confluence of decentralization, political liberalization, and the push to improve living standards, I suggest a novel source of subnational variation: progress may be made unevenly within single countries as a function of historically inherited and spatially uneven attributes.

The remaining pages of this book briefly summarize the argument before offering reflections on the implications my findings hold for ongoing decentralization reforms. I conclude with a discussion about the latent questions of determinacy and durability in the precolonial legacies I identify.

SUMMARY OF THE ARGUMENT

This book has sought to explain why local governments engage in strikingly different redistributive patterns despite inhabiting a shared formal institutional framework. My central empirical claim is that areas of Senegal that were home to precolonial states engage in spatially broader strategies of representation and redistribution. I have argued that exposure to precolonial polities generated social institutions, or norms of appropriate behavior in the public sphere that are demarcated by group boundaries, and that these norms have persisted to

Summary of the Argument

the present, carried over time by rural social hierarchies. Social institutions work because they are deeply ingrained in how actors pursue political and social strategies, informing not only what they expect of others but how they understand the value of their social relations more broadly. My theory of institutional congruence stipulates that when formal institutions spatially overlap with informal, social ones inherited from the precolonial past, politicians' behavior is reoriented toward community goals and relationships. When formal institutions are incongruent with local social institutions, we see more opportunism on the part of rural elites, specifically because their social worlds do not map onto their political ones.

Herein lies my answer to the first of two animating questions laid out at the start of this book: why are some communities able to come together to improve their collective lot while others are not? I have argued that some communities are endowed with informal social institutions that embed elites within local behavioral norms that reorient their behavior away from individual opportunism. Social institutions are carried into local governance through two mechanisms. First, precolonial states endowed communities with robust social identities that tie members together into a sense of shared fate. Shared identities imbue social institutions with meaning, but they inhere in the theory's second mechanism of cross-village social networks. Dense network ties impact elite behavior through three channels: they circulate information, they transmit rewards for well-viewed behavior and sanctions for poor-viewed behavior, and they reinforce the internalization of social institutions as actors come to see abiding by these norms as intrinsically rewarding. When social institutions embed elites from across the community within such interconnected webs of obligations, elite behavior is reoriented toward prosocial group goals, but *only* when these networks are congruent with the bounds of the local state.

This suggests that state-building at the grassroots may be uneven at least in the near term. In the wake of institutional reforms across the Global South, I suggest that attention to how local elites negotiate new political spaces of local governance can shed as much – if not more – light on macro-institutional reforms initiated by the center as can be gained by focusing on the center's own motivations. To the extent that one of the central claims of this study is that the performance of formal institutions is contingent on the impact of informal social institutions, I show how forces often conceptualized as impediments to the state-building project, such as precolonial, indigenous social organizations, may paradoxically serve to entrench the state locally by grafting it onto preconceived understandings of community. The implications of this are not only local, but seep upward to shape the strength of national political parties, the distribution of economic opportunity, and the democratic project itself.

The second question raised in this book's opening pages asked when the past matters for contemporary politics and why. I have answered by arguing that long-defunct political institutions can remain politically consequential long after their formal structures have disappeared, but that the impact of these legacies may be contingent on how contemporary institutional delimitations put these historical inheritances into relief. My central claim, that precolonial legacies persist to powerfully shape contemporary understandings of political community, risks reading as a quaint claim about a distant and idealized past but embedded within these identities and the social relations that maintain them are deeply normative questions about which citizens are the most deserving. By examining when and why the precolonial past matters, my findings will hopefully serve as a reminder that institutions inherited from the past are intrinsically political creatures, amenable to reinvention and repurposing across time.

This holds key implications for the literature on African politics in its suggestion that scholars have underestimated salient local political identities by prioritizing ethnicity as the most potent political cleavage in sub-Saharan Africa. By identifying a powerful role for place-specific identities rooted in the past, the preceding chapters encourage us to take seriously the social identities that our respondents themselves invoke to make sense of their political lives. Certainly, these may revolve around ethnicity, but in rural West Africa they appear as much – if not more – likely to draw on far more localized histories. As I have shown, intra-ethnic tensions, around clan or caste, spoil prospects for local government cooperation as frequently as inter-ethnic dynamics themselves.

This is particularly important when studying institutional change, such as that brought on by decentralization. I challenge the assumption that certain political identities are *always* politically relevant by documenting how social identities latent at the grassroots reenter political life following institutional reform. In the wake of institutional reform, therefore, we should be attentive to the ways in which identities may shift to lose or gain salience not only because new institutional environments can create new identities, but because the very shape of institutional boundaries can valorize old identities in new ways. By focusing on the spatial interaction between identities and institutional boundaries, I offer a framework for understanding why identities may generate distinct behavior at some moments of time but not at others.

Three methodological implications follow. First, and most simply, this project calls attention to the necessity of studying institutional change where it takes place. Despite widespread interest in decentralization reforms, scholars have disproportionately kept their focus on the central state or, alternatively, on the village or project level, as seen in the literature on elite capture. As a new layer of governance, decentralized local governments face unique redistributive dilemmas that are often distinct from those faced at higher or lower levels of analysis. The interests of local actors demand concerted investigation and theorization.

Second, my findings show that we can gain unique insight into political behavior by taking seriously how individuals narrate their political lives. Even if the tales of precolonial grandeur that I have repeated in these pages verge on myth and stray from historical accuracy, the collective embrace of these narratives is a valuable form of data for understanding local political and social action explicitly because the act of their retelling valorizes and reproduces social institutions. To the extent that local actors recount these narratives from their own lived experiences, they shape how social and political objectives are understood in their communities and, by extensions, the appropriate policies to pursue them. In this way, the telling and retelling of local narratives is an explicitly political act and should be studied as such.

The third methodological lesson relates more narrowly to recent criticisms that the literature on historical legacies is apolitical and atemporal.[1] I strive to offer a corrective on both fronts. Much of the social sciences' recent rediscovery of the past relies on the assumption that a historical cause, once unleashed, persists to the present in a uniform fashion. In contrast, I show that the effect of precolonial statehood in rural Senegal only appears following the exogenous institutional shock of the 1996 decentralization reforms. Embracing calls to "decompress" history, I look at *when* the precolonial past can explain distributional patterns to reveal that the social legacies of precolonial centralization may be spatially path-dependent over time, but that this does not necessitate persistent effects on the dependent variable.[2] In other words, I offer an explicitly temporal story: the long shadow of the precolonial past is at best a story of intermittent effects for local redistribution.

At the same time, I have sought to tell an explicitly political story by focusing on the mechanisms that keep social legacies rooted in the precolonial era alive within rural Senegal. Institutions always have distributional consequences, making them subject to enduring political contestation. This renders historical interactions all the more consequential, leaving the general lack of attention to how precolonial or colonial legacies play out over time puzzling. As discussed at length in Chapter 7, I find that colonial legacies have largely faded over time, while the impact of precolonial legacies on distributive outcomes has only reemerged following decentralization reforms. Although my argument is highly structural, it opens up room for the agency of the postcolonial state, which has increasingly exerted its own logics of rule at the expense of colonial legacies. Empirically, this serves as a reminder that we should (and can) test rather than assume the determinacy of the past.

IMPLICATIONS

Despite early pessimism about decentralization's potential,[3] evidence is emerging that the local state is an important site of contact between citizens and their government. Bratton et al. (2000), for example, note that many African citizens find it easier to contact their local councilors than distant state administrators. And even if the local state is just one actor among many, with decentralization "merely represent[ing] another remount in a long series of regime changes imposed from above by the state," it has nonetheless become a critical arena

---

[1] Austin (2008) and Mahoney (2010).
[2] See Austin (2008); Hopkins (2011); and Jerven (2011).   [3] For example, Treisman (2007).

where consequential decisions about citizen well-being are made.[4] Despite this "silent revolution" in statecraft, however, this is only one of a handful of studies that explores the nature of political life under decentralization.[5] What then does this study imply for these widely promoted yet understudied reforms?

The most immediate conclusion is that the political spaces generated by decentralization enable, create, and revive highly localized political interests. Local state elites are hardly mirrors of their central state counterparts and even as local actors actively engage with the central state, seeking projects, favors, and influence, these interactions do not define the totality of their political preferences. This serves as a reminder that local decision-makers are obliged to negotiate *across* villages when deciding how to distribute scarce projects and resources. Local government performance under decentralization is not reducible to the question of when local elites are able to control local positions of authority, as argued by the elite capture literature therefore, because this ignores the question of when the interests of local elites are more or less compatible in the first place. Centrally, the expansion in scope of what local agents control highlights the importance of interrogating when we expect local state actors to pursue their interests and, most importantly, when we think their own interests dovetail with those of the broader community.

This should nuance how we think about the sharp subnational inequalities documented in this book. If decentralization was designed as a means to improve transparency and representation and to aid participatory development, then my suggestion that some areas are structurally predisposed to find these tasks easier implies that we will likely see a widening gap in outcomes for core donor agendas around basic service delivery and democratic consolidation. In the worst of cases, some local elites and the villages they represent report disengaging from their local governments altogether. Of course, this may lead a village or community to mobilize local social and economic capital to find solutions to their own problems that can produce acceptable outcomes over the short term. But if decentralization was designed with an eye to facilitate the development of more robust social contracts, we should temper our expectations about the broader process of democratic consolidation that decentralization reforms are often bound up within.

In some ways, this book risks shifting its focus too heavily to the question of why elites in historically centralized areas are endowed with more prosocial preferences, which may be read by some as suggesting that all good things go together. Delivering goods broadly across space is not necessarily the ideal criteria with which to evaluate local development outcomes; highly populated villages with overcrowded classrooms could suffer if local governments prioritize giving even small, isolated localities their own school. Nor, of course, is there something inherently objectionable about politicians rewarding those who vote for them as we see in some communities.[6] Moreover, local social institutions around conflict resolution and equal voice may create "good"

---

[4] Bierschenk and Olivier de Sardan (2003, 167). [5] Fombad (2018).
[6] My thanks go to Dan De Kadt for an interesting discussion on this point.

outcomes in some ways, but they carry with them profoundly antidemocratic aspects. On the flip side of social institutions' ability to prioritize consensus and prevent political blockage of local government work, is the suppression of robust democratic contestation, which inherently relies on dissent and disagreement. In a like manner, the dense social ties or identities that serve to reproduce these institutions can be equally disadvantageous to minorities or those who do not otherwise conform. As I documented in Chapter 4, minorities and in-migrants "adopted" into congruent local governments do sometimes report weaker claims to voice in their communities.

As such, there is something intrinsically conservative in the argument laid out here. After all, the international community has been anxiously promoting participatory democracy initiatives for going on three decades in an effort to undermine the very elite and communal dynamics I identify.[7] The logical consequences of my argument for this view are at once explosive but also fundamentally mundane. It indicates most clearly that there are limits to what outsiders (international and domestic alike) can achieve in the short term and that we should approach efforts to reengineer social norms with a certain wariness. To the extent that one of the most basic lessons in the preceding chapters is that top-down reforms are conditioned by local social relations, I echo Wibbels' (2019, 21–23) recent suggestion that one reason many information and accountability experiments have fallen short of achieving their desired ends is because they fail to account for how social context intimately shapes the ways in which communities receive and act upon such initiatives. To the extent that such "social engineering" by development agencies and academics continues, we should be increasingly attentive to the ways in which it encounters local social realities that will shape the outcomes under study. If nothing else, this book has shown that large, international agendas, such as decentralization, never descend upon neutral terrain.

The argument further implies that the impacts of such social engineering are likely to vary subnationally to the extent that local communities possess distinct social networks and varying levels of cross-village solidarity. This could help resolve known noncumulative findings. Baldwin and Raffler (2019), for example, have recently observed that despite a proliferation of academic research on the subject, the impacts of the role of customary authorities in local governance and questions of development more broadly are not straightforward. Stronger traditional authorities seem to help project outcomes in some countries or regions, while inhibiting them elsewhere. As they note, outcomes seem to improve when traditional leaders are socially and geographically embedded.[8] I hope to help us move away from debates over whether customary authorities and local elites are

---

[7] This is not to obscure the ways in which international discourses have seeped into local political life; village chiefs, for example, are now frequently elected, even if only from among male family members. These initiatives have made changes, but we should be cautious in our assumptions that they will replace existing social logics, hence the language of layering or sedimentation embraced by anthropologists in studies of the region to describe how such reforms have been met locally (e.g. Bierschenk 2010).

[8] Baldwin and Raffler (2019, 76).

"good" or "bad" for development or democratic practice to recognize them as political actors responding to varied incentives. This then returns us to an animating question of this book: when are local elites more or less likely to see their social interests overlap with those of the local state?

Put otherwise, two issues are at stake: first, do our interventions target the scale at which individual and communities understand their social networks and obligations to be? And, if they are not, are we secondly willing (indeed, we may ask if it is ethically appropriate) to intervene wherever that may be? Should we conclude, for example, that we must simply find better boundaries and hunt for institutional congruence? I would caution against this as a viable solution because it risks creating infinitesimally small and non-sustainable political and economic units.[9] Nor should we presume that cross-village social institutions are amenable to construction, at least in the short term. One potential reading of my argument, therefore, is that there are deeper social processes at work than those immediately responsive to outside intervention. Decentralization does not immediately generate cohesive communities, nor can the forms of institutional congruence I study here be created at will.

In contrast, we may have to content ourselves with Eckstein's (1997, 15) observation that "incongruent authority patterns tend to change toward increased congruence." Robust social institutions and social identities can take many forms, meaning that with time, local governments could become equally viable sources of identification as the identities inherited from the precolonial past documented here.[10] This evolution will only happen, however, through politics, a necessarily unequal process that creates winners and losers. Proponents of decentralization would often be well-served to remember that decentralization shapes and redefines the fundamental ties that citizens hold with their states by design. That this generates short-term inequalities should not come as a surprise nor the fact that such reforms both "create and erode social resources."[11] These processes are deeply political, but they are also deeply social; nothing, in other words, that can be easily, quickly, or painlessly adjusted from above.

If decentralization granted an unforeseen advantage to communities with high degrees of congruence, while exacerbating intervillage inequality in others, it remains an open question as to how "stuck" these outcomes are. My evidence – from the first two decades of democratic decentralization – may describe what will prove to be a temporary outcome over the long run. We could easily imagine that the contestation and dissent that I document in many historically acephalous communities may generate stronger local governments

---

[9] In line with a recent argument by Pierskalla (2019).
[10] History offers abundant evidence of how political entrepreneurs seek to imbue administrative units with meaning in such a bottom-up fashion. To wit, MacArthur's (2016, 5–6) recent work on the historically acephalous Luyia of Kenya, who constructed new understandings of "authority, moral accountability, and political community" within the counters of colonial districts created by the British in Kenya.
[11] Hall and Lamont (2013, 65).

Implications

over the longer term if it strengthens local party apparatuses or induces more responsive leadership in the years to come. Acephalous zones certainly do not lack some cultural requisites currently possessed by centralized areas.[12] To the contrary, villages I have visited in these zones are equally vibrant and they likewise produce dynamic leaders who wish to do well by their families and friends. But in the years during which research for this book was carried out, the social ties that bind elites in historically centralized areas have the primary benefit of time and all that it brings with it: intermarriage, histories of mutual aid, and the camaraderie that can arise out of cohabitation across generations.

Ultimately, I part ways with the increasingly prominent view in economics that suggest the past traps some communities in bad equilibria. This is particularly prominent in work on the long-run effects of cultural norms by scholars of political economy of development,[13] which views historical path dependencies as leading countries or communities toward more or less productive equilibrium outcomes.[14] These accounts bear the same risks of an earlier culturalist tradition in political science, which was similarly prone to the view that communities could be ensnared in patterns of belief and behavior. But this unsatisfactorily dooms political behavior to be "mechanistic and unvoluntarist" without recognizing that many of the most important questions we study see persistence without determinism as societies change slowly.[15] To be clear, I view the long-run historical processes that create different configuration of local social institutions today as neither intentional nor something that we can create or reform from on high, but this should not be read as suggesting that these communities are not home to dynamic sociocultural changes that may move communities toward or away from institutional congruence even if formal institutions remain the same. By emphasizing the question of spatial overlap in lieu of invoking ideas of good or bad cultural equilibria, I argue we can explain why informal social institutions condition institutional performance and reform across radically different forms of government in a more productive fashion.

Indeed, the question of change is pervasive in many of the communities I have worked in. What will happen, one local government secretary mused, when the old men – who today take their horse cart out to visit old friends in nearby villages, spending the day discussing old times and contemporary problems alike before heading home at night – pass away if the youth are less likely to do this?[16] Herein lies the very fragility of the social cohesion underpinning the dynamics of my theory. Because social institutions are bound up in social identities and social networks, shifts in either or both of these components may lead local actors to question the moral obligations generated by this shared social inheritance.

---

[12] As could be implied in Hjort (2010). [13] For example, Alesina and Guiliano (2015).
[14] Nunn (2009, 75–77).
[15] Berman (2001, 247). In this way, we might expect marginal changes in local social relations to produce endogenous change over a longer term, as explored in Greif (2006).
[16] Interview, Louga Region, February 18, 2016.

As the costs of distance are eased and time passes, networks are likely to broaden. This can expand social and political horizons as rural villagers gain new information that reshapes their sense of the possible.[17] As "development" seeps further into the countryside, newly paved roads plying more and more taxis and minibuses, local elite social networks are likely to be increasingly challenged by new forms of claim-making by rural citizens. On the flip side, however, it is possible that even more communities will pull out and refresh histories that they can uniquely lay claim to. The claim to represent a deeper, "truer," or more authentically "Senegalese" history – one that communities can embrace even as the country's urban cores move full steam ahead – provides an attractive vehicle for rural communities to reclaim their status in the polity as their sons and daughters move away and as secular authority is questioned in new ways. Such dynamics are surely not to be limited to historically centralized areas; as Doquet (2006, 311) shows of Dogon communities in Mali, local officials in the commune of Dourou have actively deployed cross-village festivals and rituals, the success of which "testifies to an awareness by the population of communal unity. The gathering of villages on the same stage reinforces in their [local officials] eyes a new cultural identity." How successful such efforts to reinvigorate or create these countervailing pressures will be remains to be seen, however.

In the end, I remain agnostic as to how permanent or fleeting the social institutions I have highlighted are likely to be. Group norms rely on habituated, shared spaces of action that keep shared history and norms alive. Decentralized governance – with its meetings, its consultative drafting of local government development plans, its attempts at improving local fiscal capacity – creates numerous venues and rituals that may alter and nuance the very meaning of these communities. In incongruent communities, we may be inclined to see this as a positive, while in congruent ones we may bemoan something lost. At least in the short term, however, the existence of a bounded understanding of community in the latter has certainly helped the local state take root in a crucial early period of state reform.

In the end, this book may be read most simply as a call to study institutional reform better by asking us to think seriously about questions of boundaries, scale, and spatial delimitation. What politics are engendered by any given mode of administrative statehood and what politics do these boundaries obscure? The outcomes of top-down reforms have been repeatedly shown to be contingent on social dynamics not legible from afar and about which we often go in knowingly ignorant. To the extent we seek to aid, to improve, or to render more accountable, we should seek first and foremost to understand how individuals understand their political obligations. By starting from the grassroots and looking up at the state, I hope the argument is read as a call to take seriously how actors perceive the nested boundaries of solidarity that are created by the political delimitations of their communities and the histories those boundaries inhabit.

---

[17] As Kruks-Wisner (2018) documents in rural India.

Appendix

TABLE A.1 *Additional descriptive statistics*

	Variable	N	Mean	Range	Source
Controls: Electoral	Vote Gap, 2002	13,754	0.358	0–1	Author Coded; *Direction Generale des Elections*
	Vote Gap, 2009	13,595	0.378	0–1	Author Coded; *Direction Generale des Elections*
	Winning % Votes, 2002	13,756	0.657	0.047–1	Author Coded; *Direction Generale des Elections*
	Winning % Votes, 2009	13,593	0.659	0–1	Author Coded; *Direction Generale des Elections*
	Nat'l Alignment, 2002	14,461	0.6	0–1	Author Coded; *Direction Generale des Elections*
	Nat'l Alignment, 2009	14,461	0.67	0–1	Author Coded; *Direction Generale des Elections*
Controls: CG Favoritism	Teacher/Student Ratio, 2002	14,461	0.266	0–1	Author Coded from Ministry of Education data
	Teacher/Student Ratio, 2009	14,461	0.292	0–1	Author Coded from Ministry of Education data
	Avg. CG Transfers	14,457	23,495	13,201–86,186	*Direction des Collectivities Locales*
Controls: Ethnicity	Wolof, 2002	14,461	0.499	0–1	Author Coded
	Wolof, 2009	14,461	0.494	0–1	Author Coded
	Ethnic Fractionalization, 2002	14,457	63.84	16.66–98	Author Coded
	Ethnic Fractionalization, 2009	14,457	63.79	16.66–98	Author Coded

Controls: Social Capital	# Civic Associations, 2002	14,489	1.839	0–5	ANSD *Enquête Villages* 2002, 2009
	# Civic Associations, 2009	14,490	2.474	0–5	ANSD *Enquête Villages* 2002, 2009
Location-Allocation Models	Max. Attendance, Schools 2002–2009	285	305.63	0–2,680.3	Author Coded
	Max. Attendance, Schools 2009–2012	318	579.9	0–4,169.4	Author Coded
	Max. Attendance, Clinics 2009–2012	183	2,805.6	0–22,759.6	Author Coded
	Max. Coverage, Schools 2002–2009	285	766.31	0–5,945	Author Coded
	Max. Coverage, Schools 2009–2012	318	413.3	0–4,678	Author Coded
	Max. Coverage, Schools 2009–2012	183	639.9	0–8,580	Author Coded
Placebo Test Outcomes	New High Schools	14,509	0.002	0–1	ANSD *Enquête Villages* 2002, 2009
	Electrification	12,266	0.028	0–1	ANSD *Enquête Villages* 2002, 2009
	New Roads	12,266	0.109	0–1	ANSD *Enquête Villages* 2002, 2009

TABLE A.2 *Effect of institutional congruence on village access to new social services (Figure 5.2)*

	New primary school access, odds ratios								New clinic access, odds ratios			
	2002–2009				2009–2012				2009–2012			
	(1)	(2)	(3)	(4)	(5)	(6)	(7)	(8)	(9)	(10)	(11)	(12)
Institutional Congruence 20 km	2.762*** (0.404)	2.775*** (0.404)	2.341*** (0.355)	2.452*** (0.379)	2.035*** (0.314)	2.022*** (0.309)	1.597*** (0.255)	1.573*** (0.261)	1.662*** (0.273)	1.655** (0.271)	1.919*** (0.329)	1.850*** (0.325)
Ln Population	1.417*** (0.037)	1.387*** (0.037)	1.341*** (0.036)	1.354*** (0.038)	1.586*** (0.046)	1.551*** (0.046)	1.457*** (0.044)	1.473*** (0.046)	1.223*** (0.040)	1.229*** (0.041)	1.234*** (0.042)	1.231*** (0.043)
Dist. School Baseline (sqrt)	1.038*** (0.001)	1.038*** (0.001)	1.041*** (0.001)	1.043*** (0.001)	1.037*** (0.001)	1.036*** (0.001)	1.039*** (0.001)	1.041*** (0.001)	1.025*** (0.001)	1.025*** (0.001)	1.026*** (0.001)	1.026*** (0.001)
Population Density	1.000** (0.000)	1.000** (0.000)	1.000** (0.000)	1.000** (0.000)	1.000** (0.000)	1.000 (0.000)	1.000 (0.000)	1.000 (0.000)	0.999 (0.000)	0.999 (0.000)	0.999 (0.000)	0.999 (0.000)
% Villages Schools	1.007** (0.003)	1.009*** (0.003)	1.009*** (0.003)		1.013*** (0.003)	1.008** (0.003)	1.009*** (0.003)					
% Villages Clinics									0.174** (0.132)	0.977 (0.595)	0.832 (0.521)	
Local Economic Activity		1.045** (0.023)	1.023 (0.023)	1.025 (0.028)		1.031 (0.020)	1.019 (0.020)	1.066** (0.028)		0.969 (0.026)	0.984 (0.027)	0.959 (0.030)
Department Wealth Measure		1.054 (0.074)	1.127 (0.074)			1.064 (0.072)	1.117 (0.076)			1.158 (0.133)	1.213 (0.142)	
% Mouride		0.689 (0.482)	1.110 (0.715)			1.294 (0.866)	1.420 (0.944)					

	(1)	(2)	(3)	(4)	(5)	(6)	(7)	(8)
# Built Schools	1.144*** (0.012)	1.164*** (0.012)	1.162*** (0.017)	1.184*** (0.017)				
# Built Clinics							2.010*** (0.103)	0.996** (0.002)
Village Elevation		0.996 (0.001)	0.998 (0.002)		1.000 (0.002)	0.998 (0.002)	0.996 (0.002)	
Ln Dist. Waterway		0.958 (0.022)	0.949 (0.026)		0.966 (0.024)	0.994 (0.031)	1.005 (0.031)	1.064 (0.039)
Soil Fertility		0.989 (0.009)	0.986 (0.011)		0.876** (0.010)	0.967** (0.011)	0.998 (0.013)	0.984 (0.014)
Ln Dist. Road		0.987 (0.023)	0.975 (0.023)		0.935*** (0.024)	0.938** (0.024)	1.000 (0.029)	0.997 (0.029)
Ln Dist. Administrative Center/Market		0.737*** (0.029)	0.869*** (0.032)		0.762*** (0.033)	0.789*** (0.035)	1.165** (0.062)	1.211*** (0.066)
Local Government Capital		4.583*** (0.722)	4.636*** (0.752)		4.854*** (0.696)	4.469*** (0.646)	0.729 (0.195)	0.732 (0.196)
N	14,267	14,167	13,553	14,224	14,124	13,611	11,190	8,274
Level-2	318	318		368	368		286	
Pseudo-R²			0.146			0.132		0.074
FE			Y			Y		Y

*** p < 0.001, ** p < 0.01, * p < 0.05. Models report odds ratios and standard errors, in parentheses, from two-tailed, mixed-level logit models. All hierarchical models include a centered mean of precolonial centralization at the local government level (level 2) as well as an interaction term between village latitude and longitude.

TABLE A.3 *Effect of institutional congruence on village access to new social services, increased buffer size*

	New primary school access, odds ratios				New clinic access, odds ratios	
	2002–2009		2009–2012		2009–2012	
	(1)	(2)	(3)	(4)	(5)	(6)
Institutional Congruence 25 km	1.651** (0.266)		1.438** (0.235)		1.734** (0.349)	
Institutional Congruence 30 km		2.813*** (0.431)		1.884*** (0.309)		0.950 (0.165)
Ln Population	1.340*** (0.036)	1.342*** (0.036)	1.456*** (0.044)	1.457*** (0.044)	1.223*** (0.042)	1.229*** (0.042)
Dist. School Baseline (sqrt)	1.040*** (0.001)	1.041*** (0.001)	1.039*** (0.001)	1.039*** (0.001)	1.025*** (0.001)	1.025*** (0.001)
Population Density (3 km radius)	1.000 (0.000)	1.000 (0.000)	1.000 (0.000)	1.000 (0.000)	0.999 (0.000)	0.999 (0.000)
% Villages Schools	1.008** (0.003)	1.001** (0.003)	1.009*** (0.003)	1.009*** (0.003)		
% Villages Clinics					0.790 (0.496)	0.749 (0.469)
Local Economic Activity	1.020 (0.023)	1.021 (0.023)	1.019 (0.020)	1.016 (0.02)	0.985 (0.027)	0.984 (0.027)
Department Wealth Measure	1.104 (0.073)	1.118 (0.075)	1.105 (0.076)	1.109 (0.076)	1.218 (0.143)	1.226 (0.144)
% Mouride	1.020 (0.659)	1.028 (0.672)	1.286 (0.854)	1.270 (0.843)		
# Built Schools	1.164*** (0.012)	1.166*** (0.012)	1.184*** (0.018)	1.185*** (0.018)		

	(1)	(2)	(3)	(4)	(5)	(6)
# Built Clinics					2.008*** (0.105)	2.004*** (0.104)
Village Elevation	0.998 (0.001)	0.999 (0.001)	1.001 (0.002)	1.001 (0.002)	0.997 (0.002)	0.996 (0.002)
Ln Dist. Waterway	0.954** (0.022)	0.955** (0.022)	0.963 (0.024)	0.964 (0.024)	1.006 (0.031)	0.999 (0.031)
Soil fertility	0.989 (0.009)	0.992 (0.009)	0.975** (0.010)	0.976** (0.010)	1.006 (0.014)	1.006 (0.014)
Ln Dist. Road	0.986 (0.023)	0.987 (0.023)	0.934** (0.023)	0.934* (0.0254)	0.990 (0.029)	0.989 (0.029)
Ln Dist. Administrative Center/Market	0.722*** (0.029)	0.739*** (0.029)	0.754*** (0.032)	0.764*** (0.033)	1.157** (0.062)	1.124** (0.059)
Local Government Capital	4.660*** (0.734)	4.588*** (0.724)	4.889*** (0.701)	4.839*** (0.694)	0.741 (0.198)	0.747 (0.199)
N	14,167	14,167	14,124	14,124	10,930	10,930
Level-2	318	318	368	368	282	282

*** $p < 0.001$, ** $p < 0.05$. Models report odds ratios and standard errors, in parentheses, from two-tailed, mixed-level logit models. All hierarchical models include a centered mean of precolonial centralization at the local government level (level 2) as well as an interaction term between village latitude and longitude.

TABLE A.4 *Effect of institutional congruence on village access to new social services, reduced measure of access*

	New primary school access in 2 km, odds ratios		New primary school access in 1 km, odds ratios		New clinic access in 3 km, odds ratios		New clinic access in 1 km, odds ratios	
	2002–2009	2009–2012	2002–2009	2009–2012	2002–2009	2009–2012	2002–2009	2009–2012
	(1)	(2)	(3)	(4)	(5)	(6)		
Institutional Congruence 20 km	2.363*** (0.372)	1.549** (0.252)	2.157*** (0.378)	1.171 (0.204)	1.991*** (0.365)	2.053** (0.511)		
Ln Population	1.409*** (0.039)	1.481*** (0.046)	1.744*** (0.057)	1.766*** (0.062)	1.278*** (0.047)	1.705*** (0.086)		
Dist. School Baseline (sqrt)	1.037*** (0.001)	1.035*** (0.001)	1.033*** (0.001)	1.031*** (0.001)	1.023*** (0.001)	1.019*** (0.002)		
Population Density (3 km radius)	1.000** (0.000)	1.000 (0.000)	1.000 (0.000)	1.000 (0.000)	1.000 (0.000)	0.999 (0.000)		
% Villages Schools	1.009*** (0.003)	1.009*** (0.003)	1.012*** (0.003)	1.011*** (0.003)				
% Villages Clinics					0.781 (0.446)	1.110 (0.593)		
Local Economic Activity	1.002 (0.022)	1.021 (0.020)	1.014 (0.023)	1.001 (0.020)	0.985 (0.027)	1.008 (0.030)		
Department Wealth Measure	1.101 (0.070)	1.105 (0.073)	1.103 (0.067)	1.116 (0.069)	1.116 (0.114)	1.106 (0.101)		
% Mouride	0.525 (0.347)	1.177 (0.763)	0.553 (0.357)	1.807 (1.107)				
# Built Schools	1.154*** (0.011)	1.175*** (0.017)	1.142*** (0.010)	1.165*** (0.015)				
# Built Clinics					1.738*** (0.076)	1.545*** (0.058)		

	(1)	(2)	(3)	(4)	(5)
Village Elevation	0.999 (0.002)	1.001 (0.002)	1.000 (0.002)	1.001 (0.002)	0.997 (0.002)	1.000 (0.002)
Ln Dist. Waterway	0.949** (0.022)	0.964 (0.023)	0.958 (0.022)	0.973 (0.023)	0.995 (0.031)	0.955 (0.032)
Soil Fertility	0.983 (0.009)	0.981 (0.010)	0.982 (0.011)	0.989 (0.011)	0.985 (0.014)	0.983 (0.017)
Ln Dist. Road	0.969 (0.023)	0.937** (0.024)	0.967 (0.025)	0.947** (0.026)	0.969 (0.030)	0.954 (0.038)
Ln Dist. Administrative Center/Market	0.734*** (0.031)	0.759*** (0.033)	0.763*** (0.034)	0.774*** (0.036)	1.078 (0.059)	1.046 (0.072)
Local Government Capital	4.024*** (0.637)	4.363*** (0.627)	3.134*** (0.507)	3.905*** (0.567)	0.833 (0.221)	1.032 (0.279)
N	14,167	14,124	14,167	14,124	10,655	10,655
Level-2	318	368	318	368	273	273

*** p < 0.001, ** p < 0.05. Models report odds ratios and standard errors, in parentheses, from two-tailed, mixed-level logit models. All hierarchical models include a centered mean of precolonial centralization at the local government level (level 2) as well as an interaction term between village latitude and longitude.

TABLE A.5A *Effect of alternative explanations on village access to new primary schools, odds ratios (Figure 5.3a and b)*

	Panel A: Electoral variables						Panel B: Civic associations		Panel C: Ethnicity			Panel D: Central gov. relations		
	2002–2009			2009–2012			2002–2009	2009–2012	2002–2009		2009–2012	2002–2009		2009–2012
	(1)	(2)	(3)	(4)	(5)	(6)	(7)	(8)	(9)	(10)	(11)	(13)	(14)	(15)
Vote Gap	0.652 (0.315)			0.939 (0.445)										
Vote Gap × Ln Population	1.015 (0.088)			1.000 (0.083)										
Logged Population	1.369*** (0.055)	1.477*** (0.145)		1.570*** (0.069)	1.579*** (0.153)									
Winning % Votes		1.119 (0.917)			0.803 (0.649)									
Winning % Votes × Ln Population		0.896 (0.131)			0.989 (0.140)									
Nationally Aligned			1.013 (0.105)			1.036 (0.111)								
# Civic Associations							0.992 (0.022)	1.036 (0.024)						
Ethnic Fractionalization									0.999 (0.003)		0.988 (0.003)			

	(1)	(2)	(3)	(4)	(5)	(6)	(7)	(8)	(9)	(10)	(11)	(12)	(13)	(14)	(15)
Wolof Dominant									0.976 (0.123)		1.136 (0.142)				1.409 (0.257)
% Change Teachers per Student/Region												0.317*** (0.098)			
Average CG Transfer ($)														0.9999** (0.000)	
Institutional Congruence 20 km	2.833*** (0.421)	2.837*** (0.422)	2.552*** (0.362)	2.148*** (0.337)	2.146*** (0.337)	2.021*** (0.309)	2.774*** (0.404)	2.019*** (0.309)	2.774*** (0.404)	2.023*** (0.309)	2.019*** (0.308)	2.776*** (0.405)	2.794*** (0.408)	2.019*** (0.309)	2.018*** (0.308)
N	13,568	13,568	14,267	13,364	13,362	14,224	14,267	14,224	14,267	14,224	14,224	14,267	14,267	14,224	14,224
Level-2	313	313	318	358	358	368	318	368	318	368	368	318	318	368	368

*** $p < 0.001$, ** $p < 0.05$. Models report odds ratios and standard errors, in parentheses, from two-tailed, mixed-level logit models. All hierarchical models include a centered mean of precolonial centralization at the local government level (level 2) as well as an interaction term between village latitude and longitude.

TABLE A.5B *Effect of alternative explanations on village access to new clinics, odds ratios (Figure 5.3c)*

	Panel A: Electoral variables			Panel B: Civic associations	Panel C: Ethnicity		Panel D: Central gov. relations
	(1)	(2)	(3)	(4)	(5)	(6)	(7)
Vote Gap	1.599 (0.903)						
Vote Gap × Ln Population	0.924 (0.093)						
Logged Population	1.239*** (0.063)	1.456** (0.178)					
Winning % Votes		8.422** (8.275)					
Winning % Votes × Ln Population		0.742 (0.132)					
Nationally Aligned			1.029 (0.186)				
# Civic Associations				1.005 (0.028)			
Ethnic Fractionalization					0.999 (0.004)		
Wolof Dominant						0.882 (0.169)	
Average CG Transfer ($)							0.999 (0.000)
Institutional Congruence 20 km	1.592** (0.263)	1.599** (0.264)	1.665** (0.271)	1.654** (0.271)	1.656** (0.271)	1.665** (0.271)	1.655** (0.271)
N	10,596	10,594	11,269	11,269	11,268	11,268	11,268
Level-2	278	278	286	286	286	286	286

*** $p < 0.001$, ** $p < 0.05$. Models report odds ratios and standard errors, in parentheses, from two-tailed, mixed-level logit models. All hierarchical models include a centered mean of precolonial centralization at the local government level (level 2) as well as an interaction term between village latitude

TABLE A.6 *Trust estimates (Figure 5.4)*

	Panel B. Nunn and Wantchenkon replication				
	Relatives	Acquaintances	Local government	Neighbors	Other Senegalese
	(1)	(2)	(3)	(4)	(5)
Slave Exports per Area	0.011 (0.017)	0.053 (0.050)	0.038 (0.077)	−0.047 (0.052)	0.013 (0.081)
Age	−0.001 (0.001)	0.001 (0.003)	−0.004 (0.004)	0.000 (0.002)	0.003 (0.004)
Age^2	0.000 (0.000)	0.000 (0.000)	0.000 (0.000)	0.000 (0.000)	−0.000 (0.000)
Gender	0.019 (0.024)	0.071 (0.066)	0.115 (0.077)	−0.043 (0.073)	−0.029 (0.113)
% Co-ethnic	0.027 (0.036)	−0.005 (0.129)	−0.146 (0.167)	0.193 (0.103)	0.206 (0.165)
Went w/o Cooking Oil	−0.006 (0.012)	−0.045 (0.027)	0.018 (0.035)	0.024 (0.026)	−0.072 (0.042)
Went w/o Cash Income	0.009 (0.009)	0.031 (0.036)	0.059 (0.042)	0.003 (0.029)	−0.037 (0.052)
Went w/o Medical	0.006 (0.012)	0.042 (0.033)	−0.037 (0.045)	0.023 (0.021)	−0.052 (0.043)
Went w/o Water	−0.002 (0.009)	0.030 (0.025)	−0.051 (0.031)	−0.024 (0.021)	0.036 (0.034)
Went w/o Enough Food	−0.001 (0.006)	−0.006 (0.028)	−0.00 (0.032)	0.001 (0.022)	0.009 (0.046)
Ethnic Fractionalization	0.000 (0.001)	−0.002 (0.004)	−0.001 (0.004)	−0.003 (0.003)	−0.000 (0.003)
Education FE	Y	Y	Y	Y	Y
Religion FE	Y	Y	Y	Y	Y
Employment FE	Y	Y	Y	Y	Y
Department FE	Y	Y	Y	Y	Y
Round FE	Y	Y	Y	Rd 5 Only	Rd 5 Only
N	1,232	1,217	1,085	585	610
R2	0.129	0.251	0.121	0.170	0.128

(continued)

Panel C. Afrobarometer data

	Relatives	Acquaintances	Local government	Neighbors	Other Senegalese
	(1)	(2)	(3)	(4)	(5)
Inst. Congruence 20 km	0.004 (0.024)	-0.185 (0.118)	-0.265 (0.262)	-0.211** (0.079)	-0.239 (0.231)
Age	-0.001 (0.001)	0.002 (0.003)	-0.003 (0.004)	0.000 (0.002)	0.002 (0.004)
Age²	0.000 (0.000)	-0.000 (0.000)	0.000 (0.000)	-0.000 (0.000)	-0.000 (0.000)
Gender	0.021 (0.024)	0.075 (0.065)	0.119 (0.077)	-0.034 (0.071)	-0.021 (0.0117)
% Co-ethnic	0.033 (0.035)	0.002 (0.124)	-0.141 (0.168)	0.163 (0.103)	0.215 (0.166)
Went w/o Cooking Oil	-0.006 (0.012)	-0.045 (0.027)	0.017 (0.036)	0.026 (0.026)	-0.070 (0.043)
Went w/o Cash Income	0.009 (0.009)	0.029 (0.036)	0.056 (0.042)	0.002 (0.029)	-0.041 (0.053)
Went w/o Medical	0.005 (0.012)	0.041 (0.033)	-0.039 (0.046)	0.025 (0.022)	-0.053 (0.043)
Went w/o Water	-0.003 (0.009)	0.030 (0.025)	-0.048 (0.031)	-0.025 (0.021)	0.038 (0.033)
Went w/o Enough Food	-0.001 (0.006)	-0.006 (0.028)	-0.004 (0.031)	0.001 (0.021)	0.008 (0.046)
Ethnic Fractionalization	0.000 (0.001)	-0.001 (0.004)	-0.000 (0.005)	0.002 (0.003)	0.002 (0.002)
Education FE	Y	Y	Y	Y	Y
Religion FE	Y	Y	Y	Y	Y
Employment FE	Y	Y	Y	Y	Y
Department FE	Y	Y	Y	Y	Y
Round FE	Y	Y	Y	Rd 5 Only	Rd 5 Only
N	1,238	1,223	1,090	587	614
R2	0.127	0.251	0.126	0.173	0.133

*** $p < 0.001$, ** $p < 0.05$. Models report results and standard errors clustered by Department, in parentheses, from OLS models.

TABLE A.7 *Effect of institutional congruence on location-allocation choices (Figure 5.6)*

	Maximize attendance				Maximize coverage	
	Schools, 2002–2009	Schools, 2009–2012	Clinics, 2009–2012	Schools, 2002–2009	Schools, 2009–2012	Clinics, 2009–2012
	(1)	(2)	(3)	(4)	(5)	(6)
Institutional Congruence 20 km	−75.53 (52.86)	−27.54 (86.57)	714.01 (599.32)	−567.45*** (110.69)	−167.27** (74.55)	−685.89** (292.06)
Ln Population (LG)	267.63** (57.82)	221.65** (84.42)	1,957.9*** (466.29)	630.08** (188.13)	306.73** (118.35)	556.71** (208.05)
Population Density (LG)	−29.66 (20.01)	165.18** (56.58)	356.05 (287.78)	−228.69** (93.11)	−134.14* (48.64)	−135.52** (40.39)
# Built Schools	5.49 (8.17)	96.29*** (20.61)		−5.63 (17.36)	24.02 (11.82)	
% Villages Schools	−392.57** (110.48)	369.13 (247.9)		−1,203.04*** (291.29)	−776.42*** (146.32)	
% Mouride	502.39** (223.01)	−26.18 (235.90)		1,872.2 (885.75)	674.31 (329.39)	
# Built Clinics			506.98** (139.86)			−3.21 (53.49)
% Villages Clinics			980.44 (2,757.59)			−2,214.51** (771.46)
N	283	318	183	283	318	183
R2	0.22	0.44	0.28	0.29	0.15	0.22

*** $p < 0.001$, ** $p < 0.05$. Models report results and standard errors, in parentheses, from OLS models. Unit of observation is the local government.

TABLE A.8 *Placebo models – effect of institutional congruence on central state allocated goods, odds ratios (Figure 5.7)*

	New high schools		Electrification		New roads	
	Base	Full	Base	Full	Base	Full
	(1)	(2)	(3)	(4)	(5)	(6)
Institutional Congruence 20 km	0.998 (0.574)	1.284 (0.884)	1.070 (0.282)	0.644 (0.191)	0.775** (0.099)	0.742 (0.115)
Ln Population	12.484*** (4.74)	11.534*** (6.379)	2.133*** (0.239)	1.804*** (0.169)	1.639*** (0.085)	1.556*** (0.074)
Population Density 5 km	0.999** (0.000)	0.999** (0.000)	1.000*** (0.000)	1.000** (0.000)	1.000 (0.000)	1.000 (0.000)
Department Wealth Measure		0.864 (0.334)		2.324*** (0.544)		1.135 (0.093)
Village Elevation		1.005 (0.022)		1.010** (0.004)		0.999 (0.003)
Ln Dist. Waterway		1.002 (0.118)		1.061 (0.093)		0.876*** (0.031)
Soil fertility		0.933 (0.073)		1.052 (0.049)		0.969 (0.016)
Ln Dist. Road		1.001 (0.306)		0.738*** (0.049)		0.705*** (0.030)
Ln Dist. Administrative Center/Market		1.211 (0.615)		0.583*** (0.072)		0.849** (0.052)
Local Government Capital		21.13*** (16.516)		16.021*** (4.052)		3.644*** (0.922)
Electric Grid within 5 km			1.984** (0.505)	1.361 (0.344)		
N	1,504	1,503	11,441	11,421	11,863	11,763
R^2	0.324	0.441	0.084	0.213	0.042	0.086

*** $p < 0.001$, ** $p < 0.05$. Models report results and standard errors clustered at the local government level, in parentheses, from OLS models. Models are limited to villages with a population of 1,000 residents or higher. Models of new high school access do not include villages with baseline access. Models for electrification and new road access do not include villages with baseline access. Full models include a village's latitude, longitude, and their interaction term.

Bibliography

PRIMARY SOURCES

Administrator Chef Commandent de Cercle de Louga. October 29, 1927. "Letter to the Gouvernor Lt. General." 11D1/846. Archives Nationales du Senegal. Dakar, Senegal.

Afrique Occidental Française (AOF). 1901. "Etude sur le cercle de Nioro Rip." 1G:283. Archives Nationales du Senegal. Dakar, Senegal.

AOF. 1903a. "Etude de pays entre Djoloff et Saloum (Thies)." 1G:296. Archives Nationales du Senegal. Dakar, Senegal.

——— 1903b. "Historique du Fouladou." 1G:295. Archives Nationales du Senegal. Dakar, Senegal.

——— 1904a. "Cercle de Matam." 1G:292. Archives Nationales du Senegal. Dakar, Senegal.

——— 1904b. "Dagana (par R. Mamatche)." 1G:291. Archives Nationales du Senegal. Dakar, Senegal.

——— 1904c. "Koalack." 1G:290. Archives Nationales du Senegal. Dakar, Senegal.

——— 1904d. "Louga (par l'administrateur Forigé)." 1G:289. Archives Nationales du Senegal. Dakar, Senegal.

——— 1904e. "Monographie du Cercle de Podor." 1G:294. Archives Nationales du Senegal. Dakar, Senegal.

——— 1904f. "Niani Ouli." 1G:293. Archives Nationales du Senegal. Dakar, Senegal.

——— 1912. "Annuaire du Senegal et Dependances." Archives Nationales du Senegal. Dakar, Senegal.

——— Misc. Years. "Annuaire du Senegal et Dependances." Archives Nationales du Senegal. Dakar, Senegal.

Chef d'Arrondissement de Goudiry. September 8, 1962. "Liste des villages retenus comme pointes de polarisation dans les Arrondissements de Goudiry et de Bala." 11D1/491. Archives Nationales du Senegal. Dakar, Senegal.

Commandent de Cercle de Sine-Saloum. August 3, 1923. "Lettre à le Gouverneur Generale." 11D1/1124. Archives Nationales du Senegal. Dakar, Senegal.

Geay, L. May 21, 1953. "Rapport à Messieurs le President et les Membres de l'Assemble Territoriale du Senegal." 11D1/952. Archives Nationales du Senegal. Dakar, Senegal.

L'Administrateur de Cercle de Thies. July 17, 1897. "Lettre à Monsieur le Gouverneur Général sur le projet d'organisation du Baol." Senegal/IV/128c. Archives Nationales d'Outre Mer. Aix-en-Provence, France.

L'Administrateur en Chef Commandant le cercle du Baol. May 14, 1924. "Lettre à le Gouveneur Lieutenant-Général du Senegal." 11D1/42. Archives Nationales du Senegal. Dakar, Senegal.

Ministere de l'Interieur. 1956. "Repetoire Des Villages du Senegal." po I(4:161). Archives Nationales du Senegal. Dakar, Senegal.

Orbessier, Lt. 1896. "Rapport sur la situation politique dans les cercles de Nioro et Sine." 1G257. Archives Nationales du Senegal. Dakar, Senegal.

Rural Community of Orkadiere. 2006. "Plan Locale de Développement." Dakar, Senegal.

Senegal, Directeur des Affaires Indigenes du. (1898). "Rapport à Monsieur le Gouverneur Général sur l'organisation du Saloum." Senegal/IV/128c. Archives Nationales d'Outre Mer. Aix-en-Provence, France.

Senegal et Dependances. 1902. "Rapport d'ensemble." 2G: 20. Archives Nationales du Senegal. Dakar, Senegal.

Service de l'Enseignement Primaire. Misc. Years. "Rapport Statistique Annuel." 2G Series. Archives Nationales du Senegal. Dakar, Senegal.

Service de Sante. Misc. Years. "Rapport Annuel." 2G Series. Archives Nationales du Senegal. Dakar, Senegal.

SECONDARY SOURCES

Acemoglu, Daron, Isais Chaves, Philip Osafo-Kwaako, and James Robinson. 2014. "Indirect Rule and State Weakness in Africa: Sierra Leone in Comparative Perspective." NBER Working Paper No. 20092.

Acemoglu, Daron, Simon Johnson, and James Robinson. 2001. "The Colonial Origins of Comparative Development." *American Economic Review* 91 (5):1369–1401.

2002. "Reversal of Fortune: Geography and Institutions in the Making of the Modern World Income Distribution." *Quarterly Journal of Economics* 117 (4):1231–1294.

Acemoglu, Daron, Tristan Reed, and James Robinson. 2014. "Chiefs." *Journal of Political Economy* 122 (2):319–368.

Acharya, Avidit, Matthew Blackwell, and Maya Sen. 2016. "The Political Legacy of American Slavery." *Journal of Politics* 78 (3):621–641.

Ajayi, J. F. Ade. 1998. *General History of Africa: VI Africa in the 19th c. until the 1880s*. Paris, France: UNESCO.

Akerlof, George. 1997. "Social Distance and Social Decisions." *Econometrica* 65 (5):1005–1027.

Akerlof, George, and Rachel Kranton. 2000. "Economics and Identity." *Quarterly Journal of Economics* 115 (3):715–753.

Akyeampong, Emmanuel, Robert Bates, Nathan Nunn, and James Robinson. 2014. *Africa's Development in Historical Perspective*. New York, NY: Cambridge University Press.

Alesina, Alberto, Reza Baqir, and William Easterly. 1999. "Public Goods and Ethnic Divisions." *Quarterly Journal of Economics* 114 (4):1243–1284.
Alesina, Alberto, William Easterly, and Janina Matuszeski. 2011. "Artificial States." *Journal of the European Economic Association* 9 (2):246–277.
Alesina, Alberto, and Paola Guiliano. 2015. "Culture and Institutions." *Journal of Economic Literature* 53 (4):898–944.
Alvergne, Christel, and Daniel Latouche. 2010. "Decentralization in Africa." *Canadian Journal of Development Studies* 29 (3–4):465–481.
Anath Pur, Kripa. 2007. "Rivalry or Synergy? Formal and Informal Local Governance in Rural India." *Development and Change* 38 (3):401–421.
Angrist, Joshua, and Jörn-Steffen Pischke. 2010. "The Credibility Revolution in Empirical Economics: How Better Research Design Is Taking the Con out of Econometrics." *Journal of Economic Perspectives* 24 (2):3–30.
Apicella, Coren, Frank Marlowe, James Fowler, and Nicholas Christakis. 2012. "Social Networks and Cooperation in Hunter-Gatherers." *Nature* 481 (7382):497–502.
Appadurai, Arjun. 1981. "The Past as a Scarce Resource." *Man* 16 (2):201–219.
Arcand, Jean-Louis, and Léandre Bassole. 2007. "Does Community Driven Development Work? Evidence from Senegal." Working Paper. CERDI-CNRS. Available at: https://papers.ssrn.com/sol3/papers.cfm?abstract_id=1265231
Aubert, A. 1923. "Légendes historiques et traditions orales recueillies dans la Haute-Gambie." *Bulletin du Comité d'Études Historiques et Scientifiques de l'Afrique Occidentale Française* 6:384–428.
Austin, Gareth. 2008. "The 'Reversal of Fortune' Thesis and the Compression of History." *Journal of International Development* 20 (8):996–1027.
Axelrod, Robert. 1986. "An Evolutionary Approach to Norms." *American Political Science Review* 80 (4):1095–1111.
  2006. *The Evolution of Cooperation*. New York, NY: Basic Books.
Ayee, Joseph. 2012. "The Political Economy of the Creation of Districts in Ghana." *Journal of Asian and African Studies* 48 (5):623–645.
Azam, Jean-Paul. 2001. "The Redistributive State and Conflicts in Africa." *Journal of Peace Research* 38 (4):429–444.
Azarya, Victor, and Naomi Chazan. 1987. "Disengagement from the State in Africa: Reflections on the Experience of Ghana and Guinea." *Comparative Studies in Society and History* 29 (1):106–131.
Ba, Oumar. 1976. *La Pénétration française au Cayor*. Dakar, Sénégal: Published by the author.
Balans, J.-L. 1975. "Autonomie et modernisation chez les niominka." In *Autonomie locale et intégration Nationale au Sénégal*, edited by J. L. Balans, C. Coulons and J-M Gastellu. Paris, France: Pedone.
Baldwin, Kate. 2013. "Why vote with the chief? Political connections and public goods provision in Zambia." *American Journal of Political Science* 57 (4):794–809.
  2015. *The Paradox of Traditional Chiefs in Democratic Africa*. New York, NY: Cambridge University Press.
Baldwin, Kate, and John Huber. 2010. "Economic versus Cultural Differences: Forms of Ethnic Diversity and Public Goods Provision." *American Political Science Review* 104 (4):644–662.
Baldwin, Kate, and Pia Raffler. 2019. "Traditional Leaders, Service Delivery, and Electoral Accountability." In *Decentralized Governance and Accountability*, edited by Jonathan Rodden and Erik Wibbels. New York, NY: Cambridge University Press.

Ball, Sheryl, and Catherine Eckel. 1998. "The Economic Value of Status." *The Journal of Socio-Economics* 27 (4):495–514.
Ballantyne, Tony. 2010. "The Changing Shape of the Modern British Empire and Its Historiography." *The Historical Journal* 53 (2):429–452.
Bandyopadhyay, Sanghamitra, and Elliott Green. 2016. "Precolonial Political Centralization and Contemporary Development in Uganda." *Economic Development and Cultural Change* 64 (3):471–508.
Bardhan, Pranab. 2002. "Decentralization of Governance and Development." *Journal of Economic Perspectives* 16 (4):185–205.
Bardhan, Pranab, and Dilip Mookherjee. 2006. *Decentralization and Local Governance in Developing Countries*. Cambridge, MA: MIT Press.
Barkan, Joel, Michael McNulty, and MAO Ayeni. 1991. "'Hometown' Voluntary Associations, Local Development, and the Emergence of Civil Society in Western Nigeria." *Journal of Modern African Studies* 29 (3):457–480.
Barkey, Karen. 2008. *Empire of Difference: The Ottomans in Comparative Perspective*. New York, NY: Cambridge University Press.
Barry, Boubacar. 1985. *Le royaume du Waalo: Le Sénégal avant la conquête*. Paris, France: Karthala.
Barry, Sidi, and Sten Hagberg. 2019. "Le tsunami électoral d'Arba Diallo: ethnographie des élections couplées de 2012 à Dori, Burkina Faso." In *Démocratie par le bas et politique municipale au Sahel*, edited by Sten Hagberg, Ludovic Kibora, and Gabriella Korling. Uppsala, Sweden: Uppsala Universitet.
Bates, Robert. 1981. *Markets and States in Tropical Africa*. Berkeley, CA: University of California Press.
　1983. *Essays on the Political Economy of Rural Africa*. Berkeley, CA: University of California Press.
Bathily, Abdoulaye. 1989. *Les Portes de l'or: le royaume de Galam, Sénégal, de l'ère musulmane au temps des négriers, VIIIe-XVIIIe siècle*. Paris, France: L'Harmattan.
Bayart, Jean-François. 1993. *The State in Africa: The Politics of the Belly*. London, UK: Longman.
Bayart, Jean-Francois, Peter Geschiere, and Francois Nyamnjoh. 2001. "Autochtonie, démocratie et citoyenneté en Afrique." *Critique Internationale* 1 (10):194.
Beattie, J. H. M. 1959. "Checks on the Abuse of Political Power in some African States: A Preliminary Framework for Analysis." *Sociologus* 9 (2):97–115.
Beck, Linda. 2001. "Reining in the Marabouts? Democratization and Local Governance in Senegal." *African Affairs* 100 (401):601–621.
　2008. *Brokering Democracy in Africa: The Rise of Clientelist Democracy in Senegal*. New York, NY: Palgrave Macmillan.
Becker, Charles. 1983. *Les Premiers Recensements au Senegal et l'evolution démographique*. Dakar, Senegal: Orstrom.
　2007. "Les *Divisions* administratives du Sénégal, 1887–1960." In *L'Administration d'hier à demain en Afrique Francophone*, edited by Mamadou Badji and Olvier Devaux. Dakar-Toulouse, France: Presses de l'université des sciences sociales de Toulouse.
Becker, Charles, Mohamed Mbodj, and M. I. Sarr. 1999. "Les Sereer et la population du Sénégal." In *Paysans sereer: dynamiques agraires et mobilitiés au Senegal*, edited by Andre Lericollais. Paris, France: Editions d'IRD.

Becker, Sascha, Katrin Boeckh, Christa Hainz, and Ludger Woessmann. 2014. "The Empire Is Dead, Long Live the Empire! Long-Run Persistence of Trust and Corruption in the Bureaucracy." *The Economic Journal* 126 (590):40–74.

Bell, Andrew, and Kelvyn Jones. 2015. "Explaining Fixed Effects: Random Effects Modeling of Time-Series Cross-Sectional and Panel Data." *Political Science Research and Methods* 3 (01):133–153.

Berger, Daniel. 2009. "Taxes, institutions and local governance: Evidence from a natural experiment in colonial Nigeria." Unpublished Manuscript. Available at: www.researchgate.net/profile/Daniel-Berger-10/publication/255606155_Taxes_Institutions_and_Local_Governance_Evidence_from_a_Natural_Experiment_in_Colonial_Nigeria/links/55350e4c0cf283a8f60c8eb8/Taxes-Institutions-and-Local-Governance-Evidence-from-a-Natural-Experiment-in-Colonial-Nigeria.pdf

Béridogo, Bréhima. 1998. "Compétition des acteurs sociaux pour le contrôle du pouvoir et des ressources dans la commune rurale de Zégoua (Mali)." *Bulletin de l'APAD* 16: 1–13.

Berman, Sheri. 2001. "Ideas, Norms, and Culture in Political Analysis." *Comparative Politics* 33 (2):231–250.

Berry, Sara. 1985. *Fathers Work for Their Sons*. Berkeley, CA: University of California Press.

Besley, Timothy, and Maitreesh Ghatak. 2008. "Status Incentives." *American Economic Review* 98 (2):206–211.

Bicchieri, Cristina. 2006. *The Grammar of Society: The Nature and Dynamics of Social Norms*. New York, NY: Cambridge University Press.

Bierschenk, Thomas. 2010. "States at Work in West Africa: Sedimentation, Fragmentation and Normative Double-Binds." Institut für Ethnologie und Afrikastudien, Johannes Gutenberg-Universität, Working Papers Nr. 113.

Bierschenk, Thomas, and Jean-Pierre Olivier de Sardan. 2003. "Powers in the Village: Rural Benin between Democratisation and Decentralisation." *Africa* 72 (3):145–173.

Blasnik, Michael. 2010. RECLINK: Stata module to probabilistically match records. Working Paper. Available at: https://ideas.repec.org/c/boc/bocode/s456876.html.

Blundo, Giorgio. 1998a. "Décentralisation et pouvoir locaux. Registres traditionnels du pouvoir et nouvelles formes locales de légitimité." *Bulletin de l'APAD* 16: 1–4.

1998b. "Élus locaux, associations paysannes et courtiers du développement au Sénégal." PhD, Sociology and Anthropology, University of Lausanne.

Bockstette, Valerie, Areendam Chanda, and Louis Putterman. 2002. "States and Markets: The Advantage of an Early Start." *Journal of Economic Growth* 7 (4):347–369.

Boone, Catherine. 1992. *Merchant Capital and the Roots of State Power in Senegal, 1930–1985*. New York, NY: Cambridge University Press.

2003a. "Decentralization as Political Strategy in West Africa." *Comparative Political Studies* 36 (4):25.

2003b. *Political Topographies of the African State*. New York, NY: Cambridge University Press.

2014. *Property Rights and Political Order in Africa*. New York, NY: Cambridge University Press.

Bouquet, Christian, and Irene Kassi-Djodjo. 2014. "Les Élections locales 2013 en Côte d'Ivoire." *Echo-Géo* 1–11. Available at: http://journals.openedition.org/echogeo/13697

Branch, Jordan. 2014. *The Cartographic State: Maps, Territory and the Origins of Sovereignty*. New York, NY: Cambridge University Press.
Bratton, Michael. 2012. "Citizen Perceptions of Local Government Responsiveness in Sub-Saharan Africa." *World Development* 40 (3):516–527.
Bratton, Michael, Massa Coulibaly, and Fabiana Machado. 2000. *Popular Perceptions of Good Governance in Mali*. Cape Town, South Africa: IDASA POS.
Breuer, Anita, Laura Blomenkemper, Stefan Kliesch, Franziska Salzer, Manuel Schädler, Valentin Schweinfurth, and Stephen Virchow. 2017. "Decentralisation in Togo: The Contribution of ICT-Based Participatory Development Approaches to Strengthening Local Governance." Bonn, Germany: German Development Institute. Discussion Paper No. 6/2017 (6/2017).
Brewer, Marilynn. 1979. "In-Group Bias in the Minimal Group Situation." *Psychological Bulletin* 86 (2):307–324.
Briggs, Ryan. 2014. "Aiding and Abetting: Project Aid and Ethnic Politics in Kenya." *World Development* 64:194–205.
Brosio, Giorgio. 2000. *Decentralization in Africa*. Washington, DC: International Monetary Fund.
Bruhn, Miriam, and Francisco Gallego. 2012. "Good, Bad and Ugly Colonial Activities: Do They Matter for Economic Development?" *The Review of Economics and Statistics* 94 (2):433–461.
Burgess, Robin, Remi Jedwab, Edward Miguel, Ameet Morjaria, and Gerard Padró I Miquel. 2015. "The Value of Democracy: Evidence from Road Building in Kenya." *American Economic Review* 105 (6):1817–1851.
Carlitz, Ruth. 2017. "Money Flows, Water Trickles: Understanding Patterns of Decentralized Water Provision in Tanzania." *World Development* 93:16–30.
Chabal, Patrick, and Jean-Pascal. Daloz. 1999. *Africa Works: Disorder as Political Instrument*. Bloomington, IN: Indiana University Press.
Chafer, Tony. 2001. "French African Policy in Historical Perspective." *Journal of Contemporary African Studies* 19 (2):165–182.
Chanock, Martin. 1991. "A Peculiar Sharpness: An Essay on Property in the History of Customary Law in Colonial Africa." *Journal of African History* 32 (1):65–88.
Cheema, G Shabbir, and Dennis Rondinelli. 2007. *Decentralizing Governance: Emerging Concepts and Practices*. Washington, DC: Brookings Institute.
Chen, Yan, and Sherry Xin Li. 2009. "Group Identity and Social Preferences." *American Economic Review* 99 (1):431–457.
Clark, Andrew. 1996. "The Fulbe of Bundu (Senegambia)." *The International Journal of African Historical Studies* 29 (1):1–23.
  1999. "Imperialism, independence, and Islam in Senegal and Mali." *Africa Today* 46:149.
Clark, Andrew, and Lucie Phillips. 1994. *Historical Dictionary of Senegal*. 2nd ed. Metuchen, NJ: Scarecrow Press.
Clayton, Amanda, Jennifer Noveck, and Margaret Levi. 2015. "When Elites Meet: Decentralization, Power-Sharing, and Public Goods Provision in Post-Conflict Sierra Leone." Policy Research Working Papers. Washington, DC: The World Bank.
CNAM-SERESA. 1960. *Rapport général sur les perspectives de développement du Sénégal*. Dakar, Senegal: CNAM-SERESA.

Cohen, William. 1971. *Rulers of Empire: The French Colonial Service in Africa.* Stanford, CA: Hoover Institution Press.

Coleman, James. 1988. "Social Capital in the Creation of Human Capital." *American Journal of Sociology* 94:S95–S120.

1990a. "The Emergence of Norms." In *Social Institutions: Their Emergence, Maintenance and Effects*, edited by Michael Hechter, Karl-Dieter Opp, and Reinhard Wippler. Hawthorne, NY: Aldine de Gruyter.

1990b. *Foundations of Social Theory.* New York, NY: Cambridge University Press.

Colin, Roland. 1980. *Systèmes d'éducation et mutations sociales: continuité et discontinuité dans les dynamiques socio-éducatives: le cas du Sénégal.* Lille, France: Atelier Reproduction des thèses, Université de Lille III.

Coll, Jérome. 1997. "Des Dynamiques villageoises au service d'une 'démocratie décentralisée'. Le Cas de Mali-Sud." *Bulletin de l'APAD* 14: 1–24.

Collins, Kathleen. 2004. "The Logic of Clan Politics: Evidence from the Central Asian Trajectories." *World Politics* 56 (2):224–261.

2006. *Clan Politics and Regime Transition in Central Asia.* New York, NY: Cambridge University Press.

Colombi, Olivier. 1991. *Mémoires coloniales: La fin de l'empire français d'Afrique vue par les administrateurs coloniaux.* Paris, France: Editions La Découverte.

Colson, Elizabeth. 1969. "African Society at the Time of the Scramble." In *Colonialism in Africa, 1870–1960*, edited by Lewis Gann and Peter Duignan. New York, NY: Cambridge University Press.

Connerton, Paul. 1989. *How Societies Remember.* New York, NY: Cambridge University Press.

Cooper, Frederick. 1994. "Conflict and Connection: Rethinking Colonial African History." *American Historical Review* 99 (5):1516–1545.

2005. *Colonialism in Question: Theory, Knowledge, History.* Berkeley, CA: University of California, Berkeley.

Cornell, Stephen, and Joseph Kalt. 1995. "Where Does Economic Development Really Come From?" *Economic Inquiry* 33 (3):402–426.

2000. "Where's the Glue? Institutional and Cultural Foundations of American Indian Economic Development." *Journal of Socio-Economcis* 29:443–470.

Cowen, Tyler, and Daniel Sutter. 1997. "Politics and the Pursuit of Fame." *Public Choice* 93 (1):19–35.

Cox, Gary, and Mathew McCubbins. 1986. "Electoral Politics as a Redistributive Game." *Journal of Politics* 48 (2):370–389.

Cramer Walsh, Katherine. 2003. *Talking about Politics: Informal Groups and Social Identity in American Politics.* Chicago, IL: University of Chicago Press.

Crook, Richard. 2003. "Decentralisation and Poverty Reduction in Africa." *Public Administration and Development* 23 (1):77–88.

Crook, Richard, and James Manor. 1998. *Democracy and Decentralisation in South Asia and West Africa.* New York, NY: Cambridge University Press.

Crowder, Michael. 1964. "Indirect Rule – French and British Style." *Africa* 34 (3):197–205.

1968. *West Africa under Colonial Rule.* London, UK: Hutchinson.

Cruise O'Brien, Donal. 1971. *The Mourides of Senegal: The Political and Economic Organization of an Islamic Brotherhood.* Oxford, UK: Clarendon Press.

1975. *Saints and Politicians: Essays in the Organisation of a Senegalese Peasant Society*. New York, NY: Cambridge University Press.
Cruz, Cesi, and Christina Schneider. 2017. "Foreign Aid and Undeserved Credit Claiming." *American Journal of Political Science* 61 (2):396–408.
Curtin, Philip. 1975. *Economic Change in Precolonial Africa*. Madison, WI: University of Wisconsin Press.
Darbon, Dominique. 1988. *L'Administration et le paysan en Casamance*. Paris, France: A. Pedone.
Dasgupta, Aniruddha, and Victoria Beard. 2007. "Community Driven Development, Collective Action and Elite Capture in Indonesia." *Development & Change* 38 (2):229–249.
Dasgupta, Partha. 1988. "Trust as a Commodity." In *Trust: Making and Breaking Cooperative Relations*, edited by Diego Gambetta. Oxford, UK: Oxford University Press.
David, Philippe. 1980. *Les Navétanes*. Dakar, Senegal: Nouvelles Editions Africaines.
De Bénoist, Joseph-Roger. 1982. *L'Afrique Occidentale Française de 1944 à 1960*. Dakar, Senegal: Nouvelles Éditions Africaines.
De Juan, Alexander, and Carlo Koos. 2019. "The Historical Roots of Cooperative Behavior – Evidence from Eastern Congo." *World Development* 116:100–112.
De Juan, Alexander, and Jan Pierskalla. 2017. "The Comparative Politics of Colonialism and Its Legacies." *Politics & Society* 45 (2):159–172.
de Kadt, Daniel, and Horacio Larreguy. 2018. "Agents of the Regime? Traditional Leaders and Electoral Behavior in South Africa." *Journal of Politics* 80 (2):382–399.
Delavignette, Robert. 1947. *Service Africain*. Paris, France: Gallimard.
Dell, Melissa. 2010. "The Persistent Effects of Peru's Mining Mita." *Econometrica* 78 (6):1863–1903.
Dell, Melissa, Nathan Lane, and Pablo Querubin. 2018. "The Historical State, Local Collective Action, and Economic Development in Vietnam." *Econometrica* 86 (6):2083–2121.
Dickovick, J. Tyler. 2011. *Decentralization and Recentralization in the Developing World: Comparative Studies from Africa and Latin America*. University Park, PA: The Pennsylvania State University Press.
Dionne, Kim Yi. 2015. "Social Networks, Ethnic Diversity and Cooperative Behavior in Rural Malawi." *Journal of Theoretical Politics* 27 (4):522–543.
Diop, Djibril. 2006a. *Décentralisation et gouvernance locale au Sénégal*. Paris, France: L'Harmattan.
Diop, Momar Coumba. 1993. *Senegal: Essays in Statecraft*. Dakar, Senegal: CODESRIA.
 2006b. "Le Sénégal à la croisée des chemins." *Politique africaine* 4 (104):103–126.
Diouf, Makhtar. 1994. *Sénégal: les ethnies et la nation*. Paris, France: L'Harmattan.
Diouf, Mamadou. 1990. *Le Kajoor au XIXe siècle: pouvoir ceddo et conquête coloniale*. Paris, France: Karthala.
 1993. "Beyond Patronage and 'Technocracy'." In *Senegal: Essays in Statecraft*, edited by M. C. Diop. Dakar, Senegal: CODESRIA.
 1998. "The French Colonial Policy of Assimilation and the Civility of the Originaires of the Four Communes (Senegal): A Nineteenth Century Globalization Project." *Development and Change* 29 (4):671–696.

Dippel, Christian. 2014. "Forced Coexistence and Economic Development." *Econometrica* 82 (6):2131–2165.
Djire, Moussa. 2004. "The Myths and Realities of Local Governance in Sanankoroba, Mali." International Institute for Environment and Development. Issue Paper No. 130. IIED Drylands Programme, London, UK.
Doquet, Anne. 2006. "Décentralisation et reformulation des traditions en pays Dogon." In *Décentralistion et pouvoirs en Afrique*, edited by Claude Fay, Yaouaga Félix Koné, and Catherine Quiminal. Paris, France: Institut de Recherche pour le Développement.
Duke Bryant, Kelly. 2015. *Education as Politics: Colonial Schooling and Political Debate in Senegal, 1850s–1914*. Madison, WI: University of Wisconsin Press.
Dunning, Thad, and Lauren Harrison. 2010. "Cross-cutting Cleavages and Ethnic Voting: An Experimental Study of Cousinage in Mali." *American Political Science Review* 104 (1):21–39.
Easterly, William, and Ross Levine. 1997. "Africa's Growth Tragedy: Policies and Ethnic Divisions." *Quarterly Journal of Economics* 112 (4):1203–1250.
Ece, Melis. 2009. "Report: Access to Land at the Northern Periphery of Niokolo-Koba National Park, Senegal." *Dialectical Anthropology* 32 (4):353–382.
Eckstein, Harry. 1966. *Division and Cohesion in Democracy*. Princeton, NJ: Princeton University Press.
  1997. "Congruence Theory Explained." University of California, Irvine. Unpublished Work. Irvine, CA. https://escholarship.org/uc/item/2wb616g6
Economic Commission for Africa. 2007. Relevance of African Traditional Institutions of Governance. Addis Abbaba, Ethiopia: ECA.
Ejdemyr, Simon, Eric Kramon, and Amanda Robinson. 2017. "Segregation, Ethnic Favoritism, and the Strategic Targeting of Local Public Goods." *Comparative Political Studies* 51 (9):1111–1143.
Ellickson, Robert. 1991. *Order Without Law: How Neighbors Settle Disputes*. Cambridge, MA: Harvard University Press.
Ellis, Stephen, and Gerrie ter Haar. 1998. "Religion and Politics in Sub-Saharan Africa." *Journal of Modern African Studies* 36 (2):175–201.
Elster, Jon. 1989. *The Cement of Society: A Study of Social Order*. New York, NY: Cambridge University Press.
Englebert, Pierre. 2002a. "Born-Again Buganda or the Limits of Traditional Resurgence in Africa." *Journal of Modern African Studies* 40 (3):345–368.
  2002b. *State Legitimacy and Development in Africa*. Boulder, CO: Lynne Rienner.
Englebert, Pierre, and Nestorine Sangaré. 2014. "Burkina Faso: Limited Decentralization under Tight Oversight." In *Decentralization in Africa: The Paradox of State Strength*, edited by J. Tyler Dickovick and James Wunsch. Boulder, CO: Lynne Rienner.
Erk, Jan. 2014. "Federalism and Decentralization in Sub-Saharan Africa." *Regional & Federal Studies* 24 (5):535–552.
Fage, J. D. 1969. "Slavery and the Slave Trade in the Context of West African History." *Journal of African History* 10:393–404.
Fanchette, Sylvie. 1999. "Migrations, intégration spatiale et formation d'une société peule dans le Fouladou (Haute Casamance, Sénégal)." In *Figures peules*, edited by R. Botte, Jean Boutrais, and Jean Schmitz. Paris, France: Karthala.

2011. *Au Pays des Peuls de Haute-Casamance: l'intégration territoriale en question.* Paris, France: Karthala.

Fay, Claude. 2000. "La Décentralisation dans un Cercle (Tenenkou, Mali)." *Autrepart* 14 (3):121–142.

Faye, Valy. 2016. *Économie arachidière et dynamiques du peuplement au Sénégal : Kaffrine et le Saloum Oriental de 1891 à 1960.* Paris, France: Karthala.

Foa, Roberto. 2017. "Persistence or Reversal of Fortune? Early State Inheritance and the Legacies of Colonial Rule." *Politics and Society* 45 (2):301–324.

Foley, Ellen. 2010. *Your Pocket Is What Cures You: The Politics of Health in Senegal.* New Brunswick, NJ: Rutgers University Press.

Fombad, Charles. 2018. "Constitutional Entrenchment of Decentralization in Africa." *Journal of African Law* 62 (2):175–199.

Fortes, Meyer, and E. E. Evans-Pritchard. 1940. *African Political Systems.* London, UK: International Institute of African Languages & Cultures.

Foster, Elizabeth. 2013. *Faith in Empire: Religion, Politics, and Colonial Rule in French Senegal, 1880–1940.* Stanford, CA: Stanford University Press.

Fowler, James, and Cindy Kam. 2007. "Beyond the Self: Social Identity, Altruism, and Political Participation." *Journal of Politics* 69 (3):813–827.

Franck, Raphael, and Ilia Rainer. 2012. "Does the Leader's Ethnicity Matter?" *American Political Science Review* 106 (2):294–325.

Frank, Robert. 1985. *Choosing the Right Pond: Human Behavior and the Quest for Status.* Oxford, UK: Oxford University Press.

Frankema, Ewout. 2012. "The Origins of Formal Education in sub-Saharan Africa: Was British Rule More Benign?" *European Review of Economic History* 16 (4):335–355.

Gallego, Francisco, and Robert Woodberry. 2010. "Christian Missionaries and Education in Former African Colonies: How Competition Mattered." *Journal of African Economies* 19 (3):294–329.

Galvan, Dennis. 2001. "Francophone Africa in Flux: Political Turnover and Social Change in Senegal." *Journal of Democracy* 12:51–62.

2004. *The State Must Be Our Master of Fire.* Berkeley, CA: University of California Press.

Gardiniere, David. 1985. "The French Impact on Education in Africa, 1817–1960." In *Double Impact: France and Africa in the Age of Imperialism*, edited by G. Wesley Johnson. Westport, CT: Greenwood Press.

Garenne, Michael, and Jerome Lombard. 1991. "La Migration dirigée des Sereer vers les Terres neuves (Sénégal)." In *Migration, changements sociaux et développement*, edited by André Quesnel and Patrice Vimard. Paris, France: ORSTROM.

Gellar, Sheldon. 2005. *Democracy in Senegal: Tocquevillian Analytics in Africa.* New York, NY: Palgrave Macmillan.

Gellar, Sheldon, Robert Charlick, and Yvonne Jones. 1980. *Animation Rurale and Rural Development.* Ithaca, NY: Rural Development Committee Center for International Studies.

Gelman, Andrew, and Jennifer Hill. 2008. *Data Analysis Using Regression and Multilevel/Hierarchical Models.* New York, NY: Cambridge University Press.

Gennaioli, Nicola, and Ilia Rainer. 2007. "The Modern Impact of Precolonial Centralization in Africa." *Journal of Economic Growth* 12 (3):185–234.

Geschiere, Peter. 2009. *The Perils of Belonging: Autochthony, Citizenship, and Exclusion in Africa and Europe.* Chicago, IL: University of Chicago Press.

Getz, Trevor. 2004. *Slavery and Reform in West Africa*. Athens, OH: Ohio University Press.

Girard, Jean. 1964. "Note sur l'histoire locale du fouladou." *Journal de la Société des Africanistes* 34 (2):302–306.

Giraudy, Agustina, Eduardo Moncada, and Richard Snyder. 2019. "Subnational Research in Comparative Politics." In *Inside Countries: Subnational Research in Comparative Politics*, edited by Agustina Giraudy, Eduardo Moncada, and Richard Snyder. New York, NY: Cambridge University Press.

Gisselquist, Rachel. 2014. "Ethnic Divisions and Public Goods Provision, Revisited." *Ethnic and Racial Studies* 37 (9):1605–1627.

Glaeser, Edward, David Laibson, Jose Scheinkman, and Christine Soutter. 2000. "Measuring Trust." *Quarterly Journal of Economics* 115 (3):811–846.

Goette, Lorenz, David Huffman, and Stephan Meier. 2006. "The Impact of Group Membership on Cooperation and Norm Enforcement." IZA. Discussion Paper No. 2020. Bonn, Germany.

Golden, Miriam, and Brian Min. 2013. "Distributive Politics around the World." *Annual Review of Political Science* 16:73–99.

Goldstein, Judith, and Robert Keohane. 1993. "Ideas and Foreign Policy: An Analytical Framework." In *Ideas and Foreign Policy: Beliefs, Institutions and Political Change*, edited by Judith Goldstein and Robert Keohane. Ithaca, NY: Cornell University Press.

Gomez, Michael. 1992. *Pragmatism in the Age of Jihad: The Precolonial State of Bundu*. New York, NY: Cambridge University Press.

Goode, William. 1978. *The Celebration of Heroes: Prestige as a Social Control System*. Berkeley, CA: University of California Press.

Gottlieb, Jessica. 2015. "The Logic of Party Collusion in a Democracy: Evidence from Mali." *World Politics* 67 (1):1–36.

 2017. "Explaining Variation in Broker Strategies: A Lab-in-the-Field Experiment in Senegal." *Comparative Political Science* 50 (11):1556–1592.

Gould, Roger. 1991. "Multiple Networks and Mobilization in the Paris Commune, 1871." *American Sociological Review* 56 (6):716–729.

 1995. *Insurgent Identities: Class, Community, and Protest in Paris from 1848 to the Commune*. Chicago, IL: University of Chicago Press.

Granovetter, Mark. 1985. "Economic Action and Social Structure." *American Journal of Sociology* 91 (3):481–510.

Greif, Avner. 2006. *Institutions and the Path to the Modern Economy: Lessons from Medieval Trade*. New York, NY: Cambridge University Press.

Grossman, Guy, and Delia Baldassarri. 2012. "The Impact of Elections on Cooperation." *American Journal of Political Science* 56 (4):964–985.

Grzymala-Busse, Anna. 2011. "Time Will Tell? Temporality and the Analysis of Causal Mechanisms and Processes." *Comparative Political Studies* 44 (9):1267–1297.

Habyarimana, James, Macartan Humphreys, Daniel Posner, and Jeremy Weinstein. 2007. "Why Does Ethnic Diversity Undermine Public Goods Provision?" *American Political Science Review* 101 (4):709–725.

Hagberg, Sten. 2001. *Poverty in Burkina Faso: Representations and Realities*. Uppsala, Sweden: Uppsala University.

 2010. "Decentralisation and Citizen Participation in West Africa." *Bulletin de l'APAD* 31–32.

2019. "Introduction: Démocratie par le bas et politique municipale au Sahel." In *Démocratie par le bas et politique municipale au Sahel*, edited by Sten Hagberg, Ludovic Kibora, and Gabriella Korling. Uppsala, Sweden: Uppsala Universitet.

Hahonou, Eric Komlavi. 2002. "La Chefferie coutumière face au projet de décentralisation dans une localité de l'Ouest nigérien." *Bulletin de l'APAD* 23–24.

Hall, Peter, and Michele Lamont. 2013. "Why Social Relations Matter for Politics and Successful Societies." *Annual Review of Political Science* 16:49–71.

Hardin, Russell. 2002. *Trust and Trustworthiness*. New York, NY: Russell Sage Foundation.

Harding, Robin. 2015. "Attribution and Accountability: Voting for Roads in Ghana." *World Politics* 67 (4):656–689.

Harding, Robin, and David Stasavage. 2013. "What Democracy Does (and Doesn't Do) for Basic Services: School Fees, School Inputs, and African Elections." *Journal of Politics* 66 (1):229–245.

Hariri, Jacob Gerner. 2012. "The Autocratic Legacy of Early Statehood." *American Political Science Review* 106 (03):471–494.

Harrison, Christopher. 1988. *France and Islam in West Africa, 1860–1960*. New York, NY: Cambridge University Press.

Hawkes, Kristen, Jon Altman, Stephen Beckerman et al.. 1993. "Why Hunter-Gatherers Work: An Ancient Version of the Problem of Public Goods." *Current Anthropology* 34 (4):341–361.

Hawthorne, Walter. 2013. "States and Statelessness." In *The Oxford Handbook of Modern African History*, edited by John Parker and Richard Reid. Oxford, UK: Oxford University Press.

He, Quqiong, Ying Pan, and Sudipta Sarangi. 2017. "Lineage-Based Heterogeneity and Coopreative Behavior in Rural China." MPRE. Working Paper No. 80865. Munich. https://mpra.ub.uni-muenchen.de/80865/

Hechter, Michael. 1990. "The Emergence of Cooperative Social Institutions." In *Social Institutions: Their Emergence, Maintenance and Effects*, edited by Michael Hechter, Karl-Dieter Opp, and Reinhard Wippler. Hawthorne, NY: Aldine de Gruyter.

Heffetz, Ori, and Robert Frank. 2010. "Preferences for Status: Evidence and Economic Implications." In *Handbook of Social Economics*, edited by Jess Benhabib, Alberto Bisin and Matthew Jackson. Amsterdam, The Netherlands: Elsevier.

Hengl, T., J. Mendes de Jesus, G. B. M. Heuvelink, M. Ruperez Gonzalez, M. Kilibarda, and A. Blagotić. 2017. "SoilGrids250m: Global Gridded Soil Information Based on Machine Learning." *PLoS ONE* 12 (2): 1–40.

Herbst, Jeffrey. 2000. *States and Power in Africa: Comparative Lessons in Authority and Control*. Princeton, NJ: Princeton University Press.

Hesseling, Gerti. 1985. *Histoire politique du Sénégal: institutions, droit et société*. Paris, France: Karthala.

Hetland, Oivind. 2008. "Decentralisation and Territorial Reorganization in Mali: Power and the Institutionalisation of Local Politics." *Norwegian Journal of Geography* 62 (1):23–35.

Hicken, Allen. 2011. "Clientelism." *Annual Review of Political Science* 14:289–310.

Hilgers, Mathieu. 2011. "Autochthony as Capital in a Global Age." *Theory, Culture & Society* 28 (1):34–54.

Hjort, Jonas. 2010. "Pre-colonial Culture, Post-colonial Economic Success?" *Economic History Review* 63 (3):688.
Holzinger, Katharina, Florian Kern, and Daniela Kromrey. 2016. "The Dualism of Contemporary Traditional Governance and the State." *Political Research Quarterly* 69 (3):469–481.
Honig, Lauren. 2017. "Land, state-building, and political authority in Africa." PhD, Political Science, Cornell University.
Hopkins, A. G. 2009. "The New Economic History of Africa." *Journal of African History* 50 (2):155–177.
  2011. "Causes and Confusions in African History." *Economic History of Developing Regions* 26 (2):107–110.
Horne, Christine. 2001. "Sociological Perspectives on the Emergence of Social Norms." In *Social Norms*, edited by Michael Hechter and Karl-Dieter Opp. New York, NY: Russell Sage Foundation.
Hubbell, Andrew. 2001. "A View of the Slave Trade from the Margin." *Journal of African History* 42 (1):25–47.
Huberman, Bernardo, Christoph Loch, and Ayse Önçüler. 2004. "Status as a Valued Resource." *Social Psychology Quarterly* 67 (1):103–114.
Huillery, Elise. 2009. "History Matters: The Long-Term Impact of Colonial Public Investments in French West Africa." *American Economic Journal* 1 (2):176–215.
Hur, Aram. 2018. "Citizen Duty and the Ethical Power of Communities: Mixed-Method Evidence from East Asia." *British Journal of Political Science* 50 (3):1047–1065.
Hyden, Goran. 1980. *Beyond Ujamaa in Tanzania: Underdevelopment and an Uncaptured Peasantry*. Berkeley, CA: University of California Press.
  2006. *African Politics in Comparative Perspective*. New York, NY: Cambridge University Press.
Idelman, Eric. 2009. "Decentralisation and Boundary Setting in Mali: The Case of Kita District." IIED. Drylands Issue Paper 151. London, UK. http://pubs.iied.org/pdfs/12558IIED.pdf
Idowu, H. O. 1968. "The Establishment of Protecorate Administration in Senegal, 1890–1904." *Historical Society of Nigeria* 4 (2):247–267.
Inglehart, Ronald. 1990. *Culture Shift*. Princeton, NJ: Princeton University Press.
Innes, Gordan. 1976. *Kaabu and Fuladu: Historical Narratives of the Gambian Mandinka*. London, UK: School of Oriental and African Studies.
International Monetary Fund. 2010. "Sub-Saharan Africa: Back to High Growth?" In *Regional Economic Outlook*. Washington, DC: International Monetary Fund.
Iwata, Takuo. 2011. "Decentralisation and Elections in Benin." *Insight on Africa* 3 (2):99–115.
Iyer, Lakshmi. 2010. "Direct versus Indirect Colonial Rule in India: Long-Term Consequences." *Review of Economics and Statistics* 92 (4):693–713.
Jablonski, Ryan. 2014. "How Aid Targets Votes: The Impact of Electoral Incentives on Foreign Aid Distribution." *World Politics* 66 (2):293–330.
Jackson, Ken. 2013. "Diversity and the Distribution of Public Goods in sub-Saharan Africa." *Journal of African Economies* 22 (3):437–462.
Jerven, Morten. 2011. "A Clash of Disciplines? Economists and Historians Approaching the African Past." *Economic History of Developing Regions* 26 (2):111–124.
Juul, Kristine. 1999. "Tubes, Tenure and Turbulence." PhD, Science/Technology, Roskilde Universitet.

Kaag, Mayke. 2003. "Exploring the Context of Service Provision in Senegal: Social Dynamics and Decentralisation in the Senegalese Countryside." *Bulletin de l'APAD* 26: 1-13.
Kaberry, Phyllis. 1957. "Primative States." *British Journal of Sociology* 8 (3):224–234.
Kahan, Dan. 2003. "The Logic of Reciprocity: Trust, Collective Action and Law." *Michigan Law Review* 102 (1):73–103.
Kane, Mouhamed Moustapha. 1987. "A history of Fuuta Tooro, 1890s–1920s." PhD, History, Michigan State University.
Kasara, Kimuli. 2007. "Tax Me If You Can: Ethnic Geography, Democracy, and the Taxation of Agriculture in Africa." *American Political Science Review* 101 (1):159–172.
Kassibo, Brehima. 2006. "Mali: une décentralisation à double vitesse?" In *Décentralisation et pouvoirs en Afrique*, edited by Claude Fay, Yaouaga Félix Koné, and Catherine Quiminal. Paris, France: Institute de Recherche pour le Développmeent.
Katzenstein, Peter. 1996. "Introduction: Alternative Perspectives on National Security." In *The Culture of National Security*, edited by Peter Katzenstein. New York, NY: Columbia University Press.
Keita, Maghan. 2007. *A Political Economy of Health Care in Senegal*. Leiden, The Netherlands: Brill.
Kelly, Catherine. 2020. *Party Proliferation and Political Contestation in Africa*. Cham, Switzerland: Palgrave Macmillan.
Kendhammer, Brandon. 2016. *Muslims Talking Politics: Framing Islam, Democracy, and Law in Northern Nigeria*. Chicago, IL: The University of Chicago Press.
Kimenyi, Mwangi. 2006. "Ethnicity, Governance and the Provision of Public Goods." *Journal of African Economies* 15 (1):62–99.
Klaus, Kathleen. 2020. *Political Violence in Kenya: Land, Elections and Claim-Making*. New York, NY: Cambridge University Press.
Klein, Martin A. 1968a. "The Evolution of the Chefferie in Senegal." In *Nations by Design: Institution Building in Africa*, edited by Arnold Rivkin. Garden City, NY: Anchor Books.
    1968b. *Islam and Imperialism in Senegal*. Stanford, CA: Stanford University Press.
    1972. "Social and Economic Factors in the Muslim Revolution in Senegambia." *Journal of African History* 13 (2):419–441.
Kollock, Peter. 1998. "Social Dilemmas: The Anatomy of Cooperation." *Annual Review of Sociology* 24:183–214.
Koné, Bintou, and Sten Hagberg. 2019. "Enquête de la députation: parenté et politique dans une campagne électorale au Mali." In *Démocratie par le bas et politique municipale au Sahel*, edited by Sten Hagberg, Ludovic Kibora, and Gabriella Korling. Uppsala, Sweden: Uppsala Universitet.
Koné, Soli. 1997a. "La Décentralisation face à l'ordre ancien." *Bulletin de l'APAD* 14: 1-8.
Koné, Yaouaga Félix. 1997b. "Les Micro-communes: expression de logiques locales." *Bulletin de l'APAD* 14: 1-8.
Koter, Dominika. 2013. "King Makers: Local Leaders and Ethnic Politics in Africa." *World Politics* 65 (2):187–232.
    2016. *Beyond Ethnic Politics in Africa*. New York, NY: Cambridge University Press.

Kowert, Paul, and Jeffrey Legro. 1996. "Norms, Identity and Their Limits: A Theoretical Reprise." In *The Culture of National Security*, edited by Peter Katzenstein. New York, NY: Columbia University Press.
Kramon, Eric, and Daniel Posner. 2013. "Who Benefits from Distributive Politics? How the Outcome One Studies Affects the Answer One Gets." *Perspectives on Politics* 11 (2):461–474.
Kruks-Wisner, Gabrielle. 2018. *Claiming the State: Active Citizenship and Social Welfare in Rural India*. New York, NY: Cambridge University Press.
Kudamatsu, Masayuki. 2007. "Ethnic Favoritism: Micro Evidence from Guinea." Institute for International Economic Studies. Stockholm, Sweden. https://ssrn.com/abstract=1440303
Kusiak, Pauline. 2005. "The Machine That 'Makes the Inside Visible': Medical Instruments, Mentalities-Talk and the Politics of Technology in Colonial and post-Colonial Senegal." PhD, History, Cornell University.
Kyburz, Stephen. 2018. "The Local Political Resource Curse." Working Paper. https://drive.google.com/file/d/197gemBq5GIeot4oyCBr_z1MSlf_fOe3E/view
Kyed, Helene, and Lars Buur. 2007. "Introduction: Traditional Authority and Democratization in Africa." In *State Recognition and Democratization in Sub-Saharan Africa*, edited by Helene Kyed and Lars Buur. New York, NY: Palgrave.
Kywels, Olivier, and Marie-Paule Ferry. 2006. *Bedik: peuple des pierres*. Paris, France: Cercle d'art.
Labonte, Melissa. 2012. "From Patronage to Peacebuilding? Elite Capture and Governance from Below in Sierra Leone." *African Affairs* 111 (442):90–115.
Laitin, David. 1986. *Hegemony and Culture: Politics and Religion among the Yoruba*. Chicago, IL: The University of Chicago Press.
Lambright, Gina. 2011. *Decentralization in Uganda: Explaining Successes and Failures in Local Governance*. Boulder, CO: Lynne Reinner.
Larson, Jennifer, and Janet Lewis. 2017. "Ethnic Networks." *American Journal of Political Science* 61 (2):350–364.
Lasnet, Dr., A., A. Cligny, A. Chevalier, and Pierre Rambaud. 1900. *Une Mission au Sénégal*. Paris, France: Augustin Challamel.
Le Brun, Olivier. 1979. "Education and Class Conflict." In *The Political Economy of Underdevelopment: Dependence in Senegal*, edited by Rita Cruise O'Brien. New York, NY: Sage.
Le Meur, Pierre-Yves. 2006. "State Making and the Politics of the Frontier in Central Benin." *Development and Change* 37 (4):871–900.
Leider, Stephen, Markus Möbius, Tanya Rosenblat, and Quoc-Anh Do. 2009. "Directed Altruism and Enforced Reciprocity in Social Networks." *Quarterly Journal of Economics* 124 (4):1815–1851.
Leonard, Tammy, Rachel Croson, and Angela de Oliveira. 2010. "Social Capital and Public Goods." *Journal of Socio-Economics* 39 (4):474–481.
Letsa, Natalie, and Martha Wilfahrt. 2020. "The Mechanisms of Direct and Indirect Rule: Colonialism and Economic Development in Africa." *Quarterly Journal of Political Science* 15 (4): 539–577.
Leyti, Oumar Ndiaye. 1981. *Le Djoloff et ses bourba*. Dakar, Senegal: Nouvelles Editions Africaines.

Lieberman, Evan. 2005. "Nested Analysis as a Mixed-Method Strategy for Comparative Analysis." *American Political Science Review* 99 (3):435–452.

Lieberman, Evan, and Gwyneth McClendon. 2013. "The Ethnicity–Policy Preference Link in Sub-Saharan Africa." *Comparative Political Studies* 46 (5):574–602.

Lipset, Seymour. 1959. "Some Social Requisites of Democracy: Economic Development and Political Legitimacy." *American Political Science Review* 53 (1):69–105.

Loch, Christoph, Michael Yaziji, and Christian Langen. 2001. "The Fight for the Alpha Position: Channeling Status Competition in Organizations." *European Management Journal* 19 (1):16–25.

Lowes, Sara, Nathan Nunn, James Robinson, and Jonathan Weigel. 2017. "The Evolution of Culture and Institutions: Evidence from the Kuba Kingdom." *Econometrica* 85 (4):1065–1091.

Lund, Christian. 2006. "Twilight Institutions: Public Authority and Local Politics in Africa." *Development and Change* 37 (4):685–705.

Lust, Ellen, and Lise Rakner. 2018. "The Other Side of Taxation: Extraction and Social Institutions in the Developing World." *Annual Review of Political Science* 21: 277–294.

Ly, Boubakar. 1967. "L'Honneur dans les sociétés Ouolof et Toucouleur du Sénégal." *Presence Africaine* 61 (1):32–67.

MacArthur, Julie. 2016. *Cartography and the Political Imagination: Mapping Community in Colonial Kenya*. Athens, OH: Ohio University Press.

Mahoney, James. 2010. *Colonialism and Postcolonial Development: Spanish America in Comparative Perspective*. New York, NY: Cambridge University Press.

Mamdani, Mahmood. 1996. *Citizen and Subject: Contemporary Africa and the Legacy of Late Colonialism*. Princeton, NJ: Princeton University Press.

Manor, James. 2004. "User Committees." *European Journal of Development Research* 16 (1):192–213.

Mark, Peter. 1978. "Urban Migration, Cash Cropping, and Calamity: The Spread of Islam among the Diola of Boulouf (Senegal), 1900–1940." *African Studies Review* 21 (2):1–14.

  1985. *A Cultural, Economic, and Religious History of the Basse Casamance Since 1500*. Stuttgart, Germany: F. Steiner Verlag Wiesbaden.

Markovitz, Irving Leonard. 1970. "Traditional Social Structure, the Islamic Brotherhoods, and Political Development in Senegal." *Journal of Modern African Studies* 8 (1):73–96.

Martinez-Bravo, Monica, Gerard Padró I Miquel, Nancy Qian, Yiqing Xu, and Yang Yao. 2017. "Making Democracy Work: Formal Institutions and Culture in Rural China." Working Paper. http://personal.lse.ac.uk/padro/working-papers/scap_20170606.pdf

Marty, Paul. 1917. *Etudes sur l'Islam au Sénégal*. Paris, France: Leroux.

Masaki, Takaaki. 2018. "The Political Economy of Aid Allocation in Africa: Evidence from Zambia." *African Studies Review* 61 (1):55–82.

Maseland, Robbert. 2018. "Is Colonialism History? The Declining Impact of Colonial Legacies in African Institutional and Economic Development." *Journal of Institutional Economics* 14 (2):259–287.

Mathieu, Slyvie, and Serdar Yilmaz. 2010. "Local Government Discretion and Accountability in Burkina Faso." *Public Administration & Development* 30 (5):329–344.

Mattingly, Daniel. 2016. "Elite Capture." *World Politics* 68 (3):383–412.
Mbow, Penda. 2008. "Senegal: The Return of Personalism." *Journal of Democracy* 19:156–169.
McClendon, Gwyneth. 2018. *Envy in Politics*. Princeton, NJ: Princeton University Press.
Meagher, Kate. 2005. "Social Capital or Analytic Liability? Social Networks and African Informal Economies." *Global Networks* 5 (3):217–238.
Méguelle, Philippe. 2012. *Chefferie coloniale et égalitarisme diola*. Paris, France: L'Harmattan.
Menes, Robin. 1976. *The Dynamics of Health: Case 19: Senegal*. Washington, DC: US Department of Health.
Michalopoulos, Stelios, and Elias Papaioannou. 2013. "Pre-Colonial Ethnic Institutions and Contemporary African Development." *Econometrica* 81 (1):113–152.
  2015. "On the Ethnic Origins of African Development: Chiefs and Precolonial Political Centralization." *Academy of Management Perspectives* 29 (1):32–71.
  2016. "The Long-Run Effects of the Scramble for Africa." *American Economic Review* 106 (7):1802–1848.
Miguel, Edward, and Mary Gugerty. 2005. "Ethnic Diversity, Social Sanctions, and Public Goods in Kenya." *Journal of Public Economics* 89 (11–12):2325–2368.
Mongbo, Roch. 1998. "Décentralisation, migrations et identités: Formes de citoyenneté et dynamiques d'exclusion." *Bulletin de l'APAD* 16: 1-7.
  2008. "State Building and Local Democracy in Benin: Two Cases of Decentralized Forest Management." *Conservation and Society* 6 (1):49–61.
Monteil, Vincent. 1966. *Esquisses sénégalaises: Wâlo, Kayor, Dyolof, Mourides, un visionnaire*. Initiations et études africaines no 21. Dakar, Senegal: IFAN.
Mookherjee, Dilip. 2015. "Political Decentralization." *Annual Review of Economics* 7:231–249.
Moumani, Abdou. 1967. *L'Éducation en Afrique*. Paris, France: Francois Maspero.
Mumford, W. Bryant. 1970 (1935). *Africans Learn to Be French*. New York, NY: Negro Universities Press.
Munshi, Kaivan, and Mark Rosenzweig. 2008. "The Efficacy of Parochial Politics: Caste, Commitment, and Competence in Indian Local Governments." NBER. Working Paper No. 14335. Cambridge, MA.
Murdock, George. 1981. *Atlas of World Cultures*. Pittsburgh, PA: University of Pittsburgh Press.
Ndegwa, Stephen, and Brian Levy. 2003. *The Politics of Decentralization in Africa*. Washington, DC: The World Bank.
Nee, Victor. 1998. "Sources of the New Institutionalism." In *The New Institutionalism in Sociology*, edited by Mary Brinton and Victor Nee. Stanford, CA: Stanford University Press.
Ngaïdé, Abderrahmane. 2012. *L'Esclave, le colon et le marabout: Le royaume peul du Fuladu de 1867 à 1936*. Dakar, Senegal: L'Harmattan.
North, Douglass, John Wallis, and Barry Weingast. 2009. *Violence and Social Orders*. New York, NY: Cambridge University Press.
Nugent, Paul. 2010. "States and Social Contracts in Africa." *New Left Review* 63:35–68.
Nunn, Nathan. 2009. "The Importance of History for Economic Development." *Annual Review of Economics* 11 (1):65–92.

Nunn, Nathan, and Leonard Wantchekon. 2011. "The Slave Trade and the Origins of Mistrust in Africa." *American Economic Review* 101 (7):3221–3252.

Nzouankeu, Jacques. 1994. "Decentralization and Democracy in Africa." *International Review of Administrative Sciences* 60:213–227.

Ojebode, Ayobami, Ike Ernest Onyishi, and Fatai Aremu. 2017. "Is Election a Disadvantage? Nigerian Local Councils and Security Provision." *IDS Bulletin* 48 (2): 31–52.

Olejnik, Anton. 2005. "Transfer of Institutions: Actors and Constraints – The Russian Case in a Global Context." Hamburg Institute of International Economics. HWWA Discussion Paper No. 320. Hamburg, Germany.

Olivier de Sardan, Jean-Pierre. 2009. "Les Huits modes de gouvernance locale en Afrique de l'Ouest." LASDEL. Etudes et Travaux n. 4. Niamey, Niger. www.institutions-africa.org/filestream/20091130-appp-working-paper-no-4-nov-2009-jean-pierre-olivier-de-sardan-les-huit-modes-de-gouvernance-locale-en-afrique-de-l-ouest

Olson, Mancur. 1965. *The Logic of Collective Action: Public Goods and the Theory of Groups*. Cambridge, MA: Harvard University Press.

Opp, Karl-Dieter. 1979. "The Emergence and Effects of Social Norms: A Confrontation of Some Hypotheses of Sociology and Economics." *Kyklos* 32 (4):775–801.

Ostrom, Elinor. 1990. *Governing the Commons*. New York, NY: Cambridge University Press.

Ouedraogo, Hubert. 2003. "Decentralisation and Local Governance: Experiences from Francophone West Africa." *Public Administration and Development* 23 (1):97–103.

Oxhorn, Philip, Joseph Tulchin, and Andrew Selee. 2004. *Decentralization, Democratic Governance, and Civil Society in Comparative Perspective*. Washington, DC: Woodrow Wilson Center Press.

Page, Scott. 2006. "Path Dependence." *Quarterly Journal of Political Science* 1 (1):87–115.

Paller, Jeffrey. 2014. "Informal Institutions and Personal Rule in Urban Ghana." *African Studies Review* 57 (3):123–142.

2019. *Democracy in Ghana: Everyday Politics in Urban Africa*. New York, NY: Cambridge University Press.

Patterson, Amy. 1998. "A Reappraisal of Democracy in Civil Society: Evidence from Rural Senegal." *Journal of Modern African Studies* 36 (3):423–441.

2003. "Power Inequalities and the Institutions of Senegalese Development Organizations." *African Studies Review* 46 (3):35–54.

Patterson, Amy, and Kristen Monroe. 1998. "Narrative in Political Science." *Annual Review of Political Science* 1:315–331.

Pélissier, Paul. 1966. *Les Paysans du Sénégal*. Saint-Yrieix, France: Imprimerie Fabrègue.

Pepinsky, Thomas. 2018. "The Return of the Single-Country Study." *Annual Review of Political Science* 22:187–203.

Peterson, Brian. 2004. "Slave Emancipation, Trans-Local Social Processes and the Spread of Islam in French Colonial Buguni (Southern Mali), 1893–1914." *Journal of African History* 45 (3):421–444.

Pheffer, Paul. 1985. "African Influence on French Colonial Railroads in Senegal." In *Double Impact: France and Africa in the Age of Imperialism*, edited by G. W. Johnson. Westport, CT: Greenwood.

Pierskalla, Jan. 2019. "The Proliferation of Decentralized Governing Units." In *Decentralized Governance and Accountability*, edited by Jonathan Rodden and Erik Wibbels. New York, NY: Cambridge University Press.

Pierskalla, Jan, Alexander De Juan, and Max Montgomery. 2017. "The Territorial Expansion of the Colonial State: Evidence from German East Africa 1890–1909." *British Journal of Political Science* 49:1–27.
Pierson, Paul. 2004. *Politics in Time*. Princeton, NJ: Princeton University Press.
Piot, Charles. 2010. *Nostalgia for the Future*. Chicago, IL: University of Chicago Press.
Platteau, Jean-Philippe. 2000. *Institutions, Social Norms, and Economic Development*. Amsterdam, The Netherlands: Harwood Academic Publishers.
Platteau, Jean-Philippe, and Anita Abraham. 2002. "Participatory Development in the Presence of Endogenous Community Imperfections." *Journal of Development Studies* 39 (2):104.
Portelli, Alessandro. 1991. *The Death of Luigi Trastulli and Other Stories*. Albany, NY: State University of New York Press.
Posner, Daniel N. 2004a. "The Political Salience of Cultural Difference." *American Political Science Review* 98 (4):529–545.
  2004b. "Measuring Ethnic Fractionalization in Africa." *American Journal of Political Science* 48 (4):849–863.
Putnam, Robert. 1988. "Diplomacy and Domestic Politics: The Logic of Two-Level Games." *International Organization* 42 (3):427–460.
  1993. *Making Democracy Work: Civic Traditions in Modern Italy*. Princeton, NJ: Princeton University Press.
Quinn, Charlotte. 1972. *Mandingo Kingdoms of the Senegambia: Traditionalism, Islam, and European Expansion*. Evanston, IL: Northwestern University Press.
Raub, Werner, and Jeroen Weesie. 1990. "Reputation and Efficiency in Social Interactions." *American Journal of Sociology* 96 (3):626–654.
Reid, Richard. 2011. "Past and Presentism: The 'Precolonial' and the Foreshortening of African History." *Journal of African History* 52 (2):135–155.
Ribot, Jesse. 1999. "Decentralisation, Participation and Accountability in Sahelian Forestry." *Africa* 69 (1):23–65.
Ribot, Jesse, and Phil Rene Oyono. 2005. "The Politics of Decentralization." In *Toward a New Map of Africa*, edited by Benjamin Wisner, Camilla Toulmin, and Rutendo Chitiga. London, UK: Earthscan.
Ricart-Huguet, Joan. 2021. "The Origins of Colonial Investments in Former British and French Africa." *British Journal of Political Science*: 1–22.
Roberts, Stephen. 1963. *The History of French Colonial Policy, 1870–1925*. London, UK: F. Cass.
Robinson, David. 1975. *Chiefs and Clerics: Abdul Bokar Kan and Futa Toro, 1853–1891*. Oxford, UK: Clarendon Press.
Robinson, James, and Q. Neil Parsons. 2006. "State Formation and Governance in Botswana." *Journal of African Economies* 15 (Supplement 1):100–140.
Roessler, Philip, Yannick Pengl, Robert Marty, Kyle Titlow, and Nicolas van de Walle. 2018. "On the Origins of Spatial Inequality in Africa." Working Paper.
Romeo, Leonardo. 2003. "The Role of External Assistance in Supporting Decentralisation Reform." *Public Administration and Development* 23 (1):89–96.
Rothchild, Donald, and Victor Olorunsola. 1983. *State Versus Ethnic Claims*. Boulder, CO: Westview Press.
Rothstein, Bo. 2005. *Social Traps and the Problem of Trust*. New York, NY: Cambridge University Press.
Sarr, Alioune. 1986–1987. "Histoire du Sine-Saloum (Sénégal)." *Bulletin de l'Institut Fondamental d'Afrique Noire (serie B)* 46 (3–4):211–283.

Schaffer, Frederic. 1998. *Democracy in Translation: Understanding Politics in an Unfamiliar Culture*. Ithaca, NY: Cornell University Press.
Schaffer, Matt, and Christine Cooper. 1980. *Mandinko: The Ethnography of a West African Holy Land*. New York, NY: Hold, Rinehart and Winston.
Searing, James. 1993. *West African Slavery and Atlantic Commerce*. New York, NY: Cambridge University Press.
  2002. *"God Alone Is King": Islam and Emancipation in Senegal: The Wolof Kingdoms of Kajoor and Bawol, 1859–1914*. Portsmouth, England: Heinemann.
Seawright, Jason. 2016. "The Case for Selecting Cases That Are Deviant or Extreme on the Independent Variable." *Sociological Methods & Research* 45 (3):493–525.
Shayo, Moses. 2009. "A Model of Social Identity with an Application to Political Economy." *American Political Science Review* 103 (2):147–174.
Sheely, Ryan. 2015. "Mobilization, Participatory Planning Institutions, and Elite Capture." *World Development* 67:251–266.
Simpser, Alberto, Dan Slater, and Jason Wittenberg. 2018. "Dead but Not Gone: Contemporary Legacies of Communism, Imperialism, and Authoritarianism." *Annual Review of Political Science* 21:419–439.
Singh, Prerna. 2011. "We-ness and Welfare: A Longitudinal Analysis of Social Development in Kerala, India." *World Development* 39 (2):282–293.
  2015a. *How Solidarity Works for Welfare*. New York, NY: Cambridge University Press.
  2015b. "Subnationalism and Social Development." *World Politics* 67 (3):506–562.
Singh, Prerna, and Matthias vom Hau. 2016. "Ethnicity in Time." *Comparative Political Studies* 49 (10):1303–1340.
Skinner, G. William. 1965. "Marketing and Social Structure in Rural China: Part III." *Journal of Asian Studies* 24 (3):363–399.
Snyder, Richard. 2001. "Scaling Down: The Subnational Comparative Method." *Studies in Comparative International Development* 36 (1):93–110.
Soifer, Hillel David. 2019. "Units of Analysis in Subnational Research." In *Inside Countries: Subnational Research in Comparative Politics*, edited by Agustina Giraudy, Eduardo Moncada, and Richard Snyder. New York, NY: Cambridge University Press.
Suberu, Rotimi. 1991. "The Struggle for New States in Nigeria, 1976–1990." *African Affairs* 90 (361):499–522.
Suret-Canale, J, and Boubacar Barry. 1976. "The Western Atlantic Coast to 1800." In *The History of West Africa*, edited by J. F. Ade Ajayi and Michael Crowder. New York, NY: Columbia University Press.
Tabellini, Guido. 2008. "The Scope of Cooperation: Values and Incentives." *Quarterly Journal of Economics* 123 (3):905–950.
Tajfel, Henri, and John Turner. 1986. "The Social Identity Theory of Intergroup Behavior." In *Psychology of Intergroup Relations*, edited by Stephen Worchel and L. Austin. Chicago, IL: Nelson-Hall.
Tamari, Tal. 1991. "The Development of Caste Systems in West Africa." *Journal of African History* 32 (2):221–250.
Thelen, Kathleen. 2004. *How Institutions Evolve*. New York, NY: Cambridge University Press.
Thelen, Kathleen, and Sven Steinmo. 1992. "Historical Institutionalism in Comparative Politics." In *Structuring Politics: Historical Institutionalism in Comparative Analysis*, Sven Steinmo, Kathleen Thelen and Frank Longstreth. New York, NY: Cambridge University Press.
Tilly, Charles. 1978. *From Mobilization to Revolution*. London, UK: Addison-Wesley.

2006. *Identities, Boundaries and Social Ties*. Boulder, CO: Paradigm Press.
Touré, Ibrahima. 2012. "Autonomy and Local Democracy in Africa." *International Review of Administrative Sciences* 78 (4):757–774.
Touré, Oussouby. 1990. "Where Herders Don't Herd Anymore." Dryland Issue Paper No. E22. London, UK: International Institute for Environment and Development.
Trager, Lillian. 2001. *Yoruba Hometowns: Community, Identity, and Development in Nigeria*. Boulder, CO: Lynne Rienner.
Transue, John. 2007. "Identity Salience, Identity Acceptance, and Racial Policy Attitudes: American National Identity as a Uniting Force." *American Journal of Political Science* 51 (1):78–91.
Treisman, Daniel. 2007. *The Architecture of Government: Rethinking Political Decentralization*. New York, NY: Cambridge University Press.
Tsai, Lily. 2007. *Accountability without Democracy*. New York, NY: Cambridge University Press.
Van de Walle, Nicolas. 2007. "Meet the New Boss, Same as the Old Boss? The Evolution of Political Clientelism in Africa." In *Patrons, Clients and Policies*, edited by Herbert Kitschelt and Steven Wilkinson. New York, NY: Cambridge University Press.
Van Hoven, Ed. 1995. *L'Oncle maternel est roi: la formation d'alliance hiérarchiques chez les Mandingues du Wuli (Sénégal)*. Leiden, The Netherlands: Research School CNWS.
Venema, Bernhard. 1996. "The Rural Councillor as Development Agent: An Uneasy Connection?" *Bulletin de l'APAD* 12:2–17.
Venema, L. B. 1978. *The Wolof of Saloum: Social Structure and Rural Development in Senegal*. Wageningen, The Netherlands: Centre for Agricultural Pub. and Documentation.
Vengroff, Richard, and Michael Magala. 2001. "Democratic Reform, Transition and Consolidation: Evidence from Senegal's 2000 Presidential Election." *Journal of Modern African Studies* 39 (1):129–162.
Vengroff, Richard, and Momar Ndiaye. 1998. "The Impact of Electoral Reform at the Local Level in Africa: The Case of Senegal's 1996 Local Elections." *Electoral Studies* 17 (4):463–482.
Villalón, Leonardo. 1995. *Islamic Society and State Power in Senegal*. New York, NY: Cambridge University Press.
Walther, Oliver. 2012. "Sons of the Soil and Conquerors Who Come on Foot: The Historical Evolution of a West Africa Border Region." *Africa Studies Quarterly* 13 (1/2):75–92.
Warner, Carolyn. 1999. "The Political Economy of 'Quasi-statehood' and the Demise of 19th Century African Politics." *Review of International Studies* 25 (2):233–255.
Weber, Max. 1978 (1922). *Economy and Society: An Outline of Interpretive Sociology*. Berkeley, CA: University of California Press.
Weghorst, Keith, and Staffan Lindberg. 2013. "What Drives the Swing Voter in Africa?" *American Journal of Political Science* 57 (3):717–734.
Weiss, Yoram, and Chaim Fershtman. 1998. "Social Status and Economic Performance: A Survey." *European Economic Review* 42 (3):801–820.
Whatley, Warren. 2014. "The Transatlantic Slave Trade and the Evolution of Political Authority in West Africa." In *Africa's Development in Historical Perspective*, edited by Emmanuel Akyeampong, Robert Bates, Nathan Nunn, and James Robinson. New York, NY: Cambridge University Press.
White, Harrison. 2008 (1965). "Notes on the Constituents of Social Structure." *Sociological Forum* 2 (1):1–15.

White, Luise. 2000. *Speaking with Vampires: Rumor and History in Colonial Africa*. Berkeley, CA: University of California Press.
Wibbels, Erik. 2019. "The Social Underpinnings of Decentralized Governance." In *Decentralized Governance and Accountability*, edited by Jonathan Rodden and Erik Wibbels. New York, NY: Cambridge University Press.
Wilensky, Harold. 1975. *The Welfare State and Equality: Structural and Ideological Roots of Public Expenditure*. Berkeley, CA: University of California Press.
Williams, Martin. 2010. "The Gold Standard of Governance: Mining, Decentralization, and State Power in Senegal." *Politique africaine* 117:127–148.
Wing, Susanna, and Brehima Kassibo. 2014. "Mali: Incentives and Challenges for Decentralization." In *Decentralization in Africa: The Paradox of State Strength*, edited by J. Tyler Dickovick and James Wunsch. Boulder, CO: Lynne Rienner.
Wittenberg, Jason. 2006. *Crucibles of Political Loyalty: Church, Institutions and Electoral Continuity in Hungary*. New York, NY: Cambridge University Press.
  2015. "Conceptualizing Historical Legacies." *East European Politics and Societies and Cultures* 29 (2):366–378.
Woldense, Josef. 2018. "The ruler's game of musical chairs: Shuffling during the reign of Ethiopia's last emperor." *Social Networks* 52: 154–166.
Woolcock, Michael. 2010. "The Rise and Routinization of Social Capital, 1988–2008." *Annual Review of Political Science* 13:469–487.
World Bank. 1995. *Senegal – An Assessment of Living Conditions*. Washington, DC: The World Bank.
  2018. *World Development Indicators*. edited by The World Bank. Washington, DC: The World Bank.
  June 2019. *Togo – Decentralized Service Delivery: Status and Way forward for Strengthening Communes*. Washington, DC: The World Bank.
Wright, Donald. 1999. ""What Do You Mean There Were No Tribes in Africa?": Thoughts on Boundaries – and Related Matters – in Precolonial Africa." *History in Africa* 26:409–426.
Wunsch, James. 2000. "Refounding the African State and Local Self-Governance: The Neglected Foundation." *Journal of Modern African Studies* 38:487–509.
  2001. "Decentralization, Local Governance and 'Recentralization' in Africa." *Public Administration and Development* 21:277–288.
Xu, Yiqing, and Yang Yao. 2015. "Informal Institutions, Collective Action, and Public Investment in Rural China." *American Political Science Review* 109 (2):371–391.
Young, Crawford. 1994. *The African Colonial State in Comparative Perspective*. New Haven, CT: Yale University Press.
  2004. "The End of the Post-Colonial State in Africa? Reflections on Changing African Political Dynamics." *African Affairs* 103 (410):23–49.
Zhu, Lin, and Yongshun Cai. 2016. "Institutions and Provision of Public Goods in Rural China." *China Review* 16 (2):55–83.
Zuccarelli, Francois. 1965. "Du Canton à l'arrondissement sénégalais." Memoire, Faculte de Droit et des Sciences Economiques, UCAD.

Index

Acephalous Polities, 51–52, 54, 164
   and colonial encounter, 67–68, 86
Alliance Pour le République, 84, 161
Associational Life. See Civil Society

Baol, 50, 58
Boone, Catherine, 18, 131
Boundaries, 84–85
   colonial delimitation of, 85–89
   postcolonial delimitation of, 89–93
   redistricting under Wade, 83, 92–93, 98
Boundou, 49, 53, 56, 58, 115–116, 182
Burkina Faso, 220–221, 228, 234

Cash Crop Production, 61–62, 69
   colonial favoritism toward, 211
Caste, 32, 50, 66, 71, 105, 173
Cayor, 30, 48, 50, 56, 162–163
Central–Local Government Relations, 5, 18–19, 75, 83–84, 110, 131–132
Civil Society, 134
   elite capture of, 70
   empirical test of, 148
Clientelism, 200
   local patrons, 1, 117, 174, 177, 184
Colonialism
   French policies of direct rule, 18, 57–59
   French policies toward chiefs, 58–59, 67–68, 85
   infrastructure investments, 205
   legacies of, 57, 213
   onset of, 56–57
   revenue imperative, 203

Core Voters
   favoritism toward, 108, 177, 186, 189,
      See also Clientelism, local patrons
Cornell, Stephen, 235–236
Corruption, 183, 186
Cote d'Ivoire, 220

Data Sources
   archival data, 85, 194
   interview protocols, 158–160
   network analysis, 164–169, 184
   original survey of local elites, 96–99
   overview, 19–21
   potential bias in, 160
   quantitative data, 119, 128–136, 194–195, 224–225, 228–230
   survey and interview protocols, 96–97
Decentralization
   Acte I, 76–77
   Acte II, 77–79, 201
   Acte III, 79–81, 161
   as donor agenda, 2
   implications of argument for, 247–248, 250
   theories of, 4–5
   as two-level game, 25–26, 40, 80–83, 233
Diola, 51, 68, 105
Diouf, Abdou, 75, 77, 200
Dippel, Christian, 236
Djoloff, 48, 51, 53
Donor Financing, 77–78, 123–125, 200

Education
  colonial investment in, 202–204, 207–208
  local authority in, 78, 130, 200–201
  postcolonial investment in, 211
Elections
  2014 local elections, 161, 171–174, 182
  electoral lists, 30, 71, 83, 106–107, 114, 173, 175–176
  local electoral rules, 77–78, 172
  preferences for large winning coalition, 84
Elite Capture, 5–6
  costs of, 70–71
  evidence of, 70, 105, 232
  theoretical expectations of, 5, 24–25
Englebert, Pierre, 42, 242
Etat-civile, 177, 186
Ethnicity. *See also* Social Identities, ethnic identities
  ethnic norms, 188–189, 201
  ethnic tensions, 33, 175
  expectations of ethnic favoritism, 211
  experiences of ethnic minorities, 103, 109, 163
  theoretical expectations of, 11–12, 131–133

Fatick Region, 106
Fonds de Dotation de la Decentralisation, 79, 125, 132
Fouladou, 49, 86
Fouta Toro, 49–50, 56, 88, 92, 103

Gajaaga, 44, 49, 64
Ghana, 215, 223, 242
Griots, 66–67
Guidimakha, 49
Guinea, 220, 228

Health
  colonial investment in, 202–204, 207–208
  local authority in, 78, 130, 200–201
  postcolonial investment in, 211
Historical Legacies
  compression of history, 15, 213–214, 247
  implications of argument for, 16, 213–216
  persistence of norms, 44, 148, 216, 251
  theories of, 14–15
Huillery, Elise, 205–209, 214

Institutional Congruence
  examples of beyond Senegal, 235–238
  temporal predictions of, 9, 18, 193–201, 247
  theory of, 6–8, 26–28, 245

Kaffrine Region, 163
Kalt, Joseph, 235–236
Kedougou Region, 67
Kolda Region, 91, 133

Land
  conflicts over, 36, 111
  local government authority over, 77, 118
Liberia, 220
Local Elites
  defined, 5, 63
  relations between, 6, 28, 107–111, 248
Local Government
  boundary creation, 90–92, *See* also Boundaries
  in China, 42, 236–237
  fiscal capacity of, 78–79, 123–126, 161
  in India, 238
  on Native American Reservations, 235–236
  performance evaluations, 228–229
  political structure of local governments in Senegal, 76–77, 79–80
  as unit of analysis, 6, 25, 246
Location-Allocation Models, 150–151
Louga Region, 116

Mahoney, Jim, 16
Mali, 223, 233–234, 252
Mali's, 223
Matam Region, 72
Migration
  adoption of in-migrants, 69, 72
  bias against in-migrants, 111, 123
  effects of, 113–116, 119
  historical patterns of, 61–62, 86, 160
Missions, 60–61, 116, 204–205, 209
Mouride, 211
Mourides, 60, 68
  local political engagement of, 116–118
  as political brokers, 19, 75, 200, 210
  state favoritism toward, 61, 89, 117, 211
  Touba, 79, 116, 141, 200

Narratives, 45
  as data, 9–11, 99, 246–247
  dissenting views of, 111–112
  examples of, 102–105, 162–164, 183
  historical accuracy of, 10–11, 99–102, 188. *See* Data Sources, potential bias in
  of shared settlement or origin, 9, 32, 44–45, 64–66, 160, 233
Niani, 49, 156, 181

Index

Niger, 223, 232–234
Nigeria, 213, 220, 223, 227–228, 239
Norms. *See* Social Institutions

Ouli, 49, 182

Pakala, 49
Parti démocratique sénégalais, 77, 161
Parti socialiste, 75, 161
Political Parties. *See* Alliance pour le République, Parti démocratique sénégalais, Parti socialiste
   local party structure, 84, 161
   partisanship, 83, 106, 108, 131, 162
Precolonial Kingdoms. *See also* Baol, Boundou, Cayor, Djoloff, Fouladou, Fouta Toro, Gajaaga, Guidamakha, Saloum, Sine, Walo
   ethnic minorities within, 50
   historical variation in, 17, 44, 48–51
   measurement of, 52–55, 138–139
Public Goods Delivery
   empirical measures of, 134–135, 178–181, 194, 196–199, 225
   theoretical expectations of, 9, 23–24, 129–134
Putnam, Robert, 42, 43, 134, 148

Religion
   historical patterns of conversion, 59–61
   influence of religious leaders, 172, 176, 200
   Mysticism, 190–191
   Rip, 49, 117
Rural Social Hierarchies. *See also* Villages, social hierarchies within
   as mechanism of persistence, 8, 44, 66, 186, 239–240

Saint-Louis Region, 108
Sall, Macky, 79, 161–162
Saloum, 49–50, 53, 61, 69, 114–115
Scope Conditions, 239–243
Senghor, Leopold Sedar, 210
   government of, 74–76
   social service policies, 210–211
Sierra Leone, 241
Sine, 32, 49, 51, 58, 86
Singh, Prerna, 8, 33, 237–238
Social Identities
   ethnic identities, 12, 114, 133
   evidence of, 162–164, 183, 233–234
   inductive approach to, 13, 246

   persistence of, 32, 64, 66–67
   religious identities, 60–61
   as theoretical mechanism, 7, 31–34, 238–239
Social Institutions
   of balancing, 30, 106, 171, 176
   of conflict avoidance, 30, 103–104, 106–107, 169–170, 172–173
   defined, 6, 28–29
   effects of, 249
   internalization of, 29–30, 39, 171
   origins of, 43–45, 69
   other examples of, 234
   theoretical role of, 8, 26–30
Social Network Ties
   effect on internalizing social institutions, 38–39, 107
   evidence of, 10, 107–111, 164–170, 173, 232–234
   informational effects, 35–36, 108–109, 114, 126, 177
   persistence of, 34–35, 64–65
   reputational and sanctioning effects, 36–38, 107, 148, 170, 183, 188, 241
   as theoretical mechanism, 7, 34–40
   theories of, 36–37, 39
Social Trust, 148–150
State-Building
   implications of the argument for, 13–14, 245
Structural Adjustment, 199–200
Subnational Method, 16–17

Taxation, 78, 91, 125–126
Thies Region, 132
Tidjanes, 60, 117
Togo, 220
Tsai, Lily, 42, 236–237

Villages
   creation of new, 71–72, 178–181
   rivalries between, 92, 105, 114, 183–184
   settlement mythologies, 63–65. *See also* Narratives, of shared settlement
   social hierarchies within, 63–68, 182
   village capture, 104, 113
Vote Buying, 184, 189

Wade, Abdoulaye, 77, 80, 83, 92, 200
Walo, 49
Water and Sanitation, 178, 196–198, 227, 229

Ziguinchor Region, 105, 125

Other Books in the Series

Laia Balcells, *Rivalry and Revenge: The Politics of Violence during Civil War*
Lisa Baldez, *Why Women Protest? Women's Movements in Chile*
Kate Baldwin, *The Paradox of Traditional Chiefs in Democratic Africa*
Stefano Bartolini, *The Political Mobilization of the European Left, 1860–1980: The Class Cleavage*
Robert H. Bates, *The Political Economy of Development: A Game Theoretic Approach*
Robert H. Bates, *When Things Fell Apart: State Failure in Late-Century Africa*
Mark Beissinger, *Nationalist Mobilization and the Collapse of the Soviet State*
Pablo Beramendi, *The Political Geography of Inequality: Regions and Redistribution*
Nancy Bermeo, ed., *Unemployment in the New Europe*
Carles Boix, *Democracy and Redistribution*
Carles Boix, *Political Order and Inequality: Their Foundations and their Consequences for Human Welfare*
Carles Boix, *Political Parties, Growth, and Equality: Conservative and Social Democratic Economic Strategies in the World Economy*
Catherine Boone, *Merchant Capital and the Roots of State Power in Senegal, 1930–1985*
Catherine Boone, *Political Topographies of the African State: Territorial Authority and Institutional Change*
Catherine Boone, *Property and Political Order in Africa: Land Rights and the Structure of Politics*
Michael Bratton and Nicolas van de Walle, *Democratic Experiments in Africa: Regime Transitions in Comparative Perspective*
Michael Bratton, Robert Mattes, and E. Gyimah-Boadi, *Public Opinion, Democracy, and Market Reform in Africa*
Valerie Bunce, *Leaving Socialism and Leaving the State: The End of Yugoslavia, the Soviet Union, and Czechoslovakia*
Daniele Caramani, *The Nationalization of Politics: The Formation of National Electorates and Party Systems in Europe*
John M. Carey, *Legislative Voting and Accountability*
Kanchan Chandra, *Why Ethnic Parties Succeed: Patronage and Ethnic Headcounts in India*
Eric C. C. Chang, Mark Andreas Kayser, Drew A. Linzer, and Ronald Rogowski, *Electoral Systems and the Balance of Consumer-Producer Power*
José Antonio Cheibub, *Presidentialism, Parliamentarism, and Democracy*
Ruth Berins Collier, *Paths toward Democracy: The Working Class and Elites in Western Europe and South America*
Daniel Corstange, *The Price of a Vote in the Middle East: Clientelism and Communal Politics in Lebanon and Yemen*
Pepper D. Culpepper, *Quiet Politics and Business Power: Corporate Control in Europe and Japan*
Sarah Zukerman Daly, *Organized Violence after Civil War: The Geography of Recruitment in Latin America*
Christian Davenport, *State Repression and the Domestic Democratic Peace*
Donatella della Porta, *Social Movements, Political Violence, and the State*
Alberto Diaz-Cayeros, *Federalism, Fiscal Authority, and Centralization in Latin America*

Alberto Diaz-Cayeros, Federico Estévez, and Beatriz Magaloni, *The Political Logic of Poverty Relief: Electoral Strategies and Social Policy in Mexico*
Jesse Driscoll, *Warlords and Coalition Politics in Post-Soviet States*
Thad Dunning, *Crude Democracy: Natural Resource Wealth and Political Regimes*
Thad Dunning et al., *Information, Accountability, and Cumulative Learning: Lessons from Metaketa I*
Gerald Easter, *Reconstructing the State: Personal Networks and Elite Identity*
Antje Ellerman, *The Comparative Politics of Immigration: Policy Choices in Germany, Canada, Switzerland, and the United States*
Margarita Estevez-Abe, *Welfare and Capitalism in Postwar Japan: Party, Bureaucracy, and Business*
Henry Farrell, *The Political Economy of Trust: Institutions, Interests, and Inter-Firm Cooperation in Italy and Germany*
Karen E. Ferree, *Framing the Race in South Africa: The Political Origins of Racial Census Elections*
M. Steven Fish, *Democracy Derailed in Russia: The Failure of Open Politics*
Robert F. Franzese, *Macroeconomic Policies of Developed Democracies*
Roberto Franzosi, *The Puzzle of Strikes: Class and State Strategies in Postwar Italy*
Timothy Frye, *Building States and Markets After Communism: The Perils of Polarized Democracy*
Mary E. Gallagher, *Authoritarian Legality in China: Law, Workers, and the State*
Geoffrey Garrett, *Partisan Politics in the Global Economy*
Scott Gehlbach, *Representation through Taxation: Revenue, Politics, and Development in Postcommunist States*
Edward L. Gibson, *Boundary Control: Subnational Authoritarianism in Federal Democracies*
Jane R. Gingrich, *Making Markets in the Welfare State: The Politics of Varying Market Reforms*
Miriam Golden, *Heroic Defeats: The Politics of Job Loss*
Yanilda María González, *Authoritarian Police in Democracy: Contested Security in Latin America*
Jeff Goodwin, *No Other Way Out: States and Revolutionary Movements*
Merilee Serrill Grindle, *Changing the State*
Anna Grzymala-Busse, *Rebuilding Leviathan: Party Competition and State Exploitation in Post-Communist Democracies*
Anna Grzymala-Busse, *Redeeming the Communist Past: The Regeneration of Communist Parties in East Central Europe*
Frances Hagopian, *Traditional Politics and Regime Change in Brazil*
Mark Hallerberg, Rolf Ranier Strauch, and Jürgen von Hagen, *Fiscal Governance in Europe*
Henry E. Hale, *The Foundations of Ethnic Politics: Separatism of States and Nations in Eurasia and the World*
Stephen E. Hanson, *Post-Imperial Democracies: Ideology and Party Formation in Third Republic France, Weimar Germany, and Post-Soviet Russia*
Mai Hassan, *Regime Threats and State Solutions: Bureaucratic Loyalty and Embeddedness in Kenya*
Michael Hechter, *Alien Rule*
Timothy Hellwig, *Globalization and Mass Politics: Retaining the Room to Maneuver*
Gretchen Helmke, *Institutions on the Edge: The Origins and Consequences of Inter-Branch Crises in Latin America*

Gretchen Helmke, *Courts Under Constraints: Judges, Generals, and Presidents in Argentina*
Yoshiko Herrera, *Imagined Economies: The Sources of Russian Regionalism*
Alisha C. Holland, *Forbearance as Redistribution: The Politics of Informal Welfare in Latin America*
J. Rogers Hollingsworth and Robert Boyer, eds., *Contemporary Capitalism: The Embeddedness of Institutions*
Yue Hou, *The Private Sector in Public Office: Selective Property Rights in China*
John D. Huber, *Exclusion by Elections: Inequality, Ethnic Identity, and Democracy*
John D. Huber and Charles R. Shipan, *Deliberate Discretion? The Institutional Foundations of Bureaucratic Autonomy*
Ellen Immergut, *Health Politics: Interests and Institutions in Western Europe*
Torben Iversen, *Capitalism, Democracy, and Welfare*
Torben Iversen, *Contested Economic Institutions*
Torben Iversen, Jonas Pontussen, and David Soskice, eds., *Unions, Employers, and Central Banks: Macroeconomic Coordination and Institutional Change in Social Market Economics*
Thomas Janoski and Alexander M. Hicks, eds., *The Comparative Political Economy of the Welfare State*
Joseph Jupille, *Procedural Politics: Issues, Influence, and Institutional Choice in the European Union*
Karen Jusko, *Who Speaks for the Poor? Electoral Geography, Party Entry, and Representation*
Stathis Kalyvas, *The Logic of Violence in Civil War*
Stephen B. Kaplan, *Globalization and Austerity Politics in Latin America*
David C. Kang, *Crony Capitalism: Corruption and Capitalism in South Korea and the Philippines*
Junko Kato, *Regressive Taxation and the Welfare State*
Orit Kedar, *Voting for Policy, Not Parties: How Voters Compensate for Power Sharing*
Robert O. Keohane and Helen B. Milner, eds., *Internationalization and Domestic Politics*
Herbert Kitschelt, *The Transformation of European Social Democracy*
Herbert Kitschelt, Kirk A. Hawkins, Juan Pablo Luna, Guillermo Rosas, and Elizabeth J. Zechmeister, *Latin American Party Systems*
Herbert Kitschelt, Peter Lange, Gary Marks, and John D. Stephens, eds., *Continuity and Change in Contemporary Capitalism*
Herbert Kitschelt, Zdenka Mansfeldova, Radek Markowski, and Gabor Toka, *Post-Communist Party Systems*
David Knoke, Franz Urban Pappi, Jeffrey Broadbent, and Yutaka Tsujinaka, eds., *Comparing Policy Networks*
Ken Kollman, *Perils of Centralization: Lessons from Church, State, and Corporation*
Allan Kornberg and Harold D. Clarke, *Citizens and Community: Political Support in a Representative Democracy*
Amie Kreppel, *The European Parliament and the Supranational Party System*
David D. Laitin, *Language Repertoires and State Construction in Africa*
Fabrice E. Lehoucq and Ivan Molina, *Stuffing the Ballot Box: Fraud, Electoral Reform, and Democratization in Costa Rica*
Benjamin Lessing *Making Peace in Drug Wars: Crackdowns and Cartels in Latin America*

Janet I. Lewis *How Insurgency Begins: Rebel Group Formation in Uganda and Beyond*
Mark Irving Lichbach and Alan S. Zuckerman, eds., *Comparative Politics: Rationality, Culture, and Structure*, 2nd edition
Evan Lieberman, *Race and Regionalism in the Politics of Taxation in Brazil and South Africa*
Richard M. Locke, *The Promise and Limits of Private Power: Promoting Labor Standards in a Global Economy*
Julia Lynch, *Age in the Welfare State: The Origins of Social Spending on Pensioners, Workers, and Children*
Pauline Jones Luong, *Institutional Change and Political Continuity in Post-Soviet Central Asia*
Pauline Jones Luong and Erika Weinthal, *Oil is Not a Curse: Ownership Structure and Institutions in Soviet Successor States*
Doug McAdam, John McCarthy, and Mayer Zald, eds., *Comparative Perspectives on Social Movements*
Gwyneth H. McClendon and Rachel Beatty Riedl, *From Pews to Politics in Africa: Religious Sermons and Political Behavior*
Lauren M. MacLean, *Informal Institutions and Citizenship in Rural Africa: Risk and Reciprocity in Ghana and Côte d'Ivoire*
Beatriz Magaloni, *Voting for Autocracy: Hegemonic Party Survival and Its Demise in Mexico*
James Mahoney, *Colonialism and Postcolonial Development: Spanish America in Comparative Perspective*
James Mahoney and Dietrich Rueschemeyer, eds., *Historical Analysis and the Social Sciences*
Scott Mainwaring and Matthew Soberg Shugart, eds., *Presidentialism and Democracy in Latin America*
Melanie Manion, *Information for Autocrats: Representation in Chinese Local Congresses*
Isabela Mares, *From Open Secrets to Secret Voting: Democratic Electoral Reforms and Voter Autonomy*
Isabela Mares, *The Politics of Social Risk: Business and Welfare State Development*
Isabela Mares, *Taxation, Wage Bargaining, and Unemployment*
Cathie Jo Martin and Duane Swank, *The Political Construction of Business Interests: Coordination, Growth, and Equality*
Anthony W. Marx, *Making Race, Making Nations: A Comparison of South Africa, the United States, and Brazil*
Daniel C. Mattingly, *The Art of Political Control in China*
Kevin Mazur, *Revolution in Syria: Identity, Networks, and Repression*
Bonnie M. Meguid, *Party Competition between Unequals: Strategies and Electoral Fortunes in Western Europe*
Joel S. Migdal, *State in Society: Studying How States and Societies Constitute One Another*
Joel S. Migdal, Atul Kohli, and Vivienne Shue, eds., *State Power and Social Forces: Domination and Transformation in the Third World*
Scott Morgenstern and Benito Nacif, eds., *Legislative Politics in Latin America*
Kevin M. Morrison, *Nontaxation and Representation: The Fiscal Foundations of Political Stability*
Layna Mosley, *Global Capital and National Governments*
Layna Mosley, *Labor Rights and Multinational Production*

Wolfgang C. Müller and Kaare Strøm, *Policy, Office, or Votes?*
Maria Victoria Murillo, *Political Competition, Partisanship, and Policy Making in Latin American Public Utilities*
Maria Victoria Murillo, *Labor Unions, Partisan Coalitions, and Market Reforms in Latin America*
Monika Nalepa, *Skeletons in the Closet: Transitional Justice in Post-Communist Europe*
Noah L. Nathan, *Electoral Politics and Africa's Urban Transition: Class and Ethnicity in Ghana*
Ton Notermans, *Money, Markets, and the State: Social Democratic Economic Policies since 1918*
Simeon Nichter, *Votes for Survival: Relational Clientelism in Latin America*
Richard A. Nielsen, *Deadly Clerics: Blocked Ambition and the Paths to Jihad*
Aníbal Pérez-Liñán, *Presidential Impeachment and the New Political Instability in Latin America*
Roger D. Petersen, *Understanding Ethnic Violence: Fear, Hatred, and Resentment in 20th Century Eastern Europe*
Roger D. Petersen, *Western Intervention in the Balkans: The Strategic Use of Emotion in Conflict*
Simona Piattoni, ed., *Clientelism, Interests, and Democratic Representation*
Paul Pierson, *Dismantling the Welfare State? Reagan, Thatcher, and the Politics of Retrenchment*
Marino Regini, *Uncertain Boundaries: The Social and Political Construction of European Economies*
Kenneth M. Roberts, *Changing Course in Latin America: Party Systems in the Neoliberal Era*
Marc Howard Ross, *Cultural Contestation in Ethnic Conflict*
David Rueda and Daniel Stegmueller, *Who Wants What? Redistribution Preferences in Comparative Perspective*
Ignacio Sánchez-Cuenca, *The Historical Roots of Political Violence: Revolutionary Terrorism in Affluent Countries*
Ben Ross Schneider, *Hierarchical Capitalism in Latin America: Business, Labor, and the Challenges of Equitable Development*
Roger Schoenman, *Networks and Institutions in Europe's Emerging Markets*
Lyle Scruggs, *Sustaining Abundance: Environmental Performance in Industrial Democracies*
Jefferey M. Sellers, *Governing from Below: Urban Regions and the Global Economy*
Yossi Shain and Juan Linz, eds., *Interim Governments and Democratic Transitions*
Beverly Silver, *Forces of Labor: Workers' Movements and Globalization since 1870*
Prerna Singh, *How Solidarity Works for Welfare: Subnationalism and Social Development in India*
Theda Skocpol, *Social Revolutions in the Modern World*
Dan Slater, *Ordering Power: Contentious Politics and Authoritarian Leviathans in Southeast Asia*
Austin Smith et al., *Selected Works of Michael Wallerstein*
Regina Smyth, *Candidate Strategies and Electoral Competition in the Russian Federation: Democracy Without Foundation*
Richard Snyder, *Politics after Neoliberalism: Reregulation in Mexico*
David Stark and László Bruszt, *Postsocialist Pathways: Transforming Politics and Property in East Central Europe*

Sven Steinmo, *The Evolution of Modern States: Sweden, Japan, and the United States*
Sven Steinmo, Kathleen Thelen, and Frank Longstreth, eds., *Structuring Politics: Historical Institutionalism in Comparative Analysis*
Susan C. Stokes, *Mandates and Democracy: Neoliberalism by Surprise in Latin America*
Susan C. Stokes, ed., *Public Support for Market Reforms in New Democracies*
Susan C. Stokes, Thad Dunning, Marcelo Nazareno, and Valeria Brusco, *Brokers, Voters, and Clientelism: The Puzzle of Distributive Politics*
Milan W. Svolik, *The Politics of Authoritarian Rule*
Duane Swank, *Global Capital, Political Institutions, and Policy Change in Developed Welfare States*
David Szakonyi, *Politics for Profit: Business, Elections, and Policymaking in Russia*
Sidney Tarrow, *Power in Movement: Social Movements and Contentious Politics*
Sidney Tarrow, *Power in Movement: Social Movements and Contentious Politics*, Revised and Updated Third Edition
Tariq Thachil, *Elite Parties, Poor Voters: How Social Services Win Votes in India*
Kathleen Thelen, *How Institutions Evolve: The Political Economy of Skills in Germany, Britain, the United States, and Japan*
Kathleen Thelen, *Varieties of Liberalization and the New Politics of Social Solidarity*
Charles Tilly, *Trust and Rule*
Daniel Treisman, *The Architecture of Government: Rethinking Political Decentralization*
Guillermo Trejo, *Popular Movements in Autocracies: Religion, Repression, and Indigenous Collective Action in Mexico*
Guillermo Trejo and Sandra Ley, *Votes, Drugs, and Violence: The Political Logic of Criminal Wars in Mexico*
Rory Truex, *Making Autocracy Work: Representation and Responsiveness in Modern China*
Lily Lee Tsai, *Accountability without Democracy: How Solidary Groups Provide Public Goods in Rural China*
Joshua Tucker, *Regional Economic Voting: Russia, Poland, Hungary, Slovakia and the Czech Republic, 1990–1999*
Ashutosh Varshney, *Democracy, Development, and the Countryside*
Yuhua Wang, *Tying the Autocrat's Hand: The Rise of The Rule of Law in China*
Jeremy M. Weinstein, *Inside Rebellion: The Politics of Insurgent Violence*
Andreas Wiedemann, *Indebted Societies: Credit and Welfare in Rich Democracies*
Stephen I. Wilkinson, *Votes and Violence: Electoral Competition and Ethnic Riots in India*
Andreas Wimmer, *Waves of War: Nationalism, State Formation, and Ethnic Exclusion in the Modern World*
Jason Wittenberg, *Crucibles of Political Loyalty: Church Institutions and Electoral Continuity in Hungary*
Elisabeth J. Wood, *Forging Democracy from Below: Insurgent Transitions in South Africa and El Salvador*
Elisabeth J. Wood, *Insurgent Collective Action and Civil War in El Salvador*
Deborah J. Yashar, *Homicidal Ecologies: Illicit Economies and Complicit States in Latin America*
Daniel Ziblatt, *Conservative Parties and the Birth of Democracy*

Lightning Source UK Ltd.
Milton Keynes UK
UKHW040648141222
413898UK00014B/290